TERENCE ROBERTSON

THE
SHAME
AND THE
GLORY

DIEPPE

MCCLELLAND AND STEWART LIMITED

Contents

THE GLORY

Preface

In 1939 it seemed that Canada was on the way to achieving national cohesion, with Anglo-Saxon and French Canadian living in peaceful, if reluctant, co-existence. The nation was developing maturely towards sharply focused goals of wealth, power, and greatness, which would take only a few generations to accomplish and consolidate.

The next six years were those of change, years in which the growth of nationhood became less important than the growth of the Gross National Product.

The most damaging aspect of those war years was the loss of the core of a Canadian generation at a time when its leadership in moral, cultural, and political development was urgently needed. This core consisted of men who were either killed or confined for long bitter years in German prison camps, men who returned home to a Canada on the threshold of an amazing postwar economic expansion that was to bring changes they did not like and were powerless to prevent.

The country they had left behind five years before had vanished, drowned in a flood tide of surging progress towards a more material-istic world. Whereas their own sense of duty and patriotism had never been obscure, they have since found that new generations have no such wide, uncluttered freeway of thought to follow.

For most of them a series of events was responsible for death or enforced separation from home, the first being a single incident of war – Dieppe. Yet their presence on those bloody beaches is evidence enough that they represented then – and still do today – a generation of remarkable Canadians.

Neither intellectual contempt nor shallow cynicism can extinguish the beacon of national unity they set alight by their sacrifice. When French Canadians shepherded the civilian Dieppois to safety that day in August 1942, they were being consciously Canadian. When English-speaking Canadians risked their lives to drag the wounded commander of the Fusiliers Mont-Royal to safety behind a burning tank, they were helping a fellow Canadian, not a Frenchman.

Father Major Armand Sabourin went to Dieppe with the Fusiliers Mont-Royal and came back to Montreal to tell his people why. "We did not cross the Channel to fight for England, but to fight with her for Canada," he said. "We earned the right there to display a proud countenance from East to West, we French Canadians and English Canadians. We must try to love each other, like a husband and wife. We of French Canada represent the wife, and being weaker and more fragile we need more sympathy. English Canada is the husband and we recognize our mutual imperfections. Like a wife we should give our English-Canadian husband the impression he is running things, and we should use the intelligence, judgement, and generosity God has given us, as the wife, to exercise our influence for the common good. During those hours at Dieppe it wasn't English Canada or French Canada fight-ing separately. We went as Canadians."

If men behave at moments of crisis in accordance with the manner in which they have learned the lessons of history, then Canadians should look back in pride and quietly exult in the happy memory of those who died, those whose hearts and minds were extended to the utmost simply because their purpose was as clear to them as the sun in a cloudless sky. A nation searching for a soul cannot ignore the past, that great reservoir from which it must draw whatever national strength of character the future will demand of it. If the past is denied or the truth distorted, then the reservoir is poisoned and the nation moves on, each generation inheriting the impurity of weakness and adding to it. There is no need to place tradition in protective custody. It is there to be used as a yeast so that the present can be exploited to expand the future.

The men of Dieppe were neither ashamed nor bitter at their defeat; the outcry that followed came from Canada, not from the Army Overseas. Immediately after the raid, Canadian Postal Censors prepared an official report on the reaction of survivors taken from a study of more than eight thousand letters sent home. It said:

> The majority of the letters are found to be more serious and thoughtful in tone than usual. However there is a feeling of pride in being part of the Canadian Army, which they state has at last had a chance to show how they can fight.
>
> The morale of all appears to be very good. Regrets are not shown, but just enthusiasm, satisfaction and pride in achievement, and the Canadians' share in the raid.

A Canadian Army Intelligence Report covering the period September 4 to 19, 1942, noticed a similar reaction.

> The general morale of the Canadian Forces remains high and there continues to be evidence that the Dieppe raid has been a great incentive, and proved a stimulant and an encouragement to still greater efforts. Many writers who participated are anxious to avenge their comrades and to see further action. . . . The great majority state that, although casualties were heavy and the going pretty tough, they would willingly go over again tomorrow if they had to.

Major John Foote, VC, the revered Presbyterian Chaplain of the Royal Hamilton Light Infantry who became a voluntary prisoner of war, told me: "My lasting impression is that of the extraordinary morale of the Canadians captured at Dieppe. They were proud to have been the first to go back to the Continent and were confident they had shown the way for others to follow."

While the army settled down to a more realistic approach to the business of war, shock and disbelief reverberated across Canada, largely because the event itself was misunderstood. On the military side there was calm acceptance of the fact that such things happen in war; on the civilian side there was anger that it could be allowed to happen. Few can deny the awful futility of Dieppe as a military operation. Lessons were learned, but most of the military ones at least had been taught in previous wars and simply forgotten.

Five thousand men had been put into uniform in Quebec, Ontario, Manitoba, Saskatchewan, Alberta, and British Columbia, basically trained, and sent to England to meet an enemy who wisely stayed on his own side of the water. For another two years, vast amounts of money, energy, and equipment were expended in preparing these men for combat. When it came, the clash lasted for nine mercifully short hours in which three thousand were killed or taken prisoner while a thousand more never landed.

While the original conception of what a raid on Dieppe could contribute to victory was undeniably sound, the planning of it was so brilliantly, so appallingly detailed that it was more suited to a model exercise. When a very real enemy was so inconsiderate as to reveal a mind of his own, the actual execution of the plan proved tragically chaotic. What should have been a triumph for Canadian arms turned into a massacre. This book attempts to show how that came about.

I have avoided carrying the story much beyond Dieppe. Instead, I have confined it to the men who lit the beacon: men brought together on the winds of war – from the Canadian North, the West Coast, the Prairie Provinces, and French Canada; from the Scottish Highlands; from the plains of Texas and the snowbelts of Michigan and Vermont – and carried to the northern coast of France where Dieppe, an unattractive little seaside resort, faces the English Channel.

That Dieppe is linked by blood and an occasional feeble affection with almost every province in Canada does not make the place any more glamorous or less dilapidated. It lies in the estuary of the River Arques, really little more than a long gully between tall, white cliffs that rear up from narrow beaches and overhang them.

Its placid existence has witnessed only two momentous events. In 1066 a Norman invasion force sailed from Dieppe to conquer England; in 1942 a fleet came back from England to make it the bloody battlefield on which the art of combined operations was further refined. The Dieppois are mostly rural peasants and sturdy fishermen who have not the slightest interest in political or military belligerence. Indeed, they were shocked when the Canadians came, visited the town briefly and then retired, leaving behind a thousand dead on the pitiless, shifting pebbles of their miserable beaches.

Two men were primarily responsible for that costly experiment: Louis Mountbatten, England's most famous contemporary sailor, and Bernard Montgomery, England's most publicized contemporary soldier.

Neither the sincerity nor the professional integrity of these two gentle-men is in question here. It was, after all, their business in 1942 to undertake risks that would seem inhuman now. But this book does question the subtle means by which commanders decide the difference between calculated risk and calculated suicide.

Mountbatten has said, "I would do it again." Would he? In precisely the same circumstances? Militarists might describe this question as adolescent. Laymen know only too well how adolescent militarists can be. Montgomery has said, "I believe we could have got the informa-tion and experience we needed without losing so many magnificent Canadian soldiers." That is not what he thought when he insisted on the suicidal frontal assault across the main beaches. Mountbatten and Montgomery survived the backwash of Dieppe because greater glories obliterated their predominance over the planning of the operation, and because a scapegoat happened to be conveniently at hand.

He was Major-General John Hamilton Roberts, the Canadian mili-tary commander and the one figure upon whom the clamour for a public inquisition could be logically directed. This fine officer, a patriot in whom the roots of devotion to Canada grow deep, accepted his role silently, without protest.

The ignominy of defeat is hard to accept and political military cliques purge themselves of its presence by the cruel expedience of removing the generals associated with it. The case of Ham Roberts is no exception. Shameful treatment came later when he was made to suffer scandalously for his silence. After Dieppe it became generally believed that he had ended his final briefing with the remark, "It will be a piece of cake." This legend grew with such speed and conviction that men who were at the conference are still convinced that those were his words. If those present could be so persuaded, it is hardly surprising that a few who were not there also believe it. Among these latter were the insolent who celebrated an anniversary of Dieppe by sending General Roberts a piece of dried-out black bread.

When we talked at his home in the Channel Islands last year, Roberts denied being the author of this remark, but thought it very typical of Montgomery. The remark does, in fact, bear a striking resemblance to another Montyism addressed to the troops on the eve of D-Day. "There'll be nae bother at a', nae bother at a'," he said. In any event, there is no reason why Roberts should not have said it. Far better for him to have used this phrase as a morale booster than to warn of heavy casualties.

Roberts was, and still is, content that although Dieppe brought his own career to an abrupt end there was no serious challenge to the omnipotence of Mountbatten and Montgomery, both of whom enjoy his unwavering admiration.

This book is not intended to change anything; it is simply designed to strip the facts of embellishment, place them in perspective and, by doing so, perhaps relieve General Roberts in some small way of the burden of ill-informed, even biased, criticism he has carried for too many sad and often lonely years.

That is why *The Shame and The Glory* is dedicated to all who met the enemy for the first time on that hot summer's day not so very long ago.

"DIEPPE OCCUPIES A PLACE OF ITS OWN IN THE STORY OF WAR, AND THE GRIM CASUALTY FIGURES MUST NOT CLASS IT AS A FAILURE.... HONOUR TO THE BRAVE WHO FELL. THEIR SACRIFICE WAS NOT IN VAIN."

Sir Winston Churchill

"DIEPPE WAS ONE OF THE MOST VITAL OPERATIONS OF THE SECOND WORLD WAR. IT GAVE TO THE ALLIES THE PRICELESS SECRET OF VICTORY.... IF I HAD THE SAME DECISION TO MAKE AGAIN I WOULD DO AS I DID BEFORE."

Earl Mountbatten of Burma

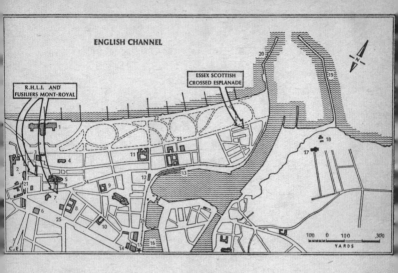

1 Casino	14 Chamber of Commerce
2 Vieux Château	15 furthest penetration by 12 men
3 Théâtre	16 Basin Duquesne
4 Town Hall	17 Notre Dame de Bon Secours
5 St Remy Church	18 Sémaphore
6 Palais de Justice	19 East Jetty
7 Post Office	20 West Jetty
8 Collège	21 Rue de Sygogne
9 Demai School	22 Boulevard Maréchal Foch
10 Sous Préfecture	23 Boulevard de Verdun
11 Tobacco Factory	24 Grande Rue
12 Fish Market	25 Rue Claude Groulard
13 Gare Maritime	26 Quai Duquesne

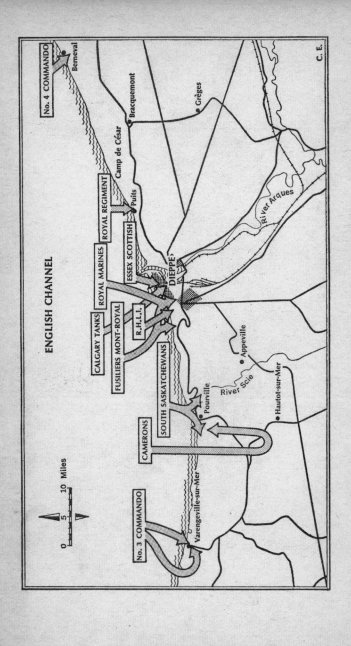

THE
SHAME

The Men

I

When the summer winds die down in the Canadian Barren Lands only space is left: a vast emptiness bound by the line where squat trees thrust up to the sky. It becomes strangely silent; and in this brief twilight all life above the ground is stilled, while below it unseen armies of insects and tiny, curious animals go about the business of survival among the roots of a bleak, scrub-filled wilderness. Their sound is only a rustle, faint at first but gathering in volume until the earth itself seems to come alive.

This was the sound two trappers heard one night when they huddled into sleeping-bags at a junction of trails four hundred miles north of Winnipeg. The younger was asleep almost at once; the older one lay tensely awake, the glowing embers of the fire between them reflecting redly from his dark, bearded face. He waited until the glow had faded into ashes, and then rose to his feet, shouldered pack and canteen, and vanished into the blackness of the surrounding brush.

Shortly before dawn, the younger one wakened and took in the events of the night with a single, swift glance. Without haste or apparent anxiety he made coffee and, squatting on his haunches, sipped it while smoking a cigarette.

When he broke camp his movements were deliberate, graceful. The simple act of standing up was an uncoiling of his slender, sinewy body with the smoothly flowing motion of a ballet dancer. He was about thirty-five years old with sandy hair, a surprisingly fleshy, pallid face, and full sensuous lips which gave him a feline, almost feminine, appearance. Yet he lifted heavy camping-equipment to his back with an ease that indicated remarkable strength.

He followed the same route south as his partner had taken, trailing over rocks and through scrub the man who had run off with six hundred dollars worth of furs, all they had to show for three months spent in the Barren Lands. His gun had gone with his partner, but sheathed at his belt was a long, wicked-looking skinner's knife.

A week later his relentless pursuit ended at the rim of a small canyon. For a brittle moment his cold, pale-blue eyes gazed down into the terrified face of a man who could recognize death. Then the knife flickered briefly in the morning sunlight and there was nothing else to do but bury its victim in the undergrowth.

On September 1, 1939, he was in Winnipeg coming out of a drunken stupor to be confronted by two pressing problems. He had no money, and for some reason the Royal Canadian Mounted Police were beginning to show interest in the fate of a missing trapper.

He became Stanley Jones that day and was welcomed as such by an eager recruiting sergeant into the Cameron Highlanders of Canada. Whatever his real name, "Private Stanley Jones" would do for the next three years; after that it wouldn't matter at all.

He had taken the first step towards something that was precariously close to a second murder – and Dieppe, where he would pay the supreme penalty anyway.

That afternoon Denis Whitaker sipped beer in the dim coolness of a bar on Toronto's Spadina Avenue. One excuse for drinking so early in the afternoon was the unexpected heatwave that had carried over from August into September. Outside were the sweating garment-makers, foreign-speaking seamstresses, and pudgy Jewish salesmen carrying racks of clothes from shops to waiting cars. There was also the dust, the dirt, and cloying dampness of a humid 90 degrees. A pair of college kids with nothing else to do jived diffidently in slow motion, their undulations made lazily suggestive by the boy's bared chest and the girl's lack of anything but a bathing costume.

Inside the bar, Denny was in shirtsleeves, the beer was ice cold, and a juke box played the latest Artie Shaw and Benny Goodman records. Sitting opposite him was Bob Isbister, and at a nearby table was a girl, legs swinging provocatively to the music's rhythm.

Neither Denny nor Bob were interested in the scene around them. Both had to have better reason than heat alone to be in a bar on the afternoon of September 1, 1939. They were football stars, trained and tempered to whiplash hardness: the glamour boys of the Hamilton Tigers and Toronto Argonauts, idols of the big league.

Denny, small, slight, dark, and wiry, didn't need beer so much as a place to sit, think, and occasionally talk. A graduate from the Royal Military College where his litheness and speed had made him spectacular on the gridiron, he was now a militia officer with the Royal Hamilton Light Infantry, a part-time occupation which had suddenly become more important than the Tigers.

Later that evening, Denny drove home to Hamilton and confided to his wife, Juanita, "I think it will come within hours now." It came two hours later when a telephone call from the Armouries brought a single word into the Whitaker home: "Mobilize."

Lieutenant Whitaker RHLI, son of an army officer and gentleman football star, was also on his way to Dieppe.

Another idol of the football grid, also the son of a distinguished military family, was waiting in Vancouver to be enmeshed by the spreading crisis in Europe. Charles Cecil Ingersoll Merritt, known on the West Coast as "Cec," was then a militia major in his father's First World War Regiment, the Seaforth Highlanders of Vancouver.

At twenty-nine, he was wide-shouldered and a burly six feet, physical attributes which made him a star of the Vancouver Athletic Club. After graduation from the Royal Military College in Ontario he had studied law, eventually becoming a barrister with a deliberate, purposeful courtroom manner, which more than compensated for his youth.

When he said goodbye to his attractive young wife, Grace, and went to his office on September 1 he had felt that a summons to action was imminent, but he was hardly prepared for the telephone call he received later that morning. A voice said briefly: "It's come, Cec. Mobilize, right now." Then the line went dead, leaving him with the receiver in his hand and a strange feeling of excitement welling up inside him.

That evening in the Seaforth Armouries, thronged with bewildered volunteers, Grace brought him sandwiches and a flask of coffee. When it was time for all wives and mothers to leave she said: "Don't try to win medals, Cec. You just come home."

They were not to be reunited as a family for six years. Cec Merritt was destined for Dieppe, and the first Canadian Victoria Cross of the war.

II

The citizen-soldiers, who would have to wait three years before confronting the enemy, were mobilized on the same day, the day that Germany marched contemptuously into Poland, and Canada proclaimed "a state of apprehended war." They mustered at armouries and public buildings throughout the country – a few in uniform but most in light summer suits – until there were enough to warrant in the region of three hundred signals to Ottawa indicating that the Canadian militia were ready for service at home, abroad, or anywhere.

As there were few guns, almost no ammunition, and not even sufficient medical forms to allow recruits to be medically examined, the appalled staff officer who received these signals noted: "We don't need an enemy. When they get enough weapons they'll kill themselves; given enough time they'll die anyway."

Political indifference had indeed achieved something close to total unpreparedness. But the citizen-soldiers belonged to a devoted generation, untamed by discipline, yet obedient to their purpose and willing to endure personal hardship, ridicule and, in French Canada, even the hatred of their fellow countrymen simply to accomplish it.

Anglo-Saxon Canada often refers sneeringly to the French-Canadian war effort. Yet one Quebec regiment recruited at a faster rate than most of its English-speaking counterparts and the Fusiliers Mont-Royal were among the first militia battalions in the country to volunteer *en masse* for service overseas. When its thirty-two officers were asked to re-attest for active service they did so without hesitation or exception. This regiment was to be slaughtered, re-formed, and then go on to fight again with a dash and fury that has given Canadian military history some of its most proud and colourful passages. At times when it is fashionable to talk of separatism and secession, people tend to forget that in Montreal some French-Canadian units had more applications for enlistment than English-speaking units but had to reject more on medical grounds. One of the slowest rates was reported in

Saskatchewan where a powerful foreign-born community was exerting pressure against Canadian participation in the war, even using the harvest as an excuse for blocking recruitment.

In Weyburn, however, the South Saskatchewan Regiment were looking with open-mouthed astonishment at Regimental Sergeant-Major Strumm who had the prairie men out on parade to hear these words:

"When I was a little child I had a set of wooden soldiers. There was a poor boy in the neighbourhood and after I had been to Sunday school one day listening to a stirring story on the duties of charity, I was soft enough to give him the soldiers. Then I wanted them back and cried, but my mother said, 'Don't cry, Sonny, some day you will get your wooden soldiers back.'" His booming finish roared out over the prairies. "And, believe me . . . *that day has come.*"

No other regiment had anything quite like Strumm in its arsenal, nor anyone quite so irreverent of army discipline and traditions as Captain Murray Osten, a dark whip of a man, whose adventurous escapades in the placid southern counties of England were to become legendary throughout the Canadian Army. A succession of despairing colonels were to agree: "There's an accident of fate we never deserved."

While this was going on in the prairies, a Toronto battalion, the Royal Regiment of Canada, was having its own troubles, most pressing of which was where to live. This was solved by taking over the International Pavilion at the Canadian National Exhibition Grounds, a building in which there were neither heat, toilets, nor rudimentary cooking facilities.

Uniforms came by instalments: wedge caps one week, fatigue trousers the next, and so on. Eventually the regiment could boast sixty complete uniforms, but since the jackets had been made in Montreal and the trousers in Toronto the shades of khaki didn't match. Their issue was delayed while strenuous efforts were made to persuade the Montreal manufacturers to provide trousers and the Toronto firm to turn out jackets. This way, it was hoped, the sixty two-tone uniforms could be boosted to a hundred and twenty, all of one colour.

Every battalion was suffering from lack of boots, clothes, palliasses, and beds. Men marched or drilled until their civilian shoes gave out, then they were excused from further training. One regiment bought its own cap badges; another had to arrange for a private supply of gloves so that men could handle rifles in freezing temperatures. One group of officers, disgusted at the total absence of any weapon larger than a carbine, built their own two-inch mortar which fired a wooden bomb – for twenty-five yards.

Incredibly, under such conditions, morale remained consistently high throughout the winter, and by the spring of 1940 most regiments were up to strength, partially equipped, and acquiring the first faint flush of a soldierly *élan*.

Yet despite all the efforts of senior officers, junior officers combined with enlisted men to frustrate initial attempts to envelop them in the straightjacket of tight discipline. They had come from lumber camps, business offices, country stores, and big city corporations; they would play the army's game just so long as they were being taught how to fight, but had no intention of catering automatically to symbols of rank. If officers commanded respect as individuals then they might get it in the form of a casual friendly "Hi."

But with time the influence of older hands and the insistent indoctrination by which armies everywhere instil discipline had their effect. Saluting, for instance, became so natural that, in order to halt an alarming rate of accidents caused by too much punctilious windmilling of arms, one regiment had to post an order saying: "As it is not advisable for an officer riding a motor-bicycle to return a salute, he will not be saluted."

Even the embryo 1st Army Tank Brigade which had attracted cat-skinners and truck-drivers from all over Canada became a model of parade-ground precision. All they really needed were the vehicles in which to be mobile.

Spurred by the efforts of the Armoured Force Association, a group of interested Toronto businessmen, the major automobile companies were persuaded to send technicians to the Canadian Armoured Fighting Vehicles School at Borden to instruct recruits in engine maintenance. As there were no armoured vehicles, they had to use engines cannibalized from elderly cars wherever these could be found.

While this was going on, the Defence Department in Ottawa remained firmly stuck in the mud of the 1918 trenches. Brigadier E. J. Schmidlen, Director of Engineering Services, announced publicly: "The ultimate weapon which wins a war is the bayonet on a rifle. . . . No one knows how useful tanks will be."

This attitude caused officers taking courses at the Borden tank school to think twice about their careers. Most of them were carried on their respective battalion lists, and to remain at a school which had not the slightest hope of acquiring a tank in the foreseeable future could result in their being passed over for promotion. One by one they quit to resume regimental duties. Finally only a handful of fanatical believers remained obstinately behind.

One of these was Major Johnny Gilby Andrews, a short, lean thirty-year-old prankster who, as a one-time bank teller, had been advised that the army might be better equipped to handle his unquenchable effervescence. Andrews had taken the advice, attended the Royal Military College and then become a fully fledged Permanent Force captain with the Princess Patricia's Canadian Light Infantry. Andrews was one of the few Canadian officers who believed that one day tanks would prove decisive in war. He staked his career on mechanized warfare, and clung to the School even when it faced extinction.

In May 1940 the 2nd Canadian Division grew into a cohesive force comprising three brigades of which the 4th at Borden and the 6th at Camp Shilo, Manitoba, were two. They included the Essex Scottish Regiment from the border areas of southwestern Ontario; the Royal Regiment of Canada; the Royal Hamilton Light Infantry; the Camerons of Canada from Winnipeg; the South Saskatchewans; and the Fusiliers Mont-Royal of Quebec for whom the General Staff were seeking a young potential commanding officer.

He came, unexpectedly and, for him, typically, from India where he had been guarding the Khyber Pass and fighting with the 4/11 Sikh Regiment in Waziristan for two years. He was burly, brash, irrepressible, and irresistible Major Dollard Menard, a professional product of the Royal Military College, who, disgruntled at the inactivity of the peacetime Canadian army, had volunteered for a steady fighting job in the remote gateway to the Orient. Joe, as he is known for reasons long obscure, resigned his commission with the Sikhs when war broke out and wrote to Ottawa requesting that he be put back on strength.

The Defence Department, startled at this emergence of a French-Canadian officer from so unlikely a trouble spot, and still thinking in terms of a six-months' war, was unwilling to spend money on his passage home. They cautiously replied that as he had been seconded to India at his own request he was no longer the responsibility of the Canadian government and would have to find someone else to foot the bill. To Joe Menard this was a typical Anglo-Saxon insult to a loyal French Canadian and, suitably annoyed, he set off from the Khyber Pass on his own to prove his patriotism.

He had more stubborn anger than money, but when he reached Bombay, friends in the British army helped him extract a free passage to Hong Kong from either the War Office or the Indian government. "I never knew which," he says. At Hong Kong he was fortunate to find that the commander-in-chief of the British army there was a General Grasset, also a graduate of the Royal Military College and a personal friend of his father's. Menard, impatient that the war might end before he had an opportunity to win it, exerted his considerable charm on the general who suggested that one way to reach Canada without paying passage might be to join the Royal Navy. Before Joe quite realized what was happening he was transformed into a sailor and appointed to a destroyer. It took many long weeks of service aboard more destroyers, a motor torpedo boat or two, and a submarine to reach Panama and then Halifax, Nova Scotia, where he discarded his naval uniform and bid farewell to the sea. By the time he arrived in Ottawa, Menard reckoned he had proved his patriotism and, to the astonishment of the Defence Department who had long forgotten the odd request from the Khyber Pass, turned up in immaculate uniform adorned by a very strange decoration and reported ready for duty.

The General Staff reversed itself, murmured polite appreciation at having the services of an experienced French-Canadian officer at no cost to the government and sent him off to a staff course without noticing that his erect military swagger was by then peculiarly aggravated by a discernible sailor's roll. Joe later became staff captain to the 5th Infantry Brigade as grooming for eventual command of the Fusiliers Mont-Royal.

By July the division was formally reported to be no further advanced than it should be in two months of divisional training, and three regiments were assigned to garrison Iceland. Because someone in the British War Office thought that Canada was itself an ice cap and that Canadians should be expert warriors on another ice cap, the rest of the division might have followed but for the intervention of Winston Churchill.

After visiting the 1st Canadian Division, then installed south of London, the British Prime Minister sent a minute to Anthony Eden saying:

> You shared my astonishment yesterday at the statement made to us by General McNaughton that the whole of the 2nd Canadian Division was destined for Iceland. It would surely be a very great mistake to allow these fine troops to be employed in so distant a theatre. Apparently, the first three battalions have already gone there. No one was told anything about this. We require the two Canadian divisions to work as a corps as soon as possible. . . .

Ottawa responded to the official representations which followed by agreeing that the 2nd Division should follow the 1st to England, and the movement of men from Canada and Iceland began in August. But it was not until Christmas that the entire division was encamped at Aldershot, the principal troop assembly point for British forces since the Crimean War.

If a coherent, partly equipped Canadian infantry division was a phenomenal achievement considering the unimpressive beginnings only a year before, another unique formation was being prepared for dispatch to England – the 1st Army Tank Brigade of which Johnny Andrews had become brigade major.

Germany's *blitzkrieg* across the Low Countries and envelopment of the Maginot Line had shattered Ottawa into sudden realization that this war was not going as predicted and would probably need a brand new set of rules. It had been belatedly decided, after the customary lengthy consideration, that bayonets on rifles would be not quite enough after all.

The citizen-soldiers were now in a theatre of war. The great beast they had come to slay remained unseen across the English Channel, but pounce he might, and they prepared to meet him on the beaches, among the forests and fields of England. All that had gone before was in the nature of a preliminary flirtation with war; if and when the enemy struck, they would fulfil the purpose for which they had endured so much.

III

When the Normans invaded England nearly nine hundred years ago they landed in Sussex and immediately claimed the rights of conquerors: out-of-season stag-hunting and unrestricted girl-chasing among the village attics. Anxious English matrons attempted, without much success, to hide their pink-cheeked daughters from the gay, lascivious Frenchmen, but practice and intuition gave these sporting knights such an unfair advantage that the process of Norman integration into the Saxon race was not long delayed.

If the intervening centuries have seen many material changes, the human character remains very much as it was. The same protective instincts were aroused in modern English mothers in 1941 when the 2nd Canadian Division moved into Sussex, and Frenchmen were once again let loose among the attics.

In no time at all the distinction between English Canadian and French Canadian blurred, and the seeds of a single Canadian character took root among the distraught Sussex matrons, most of whom were quickly convinced that Canadians generally were the most dangerous threat to youthful virginity ever encountered.

Being reasonably red-blooded, a safe distance from home, and having little else to do when off duty in the blacked-out evenings, the troops of the 2nd Division undoubtedly contributed their share of the damage. But not without the often enthusiastic co-operation of the fair young maidens of Sussex who found in these strangers from a faraway land fascinating substitutes for their own men, then mostly stationed remotely in Africa and Burma.

Friction, fighting, and some unholy brawls occurred only when these yeomen of England came home on leave to find their girls, and some of the mothers too, clinging happily to the arms of big, broad-shouldered, and wholly complacent Canadians. British indignation would then find an outlet in sneering remarks about the soft life Canadians were enjoying in Hastings, Lewes, Brighton, and Eastbourne while "We're in the bloody jungle or the bloody desert fighting this 'ere bloody war."

If anything were guaranteed to rile a Canadian soldier it was to be reminded that he had not yet fired a shot in anger. The English-speaking Canadian felt it was an unjust commentary on his interminable wait for an invasion that seemed increasingly unlikely; to the French Canadian it was an insult to his national honour and personal fighting ability.

It was rumoured that one hero of Quebec avoided such messy affairs by paying his men to bring women back to camp. This perfumed dandy in elevated heels would then escort them to his quarters in which he had installed a proper double bed complete with black silk sheets. It is still said by many of his former comrades that when the supply of local talent diminished he could make a single telephone call to London and have a squad of girls sent down to Brighton as required. Fortunately none was there the day the late King arrived unexpectedly to inspect his men.

The 2nd Division moved from Aldershot into Sussex with a standard of training that could be hopefully described as elementary. Major-General V. W. Odlum of Vancouver, who had served in the Boer War and the First World War and was quite happy to be back in the Second, had been made General Officer Commanding the Division, and it was his idea that each company commander in all the battalions should take his men on overnight training schemes to any point outside London and within fifty miles of headquarters. The emphasis was on marching, each company having to average at least twenty miles a week. Units began knocking up impressive totals well above the minimum and indeed showed an almost indecent eagerness to exercise. When local police chiefs from various parts of the country began complaining, the truth emerged. Overnight "schemes" as they were called had become far-flung pub crawls in which the 2nd Division acquired in a few months that intimate knowledge of taverns which an Englishman rarely learns in a lifetime. The result of this was that when the division exercised with the 1st Division as an army corps, they had to learn to drive trucks in blackout conditions on strange, narrow, winding country roads. Fantastic traffic jams occurred, and from then on there was less prowling and more driving.

Apart from the irritating refusal of the Germans to attempt an invasion and thereby relieve the Canadians of tedious, repetitious training and persistent boredom, 1941 was enlivened by a variety of immense "schemes" involving hundreds of thousands of troops and the introduction of battle drill, that incredible British conception in which dummy bullets were thrown away and replaced with live ammunition. This compensated to some extent for the lack of a real enemy, and if a soldier had a particular feud going, he could often settle it with the live rounds he carried quite legally. There were plenty of accidental woundings, but how many or how few were caused by malice could never be determined. Instead, the troops were ordered to approach battle drill with a good deal more care and a little less enthusiasm.

The winter of 1941-42 was the worst: a cold, wet, miserable period in which the men of the 2nd Division indulged in self-pity and suffered from a mild form of collective homesickness.

During this winter of continuing frustration, Major-General John Hamilton Roberts became the new commander of the 2nd Division. A tall, dark and thickset regular army officer from Vancouver who had served with an artillery regiment in the First World War, Ham Roberts was neither impressed by the division's efficiency nor afraid of correcting it to the point of personal unpopularity.

In 1940, when commanding the 1st Canadian Field Regiment, RCHA, he had gone to France after Dunkirk as part of the force sent in an abortive attempt to establish a second British Expeditionary Force. The regiment had landed at the Biscayan port of Brest with all its vehicles, weapons, trailers, and twenty-four pieces of field artillery and had moved inland to an assembly point.

The speed of the German advance and the imminence of a French collapse had made the British government change its mind and decide to bring the force home again. Should France surrender, the men and their equipment would be desperately needed for the defence of Britain.

But alarming reports of German armoured columns rapidly moving towards the port had thrown the evacuation organization into a confusion that came close to panic. On June 16 Roberts had brought his 25-pounders back to Brest where he was instructed to leave them in a central "parking lot" which was to be blown up as the last troops were taken aboard the waiting ships.

Ham Roberts had never lost a gun in his life; nor had he ever abandoned one without a bitter fight, and then only when all else was hopeless. He had spent the night trying to persuade the captains of ships alongside the docks to take his guns aboard. By morning they had all refused to do so without written orders from the commanding general.

That morning orders had been issued for the destruction of all guns, trailers, and transport equipment. Roberts had stormed into the astonished general's headquarters and fought for two hours to save his guns. He had achieved a brief respite, but later in the day a second order had been issued confirming the first. When he had assailed headquarters again and found the general too busy to see him, he had begun arguing and wheedling with as many senior officers as he could find.

No one had been interested in Roberts or his guns until he had discovered a senior staff officer who had attended the Royal Military College of Canada and who knew him by reputation. The old-school-tie principle had come into operation, and the general had been persuaded to give Roberts reluctant permission to load as many guns as he could within a certain time limit, which meant he had had just two hours. The regiment had rushed its guns from the parking lot to the docks, commandeered the first empty ship and, with the willing help of British seamen, loaded every item of equipment, except one gun, with thirty minutes to spare. This gun had been damaged during the withdrawal and had not returned from the repair shops – an intolerable situation for Roberts. He had led a raid on the parking lot, found a gun and trailer looking fairly lonely, and towed it down to the docks. Within minutes it was aboard, and Roberts had been grimly content that having landed with twenty-four guns he was taking the same number back. Then, looking happily along the docks, he had spotted more abandoned equipment, and before the ship had sailed his regiment had acquired seven Bofors ack-ack guns, seven artillery range finders, and a miscellaneous collection of armoured cars and Bren carriers.

Now, eighteen months later, he fixed the same bleak, uncompromising stare on his new command and set in motion events which did nothing to make the winter any happier for the 2nd Division.

He inherited reports of drunkenness, brawling, damage to civilian property, and a long record of breaking-and-entering charges in which men of nearly every regiment were involved. The Deputy Chief Constable of Brighton gave a statement to the British press saying that Canadian soldiers had been responsible for "rather serious disturbances at night" and that "our men have been extremely tolerant with the Canadians but recently they have had to draw their truncheons in self-defence." Although he referred to the 1st Division, the 2nd was included in a general order from Lieutenant-General H. D. G. Crerar, GOC 1st Canadian Army Corps, which said: "Any neglect to take prompt and firm action in apprehending, charging and court-martialling of soldiers open to the charge of desertion will have widespread and dangerous results."

Nor was it the troops alone who came under fire from Crerar. He wrote to Roberts:

> I want you to take appropriate steps . . . to impress on all your formation and unit commanders the absolute necessity of maintaining a high standard of social behaviour amongst their officers at off-duty gatherings. There is still a tendency on the part of certain officers to regard a party in the mess, or elsewhere, as an occasion when excessive drinking can be accepted, if not actually expected. That point of view must be . . . eliminated without delay.
>
> I do not wish the above statement . . . to convey the idea that I am opposed to the reasonable consumption of alcoholic beverages, to occasional mess entertainments or to other pleasant and appropriate forms of relaxation.

Roberts grinned delightedly at the oblique references to times when he himself had enjoyed the corps commander's "other pleasant" forms of relaxation. But he acted harshly, sparing no one in his determination to impose strict discipline, improve standards of efficiency, and raise morale throughout every level of the division.

Three months before, Prime Minister Mackenzie King had flown to England to meet Winston Churchill and to visit the Canadian forces.

He had spent a day at South-Eastern Army headquarters at Reigate where Lieutenant-General Bernard Montgomery, under whom the Canadian Army served, qualified his tribute to their abilities with the remark: "Your officers generally are rather too old for this war. They should be younger men, preferably around forty, so that they can put up with the rigours of the present sort of warfare."

When the Canadian Prime Minister returned to Ottawa and repeated this comment to the Minister of National Defence, the effect of it was to reach down into every echelon of the forces overseas. It reached the 2nd Division in the New Year 1942, when Roberts used a variety of excuses to remove some of his battalion commanders. Others might have followed but for the lack of suitable replacements. Commands were given to keen, youthful officers who had completed staff courses at Camberley or who had undertaken extensive specialized training with British units.

Although little in the public eye at that time, Montgomery had built up a formidable reputation among army men. He had played a significant role in extricating the British Expeditionary Force from Dunkirk and was known to be well in with General Sir Alan Brooke, Chief of the Imperial General Staff.

It is said that when Montgomery and Crerar first met, the Canadian was unaware that he was in the presence of a non-smoking teetotaller. They were travelling in the back seat of Montgomery's staff car when Crerar, deciding to smoke, pulled a pack of cigarettes from his tunic pocket. As he put one in his mouth he said, out of courtesy for a senior officer, "Mind if I smoke, sir?"

"No, certainly not," snapped Montgomery, and Crerar lit his cigarette, "but not in my car."

Crerar was utterly bewildered, more so when Montgomery ordered the driver to stop the car and turned on him, saying, "If you insist upon smoking, I shall get out until you have finished. Then we will proceed."

The flabbergasted Crerar threw away his cigarette and mumbled: "Sorry, I had no idea you really objected." It was an embarrassing initial encounter for two men who were to see much more of each other in the years ahead.

Under Montgomery, the idea of defensive warfare was replaced by a more positive approach. The title of the plan which had been the basis of all Canadian training up to 1942 was changed from "Plan for the Defence of Sussex" to "Plan for the Defeat of Invasion." The spirit of mobile defence was replaced with the spirit of mobile offence.

Montgomery's dynamic personality and unlimited energy were devoted to inculcating into the troops of his command a ferocious determination to kill every German soldier who might have the temerity to even touch the sacred soil of England; he demanded the highest standards of physical fitness, and the 2nd Division, now commanded by a disciple of this type of leadership, began to find that a static war could be strenuous indeed. Roberts was convinced that if the training were sufficiently intensive, if there were enough manœuvres and exercises, the men would have neither the strength nor the inclination to get into trouble with the civilian authorities.

It seemed he was right. Civil and military crimes were reduced sharply, and probably the most significant statistics of all showed only six convictions for indecent assault or rape in 1942 and that only one in every two thousand troops was involved in a civil crime every month. The relentless pursuit of efficiency made the citizen-soldiers of Canada hard men in whom idealism burned brightly. They were, however, still unblooded in battle and innocently unaware of the cruel realities yet to be experienced. From battalion commanders down they were so young, so eager to match their enthusiastic amateurism against an arrogant, professional enemy, that the appalled, war-weary youngsters of a friendly RAF fighter wing had expressed compassion tinged with awe in a sign placed mockingly over their mess bar. It said: "We earnestly regret that Canadian colonels under 21 cannot be served spirits unless accompanied by their parents."

Among the honorary members of that mess were seven Canadian colonels commanding between them nearly five thousand troops. Their average age was thirty-three and their life expectancy in the actuarial terms of 1942 was three years. Their youth in years was not a disadvantage because they expected to grow out of it; life expectancy was a phrase that never occurred to them. Their main problem was holding highly trained, impatient men on a leash when their natural impulse was to leap at the enemy's throat.

The moment for letting them loose was not far away. In March, when buttercups on the Sussex Downs indicated the approach of spring, the decisions of those responsible for the conduct of the war began to seep down to the poised armies, decisions which would release them from confinement in Britain and send them out swiftly at night to win bright honours from the pale-faced moon.

Reasons for
a Raid

I

Britain was a lying-in hospital for the expectant Canadian Army. Confinement was so prolonged that it seemed to the men they were the Cinderellas of the Commonwealth, ordered to stay at home while the armies of the sister Dominions and the United States comported themselves none too well at military encounters nearly everywhere between Tobruk and Corregidor.

There were good reasons for the long wait in Sussex. As late as October 1941, when most people considered a German invasion unlikely, British Intelligence had estimated that if Germany could stabilize the Russian front and enforce a stalemate, she could send fifty divisions against England. Secret reports from inside Germany, substantially confirmed by reconnaissance photographs, indicated that some eight hundred landing-craft had been built, each capable of carrying "8 to 10 tanks as well as infantry."

The Canadian government, supported by their Chiefs of Staff, agreed that Canadian troops could be used best by undertaking the most vital task of all – the defence of Britain – thereby leaving Churchill free to manipulate British and other Commonwealth forces in accordance with higher strategy. The Prime Minister of Canada, Mackenzie King, said he opposed sending troops anywhere else because "our duty is to protect their lives, our position being that we are at the side of Britain, and not to begin playing the role of those who want an Empire war." By late 1941, however, he was under heavy political and military pressure to insist that Canadian troops be put into action in some theatre or other.

In May of that year the idea of Canadian participation in raiding activities along the French coast had been mentioned for the first time. According to the Mackenzie King diaries, "Defence officials say we should ask the British authorities to have our Army put into action somewhere at once – if not in the Middle East, then on raids to France . . . even if it involved some being killed." Politically his colleagues in the government were insisting upon something spectacular to inject life into the newly launched recruiting campaign. Mackenzie King had retaliated by reaffirming that Canadian soldiers were "doing the highest service in protecting the heart of the Empire." Noble as these words had been, their sentiment was not shared by the men concerned; nor was it reflected in the growing dissatisfaction at home at the seeming idleness of the army overseas.

During his visit to England in September, Mackenzie King discussed these difficulties with Churchill and is reputed to have said, in effect: "I don't know how long I can go on leading my country while our troops remain inactive." Several days later, when speaking to three thousand Canadian troops in Sussex, he tried to off-load some responsibility for their inactivity on the British government. "You must not allow anyone," he said, "to say that it was your Government's restraining hand, but that it was the view of the Government of the United Kingdom to have you in this place of vital importance. . . ."

The Canadian Prime Minister was really echoing the advice of McNaughton who was determined that "our men should not be used uselessly or experimentally in war." The General wanted to preserve this army until the day came to liberate Europe; then he would lead it into battle personally. While Mackenzie King had to justify this wait-wait policy in political terms it did not suit the Army which began to take matters into its own hands, in a most subtle and effective way.

Intimate, prolonged contact with the British General Staff and senior

command officers was having the effect of providing Canadian commanders with a safety valve. They could rid themselves of frustrations
in the company of like-minded friends who were also in a position to
offer them action – particularly Montgomery and Lord Louis Mountbatten, who had been charged with providing the practical experience
on which planners would work out the grand design for a return to
continental Europe.

II

When Hitler signed an armistice with France on June 22, 1940, he had
declared triumphantly that Britain had been "driven forever from the
Continent of Europe."

The following night 120 Commandos carried out the first raid of the
war on the French coast. They stayed ashore long enough to give the
lie to Hitler, but had to leave without prisoners and without much
information and were landed back in England at a strange port where
military police promptly arrested them as deserters. In the mild legal
furore which followed, an officer was reported as saying, "We went
there merely to show the Hun we can go back any time we bloody
well feel like it." More realistically, perhaps, this initial raid served to
indicate that while Europe reeled under the thunderous impact of the
German *blitzkrieg*, Britain was thinking seriously about returning to
put the pieces back together again.

A month later the newly created Combined Operations Command,
headed by Admiral of the Fleet Sir Roger Keyes, was directed to undertake a program of harassing raids against the Continent designed to
gain experience in German defences. Then, in October, the Joint Planning Staff was formed, consisting of the directors of planning of the
three British services, given an underground room at the War Office,
and told to begin planning for a possible bridgehead on the Cherbourg
peninsula. At that time Churchill and his Chiefs of Staff were looking
ahead to the day when they might want to land in strength somewhere in France, stay there for a few days, and withdraw only when
Germany had been given a salutory example of what was to come.

Combined Operations is an ancient British method of waging war.
Once known as "conjunct expeditions," it was employed as early as
the sixteenth century, when Spain was the enemy and Drake used land
and sea forces to raid the West Indies; so did Lord Howard when he
assaulted Cadiz in 1596. While the lessons of these early raiding activi-

ties were always well absorbed, they were sometimes applied rather badly. For instance, the achievements of Wolfe and Saunders at Quebec in 1759 were the outcome of a "conjunct expedition" formula which was tried successfully during the Napoleonic wars and again at Gallipoli in 1915 without any success at all.

Once the British and German armies lost contact in 1940, the opportunity to return to the "conjunct expedition" formula came once more, and Combined Operations was founded upon two pursuits dear to British hearts – love of the sea and love of the chase.

While raids could irritate the enemy, keep him constantly alert, and tie down his troops in inactive areas, there was little real hope of Britain being able to return to the Continent in force until her armies had been built up and Germany's strength had been irrevocably committed elsewhere than in the west. Only when these two conditions came about would the pendulum of power swing in Britain's direction.

The second was fulfilled in June 1941 when Germany attacked Russia, and the first in December when the Japanese raided Pearl Harbour. German strength was channelled eastwards while the full might of the United States was placed alongside that of Britain in the west.

So violent a change in the strategic picture of war made possible eventual invasion of the Continent and raised Combined Operations from the level of a wildcat raiding organization to an embryo invasion headquarters.

The aging Sir Roger Keyes, who was more than seventy, was dismissed by Churchill on the ground that his irascibility was causing friction among his subordinates. Sir Alan Brooke, Chief of the Imperial General Staff, had also inspected the first Combined Operations training depot in Scotland and had reported, "It's all right as far as it goes. But the thinking behind the Command generally is far too small." Keyes was quickly replaced by a new chief, Lord Louis Mountbatten, 41-year-old cousin of the King and one of the most colourful British naval officers of the war, who became "Adviser on Combined Operations to the Defence Committee and Chiefs of Staff."

Mountbatten's directive defined his primary duties as "the preparation for the apparatus and plans for the invasion of the Continent." From then onward, raiding activities became the glamorous secondary functions through which Combined Operations could gather the experience and information necessary to blueprint eventual landings in strength.

Early in 1942, when the United States Chiefs of Staff had joined with their British counterparts to become the Combined Chiefs, a directive was issued to Combined Operations which said: "Raids in force designed to obtain information and experience in the enemy's defence system are to be pressed forward as opportunities arise." This directive was tantamount to being blessed by the Anglo-American high priests of war, and Mountbatten immediately chose as his chief staff officer the slight, dapper, forty-year-old Captain John Hughes-Hallett, Royal Navy, who was to prove one of the wonder boys of Combined Operations.

Hughes-Hallett brought to his job an amazingly precise mind which coupled imagination with cool practicality. He could strip complicated issues down to hard essentials and ended most arguments with a quiet "Let's do it and see." He gave to the war the same intense concentration of effort that artists apply to masterpieces and, being essentially sensitive, he earned the devotion of the creative non-conformists who somehow achieved astonishing results with dubious schemes pulled out of the thin air in the wild blue yonder.

As Mountbatten's naval adviser, he was also director of the Combined Operations planning syndicate, a boldly imaginative group of young officers renowned for their unorthodox procedures. In this capacity, he was to exert more influence on the Canadian Army's initial venture into battle than any other man alive. A paradoxically complex yet concise, clear-thinking officer, Hughes-Hallett conceived the two great raids which contributed so much to the invasions of North Africa and Normandy. Because the second raid would probably not have taken place if the first had been unsuccessful, the incredibly impudent attack on the French Biscayan base of St Nazaire is an essential ingredient of the Dieppe story.

On February 1, 1942, the Allies had not yet stopped losing the war; the axis upon which global strategy pivoted was one ship, the mighty German battleship *Tirpitz*. Her presence in Norwegian waters where she lay poised for a pounce into the Atlantic compelled the maintenance of British battleships in the North Sea and two United States battleships with one British in the Atlantic.

Land operations also suffered. In the two dominant theatres, Pacific and North Africa, it was impossible to plan effective counter-attacks until the initiative could be regained at sea.

Commander Robert Edward Dudley Ryder, RN, reported to the London headquarters of Combined Operations in mid February with certain misgivings. Well built with blue, wide-set eyes in a square, tanned face, he had no particular wish to be heroic or to be anything but a competent naval officer. A tall, aggressively fit-looking Commando gave his credentials a cursory, almost contemptuous glance, and showed him into the office of Captain Hughes-Hallett.

"Glad you got here quickly, Ryder. Want to show you something interesting. See that map? It's St Nazaire. Know its importance?"

"U-boat base, sir."

Hughes-Hallett shrugged impatiently. "I know that, but what else? Look, *Tirpitz* is lying in Bergen waiting for a chance to break out into the Atlantic. She can raise merry hell along the convoy routes – finish the job started by the U-boats. But once she slips out, the Home Fleet and the United States Atlantic Fleet can seal off her return through the Denmark Straits to home waters. That means she will have to be supplied, repaired, and generally sustained at sea from St Nazaire."

"Why, sir?" Ryder was still only mildly curious despite a growing uneasiness.

"Because she's 42,000 tons and there's only one dry dock cum floating dock in enemy hands that she can use – the one the French built for their passenger liner *Normandie* before the war. And that is at St Nazaire. Destroy it and they'll think twice about sending *Tirpitz* out."

Now Ryder was thoroughly alarmed. "And what has that got to do with me?"

"You, my dear Ryder, will blow it up."

From this brief conversation was born Operation Chariot, the code name for an impertinent raid in force which was to lift the innocuous commander into the forefront of fame.

The Hughes-Hallett formula for success was surprise and simplicity. An expendable ship filled with explosives would ram the dock gates while a small force of Commandos destroyed the power plants and pumping-machinery. It was a cheeky plan because the dock was 1148 feet long with gates 167 feet across, 54 feet high, and 35 feet thick. However, Mountbatten had blessed it, and when it was discussed by the Joint Chiefs of Staff in Washington, Admiral Ernest King was reported to have said: "I don't give a damn what the British do so long as I get my battleships back to the Pacific."

In London next day, Ryder, invested with new authority as naval force commander, met his co-leader in charge of the military force, Lieutenant-Colonel A. C. Newman, a large, robust Commando officer with a startling air of competence about him.

Prospects of success were remote indeed. The River Loire runs westwards out of France into the Atlantic through an estuary one mile wide which is filled with sand banks, mud banks, and shoals. These form a natural barrier to indiscriminate entry except through a narrow channel running for five miles close in along the north shore. St Nazaire lies at the end of this north channel. The Germans had mounted four batteries of three long-range guns each at intervals along the north coast so that the channel could be invested in covering fire for its entire length. More batteries on the southern shore prevented sneak attacks by shallow-draught vessels over the shoals.

These were but preliminary dangers. Once inside the harbour, light machine-gun and Bofors strongpoints had been so placed to more or less guarantee wiping out anything that moved.

The inner berthing basins were controlled against the ebb and flow of the tides by a series of locks, the largest of which was, in fact, the Normandie Dock. This vast structure had great caissons built into the gates through which water could be pumped in or out. If these were destroyed the dock would be rendered useless and the inner basins, used by U-boats, would also be wrecked. As an additional defence, however, the enemy had established a chain of coastal radar stations with an effective radius of not less than thirty miles.

When confronted with this information, Ryder was even more convinced that the cheerful planners of Combined Operations were not treating him kindly. Newman gave him no help at all.

"Getting us in there is your job, old boy," he grinned callously. "And out, too, remember?"

They retired to the peaceful port of Falmouth with a small group of young, enthusiastic technical experts to consider how best to pierce these defences. The conservatory of a sea-front hotel became their headquarters, and from this exotic, plant-filled bower went out the orders for assembling the Chariot force.

Ryder's naval force consisted of HMS *Campbeltown*, one of the fifty American destroyers given to Britain in exchange for a 99-year lease on the naval base at Bermuda. She was obsolete, expendable, and with her came eighteen little boats purloined from the Coastal Defence Forces squadrons: sixteen motor launches (ML), one motor torpedo boat (MTB), and one motor gun boat (MGB).

To ensure total destruction of the caisson gates, experts advised that five tons of explosives would have to be stowed into *Campbeltown*'s bows so that when she rammed, the full force of the explosion would come from hard alongside. Whatever happened, she must not hit and then fall away. It was decided to ram hard, scuttle the ship, and let the crew disembark into the ML's for the withdrawal. The explosives could be detonated by fuses when she had sunk alongside the caissons.

Meanwhile, Ryder had dealt with two other problems. To interfere with the enemy radar chain, Bomber Command were to launch a raid on the St Nazaire docks as the Chariot force approached. He hoped that this would divert attention from the sea approaches. It was certain that by the time they reached the harbour every searchlight in the area would be turned on them. So *Campbeltown's* two afterfunnels were removed and the two forefunnels cut down to resemble the cutaway silhouette of German destroyers. He gathered a variety of recognition flares, German ensigns, and a German-speaking signalman, Leading Signalman Pike, with the object of trying to deceive the Germans into believing they were friendly.

Ryder needed a moon to enable the force to see what it was doing; time and tide indicated that it would have to be the night of March 29-30.

At this stage in the planning, the conservatory was visited by an apologetic young man who introduced himself as a counter-espionage agent from Military Intelligence. With deprecating thoroughness, he explained that Messrs Ryder, Newman, and Co. should really pay more attention to security. An uncommonly large number of sailors and soldiers running wild around Falmouth was causing people to talk, even hazard guesses at what they were doing. Somebody might guess right and, he smilingly announced, there happened to be a German spy in Falmouth.

In very little time, the Chariot force became the 10th Anti-Submarine Striking Force training for special operations against U-boats in the Mediterranean; Newman's Commandos were rumoured to be preparing for an assault on the Channel Islands. Neither Ryder nor Newman were ever told if these cover stories deceived the enemy agent, if he really existed. They never saw the man from Military Intelligence again.

By March 21 their preparations were complete. The MGB would lead with himself, Newman, and a headquarters staff of twelve men aboard. *Campbeltown* would follow astern with the main military force, while on each beam of her would be an ML armed with torpedoes to deal with guard ships. In lines, astern of these two, would come the remaining ML's loaded with troops. The formation would steam south across the Bay of Biscay until they saw a dim white light. This would be shown by the submarine *Sturgeon* which marked the point at which they would turn directly east for the approach to St Nazaire.

The first point they would reach in the harbour itself would be the only jetty, called the Old Mole. The port line of small boats would land troops there. The starboard line would continue until *Campbeltown* broke off to ram the dock caissons and then land troops alongside nearby.

On March 25 the meteorological reports indicated that the fine weather might end within forty-eight hours and be replaced by some dirty storms. With Newman's concurrence, Ryder signalled the Admiralty that he intended sailing the next day, thereby advancing the date of the assault to the night of 27-28.

This program was approved, and next morning two fast destroyers, *Tynedale* and *Atherstone*, met the weird Chariot fleet in the Channel to escort them across the Bay of Biscay. With Ryder as fleet signals officer was a young Canadian, Sub-Lieutenant Johnny O'Rourke, for whom this raid was but a prelude to Dieppe.

That day and night they sailed southwest down the English Channel and out into the Atlantic, taking a wide turn round the Breton Peninsula to avoid reconnaissance aircraft.

Before dawn on the 27th they headed due south expecting to rendezvous with the "beacon" submarine at 8:00 p.m. Suddenly *Tynedale* increased to full speed and raced off to starboard, her light blinking urgently at Ryder in the MGB: "Sighted suspicious object. Am investigating."

On the MGB's bridge, Newman muttered: "Good God, that couldn't be a U-boat wirelessing our position, could it?"

"It could be," replied Ryder, and they waited in silence.

A signal lamp blinked furiously again from the destroyer, accompanied by the sound of heavy gunfire drifting across the rolling water: "U-boat attempting to surface. Have driven it down with gunfire."

Ryder turned to his signalman, the German-speaking Pike. "Tell *Tynedale* to sink the bloody thing. *Atherstone* to join her for the search."

He looked back at his squadron. *Campbeltown*, commanded by Lieutenant-Commander S. H. Beattie RN, was slicing easily through the calm water about two hundred yards astern. Strung out on either side of her and astern lay the two lines of small boats being tossed about by the Biscay swell.

Pike called out: "*Tynedale* calling, sir. Says 'No luck. Consider S/M made sighting report of two destroyers crossing Bay. Think it unlikely ML's were spotted. Intend returning to station.'"

Disturbed by the chance they were taking with this theory but determined to continue, Ryder was driven nearly frantic two hours later when they ran into the middle of a Spanish fishing-fleet. There were too many to sink, but one was boarded and examined. It was found to be utterly innocent, and with much cheering and waving the squadron passed on.

At 8:00 p.m. officers and lookouts peered into the night ahead searching for the *Sturgeon's* beacon light. It was a mellow night, but the beauty of it was not appreciated. Instead, the first curtain of tension fell across the 630 sailors and soldiers.

Six minutes later the beacon light shone ahead. Only the swish of water swirling from their bows intruded on the still silence. The nineteen ships swerved past the submarine, received a "good luck" from her dimmed, blue signal lamp, and headed due east: the last leg to St Nazaire and the Normandie Dock.

At 10:p.m. the loom of gun flashes and anti-aircraft fire spurted from the horizon, too early for the St Nazaire raid. "Must be some chaps passing over *en route* somewhere else," murmured Ryder. By unspoken yet common assent, all voices were pitched low although the enemy lay more than twenty miles away.

This was the time when force commanders begin to worry, to count off the things forgotten and to weigh them in the scales against success. Ryder's thoughts ran rapidly over the plan and it seemed they had forgotten nothing. He had a sense of faint unreality, as though it were a dream in which he was trapped, unable to escape back to normality.

At midnight they were still twelve miles away, but the dull roar of aircraft engines and the deep cracking thud of flak guns beat gently out to sea. The bombers had arrived on time. Above them the stars had vanished behind a thick canopy of dull grey cloud. Steadily, they drew closer to the enemy coast which bruised the dark horizon, now glowing with the continuous roll of gunfire.

Ryder called out to the MGB captain: "Time to start weaving. Only about two miles off now."

The echo sounder whirred alive and the gun boat swept from side to side along the line of advance, taking soundings of the extreme sides of the approach. Shortly after 1:00 a.m. on the 28th, the squadron sailed in under the great guns of St Nazaire. Slowly, silently, waiting for the radar-controlled batteries to tear into them, the shadows of the ships flitted eastwards into the enemy's lair.

One and a half miles to go.

On *Campbeltown's* bridge, Lieutenant-Commander Beattie, crouched at an observation slit in the heavily mattressed, armoured sides. At any moment the harbour and gates to the Normandie Dock would wing into view. Less than a hundred yards ahead the MGB continued veering from one side to the other, searching for hidden obstacles in the destroyer's path. Tiny beads of sweat ran down his taut face to gather in his damp beard.

"Tell the engine room to stand by," he called out. Once round that bend and *Campbeltown* would be on her own, heading at full speed for the target. Beattie wondered vaguely how far they would get before the enemy opened fire.

One mile to go.

Hundreds of glinting, red-lined eyes strained into the darkness at the outline of the harbour. Then it was suddenly daylight. Every searchlight on both sides of the estuary blazed at them, floodlighting the whole force in a merciless glare. Hands were raised in desperate attempts to ward off the fierce, blinding dazzle.

Each ship was clearly visible in those few vital seconds. Ryder's slender hope for a few minutes' respite had depended on his loose plan to deceive the enemy. The black camouflage of the ships was similar to that used by the Germans; the cut of the destroyer's funnels resembled German design; tattered, dirty Nazi battle ensigns fluttered at mastheads.

The last of the big coastal batteries to port fired a warning salvo, quickly followed by a burst from a heavy gun on the south side. Ryder, standing with Newman on the exposed bridge of the MGB, looked back to see smoke pouring from *Campbeltown*'s funnels as she increased speed in a frantic race against the waiting guns. If one should hit on her foredeck she could be blown into fragments.

It was Leading Signalman Pike's moment. At a muttered order from Ryder the game of bluff began.

Challenges flashed from a dockyard signal tower and from the guard vessel. Pike let off a series of coloured flares known to be a recent German recognition signal. Then, without knowing the correct reply to the challenge, he flashed back one word: "Wait."

Ryder was counting the seconds until he thought the enemy might be getting restless. He gave another order to Pike, and the young signalman launched into a long plain-language signal in German saying, "We have two craft damaged by enemy action. Request permission to proceed up harbour without delay."

The searchlights were extinguished one by one; the guns stayed silent. The ruse was working, but for how long? The torpedo-carrying ML on *Campbeltown*'s starboard beam picked up speed and pointed her bows at the guard vessel.

Ryder whispered: "Please God – just five more minutes."

God granted a vital two; then the enemy, no longer tolerant of this strange fleet on his doorstep, let loose a deluge of searchlights, streaming tracers, and screaming shells. At 1:30 a.m. the battle opened with unbelievable fury.

At that moment the bombers, no longer able to see through the thickening clouds, and forbidden by a War Cabinet order to bomb "blind" on French towns, gave up the diversion raid – just when it was most needed. The garrison, already brought from their beds by the air raid and standing by their guns, could give the small ships undivided attention. Flak guns depressed their muzzles and joined the whiplash barrage aimed at Chariot. Tracer bullets, which float so majestically when fired upwards, now streaked low across the water with frightening speed, pounding the ears with a drumming crackle; heavy shells roared above them in a continuous whine before throwing up great spumes of cordite and water among the grim, awed attackers. An explosion shuddered through the night, and Ryder turned to see the guard ship vanish in a hovering cloud of smoky spray, successfully torpedoed.

His squadron was answering back in strength now. Machine-gunners and pom-pom crews engaged their respective targets until forty distinct and separate duels emerged from the holocaust. One by one the searchlights went out under the concentration of fire until only four were left in the main docks.

The MGB pulled out to starboard to give *Campbeltown* a clear run to the dock gates, while the port line of ML's made an immaculate left-hand turn to race for the Old Mole jetty as their gunners laid a devastating carpet of brilliantly flaming tracers on the concrete blockhouses defending it.

Newman bellowed in Ryder's ear: "Soon as *Campbeltown* hits, I must go ashore."

Half a mile to go.

In the destroyer's wheelhouse, Beattie remained motionless at the slit in the armour plating. Clearly visible, fine on the port bow, were the seaward caisson gates to the dock. Bullets drummed rhythmically around the ship, but his voice was steady, even deliberate, as he shouted above the tumult at the coxswain.

"Port ten. . . . Midships. . . . Steady now. Coxswain, can you see the gates dead ahead?"

"Yes, sir."

"Right, don't miss. Hit 'em dead centre."

"Aye, aye, sir," the clipped, stereotyped reply was almost a chuckle. The words of Beattie's next order came out with relish, fully savoured. "All quarters – stand by to ram."

As he said it, a twelve-pounder shell burst into the wheelhouse and killed the coxswain. An officer leapt across to shove the body away from the wheel and take over the steering himself. Beattie's eyes were fixed rigidly ahead, failing to notice the sleek, black shape racing across the harbour to intercept.

Ryder's sweat-covered face was creased in a large grin as he watched *Campbeltown* alter course slightly and point her nose at the prize target. Nothing, he thought, could stop her now.

On the foredeck below him, a voice screamed in sudden rage from the pom-pom platform. Instinctively, he swivelled round with the gun barrels and saw the speeding, dark shape that had angered the gunner. Another harbour-defence vessel, lost until then beyond the rim of light, had guessed at *Campbeltown's* intentions and was trying to head her off. Before he could give the order, the pom-pom gunner, Able Seaman Bill Savage, was hurtling two-pounder shells at the dangerous intruder.

For about thirty seconds of eternity the fate of the operation lay in the hands of young Savage. The enemy ship was firing at the destroyer, but Savage had the enemy's range. Suddenly, she exploded and disintegrated in a roaring flash which carried away Savage's shriek of triumph. His shells had found her magazine locker.

As though the destruction of the enemy ship was a signal, the firing from shore slackened. Losses on both sides were already heavy and the ML's attacking the Old Mole were being held off by fire from the two blockhouses.

Ryder watched *Campbeltown*, fascinated in these last few seconds, as she drew near to the great caissons. At 1:34 a.m., just four minutes later than planned, there was a slight check as she crashed through the anti-torpedo net, leapt across the water gap, and smashed with a prolonged, splintering, grinding roar into the caissons of the Normandie Dock.

The first objective of Operation Chariot had been achieved; from now on the plan would have to be drastically revised, even scrapped, as the enemy's resistance stiffened.

Ryder took the MGB as close to *Campbeltown* as possible to inspect the damage. Her bows had ridden up and over the top of the gates, but below the water line they had been buckled back for 34 feet, only

12 inches adrift from the required distance. The explosives would be lying right alongside the gates.

He waved to Beattie, who was watching eighty Commandos throw scalding ladders over the fo'castle and clamber down to the dock itself. An ML ranged alongside the destroyer to take off wounded while fuses were set to the explosives and scuttling charges.

Campbeltown had suffered tremendous punishment. Eighteen of her crew were dead, twenty more seriously wounded. Yet the remainder stayed aboard with Beattie to support the ML's with machine-gun fire.

By now the harbour was a shambles of burning boats, swimming men, exploding shells, and fantastic criss-crossing of low-flying tracers. At the Old Mole the six assault ML's had been beaten off with severe losses. Four were already burned-out hulks, the dying screaming as they went down with the boats; a fifth was on fire but had managed to withdraw seawards on one engine with her entire complement of sailors and soldiers desperately wounded. The sixth had forced a passage alongside the jetty where her sixteen Commandos were pinned down on the steps.

Around *Campbeltown* the ML's from the starboard line were attempting to land troops in the face of equally destructive fire. One was enveloped in flames and ran aground; two more suffered such severe casualties they withdrew and engaged gun emplacements on the south side of the river; another sank almost alongside the destroyer, enabling the sailors and Commandos to swim ashore; while the sixth withdrew to cover the main retirement.

It became imperative to secure the Old Mole jetty. Ryder took the MGB into the fire and fury spouting from the blockhouses and ordered Savage to engage them with his two-pounder. A vicious duel developed in which Savage, without any protection, silenced first one strongpoint, then the other, while the gun boat ran in and closed the steps. In seconds, Colonel Newman was ashore with his headquarters staff to lead a rush along the jetty which overpowered the flak emplacements.

The battle had raged for nearly two hours. Ryder decided to have a last look at *Campbeltown* before quitting the harbour. He steamed up to the Normandie Dock feeling curiously alone, which was hardly surprising as the MGB was now the only boat afloat. Enemy guns swung round to concentrate on her, and Savage, at the two-pounder, found himself engaged on three sides at once. Quite coolly, Ryder boarded *Campbeltown*'s low stern and took ten minutes checking through the ship to see that no wounded had been left behind, then returned and, with a last salute at the bitterly engaged Commandos who would have to accomplish their objectives on their own, he headed for open waters. A last stream of tracer bullets hunted them from the Old Mole, and the gallant Bill Savage, who had fought so violently, collapsed over his gun, killed when the naval battle was over.

Ashore, the Germans were convinced that the Allies had launched a second front through St Nazaire. The normal harbour garrison was reinforced by an infantry battalion, a flak regiment, and a Panzer brigade – in all, 10,000-odd men. Ryder had left Colonel Newman with 169 soldiers, a large number of whom were demolition experts.

Once clear of the Old Mole, Newman sent runners around the Normandie Dock to order all parties to withdraw on him at a distinctive house about fifty yards from the sea front. As the various parties fell back on him, he decided that their best chance for survival lay in fighting a way through the city itself, then out into the open countryside inland where they could split up and make their individual ways to the Spanish border. They began running through the docks towards the town in two long lines, covered by a small rearguard party who slipped from railway sidings to houses, to bridges, to garden walls, keeping the enemy at bay.

The first big building overlooking the docks and facing the crumped *Campbeltown* was the city hall, and here Newman paused to allow the rearguard to catch up. Ammunition was running short, and the rush from the docks had cost many lives.

At the approach of dawn they were fighting through the main street of St Nazaire, dragging their wounded with them. Newman found a cellar, and the survivors tumbled down into its shelter where they could rest, tend the wounded, and eat iron rations while waiting for the Germans. Nearly an hour later they were discovered, and Newman surrendered. Only 109 were left and of these more than eighty were wounded. Only three rounds of ammunition for each man remained.

Far out in the Bay of Biscay, Ryder, Beattie, and the survivors from *Campbeltown* were safe, as were more than a hundred Commandos, half of them wounded.

One question remained unanswered. Would the destroyer blow up?

At daybreak, the Germans threw a strong cordon of troops round the docks and along both sides of the Normandie Dock. French dock-yard workers turning up for the day shifts were refused entry.

At 11:00 a.m the German admiral commanding the port, drove to the docks and boarded the destroyer. Hundreds of German officers and men were milling around her. The inspection was quick and ineffectual. No one searched for the explosives, and the admiral returned to his car to drive away.

At 12:35 p.m. a mighty roar reverberated through the town. *Campbeltown* had exploded. When the smoke and the dust cleared, the dockyards were all but demolished, the Normandie Dock was wrecked, and 380 Germans were killed in the immediate vicinity, including 60 officers.

On March 30 the mighty battleship *Tirpitz* lay in her Norwegian hideout, no longer the pivot of world affairs. The ability of the Germans to maintain any capital ship in the Atlantic was destroyed, and with it came an end to surface raiders on the convoy routes. It was not until 1949 that the French were able to repair the damage in St Nazaire.

III

While Germany reacted with "the dull, low whining note of fear," as Churchill put it, the planning syndicate of Combined Operations headquarters in London exulted. St Nazaire was the proving ground for the conviction of Hughes-Hallett that raids in strength could succeed, even against heavily defended ports, given darkness and the element of full surprise. The raid also acted as a morale-builder in rather desperate days, and Commandos on leave in the south of England were in a boasting mood. The only other troops in the area were the Canadians – still waiting for glory. When Commando met Canadian in Sussex – a drink too many, an injudicious remark, and tempers might flash.

In April the Canadian Army was straining so hard on the leash that unit officers were reporting a critical tension building up under the thin crust of discipline. To General McNaughton, the Army Commander, General Harry Crerar, the 1st Corps Commander, and the divisional commanders, the only solution seemed to be action or the promise of it before the crust cracked.

Although they were unaware of them, events were already taking shape in high places which would thrust them into the cauldron of war.

"Poor Man's Monte Carlo"

I

The British Inter-Service Joint Planning Staff, consisting of two officers from each of the three services and a political adviser from the Foreign Office, had been closeted in a bunker beneath the War Office for most of six months. They had wrestled with the problems of invasion, problems of manpower, arms production, shipping space, equipment, and landing-craft, and by March had produced plans for landings in Norway, North Africa, and on the Cherbourg peninsula of northern France.

These plans were all very theoretical, little more than academic exercises for those of the military fraternity who dreamt of that far-off day when they might lift a mailed fist from the sea and send it crashing against the walls of Fortress Europe. Churchill, enraptured by the vision of a Norwegian campaign "rolling up the map of Europe," fought bitterly for it against his Chiefs of Staff and gave up only after a protracted struggle had diverted his enthusiasm to North Africa.

The North African landing was a somewhat special case, owing to the unpredictable reaction of Vichy French troops. The various proposals concerned with the best way to get back on the Continent, however, would depend upon practical experience in large-scale assault operations, with particular emphasis on the art of taking ports before the enemy could destroy harbour facilities. The St Nazaire raid had provided some information, but its objectives had been too narrow in scope for the proponents of a full-blooded invasion.

A proposed operation against northern France known as "Sledgehammer" was not intended to please them either; it was foreseen by the British as a large-scale diversionary raid to be mounted only if the Germans, not the Russians, might be crumbling on the eastern front. In such an event the Germans would be unable to keep large reserve formations in the west, and the Allies could hope to sustain a bridgehead on French soil.

Roosevelt and the United States Chiefs of Staff viewed Sledgehammer differently, regarding it as the important basis for a full-scale offensive in France during 1942 to relieve the pressure on the Russians and prevent them being knocked out of the war.

On March 9 Roosevelt wrote to Churchill: "I am becoming more and more interested in the establishment of a new front this summer on the European Continent . . . even though losses will be great, such losses will be compensated by at least equal German losses and by compelling Germans to divert large forces of all kinds from the Russian front."

On the same day, Churchill presided over a particularly acrimonious session of the Cabinet Defence Committee with a variety of British military leaders present, including Mountbatten. Discussion centred on the Roosevelt letter, and Churchill announced that he was looking for ideas on what could be done, even if it entailed a modified Sledgehammer. One military leader after another gave it as his expert opinion that any major operation on the Continent was out of the question, mainly because nothing was known of German defences, and resources were too meagre to be staked on gambles.

Then the Adviser on Combined Operations rose and said: "We don't agree, sir. We think it should be possible to mount an effective assault on Cherbourg. My Naval Adviser and Chief of Planning Staff has prepared a paper on it."

Mountbatten explained how Combined Operations proposed to

launch the assault, and when he had finished Churchill beamed his pleasure at having someone at the committee prepared to recommend action rather than block it. After the session he underlined Mountbatten's predominance over invasion affairs by promoting him to Vice-Admiral, Lieutenant-General, and Air Marshal and by appointing him to the Chiefs of Staff Committee as Chief of Combined Operations. This was the means by which Mountbatten became a member of that intimate political-military élite responsible for the conduct of the war.

General Sir Alan Brooke thought Mountbatten's presence "rather a waste of time." In his view the youthful representative of Combined Operations should have been summoned to meetings only when his organization would be under discussion. Churchill insisted, however, and then explained Mountbatten's elevation to the summit of decision-making in a telegram to Roosevelt which said: "He is an equal member now, attending whenever either his own affairs or the general conduct of the war are under consideration. He will be the centre of . . . the joint attack on Europe."

Mountbatten attended his first meeting of the Chiefs of Staff as a member on March 10 when it was agreed to pursue Sledgehammer, if only to ensure that a plan existed which could be used as a means of capitalizing on a German upset in Russia. This meeting also decided that, in the meantime, limited resources precluded anything more ambitious than a raid of such size that the enemy might be tempted to transfer *Luftwaffe* squadrons from east to west.

Mountbatten suggested that a raid of this size on Cherbourg would not only serve to draw the *Luftwaffe* into a decisive air battle but also provide the Joint Planning Staff with the practical information they needed on which to base invasion plans for 1943.

The other Chiefs of Staff rejected this proposal on the ground that such a raid required local, overwhelming air superiority, and Cherbourg was outside the RAF's air umbrella over the Channel. The chairman, Sir Alan Brooke, instructed instead that "a landing must take place within our air umbrella, namely in the vicinity of Calais or Boulogne."

Armed with the views of the Chiefs of Staff and concurring with Mountbatten's proposal that a raid designed to draw the *Luftwaffe* into the air could also serve their purposes by having as its target a port capable of handling a large volume of sea-borne traffic, the Joint Planners compiled a list of seven French ports, labelled it "Most Secret," and sent it to Combined Operations with a request that the planning syndicate select one as a target for a sizable raid. They hoped that the resulting experience would answer some, if not all, of their invasion "ifs."

As Naval Adviser, Hughes-Hallett argued forcibly against using any of them. "We don't know how many staff officers, aides, Foreign Office people, secretaries, or even messengers have seen this list since it was typed," he told Mountbatten. "We can be sure that there's more than one copy existing, and heaven knows where the rest are. This list must be regarded as compromised from a security point of view, so let's compile another of our own including ports which would meet the same requirements."

Hughes-Hallett had his way, and his syndicate began studying the Channel coast of France, making detailed examinations of the merits or otherwise of potential targets.

The Air Adviser ringed the eastern end of the Channel and said: "Anywhere in here will suit the Air Force. We can give fighter cover in this area." Brigadier Antony Head remarked casually that it would also suit troops "because there won't be time for them to get too sea-sick to fight."

Hughes-Hallett stabbed a confident finger at Dieppe and said, "Right. Let's take the old peacetime route – Newhaven to Dieppe and back. It's less than seventy miles away."

When Mountbatten was told of their decision he asked for a summary of what was intended.

"That's easy, sir," replied Hughes-Hallett with a prim smile. "A little darkness, a lot of surprise, and we can visit the poor man's Monte Carlo for at least a day."

On April 4 the Chief of Combined Operations gave approval for a draft plan to be drawn up for an attack on Dieppe.

II

In the spring of 1942 British strategic planning for the conduct of the war rested on two plateaus: a vast Anglo-American enterprise in North Africa to expel the Germans from the Middle East, and a long-term plan for a probable invasion of the Continent in the summer of 1943. In British eyes, these were the only practical operations possible at a time when shipping, the vital ingredient of victory, was the most serious of all problems facing the Allies. The extension of the war to global dimensions had placed an appalling strain on available shipping at a time when the U-boats were having a happy time off the United

States Atlantic coast. Shipping space was rapidly vanishing because the United States navy, in Roosevelt's words, "had been definitely slack in preparing for this submarine war off our coast."

At the beginning of 1942, United States shipyards had promised to add eight million tons to Allied shipping strength. By the late spring, the U-boats had sunk in United States waters alone two million tons more than the shipyards produced. This was the problem that plagued all aspects of Anglo-American strategy.

The British, who were beginning to deal with U-boats effectively in the eastern Atlantic, recognized the problem clearly, a factor that produced friction among the Combined Chiefs of Staff and signified an end to the Anglo-American honeymoon which had flourished just so long as the United States had been an interested spectator.

On April 1 General George Marshall, United States Army Chief of Staff, and Henry Stimson, Secretary of War, presented Roosevelt with a plan for an early Anglo-American invasion of France; the author was the newly appointed head of the War Plans Division, Major-General Dwight Eisenhower.

The Eisenhower plan called for a major assault across the Dover Strait in 1943, preceded by a sacrificial landing in September 1942, if the position on the Russian front became desperate.

This secondary part of his scheme incorporated the doubtful British Sledgehammer raid on northern France and ballooned it into an attack involving ten British and two United States divisions which would be forced ashore in the hope that they could remain there throughout the winter until the main invasion took place in the spring. In any event, there would be no withdrawal, no second Dunkirk. Once ashore, the Sledgehammer force would be on its own, paying a tragic price for keeping Russia in the war.

The same day that Combined Operations planning syndicate had selected Dieppe as a target for a raid in strength, Marshall and Stimson took off by air for London to persuade the British to accept the Eisenhower concept of strategy. Had they been successful Canadian history might read very differently today. Among the ten British divisions the United States plan was prepared to sacrifice was the bulk of the Canadian Army Overseas.

The British, however, rejected this proposal and reiterated that the fundamental reason for Sledgehammer would be an overwhelmingly successful Russian counter-attack. The Sledgehammer force would then hit the Germans at a time when they were most demoralized and when they would have no troops in reserve to meet a threat in the west.

They felt that the United States interpretation of Sledgehammer as a desperate measure to forestall a Russian defeat would be disastrous because a victorious Germany in the east would react by throwing all her reserves against the west. While planning at this high level remained frozen, three conferences on April 14 consolidated the Dieppe venture as tactically feasible.

In the morning, British Home Forces Command, which would supply troops for the raid, met Combined Operations Advisers, approved the scheme in principle, and delegated its own planners to join the planning syndicate in producing a memorandum on what forces would be required and what they would be expected to do. Also that morning the British Chiefs of Staff, discussing action in Europe during the summer, agreed that "a series of medium-sized raids is the only practical solution."

In the afternoon they were joined by General Marshall who, in putting forward the United States proposals, returned to the theme by urging "repeated Commando-type raids along the coast of Europe which will harass the enemy and give experience to Allied troops."

In a cable to Roosevelt on the 17th, Churchill said: "Our agreed programme is a crescendo of activity on the Continent, starting with an ever-increasing air offensive both by night and day and more frequent and large-scale raids, in which United States troops will take part."

The following day, Anglo-American command decisions were incorporated into a document entitled "Operations on the Continent" which said: "We have already approved a policy of raids to be undertaken in the summer of 1942 on the largest scale that the available equipment will permit. These raids will be carried out on a front extending from the North of Norway to the Bay of Biscay and will be planned and launched by the Chief of Combined Operations in consultation with the Commander-in-Chief, Home Forces."

While the deadlock over Sledgehammer persisted, British planning veered toward a compromise with their United States counterparts: a raid of such strength that it would not only serve its prime original purposes, but also help Russia by holding enemy reserves in France. The almost imperceptible hardening of British opinion in this direction gave impetus and importance to the Dieppe proposal which grew in political and military stature and assumed the mantle of a major Anglo-American effort to help their ally in the east.

Roosevelt, who had been informed of its nature after the April 14 conferences, insisted that for political and prestige reasons the United States should be associated with it through a military contribution. But the demand of senior Canadian officers in England that their troops be used in the next major Allied operation had influenced British commanders who were already considering a Dieppe force combining British paratroops and Canadian infantry. When Roosevelt's request reached London it was resisted because the few American units in England at the time were all green, and provision was made instead to take along a token number of American Rangers "to gain experience in assault."

Fortune at this stage was favouring Ottawa, which could have been asked to sacrifice nearly the whole Canadian Army Overseas on the altar of Eisenhower's inexperienced and wholly callous version of Sledgehammer, but would instead cheerfully volunteer a sacrificial division to lure the *Luftwaffe* into battle over the Channel, relieve the Russian front, and unlock what Mountbatten has called "the priceless secret of victory" by showing the way back to continental Europe.

Mackenzie King and the Canadian War Committee were well aware of how close they had been to being called upon to support the Eisenhower plan and had added their objections to those of the British. They had no inkling of the wild and hopeless venture that was being hatched at Richmond Terrace. As far as the governments in Ottawa, London, and Washington were concerned then, there was nothing but a stand-off on Sledgehammer in sight.

III

When were the Canadians to fight? For how long could they be held on a leash? At what point does constant training turn men sour and put an army into decline?

These and many similar questions preoccupied senior Canadian commanders in Ottawa and London during the winter of 1941-42. They became impatient with their political chiefs who seemed blissfully unaware of increasing public criticism mirrored in national press and radio commentaries. A volunteer army had been raised to fight with the British Expeditionary Force in France, had been compelled instead to remain static in defence of Britain, and had since become the most exercised, untried army in the war. Mackenzie King's portentous pronouncements that there was no nobler task for the Army merely irritated people. More than one military critic referred cynic-ally to "our army of noble idlers" and "the taxpayers' army of remit-tance men."

Yet as early as June 1941 Brigadier E. L. M. Burns of Canadian Military Headquarters in London had discussed the future employment of Canadian troops with the Director of Military Operations at the War Office. He had been told that the Canadian Army could not be used anywhere but in the United Kingdom and had replied that this was not the position of the Canadian government, who would consider favourably any proposal for using Canadian troops in another theatre. McNaughton, it seemed, might agree to the employment of Canadians in any worthwhile expedition, but only as an army. He was obsessed by the conviction that his army was autonomous, and that continuity of Canadian command should be ensured at all costs.

Several months later, McNaughton had suggested to Colonel J. L. Ralston, Canadian Minister of National Defence, that in the spring of 1942 the entire Canadian Army should be given a fighting role else-where than in Britain. There was so much dislike between these two men that Ralston could be relied upon to reject McNaughton's advice without any additional reason.

Commonwealth forces were fighting in Africa but Churchill had no wish to have the Canadians there. "I have long feared the dangerous reactions . . . on world opinion of our seeming to fight all our battles in the Middle East only with Dominion troops," he said. He insisted that more and more British units be sent to North Africa and this could be done only while the Canadians stayed in Britain itself.

In March 1942 McNaughton visited Washington and was asked by President Roosevelt about the morale of his troops. He replied, "I have no particular anxiety on that score, nor will I have for some months to come. The force is growing rapidly and there are ample outlets for promotion and we are working the men very hard, constantly chang-ing the scene of our activities . . . and most important of all our sol-diers are a highly intelligent body of men."

Such bland optimism revealed how wide the gap was between the aloof McNaughton and reality. His prestige as a scientist was unassail-able; but as Canadian Army Commander he was to find that the repu-tations of soldiers are less inviolate, more inviting of challenge.

While this sanguine view of the military scene appealed to Ottawa and Washington, in England General Crerar was perpetually pushing for action at Montgomery's South-Eastern Command headquarters and with Home Forces Command. In the absence of any major political decision to transfer the entire Canadian force, there were only raiding operations available, and too many of these never got past the planning stages. He did, however, have the satisfaction of knowing that both Montgomery and Mountbatten were as keen on getting the Canadians into action as he was, and they both promised that any Combined Operation calling for troops from South-Eastern Command would be offered to his Corps.

Crerar's alternative was to transform training programs to match the new offensive spirit in Allied planning. In an order to divisional commands he defined his aim as "to train all ranks up to that stage of mental, physical and professional fitness needed to engage successfully in offensive battle against the Germans." He emphasized the need to raise the infantry to the highest standards of physical fitness because he could foresee the day when early invasion operations would be conducted with a shortage of transport.

A series of inter-divisional exercises followed, culminating in the largest staged battle of its kind in southern England. Montgomery directed it, and at the end General McNaughton was able to report to Ottawa:

> In the opinion of both General Montgomery and myself results reflect the satisfactory state of tactical training and endurance now reached by Canadian units and formations taking part. The exercise was specially designed to test capabilities to the limit. It lasted eleven days . . . during which some units marched on foot as much as 250 miles which is about the life of army boots on English roads. Much of the marching was tactical at forced pace. . . . Hardships and heavy tasks accepted by troops most cheerfully and though now very tired they have come through these strenuous tests with enhanced morale and confidence in themselves.

In addition to training, changes in unit commands were also having an effect. In the 2nd Division, Brigadiers Sherwood Lett of Vancouver and William Wallace Southam of Toronto commanded the 4th and 6th Brigades respectively; among the battalion commanders were Lieutenant-Colonel Merritt, the huge West Coast barrister-athlete who had taken over the South Saskatchewans; youthful Lieutenant-Colonel Robert Ridley Labatt of Hamilton commanded the Royal Hamilton Light Infantry; and Lieutenant-Colonel Joe Menard had found his spiritual home at the head of the Fusiliers Mont-Royal.

There were also Lieutenant-Colonel Fred K. Jasperson, the Windsor lawyer who had inherited the Essex Scottish Regiment; Major Douglas Catto, Toronto architect who was to command the Royal Regiment of Canada, was then second in command; and Alfred Gostling, the one-time Winnipeg radio-repair man who had been promoted to Lieutenant-Colonel of the Camerons of Canada. Johnny Andrews, though not formally a limb of the 2nd Division, was working with it as lieutenant-colonel, commanding the Calgary Tanks.

None of these men, whose ages ranged between twenty-nine and forty, would complain at being described as tough disciplinarians, hard soldiers who did everything their troops could do and more. They were as Roberts wanted them – with, perhaps, one lone exception.

The process of ridding the division of its more carefree, careless, and indifferent officers penetrated to all levels. Once the colonels were appointed they continued weeding out down to the level of NCO's.

Yet discipline remained a problem, to the extent that on one occasion Montgomery wrote to General Crerar: "Enclosed is a report about the general behaviour and discipline of –––––– Regiment. Perhaps you could move this battalion to another area."

On another occasion R. P. Wilson, Chief Constable of West Sussex, was forced to write to McNaughton saying: "Since their arrival here the –––––– Regiment of –––––– has caused me considerable anxiety. In the last seven months, 39 of the Regiment have been convicted of 53 offences and there is no doubt that many other offences have been committed though it has not been possible to bring them before the Courts."

During one exercise, a group of Canadian troops sheltering from a pelting rainstorm were forced to parade when a staff car drew to a skidding halt. In it were Montgomery and Crerar. Montgomery stood up to speak to the men and was greeted by a series of vulgar noises followed by a shouted "Hey, Monty, for Christ's sake go home willya."

Angry letters flowed from Crerar along the chain of command in an attempt to identify the culprits. The unit commander, company commander, and even platoon commanders were severely reprimanded, and a letter of apology was sent on behalf of the Corps. Montgomery replied with typical unpredictability. After thanking Crerar, he said: "It doesn't worry me a bit. This sort of thing merely results from high spirits. I don't regard it as any more serious than soldiers letting off steam and the best target is always an officer – the more senior the better."

But the strain on the leash was still critical; the time had come to give the Canadians the war they were impatient to fight. They were not the only soldiers waiting for a chance to pounce on the enemy. There were also Commandos, United States Rangers, and French Marines.

IV

In the remote, bleak hills of the Scottish highlands, where the Camerons once ranged as undisputed masters, is Castle Achnacarry, ancient, weathered, and aloof. For two centuries no English soldier had occupied the castle or the land it has dominated so arrogantly. Then in the spring of 1942, while conflicting plans for winning a war we were losing flew between London and Washington, Sassenachs returned to Achnacarry.

The old house in the heart of the highlands became notorious as the Commando Training Centre – and with the Commandos came men of strange nationalities – languid United States Rangers, stiff-legged but light-footed Irishmen, and precious, high-stepping Free French Marines.

The French were the first, arriving in March under the leadership of a burly ex-manager of the New York Branch of a Paris bank, who had returned to France at the outbreak of war, joined the French navy, escaped to England after Dunkirk, and had then persuaded the Royal Navy to make him a commander for the duration. It was agreed by all at Achnacarry that the gorgeous WREN secretary who accompanied him wouldn't last quite that long. She would retire worn out; his taste for her particular beauty would evaporate; she would tire of his Latin turbulence and settle for a solid Englishman; she would tire of him and of Englishmen as well and settle for an adoring, dollar-loaded American or, appalling as the thought was to her worshippers, she might become an accidental victim to her commander's wealth of guns and knives.

Three weeks later the French Marines received their orders: to report immediately at a secret base in the south of England prior to proceeding to the Isle of Wight for assault exercise.

The departure of the Frenchmen and the arrival of 600 United States Rangers overlapped and overloaded the training program at Achnacarry. The commandant had warned his staff that the "best, toughest men in the American Marines" were due, and that he wanted the training course to be "hard for them – very hard indeed."

This unit was the now-famous 1st United States Ranger Battalion commanded by Major William O. Darby, formed at the suggestion of General L. K. Truscott, the senior United States observer at Combined Operations Headquarters, who had been so impressed with the British Commando system that he had persuaded Washington to create a similar force of shock troops and had then weeded them from the United States divisions stationed in Northern Ireland.

Eventually, Truscott was to select from this battalion six officers and forty-four men to accompany the Dieppe force, among them Captain Roy Murray who would survive the raid to become twenty years later the colonel commanding the battalion in West Berlin; young Lieutenant Edwin Loustalot who would not survive but would become instead the first American soldier to be killed by a German; and Lieutenant George Shunstrom who would land with Lord Lovat's Commandos and be a long time recovering from the experience.

These were the first Rangers to be put through Commando battle drill. They swung across ravines on toggle ropes while bullets whizzed past their ears and grenades exploded into the depths below them; they scaled cliffs while hunks of their faces were blown out by dynamite charges; they assaulted a nearby lakeshore, with mortar bombs falling between their boats.

A long, lean corporal completed two weeks of this treatment and then sauntered over to the commandant and said: "You sure got some depot heah, suh. Ain't nevah seen nothin' like it in muh life."

He was Frank Koons of Swea City, Iowa, destined to become the first American soldier to kill a German in the European theatre and to earn the British Military Medal for bravery.

V

A plan had been conceived, a target selected. On April 14, the day it had been blessed by the Anglo-American Combined Chiefs of Staff, urged by the impetuous Churchill and approved by Roosevelt who was anxious to do something to help Russia, on this day no member of the Canadian government and no Canadian military commander had the slightest idea that a raid was in the wind.

But they knew of another called Operation Abercrombie, a small raid planned by Lord Lovat's Commandos on the French coast at Hardelot, a village south of Boulogne. The general idea was for a casual midnight descent upon the area to capture prisoners, destroy a searchlight position, and keep the defences in a state of nervous apprehension. Crerar had been so persistently determined to "blood" his Corps that British Home Forces Command inquired whether he would like to assign fifty Canadian soldiers to the raid.

Crerar leapt at the opportunity, obtained McNaughton's approval, and gave the assignment to a group of the Carleton and York Regiment under the command of Lieutenant J. P. Ensor. The operation took place on the night of April 21-22 and proved a complete fiasco. The Commandos landed, the enemy ran so fast no prisoners could be taken, and the Canadians never even got ashore. Their landing-craft lost its way on the passage across, failed to find the right beach, and eventually headed back in the direction of what it hoped was Dover. At least these select few Canadian troops had been within sound of the guns.

The Blunders Begin

I

Spring that year brought an optimism unknown since the grim promise of blood, sweat, and tears. This was 1942, and here was the spring of yesterday returned. You could almost feel the tension draining from London as that grim, grey citadel of resistance recaptured an earlier buoyancy.

Daffodils, primroses, and bluebells filled the parks; from the rubble of a hundred thousand homes in the east end blossomed clusters of weeds, gloriously coloured, giving unexpected richness to the tired, sweat-backed defenders. Slums that had known only the ugliness of too much humanity, too many unemptied garbage bins and never enough sky were suddenly gardens of yellow, green, and gold. The parasite foliage grew from the dust of shattered bricks; landscaping was by courtesy of the *Luftwaffe*. They may have been weeds, but to the gaunt people who lived, worked, and slept in the surviving rows of cracked, scarred houses, they possessed their own pathetic beauty.

A nation had been seared by fire, the fat burned off, and what remained was lean, hard, and confident. Jauntiness replaced weariness, gaiety came naturally, spontaneously, without desperation, and the spirit of the hunter surged through the corridors of Whitehall.

With this spring came the end of the lonely war, the beginning of a United Nations crusade.

It was time for offensive planning, and an astonishing profusion of plans emerged from the keen, young staffs of newborn organizations. On the higher levels of strategic planning there was Gymnast, which would become Torch when the Allies landed in North Africa; there was also Roundup, an invasion of France in 1943, which would become Overlord when eventually launched a year later.

Sledgehammer, which the British visualized as a stab in the back for a Germany being defeated in the east, was seen by the Americans as a sacrificial prop for a reeling Russia. Their differences on this operation inspired ugly petulance in Washington when Marshall and Stimson suggested turning the American back on Europe and concentrating instead on the Pacific. Roosevelt's deep sense of history thwarted this proposal, and Marshall, ashamed and regretful, sent the little-known General Eisenhower to London to join General Sir Bernard Paget, Commander-in-Chief, Home Forces, in an Anglo-American planning group for Roundup known as the Combined Commanders.

It was a happy choice. Eisenhower and Paget were like-minded men, devoted to the objective of invasion and intent upon launching it over the shortest possible route – across the narrow sea from southeast England to the Pas de Calais.

Combined Operations, unrelated to the Combined Commanders, had tasted German blood at St Nazaire and thirsted for more. But the Adviserate and planning syndicate had their eyes fixed upon the coast of lower Normandy, and from the fertile imaginations of this brilliant group emerged the boldest, most impudent plans of all.

They had one for Dieppe, one for simultaneous raids on Calais and Boulogne, another for an impertinent Commando strike against Alderney in the Channel Islands, and yet another nobly code named Imperator. This scheme called for an armoured column to be landed in Normandy from where it would move swiftly to Paris, shoot up German headquarters at the Hotel Grillon, rekindle the flame on the tomb of the Unknown Warrior at the Arc de Triomphe, and then speed back to the coast to evacuate through a covering force.

Although these plans were blessed by either Mountbatten or some other enterprising authority, the weight of objections from more cautious quarters threatened to submerge them all before they could be properly floated – all, that is, except one.

II

The plan to raid Dieppe was still only theoretical. Tactical in concept, it had to be fitted into strategic planning – a difficult task at a time when the Anglo-American symphony was producing some harsh discords – before it could be studied in practical terms. The Combined Operations conference in London at 11:00 a.m. on Tuesday, April 14, which was attended by the Adviserate and the Joint Planning Staff, was limited in scope, confined to a few basic principles.

It was agreed that the project had some merit and should be taken up by the Adviserate with the Commander-in-Chief, Home Forces, General Paget, who would be asked for troops if the plan ever materialized. The Adviserate was instructed to examine specifically a definition of the raid's objectives, an estimate of the forces required, an explanation of how they would be employed, and an appreciation of the limiting factors.

The meeting with Paget, held on Thursday, April 16, produced two plans for the raid. However, Hughes-Hallett told me: "In these early preliminaries we were thinking only in the most general terms. Our first plan was that Dieppe should be assaulted by a frontal attack delivered over the main beaches and supported by flank attacks at Pourville, two miles to the west, and Puits, one and a half miles to the east. Simultaneously, parachute and glider-borne troops were to capture the two heavy batteries situated one near the village of Berneval, six miles to the east of Dieppe, and the other at Varengeville, about four miles to the west. This plan was supported by our own military planners at Combined Operations and by the Home Forces army planners.

"The second plan was to make no frontal assault, but to land two battalions at Puits, two at Pourville, and keep two more in floating reserve. A seventh battalion would land with tanks at nearby Quiberville. I favoured this plan, as did most of the naval planners connected with the raid."

While Hughes-Hallett opposed the frontal assault strongly he did concede that if the army really wanted to land on the main beaches the navy could put them there.

This clash of opinion crystallized on Saturday, April 18, when another meeting of army and Combined Operations planners thrashed out the advantages or otherwise of the frontal assault. Hughes-Hallett was not present at this conference, at which army opinion prevailed.

"My absence had nothing to do with it," he said. "The Navy or Combined Operations could recommend, but it was hardly our job to tell the Army how to go about their business. It was quite feasible to put them ashore on the main beaches if that's what they wanted, and our chaps said so. But my view that it was a decidedly hazardous plan was well known."

On Monday, April 20, the Deputy Commander-in-Chief, Home Forces, presided over another conference at the War Office attended by the Vice-Chief of Combined Operations, the General Officer Commanding the 1st British Airborne Division, the Combined Operations Adviserate and planning syndicate, and the Home Forces planning group. Both plans were further modified so that airborne and gliderborne troops would be dropped in and around Dieppe at the moment of the main assault, which would be accompanied by a squadron of tanks to support troops who might have to clear beach minefields. Regardless of which plan was ultimately adopted it was to be a two-tide operation beginning shortly after 4:00 a.m., following heavy air bombardment of the town and the beach promenade, and would last for fifteen hours.

The conference carried over to the next day and eventually produced a broad outline for an operation in strength against Dieppe which included seven battalions of troops, a regiment of tanks, a parachute brigade, two companies of glider troops, one hundred and fifty high-level bombers, and four squadrons of low-level precision bombers. In addition to the landing-craft of various types and troop transports, the navy was to supply special anti-aircraft ships, limited naval bombardment of the wing headlands, and mortar-firing barges to support the assault across the main beaches.

Even though both alternatives were still merely summaries of intentions, a raid on Dieppe was beginning to emerge with operational possibilities. But there was no guarantee that it would ever become anything more than a planning exercise.

Intervention from another source gave it unexpected significance. The Combined Commanders had agreed that an invasion of France should be launched through six Pas de Calais ports simultaneously, reserves being poured through the most successful bridgeheads to exploit initial gains and then plunge inland towards Germany itself.

But what defences would the assault forces meet? How many troops would be needed to overwhelm the defenders? How would the assault troops be carried there and with what support? What equipment would they need and how would the enemy react in the handling of his own reserves?

There had been no amphibious assault since Gallipoli in 1915, and surely the lessons of that abortive campaign would be insufficient in 1943? The vital prerequisite was an operation that could provide enough answers to ensure a reasonable hope of success.

As the British Joint Planning Staff had done only a few weeks before, when planning a bridgehead for Sledgehammer, the Combined Commanders now sent their plan, including the list of the six ports, to Combined Operations with the request: "Please raid one of these ports in sufficient strength to persuade the enemy to react as if he were faced with actual invasion."

And also as before, the Advisers at Combined Operations destroyed the list of ports for security reasons and looked for a seventh. Hughes-Hallett took the initiative again and reported to Mountbatten: "There's only one place in terms of absolute security that we can raid in the time available and that's Dieppe. After all, we have an embryonic scheme of our own for it which could be modified to meet the objectives of the Combined Commanders.

"Besides," he added, "a raid on Dieppe will serve a double purpose as an invaluable rehearsal for both Sledgehammer, should we have to mount it in a hurry, and Roundup."

Among his many other roles, Mountbatten was an associate member of the Combined Commanders and when he put his Naval Adviser's proposal before them they immediately concurred. Dieppe, which until now had been a plan-in-principle, became at that moment a plan-in-being.

A note from Mountbatten to Hughes-Hallett said simply: "It's on."

The Naval Adviser grinned appreciatively, took the file which contained a meagre assortment of typewritten notes, all that comprised the total record of the plan to date, and scrawled across it "Operation Rutter," a code name of no particular significance. The word "rutter," meaning "a mercenary horse-soldier," happened to be the next unused one on a list of approved code names at Combined Operations Headquarters.

Combined Operations gave birth on April 24 to a tactical plan that could be fitted by unanimous consent into Anglo-American strategy.

III

Acceptance by the Combined Commanders of the Dieppe project under its code name "Rutter" as an essential ingredient of the strategic Roundup, made Mountbatten, as Chief of Combined Operations, and General Paget, as Commander-in-Chief, Home Forces, jointly responsible to the Chiefs of Staff for further planning. The result was another collision between the army and the naval planners at Combined Operations Headquarters.

Paget, in accordance with a directive relating to the command of all raiding operations, could decide which of the various Home Commands should supply the military forces required and then delegate his responsibility to the General Officer Commanding that particular area. In this instance, he selected South-Eastern Command to provide the troops and designated the area commander, Montgomery, as the responsible army authority for all military matters concerned in Rutter.

The air side became the responsibility of Air Vice-Marshal Trafford Leigh-Mallory, commanding No. 11 Fighter Command Group, the front-line squadrons confronting the *Luftwaffe* in France and the Low Countries. Of medium height and heavily built, Leigh-Mallory was one of the most attack-minded commanders in the Royal Air Force, slightly pompous in the eyes of his juniors, but always confident and self-assured. Veterans of such famous wings as Biggin Hill, Kenley, and Tangmere remember his irritating habit of standing feet apart with thumbs hooked into the breast pockets of his tunic while making caustic comments about the performance of some squadron or other. They also remember that it was he who took over No. 11 Group in 1941 when it was still defensively inclined and said: "The coast of England is not a front line. The Channel is not enemy air space. The Channel is English and so is the air above it. From now on you will operate in offensive sweeps over the Continent and fight the enemy on his side of the Channel." This policy gave Fighter Command a shot in the arm, and although many pilots and planes were lost over France, the *Luftwaffe* never again operated over England in worthwhile numbers.

Copies of the alternative Combined Operations plans were sent to South-Eastern Command headquarters accompanied by a summary of the general terms under which the Combined Commanders proposed assaulting their six selected ports for Roundup. In all cases the assaults would be on the flanks of the targets and be followed by enveloping movements. Frontal assaults were not contemplated in these plans-in-principle and, as this supported naval opinion, this was the recommendation to Montgomery for the sample operation named Rutter.

1. The main assaults should be at Berneval and Puits to the east of Dieppe, and at Pourville and Varengeville to the west. Paratroops should be dropped to the south, behind the town, and all forces should encircle Dieppe and converge upon it.
2. The effect of this movement would be to isolate the port from possible reinforcements and give the air and naval forces time to reduce the main defences of Dieppe covering the promenade and beaches by heavy bombing and bombardment.

Montgomery asked the naval planners one question: "Is it intended to stay ashore for forty-eight hours or longer?"

"No, fifteen hours at the most," they replied.

With this, Montgomery rejected the "flanks only" plan on the ground that there would be no time and too many obstacles for tanks to cover the distance between the flank-landing beaches and the port before the Germans could summon overwhelming reinforcements. To assault and capture a port quickly, he said, both troops and tanks would have to go in over the main beaches confronting the town, relying on heavy bombardment and surprise to neutralize the defences.

On Montgomery's orders the military choice was made: a frontal attack. This decision would have a decisive influence on the outcome of the operation and lead directly to such tragedy that the ripple effects would reach almost every corner of Canada.

Pretensions of infallibility are common enough in high military circles, and Montgomery could be as pretentious as anyone. For example, he insisted at his headquarters in Reigate, Surrey, that South-Eastern Command was not just part of the Home Forces but should be called the South-Eastern Army and that he should be referred to as the Army Commander, a title that rightly belonged to General Paget. Incidents such as this were giving him the first faint bloom of a reputation for being an eccentric genius, a wizard for whom glory came out of hats – any hats because he collected them.

Mountbatten argued strongly for the flank-attacks-only plan, but had to give way; presumably because as a naval officer he had no control over military planning. It was to prove the first of a series of tragic and costly mistakes, each serving to compound the one before.

At meetings of the inter-service planners, Hughes-Hallett tried again to sway military opinion away from the frontal assault. Although he was supported at these sessions by Air Vice-Marshal Leigh-Mallory, their combined efforts were not enough.

The army insisted that reliance upon flank attacks would entail such a prolonged enveloping movement that by the time the troops reached Dieppe surprise would be lost. They argued forcibly that the beaches at Puits and Pourville were unsuited to tanks, and that if they were landed at Quiberville six miles to the west of the port, they would have to cross the rivers Scie and Arques before reaching Dieppe. There was no certainty, they said, that even if the bridges across these rivers were captured in advance, they would bear the weight of a Churchill tank.

The naval staff said: "We're not convinced. It seems a pretty dangerous way of going about things."

The army ended further argument by brusquely replying that as the Army Commander at Reigate had made up his mind to take the town frontally – that was that.

Still perturbed, Mountbatten and Hughes-Hallett did what they could to lessen the hazards. A formal request was made to the Admiralty by Combined Operations for at least one battleship to be assigned to Rutter. These great ships with their immense fire-power could destroy the entire sea-front defences, take on the heavy German coastal batteries, and probably frighten the enemy into submission.

The First Sea Lord, Sir Dudley Pound, cherished his battleships, never exposing them to attack from the air if he could possibly help it. The very thought of even one leaving the wide ocean spaces for the narrow, confined and densely mined Channel was enough to reduce him to apoplexy.

The request was curtly refused. In 1942, the year the Germans had raced a battle fleet consisting of the *Scharnhorst*, *Gneisnau*, *Prinz Eugen*, and sixty other vessels through the Dover Strait – something no enemy of England had done for three centuries – the Royal Navy would permit no warship of its own larger than a destroyer in the English Channel.

To the first mistake of committal to a frontal assault had now been added the failure to provide the weight of overwhelming fire-power to support it, unless the air bombardment could be increased to compensate. Already, the plan budgeted for an air strike of "maximum intensity just before the assault."

IV

Mountbatten assumed a commanding role in the next stage by taking
the chair at a major policy conference attended by representatives of
the forces so far concerned with the broad outline plan. This was held
at Combined Operations Headquarters in London's Richmond Terrace
at 11:00 a.m. on Saturday, April 25. Also present were the Vice-Chief
of Combined Operations, the Deputy Commander-in-Chief, Home
Forces, representing Paget and Montgomery, the Operations Officer of
the 1st Airborne Division, the Combined Operations Adviserate, and
Major Goronwy Rees, Montgomery's personal liaison officer.

Hughes-Hallett, as senior adviser and director of all initial Dieppe
planning, opened the conference with a summary of the draft outline
plan. His main points were:

1. That Zero Hour would be thirty minutes after Nautical Twilight.
2. That the flank attacks at Pourville and Puits would land at the
same time that the parachute battalion dropped on the heavy
batteries at Berneval and Varengeville.
3. That glider-borne forces would land behind Dieppe at Arques,
suspected to be the main German headquarters, and support
a move to capture the *Luftwaffe* fighter ærodrome at St Aubin,
four miles from Dieppe.
4. That independent groups of parachutists would drop outside
the port itself to deal with mobile batteries and additional
targets.
5. That the initial landings should be supported by simultaneous
high-level and low-level bombardment of the town and sea
front.
6. That thirty tanks should land within fifteen minutes of the
main assault, and the bulk of the tank battalion should follow
within the next twenty minutes. Tanks would also land at
Pourville.
7. Withdrawal would begin in the harbour rather than from the
sea front at about eight hours after Zero and be completed
before dusk.

The Intelligence officers followed Hughes-Hallett with a report that
the exits from the beaches at Pourville were not as favourable for tank
operations as had been supposed, and the conference therefore agreed
to abandon the proposal to land tanks on that beach.

The minutes of this conference show that further agreement was reached as follows:

1. That while the plan should cater for listing the military objectives for bombing in the town to prevent indiscriminate bombing, there must however be a proviso *to ensure that the bombing does take place even if visibility conditions do not allow accurate identification of targets.*
2. That Force Commanders should be appointed and that the operation should be carried out under the appropriate Naval Commander-in-Chief.
3. The system of command should be Joint Command.
4. That the covering letter for the Outline Plan should include a statement pointing out the value of this operation in order to gain experience for future large-scale operations.
5. That the Outline Plan for submission to the Chiefs of Staff should be only in sufficient detail to enable them to give their approval.
6. That the Plan should include instructions for bringing back as many prisoners as possible.
7. That Intelligence should consider what means could be used to dispose of any tanks that cannot be re-embarked.

Mountbatten was satisfied with these results but still worried about the civilian population of Dieppe. The problem of civilian casualties had plagued him since he had taken over Combined Operations and responsibility for raiding generally. While the other officers were leaving his headquarters, he called Hughes-Hallett to one side and said: "John, I want you to draft a paper giving some form of formal notice that the coastal areas of occupied countries are liable to raids. Therefore, in the interests of humanity or because of international law or some other reason, the civil populations of these areas should be evacuated."

At the root of Mountbatten's concern was his personal awareness of Churchill's reluctance to approve bombing of Occupied France unless it was directed against a specific target of military value.

The plan also provided that during the night of the attack a heavy bombing attack would be delivered against the dock area of Dieppe, beginning "at a time suitable to Bomber Command and ending not later than one hour before the beginning of nautical twilight" – in other words, one and a half hours before touchdown on the flanks.

Another provision was made for Hurricane fighter-bombers to attack the main beach defences of Dieppe itself immediately prior to the frontal assault going in. There was also to be sustained fighter support against coast and beach defences during the operation and eventual withdrawal.

This latter was important because it was intended to establish and hold a perimeter round Dieppe, and the re-embarkation would take place over the beaches and from the harbour entrance.

These air strikes were at that time considered to be indispensable to the raid.

V

Once Rutter involved Montgomery it came within reach of the Canadian Army. The persistent pleas of Crerar and other Canadians for a role in the next projected operations had not gone unheard at South-Eastern Command headquarters in Reigate. The static position of the Canadians for so long, the interminable exercises, and the difficulty of unit commanders at all levels in restraining eager, tempered troops, were problems Montgomery understood.

He received his own orders to become the army authority in Rutter on April 27, and the next day General Crerar was summoned to his headquarters at Dover. It was a brief interview, conducted in the usual incisive manner.

"Crerar," he said, "you have been wanting action for a long time. Here's your chance. The Chiefs of Staff have approved a Combined Ops plan to raid an enemy-held port in strength. I've been asked to provide an infantry division and some armour.

"I've received the proposed outline plan and in my view it has a lot of possibilities. The raid is yours if you want it. If you accept, then the commander of the division you nominate will be responsible for producing a detailed plan in co-operation with Combined Ops, under the general authority of myself and Mountbatten. Do you want it?"

"You bet we want it," replied Crerar. More at home among the hunters than McNaughton, he would not allow Canadian autonomy to stand between his Corps and the chance of action and experience.

Montgomery's flickering smile was pale compared with the scarcely controlled exuberance of the Canadian.

"Then you have it. The target is Dieppe."

For reasons of military protocol they decided to say no more of the project until a request for Canadian troops had been formally made to General McNaughton, the army commander and sole authority in England over the employment of his troops.

When Montgomery visited the First Canadian Army headquarters during the morning of April 30, he said he had been "pressed to agree to a composite British-Canadian Force under a predominantly British command."

He added: "I believe it is essential to maintain unity of command; therefore the force must be either all British or all Canadian. My opinion is that Canadian troops are best suited for the job and GHQ, Home Forces, accepts my views."

Then he took the plunge on behalf of Crerar.

"I've already discussed the idea of using Canadians only with Crerar and he has offered, subject to your approval, the 2nd Division."

The War Committee in Ottawa had delegated authority to the Canadian Army Commander to provide troops for any minor operation of limited size and of a temporary nature if the need for security precluded reference back to Canada. This was one of the few occasions on which McNaughton had been called upon to exercise it and he gave immediate consent, "subject to the details of the plans being satisfactory and receiving my approval."

Soon after Montgomery left, McNaughton formally instructed Crerar to make one infantry division, a tank battalion, and ancillary units from the 1st Canadian Corps available for participation in Rutter. The same day Crerar issued "Training Instructions No. 9," a program of Combined Operations assault courses for each of his divisions, beginning with the 2nd Division. This was merely a security cover order to prevent speculation when the 2nd Division moved to the Isle of Wight for special training.

A personal message to Ham Roberts followed, inviting him to join Crerar in London as "we haven't had a chance for an undisturbed chat for a long time."

McNaughton also sent a "Most Secret" cable to the Chief of the General Staff in Ottawa referring to his authority to commit Canadian troops to "minor" operations without War Committee approval and saying further:

"Plans are now being made which involve operations of a type indicated [in terms of his authority] but on a scale which cannot properly be classed as minor. I request therefore that my authority be widened by deletion of the term minor."

The War Committee of the Canadian Cabinet granted the request, and the way was clear for McNaughton to co-operate with the British General Staff.

For the Canadians the waiting was nearly over. Only a few thousand sat within forty miles of more than a million exhilarated Germans, but they were quite confident they could pulverize any attempt to invade Britain.

Where nature had created an easy landing-place they had mined it, wired it, planted tubular scaffolding across it, and had arranged that by pulling a lever it could be blanketed by flaming oil. They had covered it with machine guns, anti-tank guns, mortars, and heavy artillery – and then they had prayed the enemy would use it.

Where the white chalk cliffs rose three hundred feet straight up from the Channel they had placed lookouts, range-finders, and radar, and had even built defences facing inland. They had mined every bridge, crossroads, viaduct, canal, and tunnel within three miles of the coast and every rail or road-cutting had its own flame-throwing fougasse. The shore ends of amusement piers had been blown to separate the rest from the shore, and the sea ends were loaded with explosives.

Ancient smugglers' caves were manned by whole sections and stocked with food and ammunition to make them self-supporting for weeks, if necessary. From the tower of Fairlight Church, near Hastings, Canadians watched men ploughing forty miles away on the cliffs near Boulogne, on clear hazeless days.

They had even enlisted the support of the Channel fishermen. The main beach used by the British fishing-fleets was in the middle of a stretch of coast held by the Royal Hamilton Light Infantry under Lieutenant-Colonel Robert Ridley Labatt who was more than a little alarmed to find that they fished on the French side of the Channel, often meeting and mingling with French fishing-smacks.

Bob Labatt was one of the "young colonels," out of the same big, muscular mould as most of the others in the 2nd Division. His father had commanded the First World War battalion from which the RHLI had emerged, and it was natural, if not inevitable, that a son so like his father, should leave school in Ottawa to join the Royal Military College.

After graduation he had accepted a commission with the RHLI and had become adjutant to the regiment in 1936, the same year that Cec Merritt became adjutant of the Seaforth's in Vancouver. It was also the year that both officers were married.

Labatt, a decisive man with a proper regard for proper things, such as discipline and efficiency, was promoted to lieutenant-colonel shortly after the outbreak of war and given command of the regiment at the age of thirty-seven. When the time came for it to defend a sector of the Sussex coast, Labatt was too determined an officer to allow ancient customs to interfere with a properly efficient defence plan.

He noticed that when the fishermen returned from their trips across the Channel, they landed their Dover sole and windlassed their boats up the beach above the highwater mark. It would be comparatively simple for an enemy agent to come ashore there, walk round the defences and then return the same way that he had come – in a fishing-smack.

The RHLI immediately halted all sailings from Fisherman's Beach, and the battle had begun. The mayor of Hastings, the town council, irate fishing-skippers, and the regional controller of the National Food Board howled for the blood of any and all Canadians.

"Our boats," they announced, "have been using Fisherman's Beach ever since there were such things as fish."

The RHLI reply was brief and pithy; and common sense and compromise rescued all parties from the dilemma. The beach was wired except for one small exit; a local board consisting of the mayor, the chief constable, and Lieutenant-Colonel Bob Labatt was set up to decide which boats could operate each day, their crews being fingerprinted, photographed, and checked out and in by Canadian military police. The scheme worked so well that by the spring, Canadians along the Sussex coast could feel that they knew everything there was to know about the defence of vulnerable shores.

But since the enemy showed no signs of coming across the Channel to test their ability, they could only hope for a chance to go themselves to see if the Germans knew as much.

Dieppe Decision

Relationships between the British and Canadian commanders were always correct and sometimes even cordial. But one cause of constant irritation was the tendency of the British to regard Canadians as part of their own army and to include Canadian units in general orders affecting chains of command.

No conscious arrogance governed this behaviour, nor was there any suggestion that the Canadians were merely colonial volunteers. It was a simple fact of life that staff college courses designed to instruct future generals in elementary international politics, British military thinking notwithstanding, had not kept pace with Commonwealth political development; and the national pride, the independence, of the Canadians would never have been understood by the British commanders even if they had been aware of it, which they were not.

For that reason, they often forgot the legally autonomous status of

Canadian officers and subjected them to the same treatment they accorded their own, an obviously dangerous arrangement which led to quarrels and only grudging exchanges of confidence.

When General Roberts reached London and reported to Canadian Military Headquarters, he found that whereas Crerar was in no mood for a relaxing tête à tête, neither could he impart much in the way of information.

As he listened to Crerar brief him on the intention to raid Dieppe in strength, Roberts became acutely conscious of the shortcomings of his division. His mind seethed with plans for preparing his men for the ordeal ahead; for as a professional soldier since the First World War, when he had won the Military Cross while serving with the Royal Canadian Horse Artillery, he had refused to accept the excuse that a man's best is good enough, believing implicitly that excellence was always possible. A raid across the Channel would mean that discordant elements among his officers and men would have to be removed more quickly than might be tactful, that the re-formation of units would also have to be postponed.

He was wondering how soon he could get away from London to put these preparations in motion when the drone of Crerar's voice broke with startling clarity through the excited thoughts whirling through his head.

". . . and, of course, you will remain here in London for further instructions from either the War Office or Lord Mountbatten. A suite has been reserved for you at the Mayfair Hotel and you are to remain in it as much as possible.

"Every time you go out increases the risk of your being followed so don't go out unless it's absolutely necessary. You are advised by the War Office to only answer the telephone, not use it to make calls.

"We'll cover your absence from divisional duties with a story that you are on a special mission in Ottawa for the Army Commander. Before you leave here today, you must sign instructions for your senior staff officers for operations and plans to hold themselves in readiness for emergency briefings in London. We'll see they get there at the right time."

Crerar could say no more, and Roberts checked in at the Mayfair, abruptly aware that after two years in a static defensive role, he had been chosen to lead the first Canadian attack against the Germans, the first Allied offensive against continental Europe.

The first few days of his confinement passed quickly enough. He was too elated by the prospect of what lay ahead to be bored. Gradually, however, the prolonged silence from the War Office and Combined Operations grew irksome. He knew that he was being kept out of sight because enemy spies were always curious about the movements of senior officers, but he was also anxious to get back to his division. He had not yet realized that in fact he had been plunged into a new form of warfare in which scientific planning of daringly novel schemes had replaced the old concept of a commander deciding his own destiny at the head of his men.

While Roberts chafed at the seemingly cavalier treatment being meted out by the War Office, Hughes-Hallett at Combined Operations Headquarters was directing the final drafting of the outline plan for submission to the Chiefs of Staff.

On a higher level McNaughton was clarifying in correspondence with Lieutenant-General J. G. des R. Swayne, Chief of the General Staff, British Home Forces Command, the proper chain of command in an operation involving British and Canadian forces.

On May 5 Swayne issued a general directive on Paget's behalf which established the chain of command and confirmed Montgomery as the responsible military commander for Rutter. Swayne reaffirmed it in a letter to McNaughton on May 7 in which he referred to the pending operation, and to McNaughton's consent to the use of Canadian troops. The letter continued:

> It is desirable to keep to a minimum the number of officers who know the details of the operation, but I propose to send information to you from time to time personally. If you desire any amplification of specific points at any time the planning staff at GHQ will be at your disposal. Please indicate if this procedure would be satisfactory to you and if not, perhaps you could let me have your own proposals.
>
> General Montgomery will be responsible for providing the Canadian Corps and the 2nd Canadian Division with such information as they may require, since he is the General Officer Commanding selected by the Commander-in-Chief to prepare the Outline Plan.

McNaughton thought this arrangement too vague to be satisfactory. It implied that the venture was to be primarily a British one, using Canadian troops but relegating him to the role of spectator. The importance of it may not have escaped him and he felt that as Canadian

Army Commander he should have a more direct connection with future developments. Next day he replied as follows:

MOST SECRET
HQ First Cdn Army
8 May 42

Dear General Swayne

I have your letter MOST SECRET dated 7 May 42.

1. I confirm my consent to the selection of 2 Cdn Div with certain attached troops from 1 Cdn Corps for operation 'RUTTER' of which I have been generally informed by Lt.-Gen. Montgomery, GOC.-In-C SECO.

2. Confirming our conversation yesterday, I intend to keep in touch with this matter by establishing close liaison with you, and for this purpose I have detailed Lt.-Col. G. P. Henderson, GSO 1 Operations First Cdn Army to maintain contact with whoever you may indicate. Lt.-Col. Henderson will keep me informed, and if the situation at any time so requires, I will get into direct touch with you.

3. Also I today instructed Lt.-Gen. Crerar, Commanding 1 Cdn. Corps to keep me fully posted from his end as a matter of *information*, it being understood that all executive action in connection with the preparations would continue to follow the chain of command – GHQ Home Forces – SECO – 1 Cdn Corps – 2 Cdn Div.

4. The Commander 2 Cdn Div under 1 Cdn Corps has now been authorized to proceed with the preparation of plans accordingly.

Yours sincerely,
[*Signed*] A. G. L. McNaughton

If McNaughton or Crerar had any objections to the selection of Montgomery as the responsible military authority, this was the moment to voice them. A word from either would have clarified the position at the outset, but they were silent on the subject and waited until the eve of the raid to create a crisis at the summit.

On May 8 there was a brief release for Roberts. His telephone rang and a staff officer asked him to report immediately to the War Office. On arrival he was joined by his chief operations officer, Lieutenant-Colonel Mann, who accompanied him to a conference with Montgomery and the army planners.

This was the first occasion on which Canadian officers were shown a copy of the outline plan. After Montgomery had explained it in more detail and had answered most of the questions which kept leaping into Robert's mind, there was a slight pause. If he thought the broad proposals laid out in the plan could be implemented with a chance of success, Roberts could accept the assignment. If he thought them impossible to achieve, then he could refuse it. This choice was his right as a divisional commander.

No moment in the life of this sincere, able officer was to mean so much in terms of career and conscience. Everything about the plan appealed to him, but for a soldier accustomed to land battles and for a gunner accustomed to artillery duels there was the dubious matter of this being a seaborne assault, a combined operation in the tradition of Drake, Hawkins, Nelson, and those other great sailors.

Now it was an army affair, and he was the officer on whom depended triumph or disaster for Canadian arms – and either would be bought at the cost of killed or wounded. It would be unthinkable, however, for any Canadian commander that spring to refuse an operation which offered reasonable hope of success. To do so would be to bring about his head the wrath of Canada, the displeasure of Parliament, the anger of his senior officers, and the contempt of his men. Even as he accepted, he was aware that he had committed himself to what might prove the hardest battle of his life.

That evening Churchill Mann took up temporary residence at Combined Operations Headquarters in Richmond Terrace to supervise the detailed military planning, and Roberts returned to the Mayfair Hotel where Major Goronwy Rees was also staying. As Montgomery's personal representative, he was also South-Eastern Command's liaison officer with Mann's planning staff.

Mountbatten, of great persuasive charm and enthusiasm, Montgomery, clever and incisive, and Hughes-Hallett, tenacious and always serenely confident, were the trio who had transformed a proposal for a raid into a practical enterprise. Now a fourth was to share in their councils and exert a decided influence on future events.

Churchill Mann, then thirty-six, would bear the main burden of the military planning for Roberts. Tall, brown-haired, and sparsely built, he was recognized throughout the Canadian Army as a quick-witted, versatile staff officer, an artist in operational planning whose briefings were models of articulate simplicity. Major Rees, who became intimately associated with him, described Mann as ". . . a pure pyknic type. . . . He was a brilliant staff officer, but what was more exceptional was that his mind had a wild and incalculable originality, and his contempt for normal military codes and conventions was extreme."

Neithr Mann nor Rees knew very much about raiding operations, so they relied solely on native shrewdness and upon calculations which only actual field exercises could prove valid.

The throng of wild, unconventional young officers of all three services at Combined Operations could give little assistance, for the simple reason that to date raiding had been confined to small-scale personal sideshows, and nothing of the magnitude of Rutter had ever been attempted.

The outline plan, being no more than its name implied, left a considerable amount of detailed planning to be done. In such circumstances, the rocklike and experienced Roberts was ably complemented by the polished, calculating Mann.

II

The outline plan was submitted to the Chiefs of Staff on May 11 with a covering letter from Mountbatten saying: "Apart from the military objectives . . . this operation will be of great value as training for Operation Sledgehammer or any other major operation as far as the actual assault is concerned. It will not, however, throw light on the maintenance problem over beaches."

Five weeks after its conception as one of many suggested raiding-targets, Dieppe had matured as a blueprint for major assaults and had reached the highest service authorities in Britain. For the handful of Canadians so recently involved it was an anxious time – and none was so impatient to begin training for it than Roberts, still waiting restlessly at the Mayfair Hotel for the stamp of supreme approval.

The plans placed before the Chiefs of Staff made these comments on the target, object of the raid, and its intentions:

TARGET

The port and town of Dieppe are situated in the bight between Boulogne and Fecamp on the north coast of France. The distance across the Channel from Newhaven is about 67 miles. The main part of the town is on the west side of the harbour at the mouth of the valley through which flows the River Arques.

Entrance to the harbour is through two dog-leg jetties with

their seaward heads 330 yards apart. The channel through them is dredged to 14 feet and leads to an outer harbour called "Avant" and an inner harbour called "Arrière."

The outer harbour is bordered by four quays, one of which, the Quai Henri IV, contains the Gare Maritime. Adjoining the inner harbour are three wet docks – the Bassin Duquesne, Bassin du Canada, and Bassin de Paris.

The town lies in a gap about a mile wide in the cliffs. Dividing the town from the sea is a built-up promenade backed by a line of hotels and boarding-houses. Between the promenade and the hotels lie lawns and gardens about 1,200 yards long and 150 yards wide. They are enclosed on two sides by broad boulevards, the Boulevard Maréchal Foch to the north and the Boulevard de Verdun on the south. At the western end of the lawns is the Casino. Immediately behind the hotels, the Town Hall and a tobacco factory, all of which lie in the Boulevard de Verdun, is the Old Town. To the east of it is the harbour, to the west of it the Vieux Château, while to the south is a public garden, the main railway station, the hospital, and the newer part of the town with broader streets. Two and three-quarter miles to the south is the ærodrome of St Aubin. On the east and west flanks of Dieppe, there are steep slopes of chalk hills and the streets on the outskirts of the town climb these slopes. The most conspicuous landmark is the Cape d'Ailly lighthouse, some five miles to the west.

Between Berneval to the east and Quiberville to the west of Dieppe, a distance of 11 miles, the coast consists of high cliffs, accessible only in places to be described later. At these places, there are very narrow stony beaches. The only considerable gap in the line of cliffs is that made by the valley of the River Arques at the mouth of which lies the town and harbour of Dieppe. At the foot of the cliffs is a narrow strip of stones and boulders bordered by a fringe of rocks. The problem of landing on such a coast is, therefore, one of considerable difficulty.

OBJECT

1. Intelligence reports indicate that Dieppe is not heavily defended and that the beaches in the vicinity are suitable for landing Infantry, and Armoured Fighting Vehicles at some. It is also reported that there are forty invasion barges in the harbour.

2. It is therefore proposed to carry out a raid with the follow-
   ing objectives:
   A. destroying enemy defences in the vicinity of Dieppe;
   B. destroying the ærodrome installations at St Aubin;
   C. destroying RDF Stations, power stations, dock and rail facili-
      ties, and petrol dumps in the vicinity;
   D. removing invasion barges for our own use;
   E. removal of secret documents from the Divisional Head-
      quarters at Arques-La Bataille;
   F. to capture Prisoners.

INTENTION

3. A force of Infantry, Air-borne troops and Armoured Fighting
   Vehicles will land in the area of Dieppe to seize the town and
   vicinity. This area will be held during daylight while the tasks
   are carried out. The force will then re-embark.
4. The operation will be supported by fighter aircraft and bomber
   action.

The naval forces were to consist of six small destroyers, a shallow-
draught steam gun boat, HMS *Locust*, seven infantry landing-ships, and
a miscellaneous collection of motor gun boats, steam gun boats, armed
motor launches, and assorted assault landing-craft. The military force
was estimated at two infantry brigades with supporting engineers, a
tank battalion, and units of the 1st British Airborne Division.

The air forces were to comprise five squadrons of support fighters,
one squadron of fighter-bombers, and "sufficient bombers to produce
extensive bombardments on selected areas and targets, to provide
carrying aircraft for parachute troops and tugs for gliders."

This meant that there would be a minimum of 150 bombing sorties,
excluding those aircraft assigned to carry the parachutists, and
two low-level attacks. Settled, fair weather for at least 48 hours was
considered essential for the operation, both for flying and to permit
the airborne troops to be dropped accurately. The earliest possible date
on which it could be launched was stated to be the night of June 20-21
or "any of the six nights following."

Although supposed to be merely an outline, the plan also listed
suggested instructions to the Force Commanders. These were:

1. You are appointed as joint Force Commander for Operation Rutter.
2. Your responsibilities will include:
   The preparation of a detailed plan and Operation Orders generally conforming with this Outline Plan. The approval of the Chief of Combined Operations, who will obtain the concurrence of the General Officer Commanding, South-Eastern Command (General Montgomery) insofar as the Military Plan is concerned, and of the Commander-in-Chief, Portsmouth, insofar as the Naval Plan is concerned, is to be obtained for your detailed plan.

In these proposals lay one of the biggest planning faults of the Dieppe raid. There were so many responsible commanders involved, each with headquarters some distance from the other, that approval for even minor changes could be delayed for hours, sometimes days.

The British Chiefs of Staff approved the Rutter plan formally on May 13, at the same time accepting the use of Canadian troops. General Roberts was named Military Force Commander; Air Vice-Marshal Leigh-Mallory became Air Force Commander; and Rear-Admiral H. T. Baillie-Grohman was designated Naval Force Commander.

They were an oddly assorted threesome. Roberts, the professional artillery officer, competent and dedicated and deliberate; Leigh-Mallory, a one-time junior infantry officer who had transferred to the Royal Flying Corps in 1917 and then risen to command No. 11 Fighter Group during the Battle of Britain, a fast-thinking, sound decision-maker; and Baillie-Grohman who had commanded the Combined Operations naval base in the Middle East for more than a year and had organized the largest Combined Operations exercise ever held. It had taken place off Suez and had involved carrying the whole New Zealand Division for three days.

Baillie-Grohman was essentially a small-ship officer who would tolerate informality only if it was accompanied by a high degree of efficiency. This pursuit of nothing less than crack quality made him unpopular with some of his subordinates, and his forceful criticism of inefficiency often brought him to the verge of serious trouble with higher authorities. On at least two occasions his frankness had been frowned upon by their Lordships of the Admiralty and might have had serious effects on his career.

At the outbreak of war he had forsaken small ships for command of the battleship *Ramillies*, an appointment he held for two years under Admiral Sir Andrew Cunningham. If this in itself was quite an achievement, inasmuch as Cunningham had a habit of ridding himself of all but the best captains available, it was even more remarkable that in January 1941 Cunningham was so impressed with his fighting aggressiveness that he was selected for promotion to flag rank as Rear-Admiral.

Baillie-Grohman had then taken command of the Combined Operations training headquarters in the Middle East, and his first job was to about face the entire organization. He became responsible for an *ad hoc* organization set up to evacuate Greece. Instead of undertaking the assault on the island of Rhodes, then being planned, he rescued 55,000 troops from under the guns of the advancing German Army and from under the wings of the *Luftwaffe*.

These three strong, capable personalities had not yet met, nor would they for some time. Leigh-Mallory was at his fighter headquarters at Uxbridge outside London, Baillie-Grohman was still serving in the Middle-East, and Roberts, after a brief talk with Mountbatten at Richmond Terrace, left London for his own headquarters in Sussex to prepare for the move to the Isle of Wight. But they were only three, and this biggest military hunt since the First World War attracted a galaxy of young, bemedalled sportsmen eager to get on with the chase and reap the rewards.

There was Crerar who, though well down in the chain of command, was determined to exercise some authority; the aloof McNaughton, playing the role of soldier-statesman between Whitehall and Ottawa; the confident Montgomery, careless of any but his own autocracy, willing to match wills wherever his concepts of war were challenged; and Mountbatten, youngest of the élite, favourite of Churchill, a peer related to royalty. There was the vaguely mentioned Commander-in-Chief, Portsmouth, who would supply the ships and approve the time of sailing; and the commander of the airborne troops who could stop or start the operation by giving a verdict on the wind and the weather.

None of these men was easily influenced or swayed, nor were their judgements infallible. They were temperamental individualists, un-ignited rockets waiting for a spark to send them into orbit.

Dieppe would be the spark. Eisenhower, only tenuously associated with it then, would reap the benefits of its lessons in North Africa and Normandy, soar for a while and then come back to settle in a famous house; Montgomery soared with him and has never settled since. Hughes-Hallett went up, switched to a political arena after the war and is still rising; Mountbatten's star also rose until he reached the highest rank his country could bestow; and the rest stuck obstinately to the ground.

Hughes-Hallett worked ceaselessly for the operation, recognizing that in the future its value might prove decisive in the scales between victory and defeat. In doing so he made as many enemies as friends, so much so that in some quarters the mention of his name even today is enough to launch a thousand tirades. I have heard it said that he may have been competent but was never above average, that he was arrogant, impatient, contemptuous, and given to theatrical stunts. One senior officer who has obviously been shaken severely by a collision with him told me: "His trouble was his conceit, just like all the breed at Combined Operations Headquarters. Everyone knew at the time that Mountbatten had a dangerous weakness – he could not judge a man and surrounded himself with most unsuitable favourites. The Admiral may have changed since, as he was really very young to hold so responsible a position; so might Hughes-Hallett."

Yet a contemporary officer of high rank who cheerfully admits to a whole series of collisions with Hughes-Hallett said: "He's got a mind like a steel trap. He can unravel a complicated problem in seconds, and once convinced of the rightness of his course he never gives up."

Certainly Hughes-Hallett didn't give up on Dieppe. He presided over its birth, pumped life into it, picked up the pieces being nibbled away by orthodox militarists who berated it, and forced it through to what has been called a disastrous end, but which should be properly described as one of the most rewarding, decisive ends of the war.

III

Lieutenant-Colonel Mann's first duty after returning to 2nd Division headquarters was to provide Roberts with an appreciation of the outline plan in which he discussed the Hughes-Hallett formula for landing tanks at Quiberville and Pourville, the beaches west of Dieppe, and rejected both for the same reasons that the Home Forces planners had given earlier: that the two rivers, Arques and Scie, might obstruct an advance into Dieppe.

Mann's comments on the landing of tanks on the main beaches facing Dieppe illustrate the gulf between the various military authorities and the naval view represented by Hughes-Hallett. Dazzled by the vision of tanks rumbling up the shingle and into the town, he said:

Such a plan, on the face of it, is almost a fantastic conception of the place most suited to land a strong force of Armoured Fighting Vehicles. It is, however, well worth evaluating with an unbiased mind.

Advantages are:

1. It, if successful, puts the AFV in easy striking distance of the most appropriate objectives for their employment.
2. Surprise.
3. Would have a terrific moral effect on both Germans and French.
4. Could be most easily supported by infantry and RE.
5. Control and information will be from front to rear, and difficulties of co-ordination to surmount obstacles, and deal with resistance would be the more easily met.

Mann further argued that by landing on the main beach, the supply of ammunition for tanks and of engineer stores for their support and for demolition tasks, could be co-ordinated. The proposed plan, he thought, had the "advantage of simplicity."

The disadvantages of the plan were recognized. The plan involved "attacking the enemy frontally," and at a point where penetration was obstructed and engineer effort was required, while "the danger of failure to penetrate through Dieppe, after the heavy air bombardment" had also to be taken into account. Mann, however, pointed out that in an English coast town a similar attack would have good prospect of success "providing the engineer tasks were suitably dealt with"; and he recalled that the known strength of the Dieppe garrison was only two companies of infantry not of the best quality, plus some divisional troops. The final section of his appreciation ran as follows:

CONCLUSION

In spite of an initial adverse reaction to the proposal to land Armoured Fighting Vehicles on DIEPPE front, it seems to have a reasonable prospect of success, and offers the best opportunity to exploit the characteristics of Armoured Fighting Vehicles in this operation.

If Armoured Fighting Vehicles were omitted from the operation it could still be very useful, but the likelihood of success in regard to the destruction of the ærodrome would be greatly reduced.

In regard to the withdrawal phase, a proportion of Armoured Fighting Vehicles as part of the Rear-guard will materially strengthen the rear-guard at a time when enemy reinforcements may be deploying for counter-attack with the object of preventing our withdrawal.

I am in favour of adopting the outline plan.

It is surprising that an officer of Mann's reputed ability and impatience with conventional thinking should have given so little credence to the naval misgivings about the frontal assault. Ham Roberts could be expected to conform to the traditional military preference for a confrontation of forces. He was, after all, indoctrinated with a healthy respect for the destructive, demoralizing effects of heavy firepower which usually preceded head-on collisions.

But Mann, that much younger and unfettered by the restrictive influences of battle experience in a bygone war, could be expected to approach the planning differently and accord greater attention to the naval argument.

Nor is it easy to understand how an involved and still uncertain plan for what its authors described as a "difficult landing" could be regarded by Mann as having the "advantage of simplicity." If indeed it had such an advantage, then presumably it was in his own expert, minute detailing which transformed it into a finished product that was both complicated and inflexible.

The personalities concerned in events leading up to the raid seem to have been obsessed with phrases which proved to be quite meaningless when eventually related to the facts. None of the battalion commanders who took men ashore at Dieppe and who are in Canada today remembers anything simple about the plan he had to execute.

When Mann, the unpredictable, reacted in predictably enthusiastic fashion, Roberts endorsed his appreciation and forwarded it to McNaughton with the advice that the outline plan be formally accepted. McNaughton took this opportunity to remind the British that the Canadian Army was an independent national force and that the 2nd Division was to be treated during the operation as a unit "combined with" the British army but not of it.

In a letter to General Swayne on May 15, he said:

1. I confirm that I accept the Outline Plan for Operation RUTTER as approved by the Chiefs of Staff Committee.

2. I confirm that I authorize the Canadian Commander to proceed with detail planning.
3. It would be appreciated if you would obtain for me a copy of
   paper giving outline plan of this operation as approved by the
   Chiefs of Staff Committee, this paper to be held by you to my
   order, for reference as I may require, and in any event to be
   handed to me on completion of operation, for transmission by
   me to my Government.
4. I suggest that in future Combined Operations involving Canadian troops, the outline plan should be placed before me
   before submission to the Chiefs of Staff Committee and that
   the Chiefs of Staff Paper should show that in giving their
   approval they take note of my acceptance; also that I should
   be included in the distribution list.

[*Signed*]   A. G. L. McNaughton
    Lieut.-General
    G.O.C.-in-C. First Canadian Army
    and
    Senior Canadian Combatant Officer
    in the United Kingdom

The precise reason for McNaughton signing himself "Senior Canadian Combatant Officer" is not clear, but to reiterate a self-evident fact
in this manner could only encourage among British commanders the
feeling that he was being unduly haughty.

Had the Canadian Army been considered an Allied force the chances
are that the most important documents relating to Dieppe would have
included in the addresses that of the Canadian Army Commander, if
only as a matter of courtesy. But the Canadians were officially regarded
as "combined with" the British army, and the proper chain of command was from the Chiefs of Staff and Chief of Combined Operations
to the General Officer Commanding, South-Eastern Command (Montgomery) and then to the 2nd Division through the 1st Canadian Corps
(Crerar) – but excluding 1st Canadian Army Headquarters (Mc-
Naughton).

If his ego had been badly bruised when he was not chosen to be the
responsible military commander of Rutter, McNaughton could have
protested more vigorously – if he really believed the issue to be an
important one. Added to the inevitable dangers of clashes of personality around a pot being attended by so many high-ranking cooks,
were the stresses of nationalistic pride and inter-army rivalries.

Groomed
to Kill

I

The mass transfer of troops from Sussex to the Isle of Wight began on May 18, under the code name "Simmer." The matrons whose daughters had so far escaped bold Canadian admiration breathed a collective sigh of relief, but those whose offspring had been captivated could only console and help wipe away the tears.

During the 2nd Division's occupation of the county, a major contribution had been made towards the total of 35,000 war marriages between Canadians and English girls; an increase in the population, legitimate or otherwise, could be logically expected, and an average of about five men had been convicted for civil crimes of sorts every month.

Most prevalent of these had been theft, larceny, burglary, and assault, and there were indications that had the occupation been prolonged English courts may have dropped their amiable attitude towards the offenders and started to hand out harsh penalties.

At McNaughton's request the Canadian High Commissioner in London, Vincent Massey, had already asked the British Home Secretary that in the interests of military discipline "Canadian soldiers charged with offences should be dealt with strictly on the merits of the case and not given special indulgence." Despite this, the army legal authorities continued to report that in practice some leniency persisted.

Yet the division left behind a vast accumulation of goodwill and affection with the people of Sussex, to the extent that the postal censors were to say later:

> There is a cheerful mail revealing eagerness for action and a fine fighting spirit. These troops are confident in themselves and confident in victory. . . . Regimental pride and a fine esprit de corps is evident. . . . References to English civilians continue to be flattering and show a very friendly spirit.

Which was hardly surprising because, after all, this was not an assembly of mercenaries, but an army united by a sense of purpose and devotion to a cause, one that may, however, have grown a little dim in the years of waiting.

The force selected by Roberts for the raid consisted of the 4th Brigade (the Royal Regiment of Canada, the Royal Hamilton Light Infantry, and the Essex Scottish) and the 6th Brigade (the Fusiliers Mont-Royal, the Camerons of Canada, and the South Saskatchewan Regiment).

Commanding the 6th Brigade was Brigadier William Wallace Southam of Toronto, a 41-year-old peacetime publisher who had served with the militia for twenty years. Bill Southam was a good administrator and a popular officer but, like so many others, he was as yet untried in action.

Brigadier Sherwood Lett, commanding the 4th Brigade, was a brilliant scholar. Born in Ontario in 1895, Lett had been educated at the University of British Columbia and, as a Rhodes Scholar, at Oxford. He had won the Military Cross in the First World War and then returned to Vancouver to be admitted to the Bar, also to become a partner in the law firm of Davis, Hossie, Lett, Marshall and McLorg. In 1939 he had been appointed Brigade Major of the 6th Brigade, accompanied it to England, and had taken a staff course at the Staff College, Camberley. He had commanded the South Saskatchewans for a while before taking over the 4th Brigade. A slim, taut man, Sherwood Lett was among the most intellectually tough officers in the Canadian Army.

First to leave Sussex were the Royals who handed over their base at Billinghurst to relief troops, entrained for Portsmouth, and arrived at Ryde on the Isle of Wight late that afternoon. Eventually, they moved close to Freshwater on the western side of the island which became battalion headquarters for the training period.

General Roberts arrived with his staff the same evening and set up divisional headquarters at Osborne Court in Cowes. The South Saskatchewans were next, Colonel Merritt establishing his headquarters at nearby Norris Castle, once Queen Victoria's favourite summer residence.

As the other regiments arrived at intervals during the 19th they went under canvas at camps distributed on the western side of the island. The 14th Canadian Army Tank Battalion followed on the 20th with units of the Engineers, Signals Corps, and Field Security Service.

Churchill Mann remained at Combined Operations headquarters to fill in the details of the military plan with the help and advice of army planners, while the naval staff allotted to Baillie-Grohman moved to Cowes where their headquarters became HMS *Vectis*, one of the most heavily guarded shore establishments in Britain. It was, in fact, the Royal Yacht Squadron clubhouse, with main offices next door in Osborne Court. Royal Marine guards barred entry or exit to unauthorized persons, and specially selected stenographers worked behind locked doors.

Hughes-Hallett had particularly good reason to be triumphant at the progress of Rutter. Combined Operations had built up a fleet of landing-craft and "mother" ships of various sizes, all designed to fill equally varied requirements and all manned by volunteer officers and sailors who had been yachtsmen, river-barge operators, and tugmen before the war. Most of them knew coastal waters intimately, but they had never acquired actual experience in the handling of these new, mostly flat-bottomed boats.

For sailors accustomed to keeping clear of rocky points and treacherous shoals, the skill they had to acquire was beaching their boats without damaging them, a technique which would be made that much more difficult when attempted under battle conditions. Hughes-Hallett had been searching for a means of pitting this unique force against the enemy for a considerable time. Now Rutter presented the opportunity.

Yet once again the incredible duplication of authority and winding lane of Command intervened. The Isle of Wight and all embarkation ports likely to be used for the operation came under the jurisdiction of the Portsmouth Naval Command. Therefore, the Commander-in-Chief, Portsmouth, who had played no part in the nurturing of Rutter, was responsible for much of the naval planning and provision of equipment.

Another curious development was the splitting of authority between Combined Operations and the 2nd Division. This meant that a junior staff officer, Lieutenant Daniel Doheny, a peacetime Montreal barrister, had to assume the role of "King's Messenger," and travel constantly between London and Cowes carrying highly secret documents relating to the projected raid. He rarely carried a briefcase. "In fact most of the time I just stuffed papers into the inside pocket of my tunic," he told me.

There was also Goronwy Rees, working with Mann, taking requests for supplies and equipment from Roberts to General Paget at the War Office – where he was subjected to some abuse because the Commander-in-Chief thought the whole plan quite mad – and reporting regularly to Montgomery.

Performing similar duties on a more senior plane was Lieutenant-Colonel G. P. Henderson who assumed the role of liaison officer between Combined Operations and McNaughton's 1st Canadian Army headquarters and Crerar's 1st Corps at Leatherhead.

II

For the next five weeks that part of the Canadian army established on the Isle of Wight under Ham Roberts was known only as "Simmerforce." Civilians with homes and businesses on the island were allowed to remain; otherwise it was sealed off from the rest of Britain. Apart from the five thousand Canadians, there were four thousand sailors, airmen, and assorted groups of various nationalities, some of whom were attached to Simmerforce and others who were there to assist in the training or waiting instructions about their future fate.

No one could get on the island without bearing proper identity papers issued specially for Rutter, and once there, no one could get off unless their absence was personally approved by Roberts or Baillie-Grohman or their security staffs.

Distributed among the battalions were seventeen members of the Free French Marine Commando led by the former banker who, somewhere between Achnacarry and the Isle of Wight, had parted company with his secretary. Unattached but also present were a group of tough-looking United States Rangers who, after their gruelling experiences at Achnacarry, would never appear quite so languid or relaxed again.

There were glider troops, paratroops, and a handful of evasive, cold-eyed individuals who rarely talked and never mingled. They were called "Phantoms," a misnomer because this was really the code name for the wireless links used by War Office liaison officers. It was rumoured, however, that these men encouraged deception, that their bosses were the espionage chiefs of Military Intelligence.

The conglomeration of languages, accents, and nationalities which comprised Simmerforce reached eerie proportions when twelve im-passive Sudeten Germans arrived and refused to discuss with anyone their purpose in going to Dieppe. They spoke only German and were accompanied by an interpreter from the Foreign Office who bore instructions accrediting them to the raid signed by General Paget.

The mystery surrounding them deepened when on one trip from London to Cowes, Goronwy Rees was ordered to stand under the clock at Victoria Station at a certain hour where he would be met by a soldier wearing a sergeant's uniform. He did as he was told, and a sergeant duly appeared in a uniform which had no regimental insignia to iden-tify it, thrust a large parcel at the startled Rees, and vanished into the station turmoil. It was not until Rees reached Cowes that he discovered he was supposed to deliver thousands of forged French francs to the Sudeten Germans. But he never managed to find the party again nor anyone who knew their whereabouts.

These were but a few of the odd parasitical groups who somehow managed to get wind of what was happening, have themselves formally attached to it, and who then refused to consult in any shape or fashion with the Force Commanders. While Combined Operations officers might be accustomed to this sort of thing during raiding operations, Roberts became acutely aware in a light-headed sort of way that what he commanded was not merely a military operation, but an adventure in which anyone who felt inclined to revisit the Continent after so long an absence might participate.

Intensive preliminary training designed to harden officers and men alike began at once among the coves and headlands of the island. The troops marched, ran, forced marched, assaulted beaches through live minefields, clambered through diabolically contrived obstacle courses, scaled cliffs with ropes and tubular telescopic ladders, and gleefully plunged bayonets at each other and into sandbags; men threw officers about in unarmed combat, they crossed rivers in breeches buoys, learned to fire pistols and Sten guns from the hip, threw themselves flat on layers of thick barbed wire while others used their backs as springboards, and engaged in wildly firing sorties through dummy towns. In all these activities they carried full assault kit which, with grenades and ammunition, weighed up to sixty pounds.

The program issued by 2nd Division headquarters laid down the training principles as general agility training, particularly up steep inclines, street-fighting with special reference to communications between interdependent companies; negotiation of wire with the use of Bangalore torpedoes or other explosive devices; attacks on pillboxes using smoke bombs and flame-throwers; rapid cross-country movement by compass; training of engineer units in destruction of masonry, concrete walls built across streets and the breaching of a 4-foot-high sea wall; co-operation between infantry and tanks; training of search parties to include Field Security Police for dealing with enemy headquarters and other offices; collection of prisoners and sorting of documents; and weapon training after strenuous exercises.

The Calgary Tanks trained with tank landing-craft, practised manœuvring on pebbled shingle, and worked with sappers responsible for blowing gaps in sea walls so that tanks could exit from beaches into towns.

On May 28, after seven days of this grim program, Roberts reported:

> Although the condition of the men is reasonably good, the assault courses and speed marches have shown that there is a great improvement to be made in this direction. In the speed marches units are able to do five miles in 45 minutes, but took from 1½ hours to 2 hours to do the remaining six miles. In the assault courses, troops were able to complete the course but were, in many cases, unable to fight or fire effectively when finished.

Behind this terse comment lay an immense, agonizing weariness. Feet were blistered and swollen, backs and legs were riddled with pain, and faces had grown drawn, haggard. Roberts pursued peak fitness relentlessly and the harder he drove them, the more grimly officers and men obeyed his orders. Throughout the Simmerforce, men helped each other, for the disgrace of one would reflect in the rest.

The speed-march target of 11 miles with full assault kit in 120 minutes was eventually reached. The battalion commanders marched at the head of their men on these occasions – with one exception. This lieutenant-colonel infuriated his officers no less than his troops by waving goodbye at the start point and driving in a jeep to the finish line, where he would be waiting with a stop watch.

The second stage of the program concentrated on landing and re-embarkation from enemy-held beaches under live fire. As the landing-craft neared shore they came under heavy bombardment: explosives attached to underwater wire went off if touched by a boat and, to get men into the habit of keeping their heads down, machine guns fired live bursts two feet above the ramps of the incoming boats. The moment the landing-craft hit the beaches, mortar bombs were fired ahead of the rushing troops while snipers' bullets kicked up sand about their feet.

For the United States Rangers attached to the Canadian battalions to gain assault experience it was Achnacarry all over again – only worse. There, it had been a case of a hundred or so men firing wildly in all directions; on the Isle of Wight there were thousands.

While Roberts watched his troops, Baillie-Grohman, who arrived from the Middle East mid way through the training, gazed bleakly at the landing-craft and began to wonder if the Navy would, in fact, ever get the Army to the proper destination. The young, inexperienced reservist officers ignored timetables, hit wrong beaches and often each other. Where there should have been orderly flotillas there was often confusion, so much so that many boats grounded stern first, and when the ramps went down, the troops, who had been keeping their heads down, dashed out into the open sea. As the days passed matters did improve slightly and, by June 6, Roberts was able to write in his war diary:

> The condition of the men had improved and better results have been secured from speed marches but it has become evident that in the short time available, training to the standard required is not possible without sacrificing other valuable training.

Driven hardest were the Fusiliers Mont-Royal whose large, dark-faced commander, Lieutenant-Colonel Menard, revelled in the simulated battles. One of his company commanders, Major Sarto Marchand, member of the prominent Montreal family of distillers, told me: "It was a difficult assignment for Joe. The battalion command had always been handed down in a sort of line of succession, and when this Permanent Force outsider arrived he was regarded with the gravest suspicion. He proved a good Quebecker and virtually hammered us into submission by his own extraordinary ability to do everything just a little bit better than the rest of us. By the time we got to the Isle of Wight he was about the most popular colonel we had experienced."

For two weeks, the name Joe Menard was cursed in French from dawn till dark. And the more vicious the words, the more Menard applied the whip. He was determined that the first Canadian troops to cover 11 miles in 90 minutes should be the Fusiliers Mont-Royal. And they were. The men's hatred for Menard soon turned into pride in themselves.

Most popular pub on the island was the Starboard Club, outside Ryde, not only for its atmosphere or ability to stay open all night every night, but because it seemed to attract the best-looking girls.

On one occasion, at least, a group of Canadian officers woke up at dawn still in the bar, suffering from acute hangovers. They shepherded dishevelled girl friends into the kitchen, gulped down hot coffee, and made it back to their respective camps just in time to fall in for a speed march involving the entire Simmerforce.

Montgomery was a frequent visitor to the island, Mountbatten less so. But one time when they arrived together a curious conference was held at Osborne Court. Only four people were present: Montgomery, Mountbatten, Roberts, and Hughes-Hallett.

Montgomery had made a few caustic remarks about the physical fitness of some of the troops and Roberts had replied with a spirited defence when Hughes-Hallett broke in suddenly: "If Lord Mountbatten agrees, I should like to go along on this show with the troops, just to see how it all looks from their level. It will also give me a chance to pick up experience for future planning."

Mountbatten, always insistent that Combined Operations staff should go to almost any lengths to acquire experience and knowledge said: "By all means, John, but it's up to the General." Roberts nodded assent, and after the conference Hughes-Hallett made his plans to become Private Hallett of the Camerons of Canada. But first he had to accompany Mountbatten on a flying visit to Washington for a double-barrelled mission – to steer Roosevelt's enthusiasm away from the sacrificial Sledgehammer and towards North Africa.

IV

On the eve of his departure for the United States, Mountbatten presided over a conference at Combined Operations Headquarters attended by

Sir Bernard Paget, Montgomery, Leigh-Mallory, Roberts, and various members of the planning syndicate. It was also Baillie-Grohman's initial introduction into the closed, intimate circle of Rutter planners. Canadian-born himself he could understand and sympathize with the keenness of the Canadian Army at the prospect of going into action. But he had just arrived from the Middle East and had been given only twenty-four hours to examine the outline plan before being summoned to the conference, otherwise cold.

It is curious that the Dieppe decision had been made and the outline plan formally drafted and approved by the highest military authorities in the land, before the Naval Force Commander was told what would be required of him. He was not put into the picture fully until June 1 – nearly two months after conception. A possible reason is that there was difficulty in finding a flag officer to act as force commander.

Combined Operations in the Middle East had reached a high peak of efficiency, and Baillie-Grohman knew how operations of this kind were mounted – he had, in fact, planned a similar assault on the island of Rhodes which had been cancelled at the last minute. He listened for most of the conference, breaking his silence only to ask two questions: where did he check for further intelligence and what were the prospects of strengthening the obviously weak naval fire support? To his astonishment he was told that the dark, Latin-looking RAF wing commander sitting on his left was in charge of Combined Operations Intelligence.

"I thought this was rather an extraordinary state of affairs," he told me," because the chap was obviously a foreigner and as it turned out he was not even of an Allied country. What really concerned me was the optimism reflected in the outline plan which said that the Dieppe defences were not strong. It seemed to me that everything being planned was based on this assumption and if it were wrong the results would be terrible."

Montgomery answered his question on fire support, saying in effect that once he had studied the air plan he would see that the very heavy bombardment being laid on by the RAF would compensate for lack of heavy naval support. Baillie-Grohman recognized that this was something new, so rather than challenge the validity of it he asked Leigh-Mallory if it could be accurately timed. Even when the reply was confidently affirmative he persisted, asking Mountbatten if it would not be best to include at least one battleship. Mountbatten had been through this argument with Hughes-Hallett and rather than explain all the objections again, he suggested that Baillie-Grohman see him privately when the conference ended.

This private meeting later that day in Mountbatten's office revealed the wide gulf between military and naval tactical thinking on amphibious operations. Baillie-Grohman repeated his request that a battleship be included in the naval force. Mountbatten said the Admiralty had been approached but that the idea had been turned down "in the highest quarters." The Force Commander also expressed his doubts about the wisdom of a frontal assault across the main Dieppe beaches.

"Mountbatten told me he had not wanted the frontal attack plan either," Baillie-Grohman said. "He said he had been keen on going in on the flanks and had fought hard for it. But the Army had insisted on the frontal attack and they had got their way because, after all, it was a military matter."

Such is the legend of Mountbatten that today his name is synonymous with influence, prestige, and authority. In 1942 he may have possessed some of each, but he was by no means as powerful as people seem to believe. Churchill and the British Chiefs of Staff undoubtedly admired his ability and his determination to make Combined Operations work, but they were not compelled to accept his advice nor were they likely to be easily persuaded by the 41-year-old baby in their midst.

Mountbatten himself was too astute to give advice on matters not properly within his own sphere, unless it was asked for. Not only was his authority strictly limited, but Combined Operations had much more to think about than Dieppe. A multitude of plans were burgeoning for offensive operations, and while all this was going on the Command itself had to be welded into an efficient, if complete, laboratory for the testing of invasion tactics.

Because of this, once a plan had been made and approved by the Chiefs of Staff it became the responsibility of a designated military authority and of the appointed Force Commanders. Mountbatten and Combined Operations teams were available only for consultation.

Later that night, Baillie-Grohman travelled down to the Isle of Wight to join the staff selected for him. His Chief of Staff, Captain T. H. Black, and his Staff Officer Operations were both very able officers, but lacked experience in the complications of the many various types of combined operational craft. He was to find that inexperience existed at all levels owing to the enormous expansion of personnel which had overwhelmed Combined Operations training establishments. The handicap, coupled with the shortage of ships, landing-craft, and instructors, made training programs inedequate and incomplete.

To Baillie-Grohman, however, none of the shortcomings were so serious as that of the potentially faulty, over-optimistic Intelligence analysis of the Dieppe defences which had led to an outside plan based on the supposition that enemy resistance would not be strong.

"Throughout these preliminary preparations," he said, "my staff and I tried to extract sound, up-to-the-minute intelligence on German defences from Combined Operations Headquarters – one request concerning such simple things as copies of pictures of Dieppe taken from the sea such as might be seen in railway compartments. Eventually they did produce a confidential book detailing all that was known. But it came out only at the last minute when it had little value and simply confirmed their over-optimistic interpretations of before.

"We found Combined Operations Intelligence slow, inefficient, and lamentable, and dealing with the apparent foreigner brought us not even the simplest information. Later we sent our requests direct to Admiralty Intelligence or to the Photographic Interpretation Unit at Medmenham."

No matter how well founded were Baillie-Grohman's suspicions at this stage, his first tasks were monumental: to plan, organize, and train a naval force for the largest military offensive launched from British shores since the fall of France, with nothing like enough ships and only three weeks in which to do it.

Weakening the Punch

I

Weapons, ammunition, and all those assorted stores required for the business of killing were issued constantly from May 23 onwards with Major H. M. Romilly, Quartermaster-General in charge of raiding supplies at Combined Operations Headquarters, as the responsible officer. Supplies were difficult to acquire, mainly because Romilly was not permitted to explain why he needed them, and this question was inevitable when so many shortages existed.

A rough formula had been worked out for previous, smaller raids by which he made contact with only one officer at the War Office, who then acted as a go-between with various depots. But the amount of stores required for Rutter was so enormous that curiosity was quickly aroused.

Trainloads of crates arrived on the Isle of Wight, each one addressed to Lieutenant-Colonel Robert King, 2nd Division's Assistant Quartermaster, care of the railway transport officer at Cowes. They bore no means of identification, nor unit names. The most difficult to supply were the Calgary Tanks who needed six-pounder guns and special waterproofing gear, too bulky to be easily disguised.

As it was suspected that the main Dieppe beaches might be mined, the detailed military plan budgeted for twenty-five mine detectors, which Lieutenant-Colonel King requested from Combined Operations. Mine detectors of all types were hard to come by because the War Office shipped almost the total production to the Middle East. When Major Romilly passed on the request to the War Office, he received a blunt refusal, as did further requests, until eventually Mountbatten spoke personally with Paget, and sixteen detectors were at last allocated to Rutter.

Romilly also prepared for the reception of the wounded who might come back from Dieppe by informing hospitals within thirty miles of the main disembarkation ports that an immense military exercise would be held between certain dates and instructing them to co-operate by holding 3,000 beds available. He also arranged with Intelligence sections to establish a prisoner-of-war cage at Lingfield, Hampshire, where captured enemy documents could be collected and prisoners interrogated.

One of the most mysterious officers on the island was a Major D. Wyatt who, so it was rumoured, was a special service officer from the War Office. No one knew what he was supposed to be doing, but he was in fact an explosives expert instructing the excrescent groups attached to the 2nd Division in the handling of a whole range of explosive devices designed to destroy special targets.

Wyatt's private arsenal was seemingly limitless. He had plastic charges for blowing down concrete walls, others for blowing up huge six-inch gun batteries, and a few for blowing in cliff faces. The caverns beneath the East Headland had been transformed by the German navy into a vast torpedo dump. Wyatt had devised limpet charges for its destruction.

As one of the objectives given to the South Saskatchewans was a radar station near Pourville, and because we knew so little about the design of German radar equipment and even less about the principle upon which it operated, the director of Radio-Location Research at the Air Ministry allotted two scientists to accompany the regiment ashore. They were to dismantle the delicate internal instruments and bring them back to Britain for examination, leaving the rest of the station to be blown up by some of Wyatt's plastic explosives.

Cec Merritt was ordered by Roberts to provide the scientists with a bodyguard commanded by one officer who would be responsible for shooting them if they appeared to be falling into enemy hands. Merritt, slightly sickened by the order, passed it on to Captain Murray Osten and did his best to forget about it. But Osten had no intention of missing the battle by playing nursemaid, so he ordered his company sergeant to see that the scientists were kept out of harm's way until safely re-embarked, and then did his best to forget about it.

The assault courses were not confined to training infantry; they were also designed to shake down the crews of the landing-craft flotillas. These mostly amateur sailors were unaware then that they would eventually become famous as the permanent assault group known as Force J that landed the troops in North Africa and Normandy.

They had to learn how to approach a beach, ground on it, and remain off it within instant call, ready to come in; and a handful of regular officers who had spent their lives looking upon beaching as the ultimate in professional incompetence now spent their days teaching volunteers how to do it. When the tide went out the landing-craft had to be eased down the beach to avoid being stranded; and when it turned and began coming in, the craft would have to be driven up with it to avoid cross-winds swinging them about.

While they had carried out endless working-up practices and landing exercises prior to Rutter, they had never contemplated being called upon to operate on such a vast scale and in such numbers.

Among the predominantly British naval force were 15 officers and 55 men of the Royal Canadian Navy, first of more than 450 who would eventually serve with Force J. There was Lieutenant John E. Boak of Vancouver and Sub-Lieutenants Gordon Bayne of Lancaster, New Brunswick, Jack Koyl of Cobourg, Ontario, and Johnny O'Rourke, originally of Calgary, but more recently of St Nazaire – each of whom would be there at dawn the day the Canadians went to France.

Their presence in the operation came about more by accident than by any intent of Canadian naval authorities. In late 1941 RCN head-quarters in Ottawa decided to build up an all-Canadian assault force, and in February 1942 sent a batch of young sub-lieutenants and ratings to England to be trained in landing-craft by Combined Operations. They went to Lee-on-Solent where Lieutenant R. F. McRae of Toronto joined them as senior Canadian officer for the course.

McRae, serving with the Royal Navy but being paid and administered from Ottawa like so many Canadian officers then, thought his small force was to operate on the same basis, as an integral part of the British landing-craft fleet. For this reason he was mildly astonished when the British officer in charge of training asked him one day: "How would you chaps like some action? We've got a show coming off and we're pretty short of men and boats. We could use you."

McRae felt it was awfully decent of this senior officer to inquire rather than order and immediately committed himself and the entire Canadian contingent. They were not to operate as a group but would be dispersed among the Combined Operations flotillas in the same manner as Royal Navy crews. It never occurred to McRae that this was not Ottawa's intention, nor did he think of informing RCN headquarters in London. After all he was a junior officer and any informing that had to be done would be handled at a higher level, particularly as the RCN had a liaison officer on Mountbatten's staff.

But this officer, Lieutenant-Commander K. S. Maclachlan, was not aware of the plan to raid Dieppe, and McRae, pledged to secrecy himself, was telling no one. In fact, the RCN, neither in Ottawa nor in London, had the slightest inkling that Canadian sailors would be at Dieppe. It was not until the casualty figures started coming in after the raid that they realized their men had sneaked off to war.

Had McRae returned from Dieppe it is highly possible that angry senior officers would have demanded his court-martial. He went to prison camp instead, and the RCN was left with no alternative but to proudly proclaim their presence on the beaches and start handing out decorations.

The training of these British and Canadian crews was not a simple matter, as it meant imposing upon them the crash programs necessary if they were to learn how to form up in columns, to proceed in close order in flotillas, and to manœuvre without warning – all in the dark and without navigation lights. Even as they learned, landing-craft loaded with troops would make dummy runs into beaches, foul each other, and create chaos.

Baillie-Grohman's staff were also plagued by the necessity for keeping assemblies of shipping hidden from German air reconnaissance flights over the south coast of England. Cowes, being a convoy-gathering port at which there were always considerable numbers of ships riding at anchor, could be used because the presence of a few more would not attract special attention. But the remainder of the 200-odd ships involved had to be dispersed over the Solent off Yarmouth, Ryde, Southampton Water, Portsmouth, and the Hamble River, ports which were miles away from each other. Nor could they be linked by wireless

or netted into harbour communications systems, in case enemy interception tactics revealed a sudden increase in signal traffic.

Although all aspects of Combined Operations were dangerous, few
were more so than the new occupations of Beachmaster (a naval
officer) and Military Landing Officer (an army officer), both of whom
had to be landed in the first flights, to work as a team ensuring that
their beach was clearly marked for succeeding waves; they had to
move forward with the first line of assault troops identifying exits from
the beach into the hinterland; and also establish an organization for
controlling vehicle traffic moving from the shore line inland. Finally,
Beachmaster and Military Landing Officer were together responsible for
calling in the boats to evacuate troops, conducting themselves in the
manner of traffic police on point duty while constantly exposed to
enemy fire.

Major Brian McCool of the Royal Regiment of Canada became head
of the Military Landing organization. He would set up headquarters on
the main beaches and have assistants operating on the immediate flank
beaches, Blue and Green.

Among his responsibilities was the allocation of priorities for strange
people who might have to be brought back to England. The scientists
with their radar loot would be one team; another involved a Field
Security unit who would raid German divisional headquarters, capture
as many documents and codebooks as possible, and report back to
McCool; a third and very hush-hush mission would make its way to
the prison and release captured Resistance workers and anyone else
accused of plotting against the Germans. They too would report back
to McCool on the main beaches with authority to re-embark with any
material they may have collected and with any civilians accompanying them, up to a limit of twelve.

McCool had only recently acquired special qualifications for this job
while undergoing Commando assault training at Hayling Island, near
Portsmouth, and in Scotland. Under him were 200 Canadians who
comprised Viking Force, really an embryo Commando troop which,
had it not been for Rutter, might have served as a permanent unit. As
it was, the unit had been moved north secretly to practise landings on
the west coast of Scotland. To divert attention from the removal of
other Canadians from Sussex to the Isle of Wight, a rumour was spread
deliberately that they had really gone to Scotland to train for a pending
campaign in Norway.

After a brief two weeks in Scotland, the force was returned to the

Isle of Wight where the personnel were dispersed among the various regiments to act as instructors in the art of beach organization.

II

For the latter part of the Isle of Wight sojourn, Churchill Mann remained at divisional headquarters in Osborne Court, Cowes, inserting details in the military plan which Roberts then included in the general training program. In this way troops were trained to the plan, each exercise serving a specific purpose. In most instances, landings and assaults were carried out as Mann envisaged them taking place in the actual operation and, once ashore, the troops headed for mock-ups of the objectives they would attempt to reach at Dieppe.

The same process applied to the naval and air plans which were drafted in co-operation with Mann's planning team so that at least the naval force could be trained with the same infantry groups they would carry during the operation and undertake with them manœuvres related to a combined plan.

Mann assumed most of the work himself, giving the same concentrated attention to the seemingly insignificant trifles as to the obviously important ones, so that in consequence the detail that eventually went into the final military plan was so meticulously prepared that it occupied more than 120 typewritten foolscap pages.

The 48-page book compiled by Combined Operations Intelligence, which listed German defences and the number and quality of the troops in the Dieppe area, and its supplement of maps and air photographs, reached him at such a late stage that its effectiveness is questionable. Each section of this "Most Secret" document was the result of an analysis of messages from Intelligence sources in Occupied France – notably the Resistance, British Special Operations Executive, and military espionage groups.

This information was reinforced by a multitude of snapshots taken by English tourists in Dieppe before the war and collected by agents of the Central Photographic Intelligence unit with headquarters in Oxford. These agents, mostly women, travelled across Britain knocking on doors and asking for any pictures the householder may have taken during prewar visits to the Continent.

When a special operation was being mounted, the unit assembled snaps of the target area for minute study. From a snap of Mum, Dad, and the kids picnicking on a Dieppe beach, it was possible to estimate the gradient of the beach, even the density of the pebbles and their ability to hold the weight of a tank; from pictures of young couples shrimping among the rocks at the foot of the headlands it was possible to pinpoint cave entrances in the cliff faces.

Photographic Air Reconnaissance squadrons flew over France, Belgium, Holland, and Norway almost daily, the extent of their operations diverting attention from the principal effort being made over the Dieppe area. These Spitfires were unarmed and stripped of armourplating to give them extra height and speed.

Their photographs were sent to the Allied Photographic Interpretation Centre at Danesfield Hall, Medmenham, Buckinghamshire, for scientific analysis. In charge of this unit was Wing Commander Douglas Kendall, a slender æsthetic-looking ærial photography expert, who is now president of Hunting Air Survey Corporation in Toronto.

"We flew missions over Dieppe continuously during the planning stage," he told me. "Most of the defences were pinpointed in the photographs, even the road blocks barring entry into the town from the beaches. We got excellent shots of the wing headlands on either side of Dieppe and it was quite clear that the guns on top of them could catch anyone landing on the main beaches in pretty murderous crossfire.

"The East Headland was particularly well defended and covered the entire promenade, beach area, and harbour entrances. That's why the Royal Regiment landing at Blue Beach had to get up there to capture these guns before they could cut down the troops landing on Red and White Beaches."

Despite this incredibly patient examination of photographs from all sources, the planners failed to reach the conclusion that the caves in the headlands might be stuffed with machine-gun nests and snipers' hideaways. No provision was made to neutralize them.

Several days were spent on a Dorset beach testing the performance of Churchill tanks on the shifting pebbles. The slope of this particular beach was steeper than might be expected at Dieppe, and the tanks behaved perfectly, manœuvring in all directions without once sinking too deeply into the shingle or losing traction. But no attempt was made to have them negotiate sea walls such as they would certainly face in the actual operation. Sappers were supposed to build timber ramps against the walls in difficult spots; but no one considered the likelihood of their being killed first. In this it seems that the Canadians were at fault, as there is evidence that Combined Operations felt such misgivings that they suggested using remote-controlled tanks filled with high explosives to blow gaps in the wall.

The detailed military, naval, and air plans were completed early in June, and by far the most complex was Churchill Mann's, which Roberts accepted with only minor amendments because he had no reason to do otherwise. After all, it was a splendid example of documented theory which stipulated the times to the nearest minute by which each unit would gain its various objectives. The sequence of events allowed only two and a half hours for the assault and occupation to be completed. By 7:20 a.m. Dieppe would be captured, the raiders would hold a perimeter round the town about four to five miles deep and all the special demolition and intelligence groups would be able to carry out their tasks unmolested by the enemy. The sheer effrontery of it was magnificent, but to base a major operation on such contempt for an enemy who happened to know how to wage war properly, was tempting fate, to say the least.

It was a hopelessly rigid plan built up from extreme confidence, extreme enthusiasm, and extreme inexperience, but then neither Roberts, Mann, nor anyone else for that matter had ever planned a raid quite so large and intricate as that on Dieppe. Failure was not even considered, and in the event of the assault forces being unable to secure their beaches, there was no alternative plan for them to follow.

"I remember it was very long and detailed," Baillie-Grohman told me, "and I never had time to go into the thing. Roberts kept me in the military picture verbally – and very well too."

III

The basic tactical plan had been laid down by Montgomery who now wanted to see for himself the approach of the landing-craft, the assault across the beaches and through the wire, the arrival of the tanks, how they came ashore, and how fast the engineers could build ramps along the sea wall for them to move onto the promenade. There were also track-laying tanks and flame-throwing tanks, so new they had not yet seen action.

He asked the Force Commanders to prepare a full-scale exercise at a place of their own choosing, and Baillie-Grohman selected the Bridport~West Bay district on the coast of Dorset. This stretch of shore closely resembled the beaches and cliffs of Dieppe and would in his view provide the landing-craft officers with useful training in the handling of their craft. In addition, the distance from the Isle of Wight was roughly the same as that to Dieppe, and the timing of the exercise could be connected with the timing of the actual operation. "I also mentioned to Roberts that it would give the troops some idea of what it is like to be cooped up in a crowded boat for a long period," he has told me since.

Although he had not been very impressed with the performance of the naval crews during earlier exercises in the Solent, and therefore expected the worst, Baillie-Grohman did not know that he had added to naval troubles by choosing Bridport. The tides during the run from Cowes were to prove far stronger than those to be encountered while crossing the Channel to Dieppe, and this factor would prove too much for the more inexperienced young officers to handle.

Code name for the exercise would be "Yukon"; and to prevent need-less speculation it was announced to the 2nd Division as a test for Combined Operations to be held on June 8 in conjunction with the Royal Navy and Royal Air Force.

It was a futile cover story. Rumours of a pending operation were spreading like bush fire, and Les Fusiliers Mont-Royal were already giv-ing other Canadians lessons in elementary French.

Heavy air bombardment of Dieppe was a vital ingredient of the military plan, but during the early planning it had been discovered that there was a British War Cabinet directive that targets in Occupied France could be bombed "only when weather conditions are such that accurate attack can be expected." The Chiefs of Staff had sent a memorandum to Churchill complaining at the broad ban this directive imposed on offensive operations and remarking that "the restriction has already proved a hindrance to Combined Operations."

They were referring to the St Nazaire raid, when bombers were prevented from attacking because clouds obscured targets in the dock-yard area and made accurate bombing virtually impossible. The minute from the Chiefs of Staff Committee explained that since such a predi-cament was likely to recur, the Cabinet ruling – designed to avoid causing casualties among French civilians – might be relaxed where Combined Operations were concerned.

On June 1 the Foreign Office replied that Anthony Eden, while still opposed to the indiscriminate bombing of French towns at night, agreed that an exception to the rule would be made in the case of coastal raids. The letter said:

"B" Your minute of the 19th May to the Prime Minister urging on behalf of the Chiefs of Staff that the Cabinet ruling that targets in France may be Bombed "when weather conditions are such that an accurate attack can be expected" might be relaxed so far as Combined Operations are concerned.

"A" The Secretary of State agrees with your proposals. At the same time he asks me to say that he is still against indiscriminate bombing at night except in connection with a coastal raid.

This letter had been submitted to the Prime Minister who had minuted on it as follows:

See that the above "A" is observed except as provided at "B."

[*Initialled*]   W.S.C.

Permission from the highest authority, to bomb Dieppe during the dark hours immediately prior to the landings, gave the frontal-assault principle validity. Heavy bombardment from the air could have the same effect as the naval bombardment denied by the Admiralty.

Then other events and personalities intervened to force the planners to delete even the bomber attack.

Behind this astounding decision was a private meeting between Leigh-Mallory and Air Marshal Sir Arthur Harris, Chief of Bomber Command. In view of the lifting of restrictions against bombing French towns, Leigh-Mallory asked for 300 bombers to attack Dieppe on the night of June 20-21 regardless of weather conditions. He wanted in particular the main weight of bombs to be dropped on the buildings facing the sea front across the promenade and on the headlands at the east and west of the main beaches. He also asked that the heavy bombing be continued in support of the initial landings.

Harris, dedicated to the conviction that Germany could be bombed into submission, had set minimum nightly tonnages to be dropped on industrial targets and regarded the provision of bombers for Combined Operations a senseless interference with this program.

"I have neither planes nor crews to spare for useless sideshows," he said.

Despite Leigh-Mallory's protests, Harris refused to be committed to 300 bombers, nor would he guarantee any accuracy in a bombing aimed at supporting the actual landings. He insisted that if cloud conditions were bad, it was possible that more bombs would fall in the middle of the town than on the sea front, and if this happened there would be no point in Combined Operations blaming Bomber Command. At one point he declined to guarantee that his bombers would even hit Dieppe at all. Leigh-Mallory left Harris's headquarters convinced that if the operation depended upon the air bombardment it would probably never take place.

On June 5 a dramatic conference was held at Richmond Terrace, with Montgomery in the chair and attended by the Combined Operations Adviserate and the three Rutter Force Commanders: Roberts, Leigh-Mallory, and Baillie-Grohman. It began quietly enough with Roberts and Baillie-Grohman demanding from Leigh-Mallory that the initial assault over the main beaches be covered by a smokescreen laid by aircraft. Leigh-Mallory replied:

"We can't do it. First, it's pretty difficult for aircraft to lay smoke accurately over a narrow beachfront, and second, we have the cannon-firing Hurricanes delivering their attack to cover the initial assault. In my view, the Hurricanes will prove more effective than a smoke-screen."

Roberts was not particularly satisfied. Deprived of a naval bombardment and being so accustomed to attacking under a heavy artillery barrage, he wanted something more than just the Hurricanes to keep the defences quiescent.

"How about the Navy?" he asked of Baillie-Grohman. "Is there any reason why you shouldn't increase your fire-power or at least lay some smoke along the shore line?"

Baillie-Grohman shook his head. "Requests for battleships have been turned down, and I've been told at the Admiralty that no warships other than the destroyers already allocated can be supplied.

"Yes, but you could carry mortars in the landing-craft and lay smoke bombs on the beach," interjected Montgomery.

"Some landing-craft already carry mortars. I'll see if I can get some more," promised Baillie-Grohman.

The minutes of the meeting recorded that more landing-craft should be equipped with mortars if possible so that they could lay their own smokescreens.

Leigh-Mallory then suggested that a small naval demonstration in the Boulogne area would be invaluable as a feint while the raiding convoy was approaching the French coast. Baillie-Grohman agreed that the Chief of Combined Operations could lay on this demonstration about an hour and a half before touchdown.

It seemed from the minutes that the naval and military Force Commanders had little to offer in the way of proposals, most of which came from Leigh-Mallory. It was, for instance, Leigh-Mallory who drew attention to the fact that the fleet would be vulnerable to air attack while lying off Dieppe and that the two fighter squadrons earmarked to cover it might be insufficient.

Montgomery agreed and suggested that Baillie-Grohman should ask Portsmouth Command to provide all ships taking part with additional anti-aircraft armament. He went further, offering to make the guns available from South-Eastern Command if the Navy could supply extra ships to carry them.

At this stage, Leigh-Mallory, uncomfortably conscious of "Bomber" Harris's attitude, dropped his own bombshell. He reported his conversation with the chief of Bomber Command and said: "There's a chance we may not get all the bombers we need if Bomber Command insists that some target in Germany that night is of more vital importance. And if we can't get overwhelming air bombardment immediately prior to touchdown, then the only likely result will be to put everyone on the alert. Inadequate, inaccurate bombing would be useless.

"I propose," he said, "that we bomb Boulogne with 70 aircraft at the same time as the naval demonstration and create an additional diversion. We might also bomb the *Luftwaffe* fighter ærodromes at Crecy and Abbeville just to occupy the radar stations which might otherwise pick up the approach of the convoy."

In this single statement Leigh-Mallory stripped away the overpowering fire support that had been promised to overcome naval objections to the principle of a frontal assault.

Mountbatten and Hughes-Hallett had concurred with the principle only if they could cover the landing with battleship fire-power. When this had been denied, they had conceded again on the undertaking that Bomber Command would provide comparable heavy air bombardment. Now this last excuse for leaving the frontal assault in the plan vanished, and not one of these senior commanders suggested it should therefore be abandoned. At least one of them, Baillie-Grohman, had been told on a high level that Churchill intended to proceed with the raid no matter what the objections, and that nothing would dissuade him.

General Roberts supported Leigh-Mallory by saying that erratic, indiscriminate bombing would only serve to destroy a large number of houses in the town itself, probably set fire to many more and prevent tanks from operating in streets choked with debris.

Roberts told me: "I knew that the fate of the operation was still uncertain, and Leigh-Mallory had warned me that Bomber Command couldn't at that stage of the war bomb from a high level with any precision. I was prepared to agree with the proposal rather than see the operation cancelled, and in any event my prime concern was the heavy batteries on the headlands flanking the beaches. If they could be neutralized, there was a good chance of the element of surprise compensating for lack of fire-power. I had reason then to believe that the Air Force and the Navy would take care of those guns."

Montgomery agreed with the abandonment of the bombing-raid, and another of the original designs for success disappeared.

The lessons of Gallipoli twenty-seven years before were forgotten, fire-power had been allowed to dwindle to nothing, and the troops would be expected to land on heavily defended beaches with only a handful of bombers and cannon-firing Hurricanes to occupy the defences.

It seemed that the authorities responsible for Rutter were so confident, so determined to get back on the Continent, so eager to get at the enemy, that they would let the troops go in with bows and arrows, cutlasses, or even bare hands, if necessary.

The remainder of the conference was anti-climactic.

Commander Ryder of Combined Operations, now holding the Victoria Cross for his leadership of the St Nazaire raid, was also going to Dieppe in the steam gun boat, *Locust*. It would be his job to get into the harbour and remove German invasion barges. He pointed out rather acidly that the naval plan had not taken into account the possibility of the barges not having enough fuel to be driven back to England. In this event, he said, his "cutting out" force would have to take the barges in tow, and perhaps some special measures should be taken to meet this contingency. Baillie-Grohman said he would see what could be done, although he was privately dubious about the whole cutting-out expedition and whether his colleagues at Combined Operations or at Portsmouth would release anything more to the enterprise in terms of ships or equipment.

There is some evidence to show that Churchill who had joined Dudley Pound in denying battleship support to the operation, also played a decisive role in the elimination of the air bombardment. It is probable that the Prime Minister, and possibly Anthony Eden, had second thoughts about the political repercussions, were the operation to result in a large loss of French civilian life. The Germans could be relied upon to make propaganda capital out of such an incident, and the British government might find it hard to counter allegations that it sanctioned an inhuman act of war knowing that the defenceless French would suffer more than the Germans. It is quite possible that Churchill demanded from Bomber Command a degree of accuracy that it could not possibly guarantee and, in the absence of any assurances that loss of French lives could be kept to a minimum, he intervened at Chiefs of Staff level to have the air bombardment cancelled.

Certainly Baillie-Grohman remains convinced that politics influenced the decision and recalls that the confirmatory order cancelling the raid mentioned that the government could not permit inaccurate bombing of French towns by night, and ended: "Reliance must now be placed on tactical surprise."

"It was obvious to all the generals," he told me, "that naval fire support was weak. But if the army was prepared to take this serious and entirely obvious risk, I felt that the navy had no option but to support them with whatever we could get. The dice were loaded against us, but to what extent it was difficult to say. We might catch them napping. The Canadians were mad keen on going in; so was Leigh-Mallory. I understood that the Prime Minister was quite determined to go ahead as well. He was largely influenced by the success of the bold St Nazaire raid which had been contrary to the gloomy predictions of many of his able advisers."

So ended an incredible conference which in a few short hours had stripped the enterprise of its mailed glove and replaced it with one of velvet. Instead of a steel fist rising out of the sea to send the enemy reeling back in disorder, a hand would emerge to lightly slap his cheek – and sting him into violent retaliation. If Churchill could change his mind and forbid not only the battleship but also the inaccurate bombing of Dieppe while insisting that the operation nevertheless proceed, then Montgomery, at this conference, could have reversed his decision on the frontal assault on the ground that it was no longer feasible.

Montgomery was to refer in his memoirs to two specific changes in the plan: an eventual switch-round of troops and the elimination of the preliminary air bombardment. He said: "I should not myself have agreed to either of these changes." Yet he had himself presided over the very conference which eliminated the bombing.

Although he missed this dramatic conference, Hughes-Hallett flew back to Britain ahead of Mountbatten in time to don the guise of a Canadian and become the buddy of a cold-eyed ex-trapper.

III

According to his papers, Private Hallett was a clerk at Combined Operations Headquarters who had been transferred to the Camerons for field training. This story covered his English accent and enabled him to explain away any insight into Commando organization that he might let slip.

He began creating his character by telling anyone who would listen of his cover background, and set about making friends. The Canadians were only too keen on being friendly, and he quickly found that they would not have been in the slightest interested had he been the Archbishop of Canterbury in disguise. All brilliance has an element of artistry, and Hughes-Hallett was able within a few days to live convincingly the life of an ordinary infantryman, remaining neutral in tent arguments, pretending ignorance on matters about which he was well informed, and nodding sage agreement at the constant nagging about officers.

The Camerons, he found, had one officer they hated with alarming intensity; another they liked, even worshipped.

"For this man," said Hughes-Hallett, "that battalion had what amounted to an abiding affection. There was nothing they wouldn't do for him, nowhere they wouldn't go for him."

This aspect of his deception had no interest for Hughes-Hallett. What the men thought of their officers, of each other, and all the other personality problems which absorb soldiers most of their waking hours were their own affairs, not to be exposed or exploited by an intruder. His only concern was to take part in the operation, even if it meant doing so in the uniform of a Canadian private.

In the oddly casual, almost indifferent manner by which comparative strangers often drift into close relationships, Private Hallett found he was sharing daily routine and most of his evenings with a taciturn private who rarely mingled with other soldiers. His name was Stanley Jones and, so he said, he came from Winnipeg. Hughes-Hallett noticed that, when he sometimes sat outside the tent in the evenings smoking a cigarette, Jones would coil down beside him and talk of the places he had seen, the beauty of the seasons in various parts of the world, of music, of books, of art.

He discussed these things without any deep understanding of them, and it was apparent that this wide-shouldered, slim-hipped, controlled man had a superficial knowledge that was largely self-acquired. His eyes were cold, expressionless, and Hughes-Hallett recognized thinly concealed cruelty in the full, sensuous lips and pallid, loose-jowelled face.

Hughes-Hallett kept pace with the rest of the battalion throughout the assault training, racing across shingled beaches, scrambling through barbed wire entanglements, staggering up steep gullies and climbing sheer rock faces. Whenever he faltered there was always Jones to give a slight smile of encouragement and, if necessary, a pull or a heave.

It happened one evening in the village of Wootten. Hughes-Hallett and Jones were drinking beer in a saloon bar. Three British Pioneer Corps soldiers were sprawled across a table at the other side of the room, arguing loudly, and getting sullenly drunk. Two very young Canadians ambled in quite amiably, ordered beer, and took it to another table, and the minutes passed with each group ignoring the others.

Hughes-Hallett cannot recall at what point the atmosphere changed or what caused it to become electric, charged with sudden friction. Jones had stopped talking, his pale eyes boring steadily into a huge Pioneer who stood up, swayed slightly, and then lurched towards the bar.

As he passed the pair of Canadian newcomers, he pretended to lose his balance, knocked against their table, and sent their glasses of beer crashing to the floor. He towered over the startled youngsters and yelled: "You Canuck bastards. Think you can trip me up and get away with it . . ."

He grabbed the nearest Canadian, pulled him to his feet and began pounding his face. No one else moved. The only sounds were the thuds of punches and the heavy breathing of the Pioneer.

The Canadian fell to the floor, his face swollen and bloody, and the Pioneer began kicking him about the head. His buddy sat wide-eyed with surprise, transfixed to his chair. The other Britishers looked on blearily, too drunk to realize what was happening.

Sickened by the unexpected brutality of the scene, Hughes-Hallett had half risen, but a hand gripped his arm tightly, pulling him down again. By now the Pioneer was standing over his moaning victim, taking a swallow of beer and then delivering another kick with his heavy army boots, repeating the process with murderous regularity.

Jones whispered: "There's a pub about a hundred yards up the road. Soon as I give the word, get out of here, go there, and order two large beers. I'll follow you a minute or so later."

It was an order that Hughes-Hallett could ignore, but if he did choose to stay, it would mean revealing his true identity.

While he waited, the boy on the floor began to cry out, and even the bully's companions were shocked into hard, brittle awareness of the brutality of the assault.

It seemed they were getting ready to put an end to it when Jones snapped: "Now . . . go."

Hughes-Hallett nodded agreement, went to the door, and paused to watch fascinated as Jones drew a knife from the top of his right boot, rose from his chair, and walked slowly towards the Pioneer.

The knife glittered under the naked electric light, and the Pioneer's expression changed to swift, ugly fear as he stumbled backwards against the bar, clutching his chest. Jones moved over him, the knife slicing this time at his face.

Hughes-Hallett turned away, sprinted to the next pub, and ordered two glasses of beer. Jones arrived a few moments later, sipped calmly at his drink, and said softly: "The bastard won't be hurting anyone else for a time."

That evening Jones told Hughes-Hallett how another man, a greedy trapper, had died years before trying to double-cross him in the Canadian Barren Lands. While Jones talked, Hughes-Hallett balanced his duty as a naval officer to have this self-confessed killer arrested, against his responsibility for the fate of Rutter.

"There was really no decision to make," he told me. "There could hardly have been any question of bringing Stanley to trial for the earlier incident. So far as he was aware, it was unknown to the police, and in any case accused persons are carefully protected from being convicted as a result of their own gossip."

Hughes-Hallett might have finished then with infantry training until the actual operation, but when he spoke to Roberts about it he was told: "We have an exercise laid on. You had better stay with the battalion just to see if you really can keep up with 'em."

IV

The operation order issued by General Roberts for Exercise Yukon said:

> 2nd Division will be the assaulting force on a part of the south of England coast and local troops will be the enemy.
>
> 2nd Division Raiding Force will seize West Bay, destroy objectives at West Bay and Bridport, destroy enemy aerodrome, exploiting to Bradpole to capture enemy headquarters. . . . The Force will re-embark at West Bay and return to I.O.W.

In this order the West-Bay~Bridport area represented Dieppe, the ærodrome behind represented that at St Aubin behind Dieppe, and Bradpole was Arques-La-Bataille where it was thought German divisional headquarters were located.

Included in the exercise were three companies of paratroops to be landed to the east and west of the assault area to capture imaginary heavy batteries which, in fact, would be at Berneval and Varengeville.

Yukon began during the night of June 11, and at 5:00 a.m. on the 12th the first troops landed – the South Saskatchewans on Green Beach, the Royal Regiment on Blue Beach, the RHLI and the Essex Scottish on Red and White Beaches, while the Queen's Own Camerons followed into Green Beach to pass through a perimeter established by the South Saskatchewans. The Calgary Tanks trundled on to the main Red and White Beaches, while the Mont-Royals remained in floating reserve until the evacuation when they landed on Red Beach to act as a rearguard covering the withdrawal.

Generals Paget, Montgomery, McNaughton, and Crerar travelled down from London to see the exercise. Mountbatten was *en route* back from the United States with Hughes-Hallett.

At sea with the raiding-force in a destroyer specially equipped with a bewildering array of radio sets which transformed it into a headquarters ship, were the staffs of the military and naval Force Commanders. In another destroyer with duplicate equipment was Churchill Mann, acting as deputy to Roberts. If anything happened to the principal headquarters ship, Mann could assume immediate command of military operations from the other. Leigh-Mallory was controlling the air operations from the headquarters of Fighter Command's No. 11 Group at Uxbridge, west of London, where radar reports of movements in the Channel and over it were plotted. His liaison officer, Air Commodore A. T. Cole, Royal Australian Air Force, was with Roberts.

If all unit commanders, from the company up to battalion levels, followed the huge dossier of details labelled Yukon, but in reality Rutter, everything should have gone without a hitch. After all, there was no honest-to-goodness enemy about to shoot the details to ribbons.

Nor were Germans necessary. Yukon, to the astonishment of the high-ranking witnesses, was an indescribable shambles with the Navy being primarily responsible. The South Saskatchewans were landed a mile from Green Beach, the Royals about two miles from Blue Beach, and the tanks arrived an hour and a half late because the tank landing-craft lost their way in the dark. It was no surprise to Baillie-Grohman. Although the run from the Isle of Wight to Bridport was more difficult than that to Dieppe, he had always been slightly shocked at what he thought to be a low standard of training of landing-craft crews. He had expected chaos, and chaos there was.

The infantry generally moved too slowly inland, reached their objectives late, and upset Mann's carefully worked out time schedule.

The frontal assault over Red and White Beaches went with precision only because the local troops masquerading as the enemy dutifully ducked for cover when the cannon-firing Hurricanes roared overhead in a mock strafing-attack.

Nothing could shake the confidence of McNaughton, Crerar, Roberts, or Churchill Mann. Ignoring the indisputable fact that real live Germans might have turned the chaos into a bloodbath, they noted that if the landing-craft crews could improve their navigation and punctuality, success could be reasonably expected. They were not to know then that what they planned was virtually impossible.

For the first time Montgomery expressed serious doubts about the feasibility of the operation and about the ability of the forces employed to undertake it. He criticized sailors and soldiers impartially, made some caustic comments about the need for a lot more training and stalked off to Reigate while the other generals made their way back to London. From this moment on, his interest in Rutter waned. He seemed to take the attitude that it was a combined operation approved by the Chiefs of Staff and therefore no longer any affair of his. If McNaughton had argued again for military responsibility the likelihood is that Montgomery would have made him a present of it.

Montgomery has become better known since 1942 as an astute, discerning general, and it is clearly recognizable now that something in the confusion of Yukon convinced him that it was an ill-fated venture.

Yukon in no way diminished the eagerness and enthusiasm of the Canadians who became even more anxious to put matters right and get to grips with a war that seemed to be passing them by. For weeks they had been swimming dressed and undressed, with and without Mae Wests. They had shot, bombed, and blasted buildings, bridges, piers, pillboxes, wire entanglements, trenches, and tunnels. They had run up 900-foot hills, scaled overhanging cliffs 300 feet high, and fought with rifles, bayonets, bombs, tommy-guns, knives, tin hats, fists, feet, and fingers. They had learned all there was to know about boats, barges, landing-craft, and lighters; they could land on any beach by day or night in complete silence and disembark in eight seconds.

Most of all they had learned how to make their unpredictable Sten guns work. These weapons jammed frequently, but the troops found that by filing down hammers and adjusting the automatic mechanism, the guns would be given some degree of reliability. As each gun was adjusted to its owner's liking, it became a treasured personal possession. The Canadians were by then convinced — with good reason — that they were capable of cracking the very same defences they had constructed along the Sussex coast.

General Paget did not share their optimism. He had such a low opinion of Rutter that he might well have ordered its cancellation but for the arrival back in London of Mountbatten and Hughes-Hallett. They were undismayed by the dreary reports about Yukon, taking the typical Combined Operations attitude that nothing is impossible if you apply ingenuity and work long enough at it.

Obviously, if the operation was to be launched on June 21, there was no time for more training. More training was essential, however, and on Baillie-Grohman's advice Mountbatten issued an order to the Force Commanders postponing the operation until the right combinations of moon and tides occurred again in July.

This decision was made at another Combined Operations conference at Richmond Terrace on June 14 at which Roberts and Leigh-Mallory were present. They both complained bitterly at the naval performance, and Roberts went so far as to say that, while he had every confidence in the Naval Force Commander, there were other senior naval officers involved who did not appear to be interested in success. At times, when he had been unable to contact Baillie-Grohman personally, he had put his problems to other officers who had replied with polite complacency: "You will have to see the staff officer responsible, sir." Even Leigh-Mallory supported Roberts and it became evident that friction at this moment was likely to develop into more of a crisis than the dismal outcome of Yukon.

When Mountbatten announced his intention of postponing Rutter, the Adviserate warned that there could be a considerable risk of loss of security, that there was a danger of men trained to a high pitch going stale.

Mountbatten replied: "Those are risks we'll have to accept. I'm not letting this operation proceed until I've had an opportunity to see another exercise myself. Roberts, I would like you to inform General Montgomery of my decision."

When Roberts telephoned Montgomery that evening the reply was curt. "I'm not surprised," said Montgomery. "The Admiral might have had three ships sunk under him but he has some good sense."

Roberts also informed Private Hallett of the decision, and thankfully the Naval Adviser of Combined Operations reverted to his proper identity. As a parting shot to Roberts he said: "And I did keep up with 'em."

The next day a further meeting at Richmond Terrace attended by Mountbatten, Montgomery, the three Force Commanders, and the Combined Operations Adviserate formally endorsed the postponement and agreed that a second exercise should be held on June 22-23 with a tentative date for the actual operation set for between July 4 to 9 inclusive.

The 2nd Division, with all its strange attachments, returned to the Isle of Wight, which was once again sealed off from the rest of the country.

Anger at the Summit

In the period of pause which followed Yukon, the conviction that their eventual destination was somehow related to the public outcry for a second front spread through the Canadians. Elated at the prospect, impatient at delays, and edgily fearful that there might be no warning, the troops speculated openly on where and when. Their training had told them how. But the rumours circulating wildly on the Isle of Wight had nothing whatsoever to do with a unique event in Sussex, where Roberts had left a skeleton division staff to "mind house while we're away on manœuvres."

In charge was a young Canadian officer who, brooding at being so abandoned by his comrades, decided angrily that the division was *en route* to open a second front and had deliberately left him behind. As there were no visitors to relieve his boredom, he acquired a cheap school atlas and occupied himself studying the northern coast of France.

With only native intelligence to aid his limited professional knowledge he began systematically crossing off those possible objectives he considered unsuitable for invasion. He was looking for a port which would be in range of fighter cover, close enough to England to avoid prolonged sea passage, large enough to handle a constant stream of seaborne traffic, and accessible across wide beaches. After four days he decided upon the only port which seemed to fulfil the requirements he had so arbitrarily established – Dieppe. He chuckled at the thought of what a fantastic coincidence it would be if the 2nd Division should, in fact, go to Dieppe and, indeed, the remote possibility of being right amused him.

Properly, then, he should have kept his thoughts to himself. Instead, he travelled to London where he was quickly picked up by a party of United States army officers celebrating at the Savoy Hotel. At the height of the party an argument erupted on the merits of a second front and he announced thickly, with mock solemnity, that he was in possession of a great and terrible secret. The Canadian Army, he confided with ponderous alcoholic wisdom, was already bound for France in the van of the Allied return to the Continent. Incensed by the jeers which greeted his proclamation, he proceeded to elaborate his theory that an armada was at sea, embroidering what he thought to be fanciful with convincing and wholly imaginary evidence. Laughter subsided, and an air of uncomfortable antagonism settled over the party.

"Where will they land?" asked one American.

"Dieppe," the Canadian replied triumphantly. "They never told me but I figured it out . . ."

When the party broke up early in the morning, he staggered back to his own room and fell asleep, but nor for long. An insistent knocking on the door brought him awake, and when he opened it a British army officer with two men in civilian clothes pushed past him into the room. While he dressed they searched his luggage and answered his mumbled question with a curt: "You will accompany us to the War Office." Once outside the hotel, he was bundled into the back of a limousine, with curtains drawn round the rear and side windows, and only then told that he was being taken to a military establishment in the country where he would be confined until further notice.

His escorts were charming and polite, and when he asked what he had done to be arrested they replied blandly, "We have no idea, old boy. But don't worry about it. You'll even like the place."

The "place" turned out to be a Canadian re-inforcement unit stationed north of London where, according to official instructions he was to be "kept under close arrest so that the temptation for him to talk would be less and until the danger period is over." Mountbatten, who had no sense of humour where security was concerned, read a report on the incident and immediately recommended that the naïve young officer be court-martialled – advice which the Canadian authorities had the good sense to ignore.

During this whimsical drama, Mountbatten, Montgomery, McNaughton, and Crerar had joined Roberts in Dorset on June 23 to watch Exercise Yukon II carried out at dawn across the same stretch of coast as before. At first light they were standing on high ground overlooking the main assault. Live bullets were whizzing across the beaches, and Hughes-Hallett was standing close to Montgomery when a two-inch mortar smoke bomb exploded between them. The startled Army Commander from Reigate allowed his mouth to fall open in astonishment.

"That one was aimed up here deliberately," he snorted. "Let's get out before they try again."

Hughes-Hallett was injured and had quite a few pithy comments to make. Montgomery didn't hear them – he was already moving out of range.

Yukon II was officially described as a comparative success, which meant that it was not much better than the chaotic Yukon. The Royal Regiment reported that landing was effected at the proper beach, and all went smoothly and according to plan. But the Essex Scottish war diary noted that "the Assault Landing Craft lose direction and we are late landing."

While Roberts was resolutely satisfied with the division's performance, he was still disgusted with the way the navy handled its role; nor was he at this stage convinced that Combined Operations were fully aware of naval failings. As a soldier he could not understand that the run to Bridport, with strong tides, was far more difficult than the actual trip to Dieppe would be.

During their drive back to London that evening, Paget and McNaughton discussed the exercise in detail, agreed that Roberts was right, and on reaching his headquarters, McNaughton put their fears in writing to Montgomery. His letter said:

> Today the C-in-C, Home Forces, expressed to me his opinion that in Exercises Yukon I and Yukon II two major faults were apparent, which he said were –

1. The lack of precision in place and time in bringing the landing-craft to the particular beaches to which they had been directed in the plans.

2. The inefficiency of smoke cover provided for the approach of the landing-craft to these beaches.

He suggested to me that these points needed correction, and I fully share his view. In both these matters remedial action lies clearly with the Naval service and I therefore request that you take them up with the appropriate Naval authorities.

Please inform me at the earliest possible date as to the action taken.

The peremptory tone of this letter reflected the growing friction between McNaughton and Montgomery. Although the overall commander of Canadian troops in England, the Canadian Army Commander still lacked any real authority in Rutter, and in these circumstances it is quite probable that by again signing the letter "Senior Combatant Officer, Canadian Army in the United Kingdom," he was expressing considerable irritation.

Next day, Montgomery replied briefly to the effect that as the responsible military authority he was attending to the points mentioned by the "Senior Combatant Officer, Canadian Army in the United Kingdom," and would let him know the result. Despite this command rivalry, the apprehension of Roberts about the naval performance was a matter of genuine concern not only to McNaughton and Crerar, but also to General Paget who wrote to Montgomery on June 24 saying:

It seems to me that Yukon II revealed three important points calling for immediate action. These are:

1. The need for better navigation arrangements in order that the landing craft may arrive at the right place and at the right time.

2. Arising out of (1) the need for more accurate timing of the various phases of the operation, e.g., the attack of our fighters.

3. The need for increased use of smoke. Our use of it is very amateurish.

These are really matters for Combined Operations Head-quarters and I suggest you bring them to their attention as soon as possible.

Meteorological experts forecast favourable weather on July 4-5, which was in the middle of the period when the desired state of moon and tides occurred, and after brief discussion it was agreed to launch Rutter on this date or on the two nights following. When consulted by "scrambler" telephone, Montgomery and Roberts returned to Cowes where the officers of the 2nd Division were summoned to Osborne Court for a special briefing.

Nearly 300 officers thronged the briefing room that afternoon of June 27 to hear for the first time of the intention to raid a French port. Kendall's Central Interpretation unit had built a scale relief model of Dieppe and its surrounding areas, about ten feet long by six feet wide. When this was unveiled an expectant hush fell over the conference as Roberts began:

"Gentlemen, we have waited over two years to go into battle against the Germans. The time has now come for a party. This scale model is the target, and Colonel Mann will brief you on the intentions of the assault. I must emphasize the need for complete security. Other ranks will not be told until they are aboard their ships."

The name of Dieppe was avoided deliberately, but while the officers were crowding round the model, examining the incredibly minute detail in the reconstruction of houses and streets, identifying what had previously seemed only imaginary objectives, and relating reality to the training they had undergone, an amazed murmur broke through the silence with the impact of a physical blow.

"Good God, I know that place."

The room became suddenly tense, while Roberts climbed slowly to his feet, gazed furiously in the general direction of the voice and said: "I'm not going to ask who said that. But forget it – right now. If any information leaks out the party will be cancelled."

Roberts emphasized the security aspect, warning against mess discussions, and saying flatly: "One colonel has already been cashiered for phoning a girl friend and telling her the party has been cancelled – which it was when Yukon resulted in such bad performance. I can tell you right now that Combined Operations pressed hard to have him sentenced to penal servitude with hard labour. So when you feel like talking, just remember we may not be lenient next time."

If anything was guaranteed to shock an audience into attentiveness it was this, and the room stilled as he continued:

"Speed is essential. You must get in and secure the beaches fast. Any hesitation will only result in senseless casualties. When you are over the beaches, run over the Boche defences just as fast as you can. You may see men fall, but if you stop once it will be much worse.

"Don't concern yourselves with being put down on wrong beaches. We've taken this up at the highest level and I don't think there'll be any more trouble. Important things are at stake. Certain pieces of equipment are needed for examination by our boys. For instance, we know the Boche has got a new four-barrelled flak gun and we'd like to see one. But overall, the information we get back may have an important bearing on the outcome of the war.

"The Staff has done a fine job in working out every detail of the operation and if you follow the principles laid down in the training you won't come to much harm. I want you to spend as much time as possible looking at your maps and photographs so that you know landmarks off by heart. When ashore you will see to it that there is no looting of houses or shops. The Germans seem to have behaved correctly towards the French in this part of the world, and we don't want to leave behind any adverse impressions about our own honesty and discipline.

"When the time comes to get out, make it quick and orderly. No scrambling for boats. If prisoners don't behave and hold up the schedule, then you have your Sten guns. Use 'em."

This was the conference at which Roberts is reported to have used the phrase, "It will be a piece of cake." I have spoken to seventeen officers who were present on this occasion, and they cannot agree who said it or that it was even said. Five attributed it to Roberts, three thought it might have been Churchill Mann, and the rest either don't remember it at all or think it may have come from the back of the room. On such flimsy evidence, a patently innocent remark has been turned into a vicious barb. Generals are usually concerned with creating optimism and confidence before a battle; they do not make a habit of voicing their private fears to junior officers.

When Roberts left the room, a ripple of released excitement broke out behind him, and the battalion colonels who would lead the assault gathered in a group to discuss the implications. Cec Merritt was beaming with pure joy; Bob Labatt had about him the look of an eager hound scenting prey; Joe Menard's English was generously sprinkled with diabolical threats against the Germans expressed exquisitely in French; Fred Jasperson, feeling it necessary to offer the benefits of his forty years of experience, cautioned against over-confidence in a voice that betrayed his own exuberant anticipation.

But three officers were not so happy at what might lie ahead: Major

Doug Catto, the second-in-command of the Royals, Alfred Gostling of the Camerons, and Johnny Andrews who, always among the most eager to get on with the war, suddenly became possessive about his tanks and solemnly pronounced it as his belief that those which got ashore would never be brought back. There was also silent but almost universal opposition to the plan among junior officers who felt that as they had been trained to defend Britain against a German landing they would be able to throw back an attack based on it. And if they could do it, so could the Germans.

The same day Baillie-Grohman assembled several hundred naval officers who would be on the raid at HMS *Vectis*, *née* the Royal Yacht Squadron clubhouse, for his briefing conference. There are two versions of what transpired next. According to the first, as the Admiral rose to his feet on a dais at one end of the conference room, an elderly reserve officer stood up at the other end and said: "Excuse me, sir, but. . . ." Baillie-Grohman cut him short with a furious glare and interrupted curtly: "You will listen to what I have to say first. Then you can ask questions."

Then he proceeded with the briefing, occasionally casting angry stares to the back of the room to silence the elderly officer who kept half rising and looking as if he were about to speak.

When Baillie-Grohman had finished, the secret was out – that the Navy were to land the Army at Dieppe; and the elderly officer was allowed to climb laboriously to his feet and say: "Thank you, sir. That was an exciting briefing. But I think you should know that I'm not part of the operation. I am the commanding officer of an anti-submarine trawler waiting to join a Channel convoy.

"My ship is anchored off Cowes, and I was ordered to attend the convoy sailing conference. I thought this was it."

In the stunned silence that followed, Baillie-Grohman advanced to the front of the dais and impaled the speaker with furious eyes: "Do you mean to tell me you have no right to be here?"

"That's about the size of it, sir. But I did try to ask if this was the right conference at the start. You wouldn't let me speak."

It was the wrong thing to say. On Baillie-Grohman's orders the errant convoy skipper was locked in a toilet and a sentry placed outside the door while staff officers tried to fathom out a way of keeping him incommunicado until after the raid.

That evening the coastal convoy reached the rendezvous off the Isle of Wight where the escort should have been reinforced by the trawler.

When it failed to arrive, the convoy commodore signalled *Vectis* requesting information concerning its whereabouts.

The convoy, so the commodore said, would be at sea for about twelve days, and in any event he refused pointblank to sail on down the Channel without the added protection of the trawler. Baillie-Grohman's staff descended *en masse* on the toilet, released the skipper, and offered him his freedom on his solemn pledge not to divulge to anyone what he had heard and witnessed at the briefing conference. He thankfully complied, and with much back-slapping the victim was escorted back aboard his trawler.

According to Baillie-Grohman himself, however, this version was deliberately spread about by one of his staff as a joke and to relieve the constantly growing tension. "What actually happened," he said, "is that as I started the briefing, the security officer in charge of screening all present for their right to be there, said: 'Excuse me, sir, I would like to double check on who's here.' I let him go ahead, and he found that three officers from a convoy escort ship were in the room thinking it was a convoy conference. Amid a ripple of laughter they were politely moved out and I continued. It happens that the author of the first version was a splendid officer and a good friend of mine. We've often laughed about it."

The briefings brought the plan into disrepute among the junior officers of the 2nd Division. Some majors, captains, and lieutenants – men who had been trained to deny the element of surprise to an enemy invader – were outspoken in their demands to know just how they were supposed to achieve it on the other side of the Channel. They felt that the Germans were likely to be as unsurprised as they would be were the circumstances reversed. Junior officers of the South Saskatchewans, for example, asked in rather forthright language how three companies could expect to pass through Pourville, move inland to the high ground on the east, and occupy positions without the enemy knowing anything about it?

Two of these officers – and it is better that they remain anonymous – have told me, "We got no answer. We were told to obey orders and ask no more questions or to get the hell back to Canada." In another mess a junior officer invented a game called "How To Surprise the Enemy Into Surrender." Officers would hide behind tables and suddenly spring into view with hands held high above their heads, shouting: "Don't shoot. You're surprised. So be nice and surrender." Another wag wrote on a notice board: "The enemy can't get away. There'll be Ger-

mans in front, Germans to the right, and Germans to the left. We'll
have them trapped."

It does seem that the discordancy at the junior-officer level amounted
to a strong movement against Canadian participation in the operation.
It was so widespread that the movement had to be stamped out by
direct orders rather than by reasoning – orders issued by more senior
officers who were not entirely sanguine themselves.

II

On the 29th, Churchill returned to London from Washington where he
had tried to convince Roosevelt and the United States Chiefs of Staff
that neither Sledgehammer nor any other landing in France would be
possible during 1942. Allied strategy, he had insisted, should be confined to Roundup, an invasion in 1943 for which Dieppe was to be an
experimental operation.

By then a most curious state of affairs had developed among the high
military commanders responsible for the general conduct of the war.
Paget as British Commander-in-Chief, Home Forces, knew all about
Dieppe; he was, however, one of the Combined Commanders team who
had planned to invest six ports simultaneously in the Pas de Calais area
with pincer movements from their respective flanks. These flanking
attacks had been the intention of the Combined Commanders, and as
an associate member Mountbatten was one of them. There is little
doubt that the other members – Eisenhower, Admiral Sir Bertram
Ramsay, and Air Marshal Sir Sholto Douglas – also knew that the Dieppe
plan now called for a frontal assault. Yet there is no evidence that they
intervened in any manner to override Montgomery by insisting on an
assault through the flanking beaches.

One member, Admiral Ramsay, did confess to personal misgivings
in a private conversation with Baillie-Grohman who has told me:
"Ramsay criticized the plan severely, mainly because the operation
as planned would use up every reserve of landing-craft in Britain."

Obviously powerful influences were working to press ahead with
Dieppe, powerful enough to silence some high-ranking officers.

The public demand in Britain, Canada, and the United States for a
second front had reached new heights following Molotov's visits to
the Western capitals, and both Roosevelt and Churchill were pledged
to an early assault on France.

Churchill had deliberately created the impression in Moscow that an invasion was imminent, and even the French were reported to be preparing to revolt once the landing took place. As a result, the Germans had shifted thirty-three divisions into northern France, and the British Chiefs of Staff regarded this "holding the line in France" as the best that could be done to help Russia in 1942.

But the fall of Tobruk and the surrender of 25,000 men to a numerically inferior enemy force in North Africa on June 21 had shaken British morale and had led to a parliamentary censure of Churchill's conduct of the war. So able a politician as the Prime Minister knew instinctively that he could survive only so many such shocking defeats, and on the evening of his return he summoned a private conference at No. 10 Downing Street to discuss Dieppe, and the consequences of failure.

Sir Alan Brooke, Mountbatten, Hughes-Hallett, and other staff officers were present, and throughout the meeting Lady Churchill remained in the room arranging flowers in the background. The Prime Minister admitted his dismay at the effect of the Tobruk surrender on his talks with United States leaders and on morale at home, and warned that failure at Dieppe could result in serious political repercussions. He wanted reassurance that the raid had a better than even chance of success. He turned suddenly on Mountbatten and snapped, "This is your show. Can you guarantee success?"

Brooke interrupted: "Of course they can't. If they could there would be no point in carrying out the operation."

"Naturally, sir, I must reply no," said Mountbatten. "In operations of this kind there's bound to be an element of risk that we have to accept. We're not going to learn a damn thing unless we try."

This was not definite enough for Churchill. He brooded silently for a moment and then said to no one in particular, "Whatever happens, we cannot have another Tobruk."

"You mean you're afraid that the troops will run away?" asked Mountbatten. "Because if that's the case I think Captain Hughes-Hallett can say something on the subject. Do you think the Canadians will run away, 'Private' Hallett?"

While Churchill looked at him in amazement, Hughes-Hallett explained why he had masqueraded as a private soldier with the Camerons of Canada, and by the time he finished the Prime Minister was grinning delightedly.

"Well," he said, "what's your answer to the Admiral's question?"

"If the ones I met are any indication, sir, why – they'll fight like hell," said the unabashed, equable "Private" Hallett.

Then Brooke intervened decisively.

"This operation," he told the Prime Minister, "is quite indispensible to the Allied offensive program. If we ever intend to invade France it is absolutely essential to mount a preliminary operation on a divisional scale. This is it."

If Churchill doubted the wisdom of Dieppe, such strong advice from the highest military authority in the land dispelled his anxieties. Montgomery spent the whole of the next day at Cowes checking the entire operation with the Force Commanders, particular attention being given to the points raised by Paget and McNaughton: naval performance and increased use of smoke.

Roberts was becoming increasingly concerned about the enemy defences on the headlands flanking the main Dieppe beaches which could catch the assault troops in a vicious crossfire unless subdued early in the raid. As the plan stood they would be attacked from the rear by airborne troops and then overrun by the Royal Regiment in the east and the South Saskatchewans in the west. For Roberts, the lack of any really heavy fire support entailed the risk of troops never reaching the headlands.

"Why can't we have a couple of destroyers engaging each headland with crossfire until all the beaches are secured?" he asked of Baillie-Grohman. The Admiral replied: "Remember, that at first, at any rate, I must have one or two destroyers handy near both our flanks against E-boat attacks. I have only six destroyers available for bombardment anyhow; they are there of course for the support of your troops. Destroyers under weigh, with only 4-inch guns, are very unlikely in my opinion to be able to knock out heavy army coastal artillery on the headlands. In the meantime, you will deprive the frontal attack on the beaches of their gunfire. Here they can do much damage to machine-gun posts, the Casino, which will undoubtedly be used as a strongpoint, and other similar positions. If you'd like to have a talk with my gunnery officer, one gunner to another, I think he will convince you, if I haven't. There will be similar positions on beaches other than Red and White where the destroyers could be used effectively, no doubt."

At that moment the angry Roberts silently resolved that it would not end there; indeed he was beginning to doubt whether he could continue to be military force commander while the Navy's performance continued to be, in his eyes, less than adequate. On Baillie-Grohman's side, he found his military colleagues completely unknowledgeable about what ships at sea could and could not do.

As Mountbatten did not always feel justified in interfering too strongly in military matters, so Montgomery was reluctant to take open issue with the Navy and, after assurances from Baillie-Grohman that steps would be taken to improve the naval performance, he returned to his headquarters in Reigate to write a report to General Paget on the Cowes conference.

His lengthy letter dated July 1 said that Baillie-Grohman had arranged to provide a "mark ship" on the British side of the Channel to simplify navigation and from which it would be a straight run in to Dieppe, to provide special radar ships to watch for enemy sea forces and to give the flank-assault forces – the Royals at Puits and the South Saskatchewans at Pourville – two experienced naval officers with special local knowledge of the coast.

"I am satisfied," he wrote, "that these arrangements should ensure accurate navigation. None of these existed in Yukon and Yukon II."

On the question of smoke, Montgomery said that Combined Operations had made available their own "smoke expert who has handled smoke problems on other expeditions" and that a number of extra smoke-making ships had been added to the naval force. His letter continued:

> I am satisfied that the operation as planned is a possible one and has good prospects of success, given:
> A. Favourable weather.
> B. Average luck.
> C. That the Navy puts us ashore roughly in the right places and at the right times.
>
> In an operation of this sort I regard "confidence" as an essential ingredient for success. I am now satisfied that, throughout the Force, Commanders, Staffs and Regimental Officers have confidence in the combined plan and in the successful outcome of the operation.
>
> I say "now" because there was a moment when certain senior officers began to waver about lack of confidence on the part of the troops – which statements were quite untrue. They really lacked confidence in themselves.
>
> You may be interested in certain notes I gave to Roberts regarding training . . . . The matter has been firmly handled.

His reference to the wavering of senior officers concerned those of the 2nd Division who had started to express doubts about the reliability of inexperienced troops in an operation of such importance. Rumours of the discontent among junior officers with consequent spreading to higher officers had reached Montgomery, at whose insistence Roberts had summoned the senior recalcitrants to his headquarters for a show-down.

"This operation will succeed only if there is dash and confidence permeating right through the ranks," he said grimly. "The troops will take their cue from you. If you lack optimism and lack any confidence at all in the plan, then the troops won't fight. Either you tackle this thing with everything you've got or get out of it now. There's still time to have you transferred and make other arrangements. When you leave this room you leave the division or lead your men."

This is what Montgomery meant when he said the matter had been "firmly handled." His letter concluded: "Mountbatten, myself and Leigh-Mallory will be together at No. 11 Fighter Group HQ, during the whole operation. The battle once begun can be influenced only by the use of air power, and that is therefore the best place for us."

Below his signature he added a postscript which said: "The Canadians are 1st Class chaps; if anyone can pull it off, they will."

Montgomery had written to the Commander-in-Chief in his capacity as the responsible military authority for Rutter, and instead of sending further letters to McNaughton and Crerar they received copies of this one. Immediately, McNaughton insisted that a Canadian should render judgement on the preparedness of the troops, and on July 2 Crerar appeared on the Isle of Wight to cover the same ground with Roberts, Churchill Mann, and Brigadiers Southam and Sherwood Lett.

At this conference, Roberts again expressed dissatisfaction at the state of naval training for the operation and discussed the need for destroyer bombardment on the East and West Headlands. Crerar was filled with buoyant confidence that the division would return crowned with the sort of glory that could prove decisive to the careers of the Permanent Force officers associated with it.

He wrote to McNaughton on July 3 saying:

> I spent yesterday with Roberts. He and his Brigadiers expressed full confidence in being able to carry out their tasks – given a break in luck. There was previously some doubt as to the ability of the Navy to touch them down on the right beaches. That has now pretty well disappeared, although I told Roberts that 100 per cent accuracy should never be expected in any human endeavour, and that some error might be expected, and should then be solved by rapid thinking and decision.

I agree that the plan is sound and most carefully worked out. I should have no hesitation in tackling it, if in Roberts' place.

I also agree that once launched the operation can only be influenced by air power. In the circumstances . . . Montgomery probably considers that he is bound to be at No. 11 Fighter Group HQ – and would like to be there anyway. I don't dispute this, but I consider that you, anyway, if not myself, have also a responsibility and should have been included in this group.

Once again the command rivalry between the Canadians and the British predominated. This time Crerar was undoubtedly right in suggesting that he should be with the other responsible commanders during the operation, that he had been overlooked only because Montgomery and Mountbatten persisted in taking the legal view that the Canadian troops were, as far as Rutter was concerned, part of the British Army. The Admiral had never served in close contact with Dominion forces before and the General was a law unto himself anyway. No matter what the technicalities, by treating Crerar as a subordinate, they showed a remarkable ignorance of the national character of the Canadian Army and the consequent insistence by its Commander on continuity of Canadian command.

Montgomery having reported to Paget that he was satisfied with the plan, McNaughton now followed suit. He wrote to the Commander-in-Chief:

I now have the reports of the Commander, 1st Canadian Corps and I am satisfied that all arrangements for Operation ——— are in order and that this operation may now proceed. . . . It is my view that, having regard to the particular Canadian responsibility in this matter and to maintain the proper channel of command to the Canadian units involved, Lt-General Crerar, Commander, 1st Canadian Corps, should be with the group of senior officers of the three Services at Fighter Group who appear to be charged with the exercise of command in this operation.

McNaughton, the inventive, dispassionate scientist, may have had no personal wish to witness the battle, even from so remote a grandstand as Uxbridge, but his strong sense of national justice demanded that Crerar, at least, should be there.

On July 4 Paget's Chief of Staff, General Swayne, replied saying that "there is no room for any more at Fighter Group HQ" but that quite apart from this the Commander-in-Chief considered it wrong that Crerar should go there.

"There can be only one man in command of the operation," he wrote, "and Montgomery will see to it that he keeps Harry Crerar in hourly touch with the situation."

Paget reinforced this rebuff to the Canadians with a personal letter to McNaughton in which he said:

> For Operation Rutter I made Montgomery responsible to me . . . I understand that in agreement with Crerar he decided to retain command of the operation himself. In these circumstances I do not think that Crerar should be at Fighter Group HQ as he will not be exercising command in the operation, though of course he will be kept fully and frequently informed of what is happening.

It was patently nonsense, even discourteous, to suggest that there would be no room at Fighter Group headquarters for Crerar. The only reason for refusing Crerar the right to be there was an attempt to make the Canadian Commanders conform to a British chain of command. It was, however, true that Crerar had not objected at the outset when Montgomery asserted his authority and it must have seemed a trifle odd to Paget that the Canadians should be getting peevish at this late stage. Individualism and nationalism from too many autocrats created the issue, confused it, and then allowed it to foster. Crerar made it critical by telephoning Montgomery to request permission to join the group at Uxbridge. When Montgomery refused, Crerar demanded that he be allowed to visit Reigate to discuss "important constitutional reasons." Montgomery agreed, and their meeting took place on the evening of July 4. Crerar's memorandum of what transpired said:

> I opened by informing the Commander, South-Eastern Army, that he was making a mistake in attempting to treat the problem of command of Canadian troops as a simple military issue, capable of solution along strictly British channels of command when, in fact, it was a complicated problem and one involving national policies and Imperial Constitutional relations.

This was forthright even for Crerar who, as a Corps commander, had introduced constitutional politics as a weapon in what was a purely military affair. He was a soldier, a servant of the civil authority in

Ottawa, and the issue was that of a military command. If anyone felt inclined to discuss the imperial relationship between Britain and Canada it might, perhaps, have been McNaughton. Both Canadian Commanders were armed with written authority from Ottawa to refer to the Canadian War Committee, if it seemed that the British were attempting to employ Canadian troops improperly. In this instance there was no question of Canadians being used improperly, so it was hardly the sort of occasion on which to brandish Ottawa's authority.

Crerar's record of the meeting said further:

> It was true that the Canadian Corps had been placed "in combination with" the South-Eastern Army and that operationally and through me, the troops comprising the Canadian Corps were under Lieutenant-General Montgomery. That situation, however, did not for one moment imply that I should be divested of my responsibility through Lieutenant-General McNaughton to the Canadian Government in respect of the manner in which these troops were committed to actual operations. No agreement between the Commander-in-Chief, Home Forces, the Chief of Combined Operations and himself, or policy laid down by the Chiefs of Staff Committee could affect the Constitutional position. In order to illustrate this point in a general way I suggested that the position of the Commander-in-Chief, Home Forces, in respect to Lieut.-General McNaughton and the Canadian Army in the U.K., was very similar to that occupied by Field Marshal Foch in relation to Field Marshal Haig and the B.E.F. in the last war.

If Crerar had been initially frank, he was now positively flaunting his authority from Ottawa, in effect telling Montgomery that Canadian troops were foreign troops in Britain and not answerable, except in special circumstances, to the British Army; they would work with British commanders but remain under the direct control of their own officers. Montgomery, only mildly interested and not provoked in the slightest, must have wondered why the usually astute Crerar should feel it necessary to wield so heavy a club for so little reason. He cautiously suggested that Crerar or McNaughton should have raised these points when first asked to take part in Rutter, when Paget had nominated him as the responsible military commander. If there were Canadian objections, he said, surely that was the proper time to air them, not on the eve of the actual operation.

Crerar, having committed himself, then complained that Swayne's excuse to McNaughton of there being no room for him at Uxbridge was not convincing, and that this letter failed to take into account "the really important factor I had previously explained concerning separate Canadian responsibility."

He urged Montgomery not to regard the issue as a "simple and narrow military problem" because he felt that if this attitude were maintained it would be "raised to the highest political levels" and the decision would go against the view apparently maintained by Generals Paget and Montgomery.

It seems that Montgomery listened quite coolly despite the thinly veiled hints at a possible constitutional crisis between Canada and Britain.

The memorandum concluded:

> Throughout the conversation, which went on for over an hour, Lieut.-General Montgomery was most frank and friendly and during the course of it gained a wider appreciation of the issues that were at stake. Towards the termination he stated that in view of what I had said he would ring up Lieut.-General Mc-Naughton and suggest that he accompany him to Headquarters, No. 11 Group, and be with him during the course of the operation. He also stated that he would be glad if I, as commander of the Canadian Corps, could also be with him. He thanked me for my frankness and for the explanation which I had given him which had put a different light on the question at issue.

No doubt Crerar succeeded in giving Montgomery a well-deserved lecture on the autonomy of the Canadian Army in Britain, but there is also little doubt that Montgomery consented to have the Canadian Commanders present at Uxbridge, only because he knew that if any intervention was needed during the operation he would give the orders and no one else.

Crerar's victory may have been pyrrhic, but he achieved something. Montgomery formally invited McNaughton who then wrote to Paget saying:

> As regard the officers to be at Fighter Group HQ during the operation, I am not particularly concerned as regards myself, although for obvious reasons I would like to see this end of the work first hand. I do, however, think Crerar should be present because the Canadian troops taking part are under his command and he therefore should not be excluded.

Montgomery's view that the issue was essentially insignificant proved correct; when the event happened, Crerar's presence at Uxbridge was totally ineffective. It is hardly surprising that Montgomery should write in his memoirs: "My own feeling about the Dieppe raid is that there were far too many authorities with a hand in it; there was no single operational commander who was solely responsible . . . from start to finish."

III

While senior commanders bickered, Simmerforce on the Isle of Wight embarked in the large infantry landing-ships to prepare for yet another exercise, this one code-named "Klondike I." In addition to these converted passenger ships, with assault-landing craft swung out on davits, there were destroyers, gun boats, radar ships, torpedo boats, tanklanding craft, and flotillas of R boats, light wooden craft capable of carrying 25 troops who might live long enough to land under fire if they crouched low, their only form of protection. By July 3 more than 200 vessels of all sizes lay off the island in Yarmouth Roads, Cowes Roads, Southampton Water, and in Newhaven. When all communication with shore had been cut, the best-kept secret in Britain was broken to the troops.

In the afternoon, the battalion colonels addressed their men. Cheers broke out in one ship, were taken up in another, the volume growing as the entire fleet joined in. Later, each ship was visited by Roberts who gave officers and men a brief talk.

"This is not an exercise," he said. "At last you are going to meet the enemy. Shortly after midnight you sail for France. The target is the port of Dieppe. This is the operation you have been trained for, so at dawn tomorrow come off those boats running and don't stop until you've reached your objectives. Your unit officers will hand around maps and photographs. Go over every detail until you know them off by heart. No documents are to be taken ashore. Good luck."

In the evening, Mountbatten toured the fleet infecting the troops with his personal magnetism and confidence. General Eisenhower, one of the Combined Commanders who had requested an experimental assault on a Channel port, visited the fleet briefly to give a few words of encouragement to the lone U.S. Rangers whom he described as "the first of thousands who will eventually go into Europe."

When Eisenhower had left for London, Mountbatten had returned to HMS *Vectis* ashore, and Roberts had reported aboard his headquarters ship, the destroyer *Calpe*, nearly five thousand Canadians and three thousand British sailors were sealed off from the rest of the world, confined in the darkened fleet riding at anchor under a canopy of stars: quiet men, fearful men, disciplined and tensed. Among the Camerons again was Private Hallett, a naval officer prepared to fight as an infantryman.

Clouds, made into grey shadows by the moon, scudded overhead; a high breeze flicked streaks of white from the crests of the choppy sea – good weather for a trip to Dieppe. Midnight came and passed, the fleet remaining silent and brooding. Dawn arrived, but instead of Fortress Europe the troops gazed at the familiar shores of the Isle of Wight. Relief, blended with bewilderment, spread through the cramped quarters of the ships. What had happened?

IV

The answer lay with the Commander of the 1st Airborne Division who that evening had sent a message to Paget which said: "Best available meteorological information indicates wind will increase in strength throughout the night from the southwest. Glider operations have been cancelled and by dawn an accurate air drop will be impossible to achieve. Accordingly, I recommend that operation be postponed."

Paget relayed the message to all Commanders concerned including Mountbatten, who had received it when he reached *Vectis* after visiting the fleet. He at once called Paget to urge that the airborne division be told to reconsider for a special effort. The Commander-in-Chief replied that he would not deliberately turn aside a divisional commander's recommendation except under extreme circumstances, and he did not believe those circumstances existed then. In any event, he had no intention of throwing a highly specialized parachute force, the only one of its kind in Britain, to an uncertain fate for the sake of a Combined Operations raid. He promised, however, to let Mountbatten know if the weather improved sufficiently to change the picture.

It was a bitter moment for the Chief of Combined Operations and his Naval Adviser, Hughes-Hallett, both of whom had exerted immense efforts to push Rutter into being, against what at times had seemed insurmountable obstacles and antagonism. Their only tools had been ability, tenacity, enthusiasm, and faith. Other operations on a much smaller scale had been abandoned simply because they had included airborne forces who persisted in calling them off unless a whole series of tides, moons, winds, and cloud conditions were perfect. Hughes-Hallett, discarding his soldier's identity for the last time, looked up at the pale moon, the stars, the light fluffy clouds, and vowed that future Combined Operations raids would call for airborne troops only if no other suitable forces were available – or when there were so many that the War Office would not regard them as too precious to risk.

On July 5, with an opportunity missed and the weather likely to deteriorate further, there was little else the Force Commanders could do but meet ashore with their staffs to decide on another date. Meteorological reports forecast fair weather with only light winds on July 8, the last day until the next month on which the moon and tides would favour the operation.

Another complication was a Combined Operations Intelligence report that the 10th German Panzer Division had moved into Amiens, only eight hours from Dieppe. In a two-tide operation the troops would be ashore fifteen hours, long enough for the armoured column to reach the port and destroy them.

The solution was compression of the entire plan into a one-tide operation, elimination of the more lengthy demolition missions, and the withdrawal of the troops by 11:00 a.m. instead of in the late afternoon. Once the Commanders had agreed to this extensive alteration of the plan, it was sent to Mountbatten and Montgomery for approval and confirmation that zero hour should be dawn on the 8th. It was a remarkable effort on the part of Roberts's and Baillie-Grohman's staffs to make and distribute these alterations in time.

But rot had set in. Montgomery sat in Reigate basking in the awe of his staff and not particularly interested in the frantic attempts being made at Cowes to keep Rutter alive; Roberts and Leigh-Mallory were in dispute with some naval authorities and might even welcome an end to the whole business; the Naval Commander-in-Chief at Portsmouth, whose sole duty besides keeping ships and craft supplied was to give the order to sail, seemed to have been ignored; Baillie-Grohman was not at all satisfied with the standards of Combined Operations naval training; and on the 6th Mountbatten attended a meeting of the Chiefs of Staff at the War Office at which he advised: "If the operation is not undertaken on the 8th, Simmerforce should be disbanded and dispersed and the whole thing started again at a later date."

Only McNaughton and Crerar seemed anxious to keep the operation alive. The 2nd Division, blissfully unaware of these doubts and troubles at the summit of leadership, remained aboard their ships – waiting.

Inevitably German reconnaissance gave this vast armada more than a cursory glance. At 6:15 a.m. on July 7 four aircraft swept in low over the Yarmouth Roads and bombed the infantry landing-ships, *Princess Astrid* and *Princess Josephine Charlotte*, carrying between them the Royal Regiment of Canada.

Both ships were hit by bombs which by some strange chance passed right through them before exploding in the water beneath their keels. The Royals suffered four minor casualties – the first and only casualties of Rutter. However, there was a slight risk of *Princess Josephine Charlotte* sinking, so the troops were disembarked, mustered ashore, and ordered to march to Cowes for further orders. The column was stopped on the way by a motor-cycle dispatch rider carrying an urgent message from Roberts which ordered the regiment to return to Brambles Camp, its training headquarters.

The air attack and weather conditions combined to deliver the final blow to Rutter. Baillie-Grohman and Roberts telephoned Mountbatten to report that there was no time to change the plan to allow for the loss of damaged ships and Mountbatten, influenced also by adverse weather forecasts, formally cancelled the operation and Roberts ordered all units to disembark.

On the morning of the 8th, instead of landing at Dieppe, the 2nd Division quit the Isle of Wight to return to previous stations in Sussex. Roberts circulated a letter to the troops which said:

> It is with the deepest regret that I have to announce that our party is off. I can assure you that everything that could have been done has been done . . . but the Gods were against us and the weather and tides have defeated our attempt.
>
> I know you will feel as badly as I do, and I now want to appeal to you to conduct yourselves in this disappointment in the same manner in which you always have, and that you will maintain the same high standard of conduct and discipline for which this Division is noted.
>
> Again I ask you to say nothing about this operation which we had hoped to carry out, because if you do not there is always the possibility that we may be able to do it again at a later date.
>
> I will do everything I can to assist you and I know your Corps Commander will do the same in the matter of leave and any other facilities we can give you in order to alleviate your just disappointment. . . .

Every man was then warned of the penalties which would befall him were he guilty of a breach of security. But five thousand Canadians were now loose on the mainland and it would be a wondrous thing indeed if not one were to mention what he had been doing.

Montgomery had the last word on Rutter. He recommended to General Paget that "the operation be off for all time." It was off – for exactly a week.

Resurrection
of a Raid

No wonder Churchill was to write of this dark July: "I was politically at my weakest and without a gleam of military success."*

The Russians were still retreating; Rommel was poised on the threshold of Egypt and there was no way of knowing that he had, in fact, shot his bolt; the Japanese were pressing through Burma towards India; shipping losses in the Atlantic totalled more than 400,000 tons; Stalin was berating the democracies for not opening a second front and the public clamour for it was developing into a trans-Atlantic crescendo.

The British Prime Minister rode out the savagely critical vote of censure in the House of Commons, but there seemed slight hope of an Anglo-American accord on future operations. The British buried Sledgehammer, while the Americans could think of nothing else. With the death of Rutter a static war seemed probable for the rest of the year.

Eisenhower, with the concurrence of his chiefs in Washington, tried vainly to slap life into his sacrificial landing in northern France, but this plan, like so many others, found its way into the graveyard of future operations.

It was a month of ugly possibilities everywhere, and no responsible leader in Britain would gamble away meagre resources in men and materials on premature landings. Yet it was recognized as inevitable that eventual Allied initiative would have to take the form of an amphibious operation somewhere – if not against the Continent, then perhaps in North Africa. The idea had its opponents, with some impressive voices in London and Washington saying that the logistics involved in seaborne assaults were so staggering as to make them impracticable, if not impossible. But in the absence of alternatives other than a stalemate the prime task was to find out what a massive cross-Channel invasion would really entail.

It was one thing for political and military leaders to decide upon no major operations in Europe during 1942, but Combined Operations, the organization responsible for acquiring knowledge of invasions, had to hunt doggedly for means to acquire the experience which the vast armies would need when the time came to move. It could not justify its existence by adopting a passive, motionless role.

Mountbatten was not the sort of commander to condone idleness; nor were his staff the sort of men to practise it. While Churchill and the British Chiefs of Staff conferred with United States leaders on future strategy, Combined Operations devised a variety of ways and means by which a limited number of units could be employed on tactical enterprises.

Rutter had been their most ambitious project. Militarily it was designed to test German reaction to a potential invasion, to discover the real strength of the West Wall, and to find out how the enemy would manœuvre his reserves. There was also the hope that it might stimulate ideas for the designs of revolutionary new machines needed to overcome obstacles on the beaches: machines such as mine-destroying tanks, flame-throwing tanks, amphibious armoured vehicles, and a host of other devices.

In naval terms the problems were how to mount an invasion, how to assemble ships, what sort of ships, how and where to train them, how to guide them through minefields, how to navigate so meticulously that troops could be put down on remote beaches. Would all this have to be done under fire? How long could a fleet hope to manœuvre off an enemy coast without being blown out of the water by enemy surface units, bomber forces, or U-boat fleets? Could this be accomplished while giving adequate fire support to the assault troops?

On the air side, could invasion forces be provided with adequate air cover and fighter bomber or bomber support? Could destruction of the enemy air forces be achieved without detraction from support of the ground forces?

Cynics of each service had said during Rutter that they were bait being used by the other two. Canadian commanders, particularly, were inclined to caustic comments about the infantry being sacrificed by the Navy and the Air Force for selfish reasons. These remarks were neither accurate nor amusing, when devoted effort was required to seek out combined knowledge, without which there was risk of a stand-off in Europe with consequent sagging of civilian morale and loss of political prestige by Allied war leaders.

II

Rutter's demise had an immediate and profound effect at all levels of British leadership. With Sledgehammer in the cemetery, the vacuum in the European theatre could not be filled in 1942; there was nothing Churchill could offer Russia or his critics in Parliament, both of whom were loud in their demands for a second front, not even a raid in strength.

For the Chiefs of Staff it meant that there could be no serious planning for a cross-Channel enterprise until Combined Operations devised some other means of acquiring essential knowledge. For the Combined Commanders it meant that there was no way in sight by which their theories could be tested in battle and proven valid or otherwise. At Combined Operations Headquarters there was a deep sense of frustration coupled with a vibrant, aggressive determination to find some means of fulfilling the prime function of unlocking the "priceless secret of victory" while at the same time stabbing at the enemy as often and as cruelly as possible.

For the Canadian regiments it meant that nearly eight weeks of incessant, gruelling training had been cancelled out by postponements no one had seemed able to prevent. Even before they moved off the Isle of Wight, the 2nd Division's Osborne Court headquarters had been abandoned.

Lieutenant-Colonel Labatt, one of the last to leave, remembers that **by early evening of the 8th the large, impassive Marine sentries, the**

WREN secretaries working behind locked doors, and the unidentifiable strangers who once came and went on mysterious errands had all vanished.

"When I visited the place for the last time it was deserted," he told me. "Doors were open, anyone could walk in or out without fear of being challenged by fearsome characters whose orders were to shoot to kill, and Rutter papers stamped 'Cancelled' were scattered everywhere. There was no doubt that the raid was off – for good."

At a higher level, however, the eager young generals, admirals, and air marshals of Combined Operations were transformed by the abandonment into a hard-faced jury of inquisitors looking for a reason why. That night of the 8th, behind the austere façade of Richmond Terrace, they met in a high-ceilinged, sparsely furnished room with an unusually grim Mountbatten in the chair.

There had been moments of greater import in Allied councils and even greater were to come; there had been, and would be, scenes of greater magnificence attended by prime ministers, presidents, dictators, and kings. But none of these, before or after, ever quite resembled this meeting on a warm July evening at a time when the war could well be lost. It was a gathering of the youthful élite, all of high rank, all proven in battle, all unswervingly dedicated to victory, all possessed of immense faith and all, that evening, consumed by bitter disappointment.

The hunters were thwarted – and drama was inevitable. Mountbatten dismissed the conference secretary, and a strangely fragile silence settled in the room. The strike of a match sounded, according to one of the officers present, "like the rasp of a file on steel."

Leigh-Mallory opened discussion with a bitter condemnation of the airborne forces.

"If we're going to hold a *post mortem* on Rutter we might as well take other abortive raids into consideration. Whenever we involve ourselves with paratroops something goes wrong. We're told conditions have to be just right – the moon, the strength of the wind, the direction of the wind, the density of cloud, and what the hell else," he said. "We could wait a thousand years for all these conditions to come about on the same night, and then they'd have another equally facetious excuse. I say we leave them out in future."

Hughes-Hallett, only the snap in his voice betraying cold anger, intervened.

"If we're ever going to find a way back to the Continent we have to to have a raid in strength – and soon. If we wait for the airborne people to give us the green light we'll never go back. I agree we should leave them out until they learn to take a few risks."

He went on to flail the weak-hearted, the over-cautious, and the unbelievers who saw non-existent obstacles in all their plans. While he spoke, layers of blue-grey tobacco smoke formed above the galaxy of young fighting Commanders who listened, hushed and expectant.

Hughes-Hallett faced Mountbatten, and in a tight, icily disciplined voice said, "It is my considered opinion, sir, that an inquiry should be initiated immediately to ascertain whether, in fact, the collapse of Rutter and other planned raids in recent weeks constitute a major defeat for the Allies."

Neither Mountbatten nor any of his staff at this conference were supermen, nor did they pretend to be arbitrators of military justice. It could be said, perhaps, that each possessed the element of the war lover, an element which flowed into full spate only in conditions of war.

In peace they might be submerged by the Establishment, by red tape, by the meanness of the Treasury, by the sheer weight of mediocrity which like hot air often rises to the top, and by lack of stimulant. In war, however, when civil control of purse strings lapsed, the militaristic hunters enjoyed freedom to use the whip, which they did with ruthless efficiency.

Each Commander present knew that Hughes-Hallett had found a diabolically cunning formula for creating a showdown on the future of Combined Operations. Did the fact that there was no knowledge upon which the Combined Commanders could pursue their planning of Roundup, the fact that there was still no insight into the problems of invasion, the fact that the Allies had no plan to hold the Germans on the French coast, the fact that there was no visible means of drawing the *Luftwaffe* away from the eastern front – did all these factors add up to a major defeat? If so, then an inquiry would be more than justified; it would be imperative, with the highest military authorities in the land standing before a bar of professional opinion. It could lead to a grand unleashing of emotions, rivalries, jealousies, and prejudices after which heads might roll in a sweeping purge of the armed forces.

Mountbatten, the young associate of the Chiefs of Staff Committee, justified Churchill's confidence that evening. Much as he might have concurred with the feelings of everyone present, much as he might have wished for a mass expulsion of the "can't do-ers" from their places of power, he rejected the proposal and, with a slight smile, suggested that his Naval Adviser would be better advised to use equal cunning in raiding Fortress Europe rather than contemplate the down-fall of the Whitehall citadel.

He knew that Churchill and the Chiefs of Staff, for both political and military reasons, urgently needed an operation against the Continent. After instructing the conference to consider other means of coming to grips with the enemy in strength, he left the room to keep an appointment with McNaughton. The Force Commanders, Combined Operations Adviserate, and the planning syndicate remained behind for an informal discussion on what could be done to fill the gap left by Rutter.

Ham Roberts made it clear at the outset that any proposals with the slightest chance of being carried out should include the use of the 2nd Division.

"I don't think you've got an entire division as highly trained as we are anywhere in Britain," he said.

There is no record of who said it first, but it was at this meeting, only hours after Rutter had been officially abandoned, that someone said in effect: "If it wasn't for the fact that security has probably gone down the drain already, I'd say the best bet still is to go for Dieppe."

Both Roberts and Hughes-Hallett recall that following this remark those present went over the experiences of the Isle of Wight training in detail and eventually agreed that if some way could be found to off-set the likelihood of security being compromised the best prospect for a raid would be another attempt at Dieppe.

Hughes-Hallett provided the only acceptable solution. "As all the troops are fully trained in their respective tasks," he said, "surely they need little or no further training. If we agree on that, then we could re-assemble them at the last minute, without previous warning. Even if the enemy did get to know that we had once planned a visit to Dieppe he would never have the chance to learn that the show was going on anyway. There would be no more training, no early assembly of ship-ping, and nothing to indicate that the raid is anything but off for all time."

It was a bold scheme, contrary to all orthodox opinion, and typical of the Naval Adviser. Roberts agreed to consider the proposal and promised to let Combined Operations know of his decision within forty-eight hours.

The risks were very real. The enemy could have heard that a raid was planned on Dieppe and might not know of the cancellation. He would therefore continue looking at his defences, improving them, and bringing up reinforcements. At least one of the high-ranking members of the Combined Commanders thought this likely and had been outspokenly thankful when the operation was to all intents and purposes called off for good.

But such opinions were not for the hunters.

III

By July 9, the 2nd Division had taken up its earlier defensive posture in Sussex and, after further warnings about careless talk, normal leave was granted to all units. Army field censors maintained strict surveillance of the mails to check on breaches of security. During the entire period on the Isle of Wight only two letters out of 18,000 censored had actually mentioned a raid on the French coast. The official report of the Army Censorship Section said: "Others wrote saying they would give details when they returned from their present station."

This is precisely what happened when security was eased. There seemed no logical reason why officers and men should not now resort to writing customary letters home and to the usual off-duty gossiping in local pubs. Who could be harmed by talk of an operation that was off?

The censors reported that "there is a continuity of censorable matter regarding operations on the Isle of Wight. . . . It could not appear, however, that these are instances of deliberate attempts to disclose information . . . but made rather in the mistaken idea that it would be permissible to write once the expected operation did not take place and they had returned to the regular camps."

Montgomery had expected something like this to happen; indeed it might be unrealistic for anyone to have hoped for complete and continuous security from five thousand unfettered troops, which was the reason why he had recommended that the operation be off "for all time."

On July 11, two distinctly contradictory events took place. Montgomery wrote to Crerar formally thanking the 2nd Division for the hardships the troops had undergone during training. After remarking that the staff work in the conduct and organization of the training had been on a very high level, he continued:

> The decision to cancel the operation must have been a bitter disappointment to all commanders, regimental officers and other ranks. The raiding force had been trained up to a high standard

of efficiency, and I have no doubt whatever that, given average luck and fair weather, the operation would have been carried through with all that élan and dash which has always been so typical of the Canadian troops.

That same afternoon, Ham Roberts telephoned Hughes-Hallett at Combined Operations Headquarters to say that after consideration of the security problem, he was not only prepared to undertake the raid without further training but was anxious to "get cracking as soon as possible."

Montgomery may have buried Rutter, but Hughes-Hallett and Ham Roberts were already disinterring the corpse, restoring circulation, and tidying it up for representation to Mountbatten. This was done formally on the evening of July 12, and subsequent events moved swiftly, with Mountbatten submitting the proposal verbally to the Chiefs of Staff the following day. With Churchill pressing hard for some sort of demonstration in the West, their concurrence was immediate. On the morning of the 14th, he circulated to the Force Commanders and Combined Operations Adviserate the following directive, in which the code name "Jubilee" was mentioned for the first time:

> The Chiefs of Staff have directed that if possible an emergency operation is to be carried out during August to fill the gap caused by the cancellation of Rutter.
>
> In order to cut down training requirements, the same forces will so far as possible be employed, and the planning of the new operation has to be entrusted to the Force Commanders from the outset.
>
> The locality and form of the new operation are being chosen so as to ensure that the training of individuals of lower formations will be as similar as possible to that which was given for Rutter.
>
> Owing to the appointment of Rear Admiral, Combined Operations [Baillie-Grohman] as Rear Admiral Expeditionary Force, and owing to the dispersal of the Senior Officers on his staff, the Naval Staff for Operation Jubilee is being provided by Combined Operations Headquarters. The Force Commanders and their staffs for Jubilee will be working for the next fortnight on the second floor, and these rooms are not to be used for other purposes.

Ham Roberts and Leigh-Mallory were enthusiastic about remounting the operation but Baillie-Grohman, who was not so keen for the same reasons as Montgomery had put forward, was given another appointment. He told me: "I was thankful not to take the job on under the new conditions. Any commander, German or British, who once got the news that there had been a plan to raid his port, whether it had been cancelled or not, would most certainly look again, not once but twice or thrice, at his defences, and they would be strengthened. The great probability that this news would leak out, combined with the absence of heavy supporting fire and poor training would, in my opinion, make this operation not feasible as an act of war. Had I been asked to take on the responsibility of naval commander once more, I am very doubtful if I could have agreed. As it was, I was kept completely in the dark about Jubilee, and when this was mooted again I was already in another appointment as one of Admiral Ramsay's Flag Officers. When Jubilee did come off, the gods were certainly on our side, in that they had prevented news of Rutter filtering through to the Germans (as they evidently did), otherwise there might have been a worse catastrophe."

Mountbatten approved the transfer of the Naval Force Commander at Admiral Ramsay's request and immediately installed Hughes-Hallett as his successor on the ground that the time factor precluded the introduction of a new officer of flag rank.

Crerar received a copy of Mountbatten's directive and at once communicated its contents to McNaughton, who reacted by sending Lieutenant-Colonel Henderson to 2nd Division headquarters as his personal representative. Churchill Mann, who had been promoted to brigadier the previous day and appointed to Crerar's staff, was loaned back to 2nd Division headquarters to ensure continuity of planning, mainly because Roberts, never a desk soldier and on the whole impatient with paper work, had come to rely upon him to a greater extent than was, perhaps, quite proper for a divisional commander.

At 3:00 p.m. that day the first formal planning conference on Jubilee was held at Richmond Terrace with Mountbatten in the chair and attended by Roberts, Leigh-Mallory, Hughes-Hallett, Henderson, and members of the Combined Operations planning syndicate. The atmosphere was crisp and businesslike, in contrast to most of the Rutter meetings which, because so many commanders were of necessity absent, had often ended indecisively. Jubilee, meaning a year celebrating release of slaves, cancellations of debts, and a return of property to former owners, usually proclaimed by the sound of trumpets, was an unfortunate code name. It implied that the raiders would sound a blast on the trumpets, the West Wall would crumble, and France would be handed back to Frenchmen – something that in 1942 could be little else than wishful thinking.

The essence of the new plan would be surprise and synchronization, to achieve the early capture of the defences on the wing headlands which covered the main beaches. As in the earlier plan the flank landings at Pourville and Puits were to be made in darkness at 4:50 a.m., 15 minutes after nautical twilight. Touchdown of the assaults over the Dieppe beaches would be 5:20 a.m., by which time the wing headlands should have been overrun.

Roberts returned to the problem of air bombardment of the sea front before dawn, but Leigh-Mallory, stressing again that as moonlight would be uncertain on any of the suitable nights accuracy could not be guaranteed, suggested that fire support from the destroyers would be more effective and reliable, if there had to be a frontal assault at all. He was never happy on this point. Roberts replied that he needed the destroyers to take on the wing headlands should the flank parties fail to reach their objectives, which prompted Hughes-Hallett to say that the destroyers would probably be too busy protecting the assault fleet from E-boats and U-boats to undertake either mission. But he promised to give Roberts all the fire support possible – which was not to be much.

The use of airborne troops was struck out of the plan on Combined Operations advice that Commando units could be substituted with absolute safety. The huge coastal batteries at Varengeville and Berneval were really more of a menace to the safety of the ships than to the actual assault on Dieppe. At Mountbatten's suggestion it was decided to treat these operations as separate assaults to be planned independently by the commanders of whatever Commando forces were selected. When Ham Roberts eventually met the two leaders involved he understood why the Chief of Combined Operations was so insistent on this point.

There was considerable argument about the wisdom of the main assault being carried out so long after those on the flanks. The air and military planners gave cautious support for the idea of simultaneous landings along the entire ten-mile stretch of coast between Varengeville and Berneval on the grounds that it would increase the likelihood of total surprise, make for simplicity in planning, ensure early control of all beaches, and provide more time to prepare for arrival of tanks on the main beaches.

The Navy, on the other hand, pointed out that the main assault forces would be left facing the sea-front defences of Dieppe without armoured support for too long, as it would be impossible to land the tanks until first civil light, and by the time they touched down there might be little left of the infantry to support. Additionally, if the guns on the wing headlands were not captured they could catch the forces on the main beaches in a deadly and probably decisive crossfire. The conference eventually decided on the main assault going in at shortly after first civil light, following the flank attacks after nautical twilight by some thirty minutes.

Nautical twilight is the sailor's dawn. Given a clear horizon at sea he is supposed to detect first light when the sun is still 12 degrees below the horizon. The laymen sees dawn, in civil twilight, much later, generally in the region of forty-five minutes after the beginning of nautical twilight.

To preserve maximum security, the 2nd Division was to be kept in Sussex until the morning of the actual sailing and then move quickly to embarkation points at Portsmouth, Southampton, Newhaven, and Seaford, from where certain units would make the entire crossing in landing-craft.

It was also agreed to limit the number of mysterious satellite parties which had previously turned up on the Isle of Wight. There would be only one radar scientist instead of two, fifteen French Commandos to act as guides through the town of Dieppe, the twelve Sudeten Germans, seven of whom would carry out missions which would take them inland, and five who would act as interpreter-translators for a Special Intelligence group assigned to raid various military and police headquarters, release French Resistance leaders from the Dieppe prison, and bring back as many secret documents as possible.

As a general rule no civilians were to be brought back to England, but the French Commandos and Intelligence groups could combine their efforts to evacuate a maximum of twelve persons who might be of specific value to the Allied cause – in special operations or political warfare. The Force Commanders then issued a memorandum to the Senior Intelligence Officer of Combined Operations which said:

> The conditions for taking these parties are that there should be no subsequent increase in their numbers and that the men concerned should only be warned the day before the operation and not join the assault ship until the afternoon of the day on which they sail. If for any reason sailing is postponed, the parties will be sealed aboard.

Neither Roberts nor Hughes-Hallett had any intention of allowing these autonomous groups the same freedom to come and go that they had enjoyed during the Rutter training.

It was also decided that from August 1, the Force Commanders and their planning staffs should move from London to Southampton to an emergency Combined Headquarters to be made available by the Portsmouth Naval Command.

Within two hours the conference had given the plan a new look, stripping it of fat and tightening it to the extent that timing became almost as essential as surprise. Chief elements were the two outer and the two inner flank attacks followed 30 minutes later by the main assault at Dieppe itself.

The landing beaches running east to west were:

Berneval	Yellow	No. 3 Commando
Puits	Blue	Royal Regiment of Canada
Dieppe (East)	Red	Essex Scottish
Dieppe (West)	White	Royal Hamilton Light Infantry
Pourville	Green	South Saskatchewan Regiment
		Cameron Highlanders of Canada
Varengeville	Orange	No. 4 Commando

In floating reserve to be committed by Ham Roberts at a time and place he felt necessary was the Fusiliers Mont-Royal. In the event that it did land, the battalion would form a rearguard to cover the withdrawal over the main beaches.

The Commando objectives were the heavy Goebbels battery at Berneval and the Hess battery at Varengeville which, if allowed to operate, would make it impossible for the fleet to remain off Dieppe. At Puits, the Royal Regiment would capture another battery known as Rommel and overrun the East Headland which the Germans called Bismarck. The South Saskatchewans at Pourville were to capture the West Headland, known as Hindenburg, and move on to take a fortified strongpoint at the Farm of the Four Winds. The Camerons would pass through their perimeter to move inland towards the St Aubin airstrip and capture what was believed to be German divisional headquarters at Arques-La-Bataille.

The RHLI and Essex Scottish, landing on the main beaches were to assist in the capture of the wing headlands, capture the town and harbour, and help the naval cutting-out party aboard *Locust* to remove the German invasion barges. They would be supported by the Calgary Tanks. In all cases, the landings were to be masked by smokescreens laid by ships and aircraft and covered by bombardment from the sea and air.

Success would depend initially on surprise; then the most vital element would be accurate timing of the various phases of the operation. Synchronization would be the keynote.

The Force Commanders and the planners who had spent more than two months on the Dieppe project at the most critical period of the war, reflected a new-found sense of urgency and direction. The winds of war had been warm, moist, and thunderous for Rutter: now they were blowing fresh, cool, and crisp for Jubilee.

When the conference was over, Roberts was summoned to a meeting with Mountbatten and McNaughton, which had been requested by the latter, now determined to become the responsible military authority for the new operation, as Montgomery had been for the old.

After he had been briefed on the conference just finished, McNaughton gave his formal approval for Roberts to proceed with further detailed planning and said to Mountbatten, "I should like to discuss the chain of command."

The Chief of Combined Operations had no wish for the bickering that had accompanied Rutter to be repeated in Jubilee. He replied that as he had not been satisfied with the previous arrangements, he would become Supreme Commander responsible for the dispatch or postponement of the fleet's sailing, thereby keeping the decision to launch the operation within the jurisdiction of Combined Operations.

McNaughton said that he would have no objection to such an arrangement but it should be so decreed by the Chiefs of Staff, and continued by saying he intended to ask the Commander-in-Chief, Home Forces (General Paget) to place the military command on a different basis. His memorandum on this meeting said:

> . . . In reference to the military chain of command I said I would ask General Paget to agree to General Crerar being named as the responsible military officer to co-ordinate and if this were done I would agree to arm him with appropriate authority as regards the use of Canadian troops. I told Lord Louis Mountbatten that the detailed proposals for the operation . . . would be subject to my approval in the same way as C-in-C, Home Forces, and Chiefs of Staff Committee had approval for operations of British troops.

In effect, McNaughton had now joined Crerar in telling the British that the Canadian Army was in Britain as an independent force, not as a part of the British Army.

Mountbatten replied that as he had confidence in Ham Roberts, the question of who was the higher military authority was not one that concerned him. Like Montgomery, he recognized that once the operation had begun, there could be little control from England regardless of who held the right to intervene. In any event, his job was to give help and advice to the Force Commanders, not to instruct them.

Before this late evening meeting broke up, Mountbatten gave McNaughton and Roberts a list of the people who knew of Jubilee. They numbered only twenty, including the Chiefs of Staff, the Force Commanders, and Mountbatten himself.

July 16 had been a momentous day for the proponents of Jubilee. McNaughton ended it with a midnight call to the War Office, in which he arranged to meet Paget. This took place on the evening of the 17th and McNaughton's record of it says: "It was agreed that channel of command would run Commander-in-Chief, Home Forces (Paget), 1st Canadian Army (McNaughton), 1st Canadian Corps (Crerar) and 2nd Canadian Division (Roberts)."

McNaughton was thereby substituted for Montgomery and he assumed his authority by saying: "I intend naming Harry Crerar the responsible military officer."

Paget nodded his assent and undertook to advise Montgomery that he was no longer responsible for further military arrangements in connection with a raid in strength on the Continent – which must have relieved the Army Commander in Reigate who so obviously wanted nothing more to do with it anyway.

From the 17th, then, apart from Paget and Mountbatten at the summit of Combined Operations leadership, the proposal to raid Dieppe was entirely a matter for the Canadian Commanders; the military aspect of it was theirs to do with as they wished. McNaughton, the Commander who would not have his men "used uselessly or experimentally in war" was now the highest military authority for a great experiment in amphibious warfare.

On Paget's instructions, General Swayne confirmed the arrangement in a letter to Montgomery which said: "The Commander-in-Chief has made the General Officer Commanding-in-Chief, First Canadian Army, the military officer responsible for the conduct of raiding operations to be carried out by troops under his command."

In this way the Army Commander in Reigate was effectively ejected from the cookhouse and his place at the pot occupied by the Army Commander from Canada. But the impression lingers that Montgomery really went of his own accord.

A belief has been fostered in Canada that the Dieppe raid was predominantly a British affair in which Canadian troops were unfortunate enough to become involved. Indeed, when I spoke to General Crerar about this he said: "It was basically a British plan. We had very little connection with it at this stage."

But both McNaughton and Crerar were fully informed of the detailed planning and if they so wished, there were thirty-three days left in which it could be altered to conform with their own ideas. The frontal assault and the question of fire support were two points which might have occupied their attention. There is no record that they did; nor is it likely that they would. McNaughton, according to many officers who served under him, was normally cold and reserved, and revealed enthusiasm mainly when talking to fellow engineers about some deeply technical problem. When the British Chiefs of Staff professed a lack of confidence in him at a later stage, Sir Alan Brooke told the Canadian Prime Minister that McNaughton "seemed to have become more suited for planning and research than for action in the field. . . . Full of inventive genius, but interested in study." Montgomery was even more blunt, telling Mackenzie King that McNaughton "was good as an engineer and for organizing purposes, but . . . not the man to command troops in the field."

On the other hand Crerar was popular with his men and quite acceptable to the British Chiefs of Staff who admired his eagerness for action. He argued persistently for Canadian army independence and for continuity of Canadian command but was too shrewd to be so obstinate about it that his own and Canadian participation in offensive operations might be jeopardized.

On July 20 the Chiefs of Staff formally confirmed the appointment of Hughes-Hallett as Naval Force Commander and made Mountbatten the sole authority for dispatching the fleet when the time came. Four days later two new figures entered the Dieppe project: Lieutenant-Colonels Durnford-Slater and Lord Lovat, commanding officers of Nos. 3 and 4 Commando troops respectively.

IV

Immediately after the Dunkirk evacuation in June 1940, Churchill had said: "We should set to work to organize self-contained, thoroughly equipped raiding units . . . with specially trained troops of the hunter class who can develop a reign of terror down the enemy coasts. . . ."

So the Commandos were born – and among the first to volunteer were tall, dark, and slender Shimi Lovat and taut, disciplined John Durnford-Slater, both possessed of an uncommon flair for raiding and both responsible for an impressive contribution to terror along enemy-held coasts.

Because they had very definite and individualistic ideas on how to go about their business they would have nothing to do with the detailed military plan, preferring instead to treat their roles as separate, independent operations and to make their own arrangements for achieving the selected objectives. As the reason for knocking out the Goebbels and Hess batteries was to secure the safety of the main fleet lying off Dieppe, there could be little objection to their attitude – the reason for Mountbatten's warning to Roberts that Commando operations should be excluded from the military planning.

They were formally introduced to Jubilee on July 24 at another Combined Operations conference in London, summoned to co-ordinate the military, naval, and air plans. They met Ham Roberts for the first time and the encounter did nothing to benefit either the Canadians or the Commandos. Roberts barely spoke throughout the meeting, revealing a pessimism that was equalled only by the reservations of Leigh-Mallory. The Air Force Commander repeatedly drew attention to the lack of heavy air bombardment in the plan and at one point burst out, "I don't like this at all, I don't think there's enough preparation in the way of heavy bombing, and someone in high authority ought to do something about it. Otherwise, I think these Canadians are going to have a bad time in the centre."

His prophetic warning reflected the feelings of Durnford-Slater who had been briefed on the enemy's defence system a few days before. He said nothing, because he was present only to comment on the role of No. 3 Commando. If anyone should have supported Leigh-Mallory, it was Roberts who was suffering the effects of unspoken yet tangible pressures within himself and from his senior officers. He was eager for battle and supremely confident of his troops. But he was worried about the lack of heavy naval fire support and the inability of Combined Operations to persuade Bomber Command to deliver an accurate pre-dawn attack on the sea front.

To make known his fears in too strong a fashion – and he had voiced them all before – would be to invite distrust from Combined Operations who could be relied upon to take drastic reprisals against anyone threatening another abandonment of the raid. He knew also that McNaughton and Crerar were jubilant at having acquired military responsibility for the raid and would react even more harshly were he to place Canadian participation in jeopardy.

It seemed to him that his best course was to stay quiet, let Leigh-Mallory make the objections for him, and if they proved futile then he could count only on the thrusting enthusiasm and efficiency of the 2nd Division and an enormous amount of luck.

Mountbatten brought up the question of the U.S. Ranger contingent and asked how they were to be employed. Lovat and Durnford-Slater established quick claims to a group apiece and promised to "blood them to the satisfaction of their masters." It meant that they would command the first American soldiers to fight in Europe during the war, and Durnford-Slater said afterwards, "They wanted battle experience; they were to get it."

The meeting ended with a unanimous decision to make zero night August 17-18 or 18-19, and Roberts left London for his headquarters in Sussex to discuss the outcome with Churchill Mann. Missing from the original Rutter team was Goronwy Rees, who had represented Montgomery, and Mann felt there was much of value this officer could contribute to Jubilee. He broached the matter to Roberts who passed along a request for the loan of Rees to McNaughton.

In a letter to Montgomery on the 25th, the Canadian Army Commander said: "General Roberts has requested that Major G. M. Rees of your staff, who has been a valuable member of the Division's planning staff for Rutter, might remain with the group to provide continuity in the intelligence work."

The Army Commander in Reigate would have none of it. He replied: "I have given this matter serious consideration, as Major Rees was my personal representative and not officially a member of any formal planning group. Now that you have taken over responsibility, I suggest it is best that I cut right clear; it is not suitable or desirable that I should have a representative in the party who reported direct to me on what was going on. . . . It might lead to trouble."

Rees was thus rescued from what promised to be an awkward predicament. There is little doubt that had he been loaned to the 2nd Division, he would have been pumped unmercifully by Montgomery who might then have found the temptation to offer advice irresistible – something that neither McNaughton nor Crerar would have tolerated.

Later that day, Mountbatten telephoned McNaughton to inform him that "the Prime Minister and War Cabinet have approved Operation J – in principle, but that neither date nor place had been communicated to the Cabinet."

Churchill was therefore the twenty-first person to know that Dieppe had been resurrected.

On receipt of this message, McNaughton signalled to Crerar: "I hereby detail you as the responsible military officer for operation Jubilee and I direct that you place yourself in contact with the Chief of Combined Operations to concert plans therefor. You will keep me fully informed of the progress of plans."

This placed the onus for planning on Crerar. If there were no significant alterations from the original Rutter plan, for which Montgomery remained primarily responsible, then Crerar must have considered them unnecessary. Had he really objected to the frontal-assault principle, he could have insisted on radical and fundamental changes which might have required further training. While it is possible that another sojourn on the Isle of Wight might have led to speculation about the raid being remounted, it could also be argued that the troops would never credit the same operation being planned and would have found another target to talk about, thereby ensuring security for the real thing.

During this buoyant period of misplaced confidence it was as if the supreme commanders needed conferences every other day to draw strength and conviction from each other and to offer silent challenges to anyone who might be presumptuous enough to introduce a note of pessimism. Leigh-Mallory, always outspoken in his criticism of the military plan and recognizing the restraining influence the presence of senior Canadian officers had on Roberts, often became even more sharply critical on such occasions.

At a conference attended by Crerar, who was being expansively genial and voicing his satisfaction with the plan, Leigh-Mallory interrupted with a flat, electrifying condemnation.

"I can't see it," he said. "Your plan may have merit in theory, but it's damned impracticable. The troops will be pinned down on the beaches at the very beginning. They'll never get going again, you mark my words."

It was just not done for an airman to contradict a soldier on purely military matters, and Crerar gave the Air Marshal a long, calculating look before replying with cutting emphasis.

"Are you speaking with the authority of an airman?" he asked.

"No bloody fear," retorted Leigh-Mallory. "Before I joined the Flying Corps in 1917 I was a subaltern. I speak as a soldier who served on the western front and who knows what it's like to go over the top without proper fire support."

The exchange is another indication that Crerar was more closely connected with the planning and training in Jubilee than is generally believed, and indeed approved of it. The fact that both he and Mc-Naughton possessed ultimate military authority and apparently did little to alter the planning, further indicates that they must have concurred with its principal features.

Yet another conference was held on the 26th at which Roberts asked Mountbatten why, if surprise were to be the key element, the landings on the main beaches could not be made simultaneously with those on the flanks? He pointed out that the change would simply put the Essex Scottish, RHLI, and Calgary Tanks ashore under cover of darkness at 4:50 a.m. instead of 5:20 a.m. Hughes-Hallett immediately explained that simultaneous attacks along the entire front were impracticable for naval reasons, that if the main attack were to go in simultaneously with the flanks there would not be sufficient sea room for the ships and landing-caft, a hazard that would be aggravated by the difference in the speeds of the various types of vessels.

To clinch his objections, he estimated that such an arrangement would mean sailing the big infantry landing-ships from Southampton half an hour earlier than planned, just at the time when German evening reconnaissance patrols were busy over the Channel.

Roberts gave way, and Hughes-Hallett was left with a problem of his own, one of which was causing him considerable embarrassment. A week previously the enemy had laid a minefield down the middle of the Channel across the path his raiding-fleet proposed to take. Arrangements had been made to sweep paths across it, but the infantry landing-ships had to be exercised in manœuvring through a minefield between marker buoys. His staff had taken the ships out to sea each night for practice runs through dummy minefields, much to the astonishment and chagrin of the Portsmouth Naval Command who had never heard of such goings on after dark, could not be told the true purpose, and therefore resented this intrusion upon their operational area.

During the first days of August, the London command group dispersed for the final "netting in" of the operation's various units and tasks. Hughes-Hallett and the Combined Operations staff moved to secret underground headquarters at Fort Southwick, Portsmouth; Leigh-Mallory returned to his headquarters at Uxbridge while Air Commodore Cole, his deputy for the raid, joined the Portsmouth team. Roberts drove to 2nd Division headquarters in Sussex where his subsequent movements were covered by a letter from General Paget requesting the 2nd Division to undertake further exercises and produce a paper reviewing the Isle of Wight training to assist in the revision of Combined Operations instructions pamphlets. The letter provided an adequate explanation for the departure of Roberts and Churchill Mann to join Hughes-Hallett at Fort Southwick. They travelled by train and were accompanied by only a driver, three confidential clerks, and their respective batmen. From then on the Force Commanders would be together almost daily.

Much was yet to be done. Behind the broad principles of a raid in strength lay the intricate technical problems of supply, communications, and equipment, all of which had to be arranged under a blanket of total secrecy.

Organizing Jubilee

I

The security list could not be confined for long to so few; signals officers, sappers, counter-intelligence officers, and quartermasters had to be informed to ensure proper organization. It is one thing to plan a raid, set objectives, and decide time and place; it is quite another to prepare and supply it under strict secrecy.

For the purpose of the raid, No. 11 Fighter Group at Uxbridge would become a temporary Combined Operations headquarters at which Mountbatten, Leigh-Mallory, and Crerar would listen-in on the battle's progress. Special "scrambler" telephones linked Uxbridge with Whitehall, but the chain had to continue across the Channel to the forces at Dieppe: from Uxbridge via Southwick to HMS *Calpe*, the headquarters ship from which Roberts would direct the battle, from *Calpe* to the beaches where Southam and Lett would set up 4th Brigade and 6th Brigade headquarters, to the battalions command posts, and to the companies pressing inland. A special ultra high-frequency radio-telephone listening-station was set up on Beachy Head to pick up and log conversations overheard during the action, for examination and analysis later.

Royal Canadian Signals would also keep the Calgary Tanks in contact with *Calpe* on another wavelength, while yet another would be used to keep Forward Observation Officers in touch with the bombarding destroyers. The Special Intelligence parties would use their own "Phantom" wavelength to transmit situation reports via *Calpe* to Uxbridge and the War Office, and the two Commando troops would be linked to *Calpe* on an even higher frequency wavelength. Radio-telephone communication between *Calpe* and the fighter squadrons was essential to enable air support to "attack on call"; then further radio-telephone contact had to be maintained between ships of the fleet. Finally, the entire bewildering system had to be duplicated to HMS *Fernie*, the reserve headquarters destroyer in which Churchill Mann would sail as deputy force commander, ready to take over immediately if *Calpe* were badly damaged and Roberts unable to continue in command.

Swift and effective communication at all levels throughout the raid was so essential that wavelengths were more precious than bullets, and the sets employed were weird, wonderful, and improvized. There were light-weight walkie-talkies, heavier walker-talkies, cumbersome sets trundled about in buggy-like carriers and accompanied by baby-carriage cable-layers, and even long-range multiple wavelength headquarters sets mounted in scout cars.

Throughout the Isle-of-Wight training for Rutter, the Signals Corps had visited each infantry unit giving illustrated lectures on the communications systems, showing how army network overlapped into navy and air nets.

Because no such large-scale raid had ever been attempted before, and the signallers had no blueprint to follow, the entire complicated organization was virtually devised from scratch by Canadians, assisted by British naval experts. When Rutter was eventually abandoned and it was thought there would be no raid on Dieppe, Mountbatten had expressed his admiration in a letter to Ham Roberts which said: "May I say what pleasure it has given me to be able to forward such a good report on your signal communications. My Chief Signals Officer tells me he has never come across a better Army signal unit."

He had repeated these sentiments in an official Combined Operations report on Rutter to General Paget. It said, in part: "Army signal communications were of a higher standard of efficiency than in any previous exercise I have ever seen. The efficiency of the communications I consider reflects credit on the Divisional Signals and the Division as a whole."

This praise from a professional sailor, once the senior signals officer in a battle fleet, is even more remarkable when the militia status of the Canadian Army is taken into account. The long wait in Sussex had not been an entire waste of time.

The communications plan was minutely detailed, ranging from establishment of beach signal stations down to the equipment to be carried by each signalman: a pair of pliers, a small roll of insulating tape, a clasp knife, and fifty yards of fine telephone wire. Verbal password along the raiding-beaches was to be "McNaughton" and a list of twelve code words all beginning with the letter V was compiled, to be used if the enemy attempted to pass bogus messages over the air.

The actual order said:

> The enemy may attempt to pass bogus orders over the wireless system. Individual officers and operators can usually recognize such interlopers by voice, and may be able to identify the speakers by asking questions that only the proper person can answer. However, a number of officers and operators are not known to each other. The following identification system will be employed. If an officer or operator suspects that he is being called by an enemy interloper he will say "Identify," followed by a number. The number will refer to one of the code words given in the list below. The correct answer to the challenge would be the code word corresponding to the number given. . . . If a station hears another station on its group using its code name to pass bogus messages it will immediately jam the interloper.

There were insufficient Canadian signallers to man such a vast and complex series of systems, and some 200 Royal Naval signallers were detailed to take over many of the beach signal stations and seaborne relay stations. Once Rutter was replaced by Jubilee and zero day set for the night of August 17-18, time was too short to recall these ratings from the ships to which they had been dispersed. Somehow, while maintaining security, a fresh naval party had to be retrained. They were assembled in a country house outside Portsmouth to prepare for what was officially described as a signalling demonstration for distinguished visitors.

The signals of the 2nd Division were hampered by the same need for secrecy. They established their network on the headquarters destroyers, *Calpe* and *Fernie*, throughout the large fleet of assorted ships and then had to ask British radio operators to do the testing in case the enemy should detect Canadian accents on the air.

Both destroyers were festooned with various types of radio-telephone sets, all of which were designed and fitted to withstand blast from enemy fire and bombing. One novel type had been built by the United States Motorola Company and had undergone vigorous testing in Combined Operations assault training. An official report on the raid issued a week after it was over said: "The two headquarters ships were connected by very high frequency R/T channels. . . . The most satisfactory was that provided by the American Motorola set which is extremely efficient and stood up in a remarkable manner to the effect of blast." This was probably the most vital link of all, because had it broken down there would have been no communication between *Calpe*, *Fernie*, and Uxbridge. As a precaution, however, both destroyers were to carry a pair of homing pigeons which would fly last messages to England should the ships be destroyed.

Another group, brought for good reason into the Jubilee picture at an early date, was the Royal Canadian Engineers party under Major B. Sucharov of Montreal. This astonishingly inventive officer commanded what was called the Beach Assault Engineers responsible for seeing that the Calgary tanks, scout cars, and blitz buggies got off the main beaches, over the sea wall, and through road blocks into Dieppe itself. They would also, with the support of one company from the Fusiliers Mont-Royal, help the assault forces find a path through any beach minefields. All told there were 94 men in Sucharov's spearhead group and another 240 demolition experts who would blow up selected targets in the town, giving special attention to the torpedo dump buried into the eastern headland.

One of these was Sergeant George Hickson of Kitchener, Ontario, a slender, dark-haired sapper of medium height who was to cut a grim swathe of death through enemy strongpoints when he landed. His target was the Dieppe telephone exchange.

Major McTavish led another group ordered to land with the Essex Scottish on Red Beach and blast their way across the docks to the East Headland where they had forty-five minutes in which to blow up the torpedo dump.

But probably the most difficult task of all was to reassemble the stores and equipment required for the raid. All weapons, ammunition, and special explosives had been returned to War Office depots after the cancellation of Rutter, and now it was necessary to get them all back, once again without telling anyone why.

As he was not prepared to go through all the difficulties he had experienced when supplying the previous operation, Major Romilly at Combined Operations Headquarters obtained Mountbatten's consent to be solely responsible for gathering up the new equipment. On August 1 he requisitioned a huge country estate in Hampshire, called Warnford Park, and transformed it into what was called "The Combined Operations Stores Department." He persuaded Ham Roberts to loan him 2nd Division personnel commanded by Major Eric Bell, formerly of Regina but now living in Winnipeg, and between them Romilly and Bell were to perform one of the most outstanding examples of secret ordnance supply in the history of Combined Operations.

From August 5 onwards supplies poured into Warnford Park at the rate of sixteen railway trucks a day for nine days, ostensibly to form the nucleus of a permanent stores depot. Once delivered, Major Bell's men had to unpack weapons, clean them, and divide the stores into blocks of crates which could be moved to the embarkation ports.

One disastrous flaw in these otherwise near-perfect arrangements was not to emerge until the raid itself. The infantry had spent weeks on the Isle of Wight filing down Sten guns and magazines to overcome their tendency to jam. These guns had been returned to the War Office and those arriving at Warnford Park were brand new. More than one Canadian on August 19 was to curse his Sten, throw it away, and pick up the nearest rifle.

Johnny Andrews was also faced with a weapons problem. His tanks were fitted with new Besa guns, none of which could be judged reliable until each had fired at least 1,000 rounds. Between August 8 and 14, Warnford Park supplied more than a million rounds for the Calgary Tanks to fire aimlessly out to sea from a small beach near Portsmouth. Among these tanks was one equipped with the Oke flame-throwing device which had not yet been tested in action. It was the only prototype in existence and had been borrowed by Combined Operations under the pretext of assessing its usefulness to raiding forces.

On August 8, the British Ministry of Supply demanded the immediate return of the flame-throwing tank as it had been ordered into mass production. The Ministry department responsible had lost the blueprints and could not carry out the order until the tank was returned and new sets of blueprints made up.

Nor was this the end of the headaches that beset the team of Romilly and Bell. Nearly five million rounds of small-arms ammunition had been supplied to the 2nd Division from a War Office depot in Wales for Rutter, and the best way of resupplying the same amount was to obtain the return of this ammunition. The depot obstinately refused to part with it for a second time. Despite all Romilly's blandishments they remained adamant, and another five million rounds had to be extracted from a less inquisitive and more generous arsenal.

Deadline for all supplies to be delivered to Warnford Park was August 15; the last railway truck was checked in at 9:37 p.m. on the 14th.

II

As one of the key elements for success was surprise, the security of the raiding force was of prime importance; and responsible for maintaining it were the senior Intelligence officers of Combined Operations and British Military Intelligence, assisted by Canadian 1st Army Intelligence and 2nd Division Field Security.

While the Canadians lingered in Sussex, plainclothes counter-espionage agents mingled with them in pubs, hotels, at dances, taking note of careless talk. Daily reports were funnelled into a central analysis room at Combined Operations Headquarters where they were studied by M.I.5 (Counter-Intelligence) experts who then advised on whether there was anything to indicate that the operation may have been compromised. Jubilee was known to only a few, but full details of Rutter had been known to many, so it was more or less inevitable that the agents should overhear some gossip concerning a raid on the French coast. They had to determine if it was merely in reference to the cancelled operation or whether the talkers possessed unauthorized foreknowledge of Jubilee.

The ships that would take part in the operation were kept widely dispersed at the embarkation ports of Southampton, Portsmouth, Newhaven, and Shoreham, the landing-ships being disguised as merchant vessels awaiting convoy down Channel. The tank and personnel landing-craft were issued with stores and equipment accompanied by letters to their commanding officers informing them that these were to be standard stores for their ships.

On August 12, M.I.5 agents in the Shoreham-Newhaven area, where most of the 2nd Division were congregated, carried out a snap two-day check and set alarm bells ringing at Combined Operations with a report which said: "There was much indiscreet talk. Canadians of the Calgary Tank Regiment were heard to say that their tanks had been water-proofed and that Commandos were involved in a pending operation."

On Mountbatten's orders a censorship blanket was draped over southern England, from the Thames estuary to Weymouth. Within three days nearly 40,000 letters were intercepted, and to the relief of all concerned it was found that although mention was frequently made of an offensive against France, the date August 18 was referred to no more often than others.

The analysis said: "Although stories of an expectant operation and of a Second Front have been seen in many letters, very few were in any way specific . . . as far as the small percentage of mail examined goes, the secret is well kept."

During this early August period some indiscretions were considered serious enough to warrant action. A private of Durnford-Slater's No. 3 Commando left the unit's training area in Seaford to visit a friend with Lord Lovat's No. 4 Commando in Weymouth. He was reported to have discussed a pending operation loudly in a public hotel lounge and had to be severely reprimanded. A Royal Navy Lieutenant who was to command a landing-craft met a girl at the Queen's Hotel, South-sea, near Portsmouth, confided details of the operation to her over drinks, and told her even more when she took him to her room. He should have been more careful in his choice of girl friends. This parti-cular one was not just a prostitute but a patriotic one who made a point of reporting the confidences of her clients to proper authorities. The officer found himself transferred suddenly to a remote theatre of operations until the raid was over.

Following this affair, a lieutenant in No. 3 Commando boasted to two naval officers at Newhaven that within days he would be ashore in France. He was severely reprimanded by Durnford-Slater, later court-martialled, and then expelled from the Commandos to be returned to his regiment.

Two signallers of 2nd Division's headquarters staff spent a night with two girls from the British ATS and asked them to be "faithful until we return from a raid to France." The girls were faithful to the extent of reporting their boy friends who were quickly dispatched to the Canadian Re-inforcement unit where the young officer who had guessed at Dieppe when it was Rutter was already in residence.

On August 15, two Canadian infantrymen were arrested by the police in Seaford on charges of assault. When placed in cells they announced: "You can't keep us here. We're going on a raid to Dieppe next Wednesday." At the request of Roberts, this pair was kept in jail until the raid was over.

One of the most serious breaches occurred when the Intelligence Section of the Royal Regiment of Canada handed over a security area to the Intelligence Section of the 48th Highlanders with the remark: "You can have the job. We're going to Dieppe." The innocent recipients of this titbit had to be confined to their camp until after the raid, when disciplinary action was taken against the offenders.

Another court-martial followed the stupidity of a sergeant in the Fusiliers Mont-Royal who, unbeknown to his comrades, rented a room in a Brighton boarding-house where he entertained girl friends. Four days before the raid he paid his rent up to date and moved out, telling the landlady that he was going on a raid to France and would not be back. Indignant at such careless talk, she called the Brighton police to report the indiscretion.

But most serious of all was the amazing disregard of elementary security by a senior Royal Navy lieutenant-commander who had been briefed on August 10 and given a copy of the naval operations orders to study. He placed them in his pocket the next evening and went ashore in Newhaven to meet friends at a local hotel. He became drunk, took them out of his pocket to show off before his friends, and left them lying on the bar when his party moved on to another place. About a minute later officers of the Royal Regiment arrived, saw the orders, and were about to take action when the naval officer rushed back to claim them. He drank so heavily that night that when he returned to his ship at dawn he could not remember where he had been. Security agents placed him under arrest until after the raid. Because medical evidence revealed him to be on the edge of a nervous breakdown, he was subsequently invalided out of the service.

The security problems were innumerable, and one of the most awkward concerned the question of press representatives on the raid. The effect of a military operation upon public opinion was considered to be inseparable from the operation itself. The Germans had repeatedly employed their own interpretation of military operations to portray successful British actions as failures, and on this basis the public relations aspect of Jubilee was an essential part of the military plan.

On August 12 a meeting was held at the War Office, attended by representatives of the Political Warfare Executive, the British Ministry of Information, 1st Canadian Army headquarters, and Eisenhower's public relations staff.

Their discussion centred on how best to publicize the raid once the troops returned to England and how to counter enemy attempts to belittle it, whether it were successful or otherwise. It was agreed that the Political Warfare Executive should broadcast to the French people as soon as possible after the raid had started, warning them that it was not an invasion. This was thought necessary to avoid costly uprisings leading to German reprisals.

It was also intended to play down the raid in news releases so that it could be judged in proper perspective in relation to other areas of the war. No press interviews were to be permitted with the fighting personnel taking part except in specially selected cases. On the other hand, as comprehensive a press coverage as possible was needed so that the stories of independent observers could be used to counteract enemy propaganda. It was eventually decided to invite nine correspondents: two British, three Canadian, and four American.

As only a few U.S. Rangers would be involved, Eisenhower's team had asked for space for only one American correspondent. But Mc-Naughton's representative, Major C. S. Wallace, insisted that there should be wider coverage in the United States and offered to accommodate three more, because McNaughton "wished to have U.S. correspondents with the Canadian party."

It was further arranged to provide space for one Canadian photographer, one American magazine writer, and three broadcasters, one each from Britain, Canada, and the United States.

At Eisenhower's personal intervention the number of American troops participating should be kept secret, ostensibly to prevent alarm and despondency in the United States if a good number of them were to be killed, wounded, or captured. In his capacity as the Commanding General, European Theatre of Operations, he insisted that the handful of Rangers be referred to in all communiques as "a detachment from a U.S. Ranger Battalion" and that all news releases concerning them should be issued by United States Army headquarters.

When the Anglo-Canadian representatives agreed to these conditions the way was clear for United States public relations experts to flagrantly expand the "detachment" into the bulk of the force. Combined Operations were to admit too late and very ruefully that they should have countered by insisting that a "guidance memorandum" be issued to American newspapers "making clear that a small number of American troops were participating. Failure to do so caused a temporary over-emphasis in American newspaper headlines . . . ," a polite way of saying that their own public relations team had been outsmarted. It is difficult to imagine how they could have controlled the Americans anyway when the story involved such historic impact as the first American soldiers to land in Europe since 1917.

Special security arrangements were made to cover the assembly and departure of the press party. They were to be conducted to destinations far away from the actual embarkation ports where they would stay until the last minute. When actually sealed aboard their ships they would be briefed and informed that "as representatives of a Free Press they could report events as they saw them, honestly and fearlessly, within the limitations permitted by considerations of security."

The Political Warfare Executive was also asked by the conference to invite a Russian war correspondent, Leon Bondarenko, then in London, so that the Soviet Union might have an accurate report by its own eye-witness newspaperman. This was a direct instruction from the War Cabinet, designed to mollify Russian demands for a second front. Bondarenko was summoned to the Foreign Office on August 14 and told that if he cared to hold himself in readiness, Combined Operations would be delighted to have him as a guest on their next operation.

He replied: "I require a full briefing for submission to my editor in Moscow. He will decide if I should accept."

It was explained that for security reasons such a briefing would be out of the question, but that other Allied newspapermen had accepted the conditions and he would be welcome in their ranks."

"I must have the briefing," he said. "Also unless the operation you talk about is the second front, and your armies are going across the Channel to stay, I will not go. The Russian people are not interested in your raids. We are interested only in invasion."

Bondarenko reiterated this position at two more meetings, and eventually the Political Warfare Executive reported to the propaganda planners: "In view of Mr Bondarenko's attitude we do not consider it in the best interests of security to discuss the battle plan with him. We regret to advise that his refusal to go be accepted."

The political propaganda aspects were particularly troublesome. The operation was to be undertaken at a time when the public were demanding an end to pin-prick raids and the launching of a second front; the Prime Minister was preparing for a visit to Moscow, and his talks with Stalin would be associated with the raid; and because Canadian troops were involved, there was the probability that the enemy would claim that Britain was fighting to the last Canadian.

It was obvious that the Germans would be quick to say the raid had been an attempted invasion and they would point to the use of tanks as clear evidence that this was the case. In consequence the British public, then in a militant mood, could be expected to growl that "if they can stage one this big, what's wrong with going the whole hog?"

The propaganda experts of the Foreign Office were unanimous in their opinion that the best solution to the problem lay in having no raid at all just then. The next best thing, of course, would be a sensational military success, but at the very least they would require the accomplishment of objectives which would be so obviously important that they could be easily explained to the public. In fact, of course, the objectives were not of a type to capture public imagination, and the vastly more important intangibles of experience gained and lessons learned would have to be carefully worded to counter-balance any large loss of life.

Having considered these possibilities, there was nothing the Foreign Office could do but wait for the outcome, pounce upon the successes, and exploit them before the German propaganda machine could begin to denigrate the raid. Whatever happened, Allied propaganda would have to be swift, comprehensive, exciting, and believable. Having reached such obviously intelligent conclusions, this extremely active and thoroughly professional group of political propagandists was to lose the initiative from the outset and never quite regain it.

III

While these organizational activities were taking place, planning was continuing at the Force Commanders level, and units of the 2nd Division were being given further intensive assault training – away from the coast.

The shapes of landing-craft were marked out in white tape on the slopes of the Sussex Downs, and dummy embarkation and disembarkation drills went on from dawn till dusk, punctuated only by forced marches or occasional dashes into the face of "defenders" firing live ammunition.

They speculated no more than was usual among troops removed from battle; rumours were inevitable – they always are – but they were generally convinced that like other divisions in the growing armies occupying Britain they were being kept in a state of readiness for a second front, should it prove feasible at some future date. There were rumours of another raid, but it seems that only a few ever considered the possibility that they might still go to Dieppe.

The first briefing conference was confined on August 1 to Brigadiers Southam and Sherwood Lett, and Johnny Andrews who, as tank commander, had to be briefed early. Roberts opened proceedings with a warning that an emergency operation, planned for that month, might be ordered to take place at short notice. He said the same personnel would participate as in the case of Rutter, and that the objectives would be as before. When Churchill Mann unveiled the same model of Dieppe that they had seen on the Isle of Wight, these three senior 2nd Division officers were shocked into murmurs of astonishment.

Sherwood Lett, now Chief Justice of the British Columbia Supreme Court, told me: "I had originally thought that while it would be a difficult and risky operation, if the passage by sea could be made safely and tactical surprise could be attained, it had a chance for success. But after the exercises on the Isle of Wight I had realized that even with good luck casualties would be extremely heavy. When the fact that the actual Dieppe operation was on again sank in, I knew at once that we were in for it."

After the changes in the plan had been explained, the three listeners protested forcibly at the loss of heavy air bombardment. Both Roberts and Mann did their best to convince them that the essence of success would be surprise, that it was more important to preserve this element than to alert the enemy with indiscriminate bombing prior to the landings, but neither Lett nor Southam nor Andrews were impressed, and said so.

They were, however, somewhat mollified by the switch to a one-tide operation entailing only five hours ashore, and the conference ended with all three expressing serious doubts about the wisdom of the plan as it now stood.

Three days later Roberts held a second briefing which this time included the brigadiers, accompanied by the battalion commanders, a few selected RAF officers who would be concerned with giving air support, and by the Commando leaders, Durnford-Slater and Lovat. Flanking Roberts on a raised dais were McNaughton and Crerar, who had decided to be on hand should there be serious objections raised from the floor of the meeting.

The scale model of Dieppe was displayed again, with special markers pointing to changes in the positions of enemy defences. During the intervening weeks, the Photographic Interpretation Centre had carried on a continuous examination of photographs taken daily by air reconnaissance. Kendall, commanding the Centre, had found that these later photographs revealed some minor differences from the earlier ones and had altered the model accordingly.

The articulate Mann, acting as briefing officer for the unassuming Roberts, explained that all officers going ashore were to leave their identity cards and personal papers with the senior officer of the ship in which they sailed; it would be unwise to collect them prior to sailing in case of rumours being spread in consequence. Other ranks were to carry only their paybooks ashore, a strange instruction because the Canadian Militia Paybook contained details of a soldier's unit, his training, and date of mobilization and constituted, in fact, a complete record of his service. This sort of information was in direct contradiction to the "name, rank, and number" policy which had been instilled in all Allied formations.

Mann also distributed copies of his military detailed plan which included an order permitting Southam and Lett to take ashore two copies each. In retrospect the risks inherent in such an order seem too self-evident to need comment. The very idea of a heavy book of operational orders being taken ashore on the most hazardous raid yet contemplated is ridiculous. Were the brigadiers to prowl the beaches, checking the positions of their units against pages so-and-so of the military plan? Were they to time-check the movements of their men by constant reference to these bulky books?

General Roberts has since told me: "I recognized immediately after this conference that perhaps the taking of orders ashore might be unwise. I instructed Church Mann to amend the order to say that no copies were to be taken ashore, but certain commanders could take extracts out of the plan if they thought them necessary for the proper execution of their duties. Having given this order I had no time then to check whether it was carried out. Apparently, it wasn't."

The order, as it was retained, read:

> Each Brigade headquarters is authorized to carry ashore two complete copies of the Military Detailed Plan. . . . No other copies will be taken ashore and any information required for the conduct of the operation will be carried as notes. Maps and photographs will be carried as required for operational purposes. *All ranks will ensure that no orders, maps, photographs, operational documents or notes fall into enemy hands.*

Among the copies of the plan distributed were Nos. 37 and 38, both given to Brigadier Southam. Copy No. 38 was to be handed back to

Intelligence officers in England after the raid by a naval officer who had found it in a derelict landing-craft; the other was to lead to bitter exchanges between the Canadian, British, and German governments, which resulted in Canadian prisoners being shackled in German camps and German prisoners being shackled in Canadian camps.

Copy No. 37 did just what it was not supposed to do by falling, almost literally, into enemy hands, and the Germans were not long in finding Appendix L, paragraph 4, No. B/2. This was an order to the assault forces saying: "*Wherever possible, prisoners' hands will be tied to prevent destruction of their documents.*"

This was not a Canadian order, nor was it approved in any manner by General Roberts. He had opposed its inclusion in the detailed plan during Rutter but had been told that as Combined Operations raiders had found it to be sometimes necessary in the past, it should be inserted to ensure that the special parties were not deprived of valuable papers.

Early in August, Roberts had instructed Churchill Mann to remove the order from the plan for Jubilee, yet it remained. Ham Roberts has since said: "I even spoke to Mountbatten about it, but he replied that one of the main purposes of the operation was to bring back information. It should be left in to ensure that captured documents were not destroyed. As far as I can remember, Church Mann mentioned my instruction to Mountbatten who then said it had to stay. Church probably knew that if he brought this reply back to me there would be a crisis with Combined Ops. Thinking back, it's probably correct to say that the order was retained at Mountbatten's insistence."

Roberts was not alone in objecting to the order. Following this conference, one of his divisional Intelligence officers visited each unit to give lectures on how to bind prisoners. He was Captain T. H. Insinger, a short, round, former Dutch army officer who had emigrated to Canada in the early 'thirties. He demonstrated how to tie a man's thumbs behind his back, with the binding passed round his neck in such a way that if he attempted to free his hands his neck might snap, and if he should jerk suddenly forward he could easily break his thumbs.

Cec Merritt told me: "He seemed to really enjoy showing us how effective this method could be. But he really excelled himself with demonstrations on how to stick toothpicks beneath a man's finger-nails to persuade shy prisoners to talk. Needless to say we threw away the toothpicks he left with us." Insinger's role in the raid was to go ashore with Lett's 4th Brigade headquarters and establish a prisoner-of-war cage on White Beach.

Jubilee gathered momentum as preparations entered their final

stages. At a third briefing, which included 2nd Division company commanders on August 10, the battalion officers gave vent to their feelings
about the order to bind prisoners.

"Forget it," snapped Roberts, impatiently. "You've got pistols or Sten
guns. If your prisoners give you trouble, use 'em."

Crerar was also galvanized into a whirl of activity. That morning
he saw Mountbatten, in the afternoon, Leigh-Mallory and Hughes-
Hallett, and wound up in the evening at Horsham with Roberts and
Churchill Mann. Next day he wrote to McNaughton:

> I have to day gone over in detail the plans for the exercise, as
> now agreed to by Naval, Army and Air Force Commanders and
> am satisfied that the revisions in respect to the previous exercise
> plans add, rather than detract, to the soundness of the plan as
> a whole. I am, therefore, of the opinion that given an even break
> in luck and good navigation, the demonstration should prove
> successful.

Crerar was writing as the immediate military authority over Roberts
to the highest military authority over Jubilee. His comments implied
approval of the plans, satisfaction with Roberts and the units he commanded for the operation, and confidence in the outcome.

All it needed for the raid to become officially timed for dawn on the
18th or 19th were McNaughton's acceptance of the military plan and
formal consent to the use of Canadian troops. Leigh-Mallory and
Hughes-Hallett informed Mountbatten on the 16th that the naval and
air force plans were ready, and that afternoon the Canadian Army
Commanders drove to 1st Corps headquarters at Leatherhead for a final
review of the overall combined plan with Crerar and Roberts. He returned to London the same night and wrote officially to Crerar:

> I now confirm that I am satisfied with these plans and with the
> arrangements made in all respects, and I sanction the participa-
> tion therein of elements of 2nd Canadian Division, 14th Cana-
> dian Army Tank Battalion and other attached Canadian per-
> sonnel as detailed by you.

McNaughton has since explained that while he accepted full responsibility for what subsequently happened, he had done so only on the
general basis of his confidence in the officers concerned – in an immediate sense, Crerar, and Roberts. In practice, he has said, the extent of
his actual control over the planning was very slight.

This is not quite the case. Both he and Crerar had been associated with the enterprise from that moment three months before when they had become involved in Rutter planning. Both had intervened strongly then to keep control over the employment of their troops and both had been kept fully informed by the Combined Operations Adviserate and planning syndicate. Both had attended the various rehearsal exercises and had criticized freely; in fact, McNaughton had been so impressed with the final form of Rutter that he had formally sanctioned the Canadian role, while Crerar had not only been in the chain of command throughout, but had once written that he would undertake it himself.

From mid July, McNaughton had been designated the responsible military commander for Jubilee, an authority he had delegated to Crerar, who had played a Montgomery to his Paget. During the entire period of Rutter-Jubilee they had made no attempts to either condemn or amend the military plan.

It is true that the month of Jubilee gave little enough time in which to retrain troops had the frontal assault been omitted, but that does not mean it could not be done. An alternative plan, for flank attacks only, existed at Combined Operations Headquarters and could have been dusted off if either had really wanted it. Security, moreover, would have been less of a problem because training in different assault procedures would have been associated by the troops with a different target.

It seems strange indeed that these two very senior and distinguished Canadian officers should so depreciate their share of responsibility for the planning. They may never have made a decisive impact upon the plan, but their encounter with it was far more than a mere gentle caress.

Equally important was the lack of heavy air bombardment and naval fire support to soften the defences, a problem that could have been tackled forcibly without fear of jeopardizing the plan. Oddly enough, everyone was concerned about it and no one did anything to give the assault the sort of fire support it must have to succeed.

IV

The profusion of Allied plans, proposals, counter-proposals, and projects for taking the initiative in the conduct of the war crystallized that second week in August into two definite operations for 1942:

Dieppe and North Africa. Eisenhower quit the ranks of the Combined Commanders to start planning for the North African venture; the Army Commander of Reigate bade farewell to the Canadians in his South-Eastern Command and left England to seek out a more romantic title – Montgomery of Alamein. There is little doubt, if some of his former staff officers are to be believed, that he was almost grateful to Mc-Naughton for ridding him of responsibility for Jubilee; it is also likely that it was the sort of gratitude the Canadian Army Commander could do without.

Montgomery, having once recommended that the operation be cancelled for good, would not have accepted any further responsibility for it anyway, and it is apparent in retrospect that he held the new chain of command in no esteem at all. But what Montgomery could not have known at the time was that Churchill had the raw mission of breaking the news to Stalin that there would be no second front in 1942 and had virtually demanded of his military advisers that something be undertaken to make it more palatable. There had to be a demonstration of Allied offensive intentions somewhere soon, and there was nothing available to the generals, the admirals, and the air marshals but Dieppe.

Diplomatic niceties required that the Stalin-Churchill talks should not be linked in any way with a raid in strength against France; to do so would be tantamount to admitting that Britain and America were dancing to Russia's tune, that they were willing to gamble away lives on some reckless operation simply to placate their Eastern ally.

Yet the relationship between the two events is too striking now to be ignored, so much so that the impression of Dieppe being directly connected with these talks on August 12-13 is both powerful and persistent. It is even encouraged by Churchill himself who wrote in his memoirs: "General Montgomery . . . was strongly of the opinion that it [Dieppe] should not be remounted, as the troops concerned had all been briefed and were now dispersed ashore. . . . However, I thought it most important that a large scale operation should take place this summer. . . ."

If the explosive impetus given to Jubilee was, in fact, generated from No. 10 Downing Street, it mattered not one whit whether Montgomery approved or not. Not even this, however, can explain satisfactorily why the legacy of a frontal assault, without adequate prior naval or air bombardment, which he left behind in England, should have been so readily accepted by his heirs, the senior Canadian commanders.

Before handing over his command, Montgomery made a minor concession of goodwill to Jubilee by obtaining from Roberts permission for Goronwy Rees to join the force as an observer. This officer, who had been his personal representative in the Rutter planning group, arrived at Portsmouth in mid August after an unpleasant trip by car from London.

His fellow passenger had been an American war correspondent who, according to an account he has written since, "grumbled at the inadequacy of the arrangements for the Press. This seemed to be for him the criterion by which he judged any military operation. . . . His criticisms seemed to leave a sour taste in his own mouth as well as mine and he washed them down with large draughts of whisky from a pocket flask. He was loud-mouthed, arrogant and over-bearing. . . . I did not like him and refused his offer to share his whisky."

At the tiny Channel port of Seaford, however, there was a sort of loose, brawling Anglo-American-Canadian accord between troopers of No. 3 Commando, U.S. Rangers under the command of Captain Roy Murray, and units of the 2nd Division.

Through Murray, the Commandos handled the Garand automatic rifle for the first time, Durnford-Slater being so delighted with it that Murray gave him one as a present and then had to distribute others among the blatantly envious officers of the unit.

Murray's orders, signed by Major Bill Darby on August 1, instructed him to place himself and his men under the temporary command of Durnford-Slater. While on this special duty the United States Army would pay the Ranger officers an allowance of six dollars a day and enlisted men four dollars. Second Lieutenant George P. Sunshine, adjutant of Darby's Rangers, was to ensure that Murray's men were not absent for longer than three weeks without an explanation in writing.

Major Peter Young, second-in-command of No. 3 Commando, remarked cheerfully: "There's no doubt about this show going on. The Yanks have set a time limit on their expense account."

The Canadians had been resident in the Seaford area ever since taking over the Sussex defences eighteen months before. Now they were treated to the sight of girls regarded as Canadian property parading with soft gaiety on the arms of Commandos and Rangers. Something had to give – something like the collective temper of a hundred-odd Canadians one night at the White Horse Hotel where two Ranger lieutenants had taken a pair of WRENS to dinner.

Two Commando troopers, who knew the girls and had been tossed aside once the Rangers arrived, attempted to break up the party. In the resulting *mêlée* the girls were kidnapped by Canadians who started a party of their own in the saloon bar. All would have ended merrily had the Canadians not also absconded with every bottle of wine in sight on the dining-room tables.

To the *maître d'hôtel* the theft of the girls was insignificant compared with the theft of the wine, and he summoned help, which arrived in the form of local police flying-squads and a company of Canadian Military Police. The wine was returned with good-humoured apologies on all sides, the police eventually retired without making arrests, and the remaining troops returned to the serious business of having fun. Only then was it discovered that the WRENS, by far the most attractive in Seaford, had been purloined by two Commandos and had been spirited away to continue their dinner elsewhere.

Brawls of this kind became so frequent in the days immediately prior to Jubilee that they hardly warranted attention, let alone the dignity of punishment. They were mostly good-natured affairs, and Durnford-Slater was never concerned about them until the night he was wakened in his billet by a noise beneath his bedroom. Putting on slippers and still only in pyjamas he crept downstairs to find what he described as "an enormous Canadian walking round the hall."

His account continued: "He had broken in through a small window. Fortunately he was extremely drunk, so I spoke to him nicely and gave him a little push into a comfortable armchair, where he slept most amiably. I started to telephone for the police and most unwisely ended my message with the words: 'I will detain him until you come.' This brought the Canadian to life in a big way and he jumped to his feet shouting, 'Detain me nothing. Say, I could knock hell out of you.' "

Durnford Slater, hardly a big man, was inclined to agree and faced the angry intruder with the intention of hitting him below the belt. There was, however, no need for such drastic action. The big Canadian became suddenly pleasant again and the Commando colonel was able to place a finger against his mighty chest, to push him gently back into the armchair. He slept there heavily until aroused by an elderly local constable with whom he departed in the best of humour.

It was in this period that the Jubilee planners decided to give the assault troops on the main beaches additional covering fire by mounting heavy machine guns in the bows of landing-craft. As they approached the touchdown, the machine guns would spray the buildings facing across the promenade and engage "targets of opportunity" while the ramps went down and the troops spilled out. The performance would be repeated during the withdrawal when the craft came in to re-embark the troops.

The Toronto Scottish (M.G.) Regiment, commanded by Lieutenant-

Colonel Guy Standish Gostling, was asked to provide 40 machine guns and 120 gunners to perform these duties. Before moving to Toronto in the late 'thirties, Guy Gostling, whose brother commanded the Camerons, was a well-known Winnipeg athlete who had been champion amateur wrestler of Manitoba, a prominent tennis-player, and captain of the Manitoba rugby team. When appointed to the Toronto Scottish he had promised his men they would never go into action without him.

With his regiment now brought into Jubilee he called on Roberts at Horsham and demanded to be allowed to accompany his men on the raid. Roberts demurred, but Gostling insisted until he extracted permission to cross the Channel in *Calpe* and transfer later to a landing-craft.

Young Daniel Doheny, who had been the "King's Messenger" between Churchill Mann's initial team at Combined Operations Headquarters in London and General Roberts in Cowes, was also to be rewarded for his services. While on leave in London he received a telephone call from 2nd Division headquarters telling him to report to Portsmouth for "a party." He packed his bags hurriedly, checked out of his hotel, and caught the next train from Victoria Station, by this time thoroughly excited and wondering what use he could possibly be to a couple of brigades of raiders. Other groups, sprinkled about London and the south of England, were receiving equally strange telephone calls inviting them to converge on Portsmouth for "a party."

The radar scientist who was to sail with the South Saskatchewan Regiment entrained from London without knowing that a member of the Special Operations Executive was in another compartment on the same train.

The mysterious jungle drums of the grey half-world of security agents, spies, and counter-spies, had somehow warned Air Ministry Intelligence of the distaste and reluctance with which Cec Merritt and Murray Osten were approaching the question of ensuring that their scientist didn't fall into enemy hands. They passed the problem to London's Baker Street where the colourful and secretive Special Operations Executive had its headquarters. The SOE was only too delighted to oblige by providing a secret agent who would not hesitate to kill, were it absolutely necessary, but actually there was another motive. The raid, it was promptly decided, would be an excellent opportunity to insert one of SOE's agents into France.

Combined Operations were also worried about the fate of the scientist and had sent a naval Intelligence officer to Horsham to make contact with Captain Insinger. The two verbally agreed that a Canadian Field Security sergeant should accompany the scientist ashore to see that he returned alive – or stayed behind, quite dead.

It can be assumed with some certainty that the scientist himself was quite unaware of what was planned for him; that Combined Operations had no idea what the Air Ministry had arranged; and that neither knew what soe intended. It is interesting to speculate on the consequences had the Canadian Field Security sergeant spotted the soe agent about to shoot the scientist. Perhaps it is better not to. The situation was much too weird for sane contemplation.

Other extraneous groups consisting of Ministry of Economic Warfare and Political Warfare Executive experts were also assembled at the embarkation ports and joined by detachments of Field Security personnel. Once landed, these groups would make their separate and independent ways into the town for scientific searches of hotels suspected of being German battalion headquarters or officers' billets.

Near Brighton was haughty Roedean, the famous girls' school which before the war had turned the daughters of England's noble families into well-mannered young ladies. Now its dormitories were occupied by odd, tensed characters who came for a few days, spoke little, and then vanished, often not to be seen again. Two special agents stepped out through its graceful portals one August morning, climbed into a waiting car, and drove to Newhaven where they were met by a four-man detachment from the 8th Canadian Recce Regiment, their bodyguard during the dash they would make across the main Dieppe beaches. Once in the town itself the agents would be on their own, with three hours in which to capture a senior German officer. Their purpose was disguised in orders by a cover story that they were to bring back samples of German uniforms so that the materials could be examined for evidence that German industry was running short of pure fabrics.

The French Commandos under the bank manager from New York, who had been confined to East Bridge House in Hampshire, another country mansion taken over by obscure, twilight organizations, left the same morning in a truck, bound for Newhaven. Seven of these were to interrogate French civilians, select up to twelve for evacuation and distribute among the population leaflets warning them that the attack was not an invasion but a reconnaissance in force.

Certain members of these curious groups were armed with flimsy pieces of paper on which Churchill Mann had written instructions in long-hand giving them priority for evacuation over everyone else in the raid. If captured, the troops would become prisoners of war; but if these men fell into enemy hands they would be treated as spies and,

at best, shot; at worst, tortured. Apart, therefore, from the value of
any information they might have acquired, it was considered proper
that they should have every help in getting away from the enemy and
back to England.

At the completion of their tasks they were to return to the main
beaches, get in touch with Brian McCool, the Principal Military Landing Officer, and produce these tissues of paper. McCool would then
arrange for their departure in the first available boat.

One such document, actually issued during Rutter, read:

SECRET   HQ 2 Cdn Div.
                                      28 June 42

To all concerned:

1. This is a written order to all ranks under comd 2 Cdn Div
   to provide accommodation for Capt James King RE and
   Lieutenant Jean Dupont *in priority to any other troops or
   persons wishing to leave the beaches. This includes their kit
   bags.*

2. It covers civilians under their authority NOT exceeding four
   i/c Capt. King or Lieut. Dupont.

[*Signed*]   Churchill Mann
             Lt-Col

Another of these documents signed by Mann instructed all ranks of
the Canadian forces to accord the bearer(s) every assistance in their
work, to help them with any materials or persons in their possession,
and to evacuate them freely.

Precisely what Captain King, Lieutenant Dupont, and the other
bearers would be carrying is not stated in records, but they could be
expected to bring back code books and files from various German
headquarters. I have been told privately by a source which must
remain anonymous that the limit of twelve civilians who could be
evacuated was set because it was known in advance who they would
be. It is possible that they were Allied agents warned by clandestine
radio to get out of Occupied Europe via Dieppe, or they may have
been Resistance leaders who could no longer operate successfully in
France but could be invaluable in England.

The Combined Operations policy on the question of whether or not
to evacuate any of the civilian population was, as a matter of principle, to avoid taking off anybody. Certain personnel selected in each
battalion were supplied with posters and leaflets informing the French

that no help from them was required. The military plan, however, admitted that some civilians might create scenes during the withdrawal in their attempts to be evacuated; therefore last-minute evacuation of "such individuals as cannot reasonably be left behind may be made on humanitarian grounds."

It said further: "Fisherfolk who have their own craft . . . should be permitted to put out to sea to return to England under the escort of our own forces. . . . No action should be attempted against French Quislings and all denunciations should be answered by stating that the French people themselves must deal with the matter."

Referring to questions about the establishment of a second front, all ranks were instructed to reply along these general lines: "You will be told when the time for action arrives. Meanwhile do nothing impetuous that may endanger your life or liberty but wait for the call to action. Take cover now, there is no occasion to join in this battle."

Unit commanders were warned that looting in any form would be strictly forbidden, as the political effect of any stories concerning looting might prove disastrous. "The German occupying troops," said the plan, "have set a high standard of individual behaviour, in spite of the organized looting of France. By this standard we shall be judged. Special passes will be signed by the Military Force Commander and issued to those individuals or parties who are authorized to bring back any articles."

The pieces of a plan hopefully called Jubilee were falling neatly into place; in a few days the mosaic of what was to be the most ambitious amphibious operation since Gallipoli would be complete.

V

The same night that McNaughton sanctioned Canadian participation, Hughes-Hallett mounted a minor raid, which had the unintended effect of drawing German attention away from the Dieppe area. For some time he had been the operational authority for a small select band of specialist raiders formed to probe the enemy and frighten him as swiftly and as often as possible. By mere chance the commander of the Raiding Force, as it was known, was ready for this excursion just at that time, and Hughes-Hallett, seeing no reason for it to interfere with Jubilee, sanctioned it. The raid was launched against the eastern side of the Contentin peninsula by six men, their faces blackened, their blue pullovers blending with the darkness; grenades and sub machine guns were their only weapons.

They came out of the mist on a particularly dark night at 3:00 a.m. on the 15th, landed from a motor gun boat in a small creek near Barfleur, and vanished into the dense thicket fringing the shore.

The German sentry manning a machine-gun post overlooking the beaches heard nothing until 3:40 a.m., when a noise in the brush at his rear snapped him awake. He swung his gun round and shouted: "Password – Give the password." Instead, he received four hand grenades and a burst of automatic fire.

The din wakened Sergeant Junge and six men sleeping in a guard hut two hundred yards to the north, alarming them so much they sprinted out to see what was wrong and found the machine-gunner firing wildly inland. They fired Verey lights and the glare revealed a group of men racing across a clearing in the brush. They gave chase, but the undergrowth was so thick pursuit soon became hopeless.

By now defences along the entire stretch of coast were alerted, and Junge's party returned to their action station at an anti-tank gun emplacement. As they manned the post, four dark figures rose to the rim of the sandbag parapet, loomed over them briefly, and then began firing. Only Sergeant Junge survived.

Another hundred yards away, four Germans manned a flak battery surrounded by barbed wire. Two raiders cut gaps in the wire, slithered through them, and flopped into the emplacement, firing up from the ground as they fell.

There were no German survivors this time. At 4:40 a.m. the roar of the gun boat's engines shattered the silence and the raiders were gone, leaving behind in the undergrowth pocket lamps, signal horns, explosives, grenades, and ammunition – enough to convince the Germans that a beach reconnaissance had taken place.

The official report of the German 589th Infantry Regiment stationed along that sector of the coast confirmed the success of the feint.

". . . the object of the British Commando raid was obviously a reconnaissance of the defence posts on the North-East coast in preparation for a subsequent larger operation," it said. "The whole enemy undertaking . . . bore the stamp of lack of planning, ignorance of the terrain and of haste. The raiders took no safety precautions and threw grenades at random. If they return in strength we shall be ready for them."

The raiders had achieved, in fact, a perfect feint for the big job at Dieppe. From the 15th on, the German army in France was placed in first-degree readiness for invasion along the Contentin peninsula and the coast of Normandy: the precise sectors that the Allies were to use for invasion two years later. At Dieppe only normal precautions against possible raids were in force.

Not even Field Marshal von Rundstedt, Commander-in-Chief, considered Dieppe the sort of port an invading army would use. "Most unsuitable place for invasion," he had told staff officers in Paris earlier that year.

Ready for the Punch

I

On April 6, only two days after a raid on Dieppe had been first considered at Combined Operations Headquarters, a British secret agent in Marseilles instructed a French Resistance network to report on the movements of German panzer columns in the Rouen-Amiens-Dieppe area. A traitor in the network reported the assignment to German Intelligence headquarters in Dijon, and arrangements were made to feed the agent with false information. This was the first of sporadic attempts to utilize spies as a source of intelligence on enemy defences at Dieppe.

Throughout Rutter and Jubilee, planning was based mainly on information derived from air reconnaissance photographs by Wing Commander Kendall's Photographic Interpretation Centre. This unit's work had begun at the moment the raid was blessed by the Chiefs of

Staff, had continued without halt ever since, and would not end until the last photograph had been analysed on the eve of the raid itself.

Information from spies was sketchy, impossible to check, and therefore unreliable; spies could be instructed in only the most general terms and had to be kept in ignorance of specific Allied intentions so that in the event of capture they would not possess secrets which might be extracted by torture.

Secret agents, however, did constitute a source that could not be totally ignored, and on April 30 another attempt was made to use their services. A spy based in Grenoble was ordered to find out what German units were stationed along the Channel coast, particularly in the Pas de Calais area. His contact in Vichy France proved to be yet another German counter-espionage agent and, although he never knew it, his replies to London were drafted by German Intelligence.

On July 22, another British agent met a renowned and trusted French Resistance leader in Angers and impressed upon him the need for a continuous flow of information concerning German defences along the Channel coast. The Frenchman, however, was actually the district head of German Intelligence and is known to have so interested his superior with an account of the meeting that he was taken to Paris to give a personal report to Field Marshal von Rundstedt, German Commander-in-Chief, West.

London was not entirely unaware of the extent to which German Intelligence had infiltrated into French Resistance groups, and information from agents was never accepted unless supported by evidence from more reliable sources, such as interrogations of prisoners-of-war or foreign businessmen with impeccable reputations.

Kendall's team at Medmenham was, therefore, the prime source, but there was an obvious limit to what information could be obtained from a photograph. This is partly confirmed by German Intelligence documents captured after the war, one of which said:

> Enemy inquiries during the four months prior to the raid did not, however, admit the presumption that it was at Dieppe that the enemy would attack. For there are also numerous other enemy inquiries on record at Intelligence agencies in France, and in addition to this, many intercepted traitors' messages referring in similar fashion to almost the entire coastal area of Europe.

Despite the complete lack of eye-witness reports from secret agents, the maps and photographs compiled and analysed at Medmenham were remarkably accurate up to a point. They showed enemy artillery installations, machine-gun nests, road blocks, anti-tank emplacements, flak batteries, barbed wire fences, and obstacles blocking exits from the beaches and promenades into the town of Dieppe and its adjacent villages.

But the numbers of guns and their calibre were in some instances seriously under-estimated; a considerable number were not even located. This was not Medmenham's fault, but rather that of the Canadian and Combined Operations planners who failed to take these omissions of interpretation into account.

Throughout the planning, air reconnaissance photographs had revealed entrances of the caves in the cliff faces of the wing headlands overlooking the Dieppe beaches. Apart from drawing attention to the possibilities of underground passageways leading into the town itself, and indicating that one immense cavern under the East Headland had been turned into a torpedo storage dump for local units of the German navy, the planners gave these caves only cursory attention.

The assault forces were to make the costly discovery that each one held a heavy, long-range machine gun and that the cliff faces were riddled with fire-power, often difficult to pinpoint and on the whole impossible to destroy.

Information from espionage sources was mostly old, some of it dating back to the summer of 1941. It had been analysed by Combined Operations and compiled into a document which eventually reached Major Reginald Unwin, of McNaughton's staff and one of the few professional Intelligence officers in the Canadian Army, who became the expert adviser on German defences at Dieppe to the detailed military planners. A cautious realist, Unwin tended to see guns behind every rock or bush shown on the maps and often warned that the absence of confirmed enemy defences in an area did not preclude the possibility of it being heavily defended.

As the eager planners regarded him as too pessimistic, a wide gulf developed between them – so wide, in fact, that when the final appreciation of Dieppe's defences was submitted for inclusion in the plan, Unwin refused to sign it. Because Unwin has since died, I have relied upon Major John Robinson, now of Ottawa, who was then an ærial survey specialist acting as liaison officer between Kendall's photographic interpreters at Medmenham and the military planners, to explain why Unwin took this peculiar stand.

"Reg was very worried about what he considered unjustifiable optimism about the defences," Robinson told me. "He didn't accept the Combined Operations analysis at face value and inserted into it warnings of his own. I'm pretty certain that he drew attention to the dangers of the caves in the cliff faces and felt they were not properly appreciated. In any event, his subsequent detailed report on Dieppe's defences was passed from one staff to another until it finally came back with most of his warnings discounted, even deleted. On this basis he simply felt it was impossible to take responsibility for what he firmly believed to be other people's mistakes and so declined to sign it."

There was also a serious under-estimation of the strength of German units guarding the ten-mile stretch of coast between Varengeville and Berneval, including Dieppe itself, for reasons best known to those who took part in the shadowy war of subterfuge and treachery.

In the confusion that followed the fall of France in 1940, an enterprising French pigeon-fancier had managed to escape in a fishing-boat, bringing with him to England several cages of his pets. By some devious means he and his homing pigeons found their way into a mysterious organization which could put his pets to some use. If his loft in France were cared for by friends, the pigeons could be used to fly in messages to be picked up by couriers and delivered to a secret destination in Paris.

Some weeks were spent in placing the loft in reliable hands and establishing a new pigeon postal system to be used as a spare means of communication with Occupied Europe, mostly to send confirmations of brief radio signals.

All might have been well but for the bad form of Abwehr (German Military Intelligence) agents who, late in 1941, broke British codes used in clandestine wireless contact between London and Paris which, in turn, led them to the terminal loft of the pigeon post. One of the first carrier pigeons they caught arrived in February 1942, carrying a message confirming that London wished to know which ports between Calais and Le Havre were being used as torpedo-boat bases. The message was picked up by an unsuspecting courier who was followed to Paris, where he visited a Special Operations Executive radio operator. Both were captured and the radio man bought his life by promising to continue to work under German instructions. Since then, the Abwehr Central Intelligence Control Station (France) had been playing GV Radio Game Porto 11 – participation in secret British wireless traffic by intercepting real messages from London and dictating false replies for their obliging captive operator to send.

This was the method used to misinform British Intelligence about the strength of defences in the coastal areas of France, that of Dieppe included. Abwehr counter-espionage agents concocted a series of emblems for mythical divisions and sent their descriptions to London, one of which said that "there are troops in the area of Dieppe who carry as their totems on vehicles a white church with a small tower." In sending this message, the operator used the term *nef* (nave) which can also be interpreted as barque or ship. British Intelligence searched its files and found that the German 110th Infantry Division displayed a white Viking galley as an insignia, and informed Combined Operations that this division manned the Dieppe defences. Partial confirmation came from the interrogation of a junior German infantry general captured in North Africa who admitted having served on the Russian front prior to being transferred to the Afrika Corps. He said he had seen this insignia on vehicles of the 110th in the East, but understood that the division had been withdrawn to France for regrouping. Further secret radio reports from France indicated that the 110th was holding the Dieppe defended area with fewer than two thousand troops in the port itself, a believable figure because it implied that the division had been badly mauled in Russia.

It was not until the raid was over that the mistakes became all too clearly evident, that in fact Dieppe was garrisoned by nearly twice as many troops comprising the 302nd Infantry Division, the 110th being on the Russian front. The 302nd Division had occupied that stretch of Channel coast since April 1941, when it had taken up defensive positions there in accordance with a High Command order that said: "The use of strong Army and Air forces on the Eastern Front may induce the British to launch summer operations against the coast of the occupied West area or against Norway. . . . Daring British action can be expected."

The division was commanded by a professional soldier with a considerable reputation for offensive action and an impressive record of victory behind him: Major-General Conrad Haase, a tall southern German dedicated to the proposition that if Hitler wouldn't let him cross the Channel to occupy England, then no Englishman would set foot in Occupied Europe. Rather hopefully, it might seem, a few days after taking over the Dieppe sector, he issued a divisional order saying:

> In view of the fact that the endangered ports of Le Treport and Dieppe will not be attacked directly by the enemy, but rather by landing attempts at nearby points and the formation of a bridgehead, these aspects must be explored and preparations made for fire on the areas in question.

The order went on to define the three stages of alert which would warn of pending action: Continuous State of Alert (normal routine); Threatened Danger (officers and men to be ready within reach); and Highest Degree of Alert (action stations).

In September 1941 the Todt Organization moved into the Dieppe area to begin construction of a sector of the West Wall, building gun emplacements, pillboxes, artillery strongpoints, and concrete fortifications. General Haase held exercises in which his troops carried out dummy attacks on the Puits, Dieppe, and Pourville beaches to test the defences, and as a result ordered that barbed wire and brick walls were to be built across every gully giving exit from beaches.

During January, February, and March 1942, the wing headlands on either side of Dieppe were turned into fortified strongpoints; artillery emplacements were erected at the "Farm of the Four Winds" between Dieppe and Pourville; and the caves in cliff faces along the entire stretch of coast were filled with machine guns, anti-tank guns, ammunition, and provisions. Their crews could be self-supporting for a minimum of forty-eight hours and had the advantage of being able to run their guns forward to fire and then withdraw them for protection against counter-bombardment. An obsolete French tank, which could still be used as a pillbox, was cemented into a harbour mole with its gun turret capable of covering an arc ranging from seaward to the beaches.

On March 10 Haase issued another order declaring the area "Fortress Dieppe," with the town itself garrisoned by two battalions of the 571st Infantry Regiment, then spread between Dieppe and Pourville for a depth of seven miles. Defences in the town consisted of a series of pillboxes lining the promenade and covering road junctions for a width of 1,500 yards, while the beaches themselves would be swept by enfilade fire from the wing headlands.

Defence posts in buildings along the sea front were positioned to fire only at approaching or retreating landing-craft. They were to act as decoys to draw enemy fire, while the crossfire from the wing headlands cut down attackers who managed to land. Sprinkled among the beach and promenade defences were special positions for snipers and grenade-throwers.

The concrete pillboxes were built to standard German army requirements: more than six feet high, one and a half feet thick, and embedded into the ground so that only four feet showed above it. The road blocks denying exit from the promenade were eight feet high and four feet thick, with snipers' platforms built into the rear sides.

Two rows of barbed wire about fifteen feet apart covered the main beaches, the first row nearest the sea consisting of triple dannert backed by a single apron fence, and the second lying along the sea wall was seven feet deep. The wire was heavy concertina type which would spring back into place even after it had been crossed by tanks.

Some 14,000 mines had been laid in the Dieppe area, but mostly in small coves with gullies leading inland and in the vicinity of Le Treport. There were no mines on the main beaches, at Pourville or at Puits, but the Varengeville and Berneval beaches were sparsely mined.

Booby traps were scattered liberally along the coast. Dummy cans of pineapple, purporting to come from Malaya and British Guiana but actually filled with anti-personnel explosives, were left lying about the beaches as though forgotten; trip wires were strung through the grass atop the headlands with charges clipped at intervals along their lengths; and other types of explosive traps were connected to the doors of empty houses or left lying in drawers or cupboards.

Surprisingly at such a critical time, one in which the Germans expected the Allies to take the initiative, the 302nd Division had more than its usual share of raw recruits, some of whom had been through only four weeks of training before being sent into forward defence positions. Thirteen hundred had arrived in late July and eleven hundred more on August 12; indeed there were so many recruits that the division had been given a special recruit training officer to institute such basic classes as one entitled "Recognition of Badges of Rank."

Although the units were up to strength, some even over their proper establishment, the German element was thinned down by the addition of Poles, mostly of poor physique, some having been rejected for service in the Polish army prior to 1939. The 571st Regiment had two Poles for every eight Germans, and in one battalion the ratio was as high as fifty-fifty.

While Haase's own headquarters were at Envermeu, inland from Dieppe, the 571st Regiment responsible for the Dieppe-Pourville area consisted of one headquarters battalion, two infantry battalions, one engineer battalion, one artillery battalion, three batteries of coastal guns, fifteen batteries of heavy howitzers, numerous light howitzers, flak and mortar batteries, and innumerable machine-gun posts. Ancilliary units included German navy marines, a penal company of two hundred soldiers serving hard labour as punishment, and sixty military police guards.

In reserve along the entire 45-mile front occupied by the division were four infantry regiments totalling approximately six thousand

men and a tank company. If he needed it, Haase could call upon the
10th Panzer Division at Amiens to deliver the final annihilating blow
to presumptuous invaders.

The heights overlooking Dieppe and the sea front itself were transformed into six major strongpoints, each blocking approaches from
inland as well as from the sea and designed to meet Field Marshal von
Rundstedt's orders that landing forces should be "defeated while still
off the coast if possible, but on the beaches at the very latest."

After the Combined Operations Commando raid on St Nazaire at the
end of March, enemy coastal defence units became extremely nervous
and sensitive to rumours of further Allied raids along the Channel
coast. The German High Command issued a directive saying that the
St Nazaire incident should put "all soldiers on their mettle" and concluded: "The Fuehrer has information from abroad to the effect that
the British and Americans are planning a great surprise. He sees two
possibilities: either a landing or the use of new massed bombers."

This typical piece of intuition from Berlin was followed by a period
of intensive defence construction along the entire West Wall, various
types of fortifications being clearly defined. Dieppe defences were of
three categories: "Resistance Nests" were fortified machine-gun emplacements or pillboxes, completely self-contained and designed to
cover a pre-arranged line of fire; "Strongpoint" was the name given to
several Resistance Nests, manned in total by about seventy men, and
including flak batteries and light artillery, also with predicted lines of
fire; and "Defended Areas," defined as all-round defence systems including concrete fortifications and embracing entire ports.

Under this pattern, the heavy coastal batteries at Varengeville and
Berneval and the airfield at St Aubin were transformed into Strongpoints; Puits and Pourville defences were divided into three Resistance
Nests apiece; and Dieppe, as a Defended Area, included in its defences
all the other types.

Records of the 302nd Division disclose that General Haase was
acutely conscious during April of the probability of Allied landing
operations, and in the next few weeks rumours and predictions began
to circulate wildly. Haase's diary has an entry for May 19 saying that
"a British landing operation under the command of Vice-Admiral
Mountbatten is being planned"; another entry on the 24th said that the
German Foreign Office had warned of an imminent British landing on
the west coast of Jutland.

The flood of rumours reached full spate by the middle of June when
Haase recorded that according to reports of German secret agents,

large-scale landings could be expected "around June 20" near the Hague, near La Rochelle, and "possibly at Le Treport."

The latter was of particular interest to Haase because it was within his defence sector and close to Dieppe. During June-July the Allied clamour for a second front led the Germans to believe that this was the "great surprise" envisaged by Hitler, Haase being so convinced that he issued an order which said:

> According to reliable sources the British intend the installation of a Second Front in Belgium and France prior to June 22. This is confirmed by other reports which indicate that preparations for an invasion are being carried out in England at high pressure.

In those critical weeks, British Intelligence replied to the false information it was receiving from France by feeding German Intelligence with equally false information through known agents. The Political Warfare Executive of the Foreign Office deliberately intensified its war of nerves on the German occupation forces, using the psychological principle that the more likely a major operation in the near future was made to appear, the more alarmed the Germans would become, wearying their forces in the process of sounding the Highest Degree of Alert almost every night. They succeeded to the extent that had the raid on Dieppe taken place as originally contemplated in Rutter it is quite probable the outcome would have been precisely the same, or even worse than it was in the end.

An appreciation of Allied invasion intentions made by von Rundstedt's staff on June 23 drew attention to air reconnaissance reports of large assemblies of shipping off the south coast of England in the regions of Portsmouth, Poole, Southampton, and Portland. They coupled this information with an outbreak of French Resistance sabotage of railway tracks in the coastal areas and with the arrest of twelve Resistance leaders who were alleged to be planning a major outbreak of sabotage activity between Calais and Cherbourg. Their report said: "These incidents can be linked to indicate a planned British landing operation."

There was some justification for the fears of the German High Command that an invasion attempt was about to be launched. The *Luftwaffe* reconnaissance squadrons, in the finest bravado tradition of that service, had reported the number of Allied ships assembled at 2,802 – a ridiculous implication of meticulous counting by the pilots of the few reconnaissance aircraft which came even close to British shores.

Yet it had such a ring of Aryan thoroughness about it that Hitler immediately believed a major operation to be pending. On June 29 he directed that defences along the French coast be strengthened as a "large-scale Anglo-American landing must be reckoned with, which will have as its object the creation of a Second Front, this being required from the enemy's point of view for political reasons, both internal and external."

During July things went well for the Germans on the Russian front, and the more successes they piled up there the more jittery they became in the west, their apprehension being constantly deepened by British subterfuge. Von Rundstedt, taking his cue from Hitler, signed a proclamation on July 3 saying that the Channel coast forces had the duty of defending the backs of their comrades in Russia and must prevent at all costs the creation of a second front.

Haase added an order of his own to the 302nd Division that "a counter-thrust or counter-attack must hit the enemy before he has enough heavy weapons ashore at his disposal. In case of an enemy landing, each Regiment and each battalion is responsible for restoring the situation by prompt counter-thrust."

It is remarkable, to say the least, that Mountbatten, or any of the host of Canadian and British authorities with a voice in Jubilee, should have allowed obscure Intelligence departments to instil so much fear of invasion into the German army in the west. The political broadcasters were permitted to gaily warn the enemy against imaginary landings; bogus radio messages were sent out daily for the Germans to intercept and become even more alarmed at the prospects of invented operations; and stories planted in Allied newspapers referred to the imminence of the second front.

One night, during a motor-gun-boat battle close off the French coast, a British officer dropped a small waterproofed bag overboard. When it was washed up on the shore and picked up by the Germans it was found to contain secret orders for an invasion of Norway and a feint operation in the Bay of Biscay. That these false documents were believed by the Germans and resulted in more attention being paid to the defences in the areas concerned is no excuse for exhorting them into a high pitch of anticipation just at the time when the first major amphibious assault of the war was being planned. By then the Dieppe raid was, *ipso facto*, certain to take place, and it seems incredible that no steps were taken to create an opposite effect on the defenders of Fortress Europe, one which might lull them into a sense of false security. The only answer appears to be that no one connected with Rutter or Jubilee knew what was going on in the Intelligence war, whose proponents were mostly theatrical amateurs recruited from the fields of journalism and public relations. They gave so little heed to the main war effort that the military planners were left to contemplate victory over an alert enemy who, if not forewarned, was at least forearmed.

The propagandists, political warfare experts, and Intelligence agencies did their work so effectively that von Rundstedt's war diary recorded:

> Information accumulating as a result of photographic and visual reconnaissance . . . and reports from agents confirm an assembly of numerous small landing-craft on the South coast of England.
>
> No further data – except from agents' reports of an English operation, which could not be checked – could be obtained up to 15 August. In spite of this G.H.Q., West, appreciated that the situation from the middle of June to be such that it had to reckon with the possibility of an enemy operation, even a major undertaking, at any moment, and at any point on its extensive coastal front.

In early July one of those melodramatic ceremonies so beloved by German militarists was held in Dieppe. On orders from Paris, Haase summoned divisional officers, from junior lieutenants up, to his head-quarters and made them solemnly swear to defend their positions under any and all circumstances to the last man and with their own lives. When the last of the junior officers had been pledged, Haase himself took an oath to die rather than retreat or surrender.

Germans are also prone to paradoxical behaviour, a characteristic that was to prove significant on July 7 when von Rundstedt ordered a general alert along the Channel coast from the 10th to the 24th because "it is a most favourable period for enemy landings." In the same order he downgraded Dieppe from a Defended Area to a "Group of Strongpoints" on the ground that "due to the small capacity of its port, it is not the type of harbour the Allies are likely to choose as an invasion base."

This was meaningless in terms of defences, which remained intact, but did indicate that the High Command was giving priority to the defences of other ports. Hitler, however, reversed the thinking of his generals by experiencing another moment of intuition which led to a Fuehrer's directive on July 9, drawing attention to the gathering of landing-craft on the English side of the Channel. It said:

The areas particularly threatened are, in the first place, the Channel coast . . . between Dieppe and Le Havre, and Normandy, since these sectors can be reached by enemy planes and also because they lie within range of a large portion of the ferrying vessels.

The result of this was an immediate reinforcement of the Dieppe defences with additional anti-tank guns and mortars. But as was so often the case when the Germans were ready and waiting, nothing happened; in fact, Rutter had been cancelled, and the fate of Jubilee was still uncertain.

Tension eased slightly in the Dieppe sector towards the end of July, and for the first ten days of August all was relatively quiet, providing Haase with an opportunity to undertake exercises at regimental and divisional levels. The respite, however, was interrupted by von Rundstedt who ordered the 302nd Division to readiness at the "Threatening Danger" alert stage from August 10 to 20, as "lunar and tidal conditions are such in this time-span that they could be favourable for an Allied landing."

Haase complied by having Dieppe's defences fully manned from high tide at night to sunrise every day during the critical period, which included the day when the Jubilee planners hoped to achieve complete surprise.

The Dieppe raid was not betrayed, nor was security broken. A steady, undetected build-up of German reinforcements had taken place since the beginning of the raiding season and, if their quality in training and morale was low, they were still perfectly capable of undertaking such manual and menial labour as firing guns from protected positions. An intelligent enemy, more numerous and more heavily armed than Anglo-Canadian planners had thought, was ready for an attack, which he had been encouraged to expect by British experts in deception who were innocently unaware of the trap they were helping to bait.

II

The weather was dull and grey over the Channel, forecasts were ominous, but there was still hope that it would clear in time for the raid to take place as planned at dawn on the 18th. Weather requirements were strict. The strongest wind that could be tolerated was ten knots and if it blew from the west at this strength difficulties could be expected on the beaches. Light winds had to continue at least until after re-embarkation of the forces at about midday. Clear visibility was required for the outward voyage; cloud and rain could be accepted for the return. Two covering orders were issued, one from McNaughton instructing the 1st Canadian Corps to place the 2nd Division and ancillary units at instant readiness for an assault demonstration based upon experience gained on the Isle of Wight, and another from Combined Operations Headquarters giving embarkation time for the demonstration as the evening of the 17th.

Repeated talks in the interim between the Force Commanders underlined the concern of both Roberts and Leigh-Mallory at the weakness of the fire support to be given on the main beaches, and at the request of the latter another conference was held at Tangmere, an RAF Fighter Command station on the south coast, to thrash out the problem.

Leigh-Mallory again emphasized that he could arrange for limited air bombardment immediately prior to the landings, if Roberts was prepared to accept indiscriminate bombing. Bomber Command, he said, could not guarantee accuracy. Roberts replied that he could not accept indiscriminate bombing, that although he wanted air bombardment, desperately so, it would have to be heavy and accurately placed along the sea front of Dieppe and on the wing headlands. Anything else would merely serve to alert the enemy and cause such destruction that the rubble would make it impossible for tanks to get into the town.

Throughout the planning it had been stressed that bombing could be carried out only by night and that accuracy could not be guaranteed. Roberts had protested with monotonous regularity that inaccuracy resulting in debris blocking the passage of tanks into Dieppe would leave the infantry without adequate armoured support, something he could not tolerate. Bomber Command, however, were adamant, refusing to offer hope for even partial accuracy, once suggesting that unless conditions were ideal they might miss Dieppe altogether. On this basis Roberts had said he would prefer to do without it.

Hughes-Hallett then proposed that Bomber Command should provide fifty bombers as a reserve stand-by force which could remain in orbit over the Channel, on call to attack specified targets. The Command's representative at the meeting rejected the proposal on the ground that a force of such size could not be spared from the nightly assault on German industry. Hughes-Hallett, supported enthusiastically by Roberts and Leigh-Mallory, then suggested that perhaps twelve

Stirling bombers could be made available to orbit on call. Bomber Command refused again because, so it was claimed, such a weak force would be quickly shot down. Leigh-Mallory angrily replied that he could guarantee adequate fighter protection, but Bomber Command insisted that, in their experience, fighter protection for bombers in orbit was rarely adequate. The bombers, they said, would have to fly at slow speeds, and the fighters would never be able to give close protection. The Force Commanders were unconvinced but in the face of blunt, impatient refusal there was little further object in pursuing the matter.

The conference broke up at 4:00 p.m., with no one really satisfied at the strength of the fire support and Hughes-Hallett feeling particularly disgusted at the cavalier treatment his request for a stand-by bomber force had received. He felt so strongly that acceptance of his proposal might influence the operation decisively that he decided to put his reasons on record and in writing, coupled with a list of the circumstances in which he might call off the raid during passage across the Channel.

He knew that were he to be responsible for taking such drastic action, regardless of how good his reasons, there would be serious repercussions at Combined Operations Headquarters followed by a formal inquiry. In April a raid in strength on the island of Alderney had been cancelled because the commanders concerned could not agree on its timing; in May a raid of even greater strength at Bayonne had been abandoned, when the first assault waves were only 100 yards from an undetected touchdown, because of undue alarm in high quarters. In June Rutter had been postponed because the forces were not fully trained, and had been eventually called off because the airborne forces had not liked the weather. His own view that these incidents, when added together, amounted to a major defeat had been endorsed by the Prime Minister who was growling for the blood of anyone responsible for another abortive operation. Jubilee was a raid that had to take place for political as well as military reasons, and once the force had sailed, the commander who failed to follow through would have to produce impeccable reasons.

In the unlikely event that he might be that commander, Hughes-Hallett was determined that his own attitude should be well known and the blame properly apportioned. Skilled in the ways of the services, he knew that the wise commander protects himself against possible recriminations well in advance by making his intentions unequivocally clear prior to an operation. In a letter to Mountbatten, with copies going to the Admiralty and his co-force commanders, he outlined the circumstances in which "I intend to abandon the operation (should there still be time to do so) in consequence of loss of Infantry Assault Ships during passage."

His principal arguments were that as the South Saskatchewans were to be carried in *Princess Beatrix* and *Invicta*, the loss of these ships would mean that no landings would take place at Pourville, there would be no chance of capturing the West Headland, and the assault of the main beaches would be consequently endangered.

"In these circumstances, I intend to abandon the operation in the event of both *Princess Beatrix* and *Invicta* being lost in passage," he said.

The Royal Hamilton Light Infantry were to be carried in *Glengyle*, and Roberts had already said that if she were sunk, the landing on White Beach could still be carried out by the tanks and troops in the tank landing-craft. Hughes-Hallett said that in view of the Military Force Commander's opinion, "my intention is to proceed with the operation in the event of the loss of *Glengyle*, provided she were to be the only Infantry Assault Ship which is lost. If, on the other hand, another Infantry Assault Ship is sunk besides, I consider that the proportion of the total which is lost would be too high to continue."

The Essex Scottish were to travel in two ships, *Prince Charles* and *Prince Leopold*, and Hughes-Hallett said he would disregard the loss of one of them completely, and both of them, providing *Duke of Wellington*, which would carry a Royal Marine Commando as a military reserve, were still afloat.

"It is feasible," he wrote, "to divert the *Duke of Wellington*'s landing craft to Red Beach and they should have little difficulty in effecting a landing at about the same time as the *Glengyle*'s craft land at White Beach. If, however, all three vessels are lost on passage I intend to abandon the operation."

The Royal Regiment would embark in *Queen Emma* and *Princess Astrid* and, after consulting with Roberts, the Naval Force Commander decided:

> I agree with the military view that the operation can proceed notwithstanding the loss of one of these two vessels and I note that from a purely military point of view they consider it feasible to continue even if both vessels are lost. When, however, the added naval risks that would result from a failure to assault the East Headland positions altogether are taken into consideration,

I have reached the conclusion that it would not be justifiable to
continue with the operation in such a contingency. This being so,
I intend to abandon the operation in the event of both the *Queen
Emma* and the *Princess Astrid* being lost on passage.

Behind this emphasis on the threat from the East Headland, was a
growing conviction that the plan was too rigid, a conviction which
he recognized but which he could not, as a sailor, argue successfully
with the military. When we discussed it in one of our many meetings
during my research, he told me: "There's not the slightest doubt that
the rigidity of the plan was a dreadful mistake. It could be upset by
something going wrong, causing a chain reaction of wrongs which
would then all jam in the neck of the bottle because there was no way
of taking out the cork. There was no room for improvization or for
changing schedules to take advantage of unforeseen circumstances or
for getting out of a mess.

"Perhaps the most serious example of this, one that was becoming
clearer to me hour by hour as zero hour approached, was our failure
to have an alternative plan in case the attack on the East Headland
failed. I blame myself for this because I had always attached more
importance to the East Headland than had the Army, simply because
it dominated the harbour entrance and the inner basins."

It may be that Hughes-Hallett is open to criticism on this point, but
only in conjunction with those responsible for the military plan: Montgomery, Crerar, McNaughton, and Roberts.

The last paragraph of Hughes-Hallett's letter revealed his shrewd
insight into what would be the inevitable consequence of the operation
being called off. He wanted it on record that the provision of even a
limited bomber force on stand-by would have so changed the position
in relation to losses of ships, that abandonment may have depended
on different circumstances. In effect, he placed responsibility for heavy
naval losses, owing to failure to capture the East Headland, squarely
on the Royal Air Force.

"Finally," the paragraph said, "I wish to place on record that the
foregoing conclusions would have been profoundly modified had it
been possible to have a number of bombers to call in the area from
dawn onwards with a view to making low-flying daylight attacks on
enemy batteries in the event of an emergency."

Then, late on the 16th, forecasts of worsening weather with winds
up to twenty-five knots forced yet another postponement – this time
for twenty-four hours, to the 18th-19th.

III

Roberts had left an afternoon meeting with his staff on the 17th, with twenty-four hours in which to use the lack of adequate fire support as an excuse for calling off the raid or to accept the risk this weakness entailed and rely upon surprise alone.

To this usually calm, unruffled soldier, facing his first major encounter with the enemy as commander of an amphibious operation involving ten thousand Allied soldiers, sailors, and airmen, it must have seemed that the night of the 17th would never end. He lay down, tossed about, rose to stalk the floor of his room, and then threw himself back on the bed again, repeating the restless ritual, hour after hour until the grey pallor of dawn crept faintly into the darkened sky.

An equation with many variations coursed through his mind, the answers always elusive. Would surprise minus fire support equal success? Or should it be surprise plus powerful fire-power, which would need a revision of the plan to validate the equation?

Surprise, the hinge upon which everything turned, should give him the wing headlands occupied from Pourville and Puits, but would it actually relieve the main assault from the expected crossfire from the batteries on top of them? Were there defences he knew nothing about?

His anxiety about the ability of the Navy to hit the right beaches at the right times developed into a persistent, nagging worry. Nothing about the plan was neatly separated, each fragment of it interlocking with the rest because it insisted that everything should depend upon something. Most important of all was the dependency of surprise upon the punctuality of the landings.

He had hoped to increase the chances of achieving total surprise by changing the plan at the last minute to budget for simultaneous landings along the French coast while there was still sufficient darkness to cover the assault across the main beaches. Hughes-Hallett had rejected it on the ground that from a purely technical point of view the Navy could not cope with simultaneous landings. The density of shipping during the approach to the beaches would be too great – it proved to be greater than any operation before or after, including D-Day – and the craft involved were capable of such a variety of performances that the operation would have to be rescheduled to the speed of the slowest.

It was not for Roberts to say what the Navy could or could not do and, faced with this opposition, coupled with the need to keep the time-gap between the main assault and the tank landings as narrow as possible, he had reluctantly abandoned the proposal.

On another occasion he had argued strenuously for a concentration of the destroyer fire-power on the wing headlands, but once again he had been defeated by naval reasoning. Leigh-Mallory had supported him at this meeting, remarking caustically that as the plan stood, the main assault troops would be slaughtered.

While these images of what had been said and done, unsaid and undone, raced in a bewildering kaleidoscope before him, he tried desperately to keep personal considerations divorced from the tactical problems of the day ahead. How would his superiors, military and political, react were he to demand, on the actual eve of the operation, its postponement and revision?

The Canadian Army, like others on which it was modelled, was fiercely competitive, with promotions dependent upon a multitude of virtues and a minimum of sins. Within three years the youthful, vibrant officer class had matured into a career-conscious élite corps reflecting all the normal human frailties such as ambition, jealousy, greed, courage, strength, pride, and weakness.

In such cut-throat company, familiar in armed forces everywhere, Roberts was content to be judged on past performances, on merit rather than political acumen, but he could hardly afford to ignore the consequences of a wrong decision. If he were responsible for delaying Jubilee, there was every chance that he would be confronted with a Court of Inquiry, followed by ostracism and eventual oblivion, a lingering penalty reserved for commanders who turn their backs on battle no matter how justified the reasons. In the event that the operation proceeded as planned and ended in defeat, he would be blamed and subsequently removed from the presence of those senior officers who had no taste for association with failure. Perhaps it was this narrow choice that resolved his lonely struggle on the edge of daybreak, enabling him to end his night-long vigil in deep, undisturbed sleep.

Thoughts of Roberts and of what he must be privately enduring added to Hughes-Hallett's troubles. He had tried to help the Military Commander when he had requested the Admiralty to provide the overwhelming fire support of a battleship. He had been turned down because the Royal Navy was so desperately short of warships that none could be gambled on an adventure which offered no immediate assistance to the protracted war at sea. U-boats dominated the North Atlantic; surface raiders prowled the South Atlantic; the German battle fleet had to be contained in the North Sea; Japanese task forces threatened the Indian Ocean; and the Italian navy, supported by the

German *Luftwaffe*, ruled the Mediterranean where Malta-bound convoys were being massacred at each attempt to relieve the beleaguered island citadel.

It is difficult, however, to understand now why one capital ship could not have been spared for a fleeting, surprise visit to the Channel in support of the raid. So much had been committed in terms of men and materials that any risk would have been justified to give Roberts more favourable odds. The Admiralty had slammed the door on repeated requests from Baillie-Grohman, Mountbatten and Hughes-Hallett. If anyone might have levered a battleship from the reluctant Admiralty it would be Mountbatten. If, indeed, he did exert his considerable influence with the supreme authorities he must have been rebuffed by Churchill, who would naturally support Sir Dudley Pound, the First Sea Lord, for whom the Prime Minister held enormous respect, and against whom he would not be swayed. Both Baillie-Grohman and Hughes-Hallett recall that their requests were turned down "in the highest quarters."

Leigh-Mallory also recognized the turmoil raging in Roberts. He had always been vocal in support of the Canadian's demands for heavier fire support. He had gone to Bomber Command, argued forcibly with Sir Arthur Harris for accurate and heavy air bombardment, and when refused had gone back for a stand-by force of fifty bombers and finally for twelve. Then he too had been forced to acknowledge that nothing more could be done without exceeding his authority, and he had come dangerously close to doing so when voicing his fears to Mountbatten and Montgomery during the planning of Rutter.

Roberts would have to resolve his own dilemma, bearing in mind that the Army's prime function was to test the enemy's defences so severely that he would have to resort to a vast movement of reserves and by doing so reveal his intended methods of counter-attacking a serious invasion attempt. What complicated the issue was the insertion into the plan of so many secondary and largely useless objectives in which many lives would be risked for reasons of questionable merit. In order that these ineffectual, minor forays could be undertaken, an ambitious plan was scheduled tightly, leaving Roberts with no room to improvize or manœuvre. He could not withdraw once a crushing disaster became apparent, simply because the timetable was too rigid to be rapidly altered.

McNaughton and Crerar knew it; Mountbatten, Hughes-Hallett, and Leigh-Mallory knew it. Roberts was agonizingly aware of it, but could see no way out other than the distasteful and abhorrent alternative of relinquishing his command. The planners had thrown a plank across the Channel; he would walk it – with surprise as the solitary strand of a frail and slender life-line.

August 18 was a nervous day, a day when over-taut nerves led to jitters in unexpected places, as Roberts discovered in the morning when one of his first visitors was Bob Labatt, whose own drawn appearance betrayed another sleepless night.

"What is it, Bob? Let's be brief this morning."

"Can't something be done about the fire support, sir?" replied Labatt. "We can do this thing, but by God we need something better than a handful of destroyers to keep those headlands saturated if anything goes wrong."

"Well, we can't get it."

"Why not, sir? We'll be murdered if the Royals and the South Sasks don't get there on time."

Roberts looked bleakly at the young colonel of the RHLI. "Does it bother you, Bob? If so, perhaps you'd better not go. It's not too late to have you relieved."

Labatt stiffened formally to attention.

"I'm going all right, sir," he said with hard emphasis. "I just thought you ought to know how I, for one, feel."

The interview was over, and when Labatt had gone Roberts was alone again, an aloof commander who would not share his personal troubles even if a willing listener had been at hand, but whose appearance was that of eagerness to get on with the business of war.

Another example of immediate pre-raid concern that all was not quite as it should be emerged during a brief conversation that morning between Hughes-Hallett, who had slept soundly during the night and had taken his customary morning run, and Commander Ryder, who had probably slept less soundly because he would sail in the gun boat *Locust* and be responsible for the cutting-out force. Ryder would take *Locust*, another gun boat, and seven French *chasseurs* into the harbour entrance under the guns of the East Headland, penetrate into the inner harbours, take in tow as many invasion barges as time allowed, and then get out – once again under point-blank fire from the East Headland.

It was no less hazardous an operation than St Nazaire, where his cool courage had earned him the Victoria Cross, but memories of that frenzied night were still very vivid, particularly those caused by lack of air bombardment. Ryder was worried about the East Headland and said so.

He told Hughes-Hallett that lack of air bombardment would be disastrous, that the destroyer fire-power was utterly insufficient to cover his movements. Hughes-Hallett, too shrewd a judge of character to use persuasion on so strong-willed a man, relied instead on his own non-committal attitude to give Ryder an opportunity to argue himself into the belief that his objections might prove less justified than they actually were, which is precisely what happened.

Hughes-Hallett, the man who for so long had been intimately involved in all the vicissitudes, vacillations, and internecine strife that had plagued the enterprise from the start, gave little outward signs of anything but confident anticipation. It was by this time clear that the weakness of fire-power worried everyone from the Force Commanders down and no one from the Force Commanders up; that the eager hunters were now trapped by the initial over-enthusiasm and over-confidence with which they had approached the hurdles. Their plan had made no allowance for second thinking, they had silenced the cautious, and only time would tell if the spurs had been put to Jubilee too early.

Flare-up
at Sea

I

At 10:00 a.m. that Tuesday, the Force Commanders lifted their trumpets, sounded the opening bars of the jubilee, and staff officers scrambled for telephones to send a brief order crackling across southeastern England: "The show is on – Now." Ten thousand men in army camps, on airfields, at the embarkation ports – Southampton, Portsmouth, Shoreham, and Newhaven – were galvanized into that sudden state of chaos which military men require as the normal order of things. The vast majority blasphemed cordially, consigned to the devil those VIP's for whom they were supposed to demonstrate amphibious landings, and cut corners wherever possible.

No old hand would go on exercise without lightening his load, and the Canadians from exercising so often were artists at lightening loads. One entire battalion could see no good reason for taking along heavy boxes of live ammunition, so they emptied them; another decided to lighten individual packs by leaving behind field rations, field dressings, and trenching-tools. Then truck convoys set out from such unmilitary places as Lewes, Horsham, Littlehampton, Seaford, and Billingshurst, and before local inhabitants were quite aware of it the Canadian lodger had flitted.

The Calgary Tanks, accompanied by blitz buggies and scout cars for the signals group under Major Gordon Rolfe, and the beach sappers under Major Sucharov and Lieutenant J. E. R. Wood, had embarked the previous day at Portsmouth and Newhaven in the twenty-four tank landing-craft in which they would cross the Channel. Tank crews had been sealed aboard overnight and briefed at noon on the real purpose of the exercise.

Next to board at Newhaven were the Camerons who would cross in small, wooden landing-craft personnel (LCP's) which were neither armed nor armoured and carried approximately twenty men each, complete with sixty-pound packs, ammunition, and small arms. They were briefed by Lieutenant-Colonel Alfred Gostling while assembled in the dockyard immediately prior to taking their places in the LCP's.

The 619 officers and men of the Fusiliers Mont-Royal, also making the passage in LCP's, congregated in a schoolhouse at the village of Lansing where Lieutenant-Colonel Menard gave them a melodramatic briefing in French which began: "*Mes gars, ça y est.*" While the men cheered, he handed Father Major Sabourin a mess tin filled with more than six hundred Blessed Hosts procured three days previously from a local monastery. The priest then held Holy Communion for the entire battalion including, as Menard told me, "one officer who hadn't been to church for years and who was among the first to be killed the next morning." Among them too was Major Paul Savoy, a prominent businessman from St Jean, Quebec, who was considered too old for the raid. He had been with the regiment for fifteen years and, alarmed at the prospect of it going into action without him, had begged Menard not to leave him behind. Knowing he could do little officially, Menard had replied: "I do not want to see you again – until after we have sailed." He was to see Savoy off the coast of France at dawn; after that the elderly Canadian officer would not be seen by anyone again.

Following the service, the battalion embarked at Shoreham with the men filled, according to Father Sabourin, "with such enthusiasm as I had never witnessed before and never will again."

Early that afternoon, Brigadier Head of Combined Operations telephoned Durnford-Slater at Seaford to say, "You'll have to pick up your stores tomorrow, Wednesday the 19th." That was the prearranged code signalling the start of the operation for No. 3 Commando, which would sail in the tiny LCP's from Newhaven.

At Southampton Lord Lovat's No. 4 Commando boarded *Prince Albert*, the RHLI embarked in *Glengyle*, the Royal Regiment in *Queen Emma* and *Princess Astrid*, with their attached reserve from the Black Watch of Canada aboard *Duke of Wellington* which also carried the Royal Marine Commando destined to be the military floating reserve. The Essex Scottish embarked in *Prince Charles* and *Prince Leopold*, while the South Saskatchewans were spread between *Princess Beatrix* and *Invicta*.

By 4:00 p.m. the last of the battalions were aboard and ships sealed, except for a few special groups yet to arrive. The colonels briefed their men, and the faults of a secret too well kept were revealed. The battalion which had brought empty ammunition boxes had to borrow Sten gun ammunition from the ship's stores. There were howls of rage when men broke open crates and found brand new weapons uncleaned and covered with thick layers of grease. Most of the night would have to be spent cleaning the guns and taking whatever precautions were possible in the limited time left to prevent them jamming. In every ship and landing-craft, angry troops who had spent days on the Isle of Wight filing down and adjusting the firing mechanism of these temperamental weapons shouted to officers and NCO's: "Why the hell couldn't we have kept our own guns? These are going to be bloody useless."

Aboard *Duke of Wellington* the Black Watch were in the middle of sorting out issues of Mae West lifejackets and eating-utensils when they were ordered to prime hand grenades. There was immediate confusion as men struggled into lifejackets and received tin plates in one hand and grenades in another. Private Harry Smith of Montreal primed a grenade, put it down to take an issue of forks and spoons, and then, forgetting that he had primed it, picked up the grenade and began priming it again. For a brief moment he looked at it as if stunned and then suddenly threw it towards an open porthole. He was too late. The grenade exploded in mid air, and the force of the explosion in cramped quarters reaped a dreadful harvest of casualties among the closest troops. Private E. P. Williams was so severely wounded that he later died in hospital; nineteen others were injured so badly they had to be rushed to local hospitals in trucks. Neither they, nor the men who accompanied them, were to visit the seaside in France.

Corporal Farrell, in charge of the patrol which helped move the wounded, returned to the docks from hospital and found his ship had sailed. His report of the incident said: "We made several attempts to get on another ship, but they wouldn't have us. So we had to stay behind."

Colonel Guy Gostling's Toronto Scottish machine-gunners set up their weapons in the bows of the assault landing-craft and added their own incensed grumblings to the general outcry. To cover the landings by keeping down enemy gunners on the sea front and to take on "targets of opportunity," they needed tracer bullets. Not one ammunition belt in their stores included tracers. The effects would be worse when they tried to shoot down low-flying aircraft without knowing how wide they were aiming.

Colonel J. D. McBeth, the 2nd Division's signals commander, who had been watching the embarkation from the quayside, made a hurried visit to the Dockyard Security Office and reported a civilian he thought to be taking an unusual interest in the ships. A patrol went out and returned a few minutes later with the man McBeth had noticed. There is no evidence that the bewildered suspect was ever more than an innocent bystander, but he paid for his curiosity by being locked up in the guardhouse for the next twenty-four hours.

While the briefings were proceeding aboard the infantry landing-ships, the special mission groups began to slip unobtrusively aboard and vanish into pre-selected cabins where they would have no contact with the troops. They had been gathered at East Bridge House outside Southampton, which had been turned into a special service assembly point. Five U.S. Rangers, led by Lieutenant Robert Flanagan and supposed to be with the raiding force, had been sent there accidentally and were met by a Royal Marine liaison officer who had no idea who they were.

When the misunderstanding had been cleared up, Flanagan had time to look about him and take some notice of his companions. "Among the personnel at this place were members of the Royal Marines, the Royal Navy, some army men of a strange breed known as Phantoms, Fighting French, Sudeten Germans [possibly those for whom Goronwy Rees had collected thousands of forged French francs and had since been unable to find], and a Russian in charge of others of indeterminate nationalities disguised as Canadian soldiers," he wrote later.

There is no other evidence to suggest who the Russian might have been or what his group was supposed to do. These extraordinary groups were so obsessed with the need for secrecy they rarely communicated with anyone outside their immediate circles or with each other, and one is always left with a sense of fantasy when their machinations are mentioned. It is highly probable that many of these so-called mystery organizations mushroomed, because even crooks, cranks, misfits, habitual perverts, juvenile delinquents, and mentally retarded youths have a place in total war, and the only way to let them participate seems to be by creating organizations which owe allegiance to no one and which subscribe to the cult of the hush-hush simply to hide their collective oddball character.

It must have been a weird experience for Flanagan's small party to get mixed up with so strange a collection for no other reason than changes in the distribution of an increased number of Rangers among the raiding force.

There would be four officers and fifteen men attached to No. 3 Commando, one officer and six enlisted men with No. 4 Commando, and another twenty dispersed among the Canadian battalions – the RHLI, for instance, who took along seven Rangers. These first United States infantrymen to fight in Europe were to be accompanied by General Truscott, at whose suggestion their special formation had been created, and Colonel Loren B. Hillsinger, both of whom were to act as official American spectators. Truscott joined the reserve headquarters team aboard HMS *Fernie*, while Hillsinger embarked in another destroyer, HMS *Berkeley*.

Odd types were arriving at the embarkation ports singly or in pairs; Goronwy Rees, lately of Montgomery's staff, boarded the destroyer *Garth* with the United States war correspondent he had come to detest still trailing him; Dan Doheny, erstwhile "King's Messenger" between the Isle of Wight and London, arrived in an army truck after making a diversionary forage at Warnford Park for special stores. He arrived late in the evening to find sentries guarding gangways and at once realized that his army driver must guess that something big was in the wind. He handed out a carton of cigarettes and warned: "Now don't you say a word about this to anyone, understand?" The blank-eyed British soldier stood stiffly to attention and replied stolidly: "It's all right, sir. I never says anything to nobody of what I 'ears, sees or does." By the time Doheny boarded the headquarters destroyer *Calpe*, he found that the press team were already in possession of the wardroom and the bar.

While the forces of Jubilee were gathering from across southern England, a brief but significant drama was being played out in the underground headquarters at Fort Southwick where Mountbatten had called an emergency, last-minute conference of Force Commanders at 4:00 p.m. The most important person at this last-minute meeting of the offensive-minded élite was a very junior naval officer then making a brief but decisive contact with the assault against continental Europe. His presence was to have an immense impact upon Canadian military history.

Lieutenant Ronald Bell RNVR, who is now a British Member of Parliament, was at the time a young meteorological officer at the Royal Navy's Fleet Air Arm base at Lee-on-Solent, on the south coast. He had been summoned to the meeting because of his specialized knowledge of local weather conditions in the Channel area, particularly that between Portsmouth and Dieppe – and the weather had suddenly become once again a decisive factor.

Official weather forecasts from the Admiralty and Air Ministry were so unfavourable that, although Jubilee was already in motion, it could be stopped and reversed. Mountbatten announced that a decision on the cancellation of the raid had to be reached at once and left it up to the Force Commanders. In his turn Roberts left it up to Hughes-Hallett and Leigh-Mallory, on the ground that if the Navy could get him there and the Air Force could cover him, then his 2nd Division would fight. The Naval and Air Commanders, in their turn, placed the future of Jubilee in the hands of the most junior officer there, Lieutenant Bell. There was no doubt that any decision to cancel would result in the operation being called off for all time. It must have been an awesome moment for Bell, whose two stripes on each sleeve would have been alarmingly dimmed by the gilt surrounding him. He could plunge the Canadian Army into its first battle of the war, or he could bring months of planning and training to an uneventful end.

He barely hesitated, saying in effect: "In my opinion there will be fair weather over a small area of the central Channel until maybe four o'clock tomorrow afternoon." By then the operation would be over, and the force on its way back to Britain. Hughes-Hallett and Leigh-Mallory, only too ready to accept even the faintest chance of good weather, accepted the young officer's personal opinion, and he was dismissed from the conference, unaware then that he had influenced the course of an operation which would pass into history as one of the most controversial incidents of the war.

"As Bell referred specifically to the Portsmouth-Dieppe area," Hughes-Hallett told me, "Leigh-Mallory and I decided to go ahead. We all dispersed for the drive down to Portsmouth for embarkation. The last message I received before leaving Fort Southwick was a telephone call from the Admiralty begging us to cancel the operation in view of threatening weather."

The Naval Commander turned a Nelsonic "blind eye" on the message, and Jubilee was on.

Roberts, Hughes-Hallett, and their staffs boarded *Calpe* at 7:00 p.m., where they were joined by Air Commodore Cole, representing Leigh-Mallory, who was to be at Uxbridge. Mountbatten and Crerar would also watch the progress of the battle from the Uxbridge control room, but neither would be in a position to intervene. It was a Combined Operations rule of procedure that once a raiding force sailed, the Chief of Combined Operations and the responsible Military Commander delegated all further authority to the Force Commanders. Churchill Mann, Colonel Henderson, and their duplicate staffs were already aboard *Fernie*, and the total military, naval, and special personnel had embarked.

At 9:30 p.m. infantry landing-ships hoisted false funnels and superstructure to transform their appearance from the air, slipped their moorings and, looking for all the world like peaceful merchant vessels, headed out to sea, leaving behind the sound of shrieking air-raid sirens warning of the approach of German evening reconnaissance.

It was a warm, cloudless evening; the dying sun reflected softly on the hills behind the shore line, inspiring in the men a sudden urge to take a last look at the friendly coast. As if pulled on the strings of a master puppeteer, they swarmed to the sides of their ships – quiet, thoughtful men, each occupied by private thoughts of the day ahead, by imagined fears, and by wistful speculation on when they might see this sight again.

They were unaware of how close they had come to being sent back to their camps; and none of them had ever heard of a local weatherman called Ronald Bell, whose personal expert opinion had counted for more than the official views of the service ministries.

II

At Boulogne on the other side of the Channel another force cleared harbour at precisely the same time: a German six-knot convoy consisting of five motor vessels escorted by three sub-chasers. Their destination was Dieppe; time of arrival was estimated for 4:30 a.m., the very minute that Durnford-Slater's No. 3 Commando would begin the run into Yellow Beach at Berneval.

The possibility of the fleet encountering enemy forces while still on passage had not been ignored. Radar stations at Beachy Head, New-haven, and Portsmouth had been warned to keep *Calpe* informed of any suspicious sightings in the Channel, but there was a limit to shore radar's usefulness. Maximum effective range was mostly forty miles, sometimes up to fifty in favourable weather conditions. When the fleet reached the start line ten miles off Dieppe, it would be at least fifty-seven miles from England and therefore beyond the range of radar. For the final few miles it would rely on the radar sets carried in the individual destroyers which, in 1942, were still comparatively primitive and subject to unseemly displays of temperament at times when they were most needed.

Furthermore, Hughes-Hallett had laid down the measures to be taken in the event of an encounter in his Naval Operation Order No. 1 which said: "Senior officers of Groups in company and senior officers of detached Groups must take drastic avoiding action if contact is made with enemy forces or to avoid contact if the enemy are known to be in the vicinity. But the proper course must be resumed as soon as it is considered safe to do so as timely arrival . . . is vital to the operation."

This was an unequivocal instruction leaving no room for misinter-pretation on grounds of ambiguity. Yet at least one senior group officer was to issue orders in apparent contradiction.

III

Aboard *Calpe*, Roberts chattered amiably with the American war correspondent, Quentin Reynolds who, with his press colleagues, had been given a deliberately vague and general briefing on what was to happen at dawn. Now that time and events had banished his doubts, Ham Roberts was relaxed, confident, even cheerful.

"How do you really feel about this operation, General?" asked Reynolds.

"If the Navy gets us there – and there's no reason in the meantime for calling the show off – it will be a success," replied Roberts. Then he smiled a little thinly and added: "The point of no return is reached at 3:00 a.m. After that it becomes our show, and it will take one hell of a lot to cancel it."

"Do you think you'll suffer heavy casualties?"

"We're prepared for casualties and I'll accept them. You can't win battles without casualties. This show has to succeed, and everything's been done that can be done to make it successful. The plan is good, the men are keen, and they know what to do."

Doheny, who had been listening, wrote later in his diary:

> The General's main worry centred on the Navy. He seemed so eager to get on with the show that he kept coming back to the possibility of Hughes-Hallett cancelling the raid before the decision passed into his own hands after 3 a.m. He repeated several times that the essence of success would be the Navy putting the troops ashore at the right places at the right times. Each time, he stressed that the Naval Force Commander had assured him all would be well and that he was satisfied. But he stressed the point too much for my liking and I for one became quite worried about the Naval arrangements.

Air Commodore Cole joined the group in the wardroom and asked Roberts if he were satisfied with the air support. The 2nd Division staff members present were treated to their first glimpse of the extent to which Roberts was concerned at the lack of heavy air bombardment.

"I'm satisfied that Leigh-Mallory and yourself have done all you can," said Roberts. "But by God if we get hammered because there's been no softening up of the defences, I'm going to have a hell of a lot to say about it."

He swung round abruptly to McBeth and ordered: "I want duplicates kept of all signals sent to Uxbridge tomorrow." Cole was left in no doubt at all that Bomber Command would hear all about Dieppe in the event of failure.

The Shoreham and Newhaven forces met at 11:30 p.m. and headed towards the easterly swept channel through the minefield; the South-ampton-Portsmouth force sailed for the westerly channel, the nine infantry landing-ships hauling down their camouflage and wheeling into columns for the crossing. Fifteen minesweepers had turned in a faultless performance, using taut-wire-run procedure for establishing start points off the English coast from which they swept along a direct line to Dieppe and laid dimly lighted marker buoys on either side of the cleared passages. By the time they had finished and turned for home, both forces were nosing towards the first sets of markers.

No combined British fleet of such size had sailed the English Channel since the outbreak of war; if nothing else, this fact alone was evidence enough that the initiative had passed into Allied hands. It consisted of 237 ships, which sounds formidable, but which was really woefully weak. The largest were the infantry landing-ships, whose assault craft were already swung out on davits; the eight 900-ton "Hunt" class destroyers: *Calpe, Fernie, Brocklesby, Garth, Bleasdale, Berkeley, Albrighton,* and the Polish ship, *Slazak,* each of which mounted four 4-inch guns. Even more puny were the 500-ton ex-river gunboat *Locust,* which mounted two 4-inch guns and a 3.7-inch howitzer, and the 700-ton sloop *Alresford,* which carried a single 4-inch gun. For the rest, there were four small steam gun boats, sixteen motor launches, twelve motor gun boats, twenty-four tank landing-craft, seven French *chasseurs,* eighty-one assorted assault landing-craft, and seventy-four LCP's, these last being totally unarmed and unarmoured.

This was the peashooter armada which was carrying into the boldest raid against Fortress Europe yet planned some 298 officers and 4,663 enlisted men of the Canadian Army; 65 officers and 992 other ranks of No. 3 Commando, No. 4 Commando, and the Royal Marine Commando; 18 members of the Inter-Allied Commando; 50 U.S. Rangers under Captain Roy Murray; and a handful of odd, mysterious persons – a total of nearly 6,100 of all ranks.

If the fleet had any strength at all it would be in its training and the flexibility of the naval plan. Success at sea would depend largely upon the individual actions of the commanding officers when confronted by sudden, unforeseen situations, on how well they complied with their primary functions: to get the Army ashore in the right places on time, to protect the infantry landing-ships and landing-craft, preserve them for the withdrawal, and at the same time provide maximum support to the troops ashore.

Hughes-Hallett had organized the force into thirteen groups, of which the first four comprised the infantry landing-ships and their escorts of MGB's, MTB's, and ML's. Groups five, six, and seven consisted of the LCP's carrying the Camerons, No. 3 Commando, and the Fusiliers Mont-Royal, and numbers eight to twelve were the tank landing-craft and their escorts. The thirteenth comprised the seven Free French *chasseurs* led by the destroyer HMS *Alresford.*

The beginning was not auspicious. Ships lost themselves in the darkness, some passing through the wrong swept channels across the minefield, others not even finding the channels and crossing the actual minefield without incident mainly because of incredibly good fortune and shallow draughts. Miraculously, however, a series of signalled rebukes from Hughes-Hallett sorted them out on the French side of the minefield and the fleet proceeded towards the target in reasonable order.

Below decks, the troops slept, ate sandwiches, talked in desultory monotones, or wrote last letters home; but most of them were lying down silent and awake, preoccupied with their private thoughts.

Lieutenant Jerry Wood, Royal Canadian Engineers, commanding a beach assault group which would help the tanks get onto the promenade, lounged below deck aboard his tank landing-craft reading a pre-war thriller called *Last Train from Berlin*. He had briefed his unit, who had received the news that they were going to Dieppe with stolid, dead-pan expressions, gulped down a hot dinner of soup, bully beef, biscuits, jam, and tea, and had nudged himself down into a crowded corner of the deck.

"Though tired, I was loathe to hit the hay," he recalled. "It looked as if the show would be on all right. The captain of our craft felt it wouldn't be cancelled no matter what. It was a beautiful, moony, balmy night, so peaceful that it was hard to believe we'd be working at our trade in the morning."

Before turning in, Wood burned his orders in the galley stove and stood on deck, enjoying the stars, enjoying the quiet and the soft sound of lapping water, as were thousands of his fellow countrymen in other ships.

There was a moment of consternation aboard *Invicta* when troops of the South Saskatchewans broke open a case of grenades still covered in grease and attempted to clean them; one went off, as had happened on *Duke of Wellington*, but this time although seventeen soldiers were injured none was killed. These, however, were minor incidents which could not be helped and had so far proved remarkably rare.

The sea was calm, the swell slight, and the wind light out of the west-southwest – a still night with occasional white clouds moving slowly overhead and the stars glittering with startling brilliance against a pitch-black setting. In each ship, only the sounds of the engines throbbed steadily through the otherwise silent night and, from the decks of the larger ships, the tank landing-craft could be seen as low black silhouettes with square, snub noses creating a foamy turbulence around their bows.

Weather forecasts hinted at a general deterioration by noon of the 19th followed by overcast skies and rain. But by then the raid should be over and the force heading back for home. The time of no return was 3:00 a.m., and in such near-perfect weather conditions it was an artificial limit without practical significance. There was not the slightest apparent reason for cancelling the raid, and Hughes-Hallett had already decided that while the decision remained a naval one he would turn yet another blind eye to any awkward signals from England.

Dieppe was no longer just an idea or a plan, it was a pulsating, living operation which nothing could prevent.

IV

The fleet cleared the minefield shortly before 3:00 a.m., order was restored, and the ships proceeded in their appointed stations towards the target. In the south of England it was breakfast time for hundreds of Fighter Command pilots who had been briefed the night before and then confined to their bases – Biggin Hill, Tangmere, Hornchurch, Kenley, Duxford, Debden, and others made famous during the Battle of Britain. Tomorrow would be their first opportunity since those grim weeks of 1940 to meet the *Luftwaffe* in strength and destroy it.

Group Captain Bobby Oxspring, one of the Battle's great aces and now commanding No. 222 Squadron's eighteen Spitfires, sipped scalding coffee with his Wing Leader, Wing Commander E. H. Thomas. Both pilots had fought dog fights over France on the previous two days during scouting flights in preparation for the raid. They were joined by Major M. L. McNickle, commander of No. 307 U.S. Army Air Force Spitfire Squadron, newcomers to the air war who would fight their first major battle over Dieppe.

At Hornchurch, Commandant B. Duperier of No. 340 Free French Squadron, veteran of a dozen fighter sweeps over his native soil, shared breakfast with his RAF opposite numbers, Squadron Leaders W. G. G. D. Smith and J. R. C. Killian. All three were to return at dusk that night flushed with victory.

Forty-five minutes before first light, hundreds of fighters began forming up on a dozen runways with navigation lights burning and the throb of their engines creating a deafening din across the sleepy English countryside.

Bobby Oxspring told me: "My squadron was taking off later, so I watched the first formations take off in the blackout. It was a most spectacular sight to see three or four squadrons, with each aircraft burning red, green, and white lights, form up in the dark. The associated noise of engines was all the more impressive. It was quite a show."

On the other side of the Channel, a weather report reaching headquarters of the *Luftwaffe*'s No. 3 Air Fleet heralded a fine morning but a gloomy, overcast afternoon. It was not the sort of weather in which offensive operations could serve any useful purpose, so one pilot in three was granted twenty-four hours leave. A similar weather forecast had a different effect on von Rundstedt's staff, and the Commander-in-Chief's war diary comments: "The night 18-19th can be regarded as suitable for enemy raiding operations. Commanders of coastal defences to maintain troops at the Threatened Danger alert."

While the Army stood to, the *Luftwaffe* stood down, most of the lucky pilots spending their night off at a village forty miles from Dieppe where the *LN-Helferinnen* (Women's Auxiliary Air Signals Corps) was based. During the day a score of war correspondents, film cameramen, and magazine photographers had been taking pictures of the girls and writing stories which would inform the fatherland of the magnificent job they were doing in bolstering the morale of the *Luftwaffe*. The press tour had been arranged to encourage more Aryan girls into the Corps by showing what a good time they would have helping war-weary pilots to relax.

In the evening, the charming hostesses entertained the war correspondents at a huge dance to which all off-duty airmen had been invited. It was a gay affair with the girls in evening dresses instead of uniforms and the men in white dinner jackets or white summer mess tunics. At 3:00 a.m. the party had developed into a typically frenetic all-night revel, as if there were those present who sensed the mailed fist was about to strike from the sea, that this was to be their last night on earth.

At Dieppe itself, Corporal Fritz Palowski from East Prussia sat outside the Casino on the promenade nursing a grievance. He had spent most of the day teaching raw recruits how to recognize badges of rank in time for them to take part in an anti-invasion exercise scheduled by the 571st Regiment for the 20th. Because of this his latest request for long overdue leave had been denied again and Corporal Palowski was feeling surly and rebellious. He could have used these last few hours of his life to better purpose, if only to make dying at sunrise easier on his soul.

At the Varengeville heavy coastal battery, Sergeant-Major Holzer had ended a routine day with a minor diversion at the camp occupied by sappers. After dark, an orderly had informed him that a woman was screaming in one of the tents, so he had taken a patrol to the scene where a young soldier pointed to a cowering French girl and claimed she had tried to knife him. Naturally, Sergeant-Major Holzer admonished the soldier for fraternizing with French civilians on military property and then arrested the girl as a spy. It may be that the girl had really intended to use her knife, perhaps not. Or perhaps she didn't even own a knife. It didn't matter in the end because her assailant and Sergeant-Major Holzer would die at dawn with Commando dagger thrusts in their throats.

At General Haase's headquarters in the village of Envermeu behind Dieppe, officers manned the telephones in accordance with the state of "Threatened Danger." On the notice board was a copy of the divisional commander's Order of the Day, a fruity, fulsome document dated August 10 which by its wording was obviously aimed at stimulating fervent patriotism in the recruits. It said:

> The information in our hands makes it clear that the Anglo-Americans will be forced, in spite of themselves, by the wretched predicament of the Russians to undertake some operation in the West in the near future.
>
> They must do something –
> (a) in order to keep their Russian allies fighting;
> (b) for home front reasons.
>
> I have repeatedly brought this to the attention of the troops and I ask that my orders on this matter be kept constantly before them so that the idea sink in thoroughly and they expect henceforward nothing else.
>
> The troops must grasp the fact that when it happens it will be a very sticky business.
>
> Bombing and strafing from the air, shelling from the sea, commandos and assault boats, parachutists and air-landing troops, hostile civilians, sabotage and murder – all these they will have to face with steady nerves if they are not to go under.
>
> On no account must the troops let themselves get rattled. Fear is not to be thought of.
>
> When the muck begins to fly the troops must wipe their eyes and ears, grip their weapons more firmly and fight as they have never fought before.
>
> THEM or US
>
> must be the watchword for each man.
>
> The Fuehrer has given the German Armed Forces tasks of every kind in the past and all have been carried out. The task which now confronts us will also be carried out. My men will not prove the worst. I have looked into your eyes. I know that you are German men.
>
> YOU WILL GLADLY DO YOUR SIMPLE DUTY TO THE

DEATH. DO THIS AND YOU WILL REMAIN VICTORIOUS.
LONG LIVE OUR PEOPLE AND FATHERLAND.
LONG LIVE THE FUEHRER, ADOLF HITLER.
[*Signed*]   Your Commander, HAASE.
                   Colonel General.

V

Group 5, consisting of 23 LCP's and a flak ship, through which 460 troops
of No. 3 Commando were dispersed, was led across the Channel by SGB
5, with Commander D. B. Wyburd, the senior group officer, Durnford-
Slater, and Captain Roy Murray, U. S. Rangers, on board. The group
formed into four columns for the trip across the minefield, ran into
the returning minesweepers, and the resulting mix-up so delayed their
progress that Wyburd ordered a slight increase in speed to make up
lost time. The LCP's found it difficult to keep up, and by 2:30 a.m. only
fifteen were in sight astern of SGB 5.

On the gun boat's bridge, Wyburd discussed the situation quietly
with Durnford-Slater and Murray, both of whom, being army men,
were slightly concerned at this casual misplacement of eight LCP's
crammed with soldiers.

"Can't help it," said Wyburd. "We've got to touchdown on time with
as many landing-craft as possible. The rest will follow us somehow.
Main thing is to get as many of you chaps ashore on time as we can."

The Commando colonel and his American protégé, their faces blackened in accordance with raiding custom, nodded agreement but privately hoped that the missing eightsome were not too far behind.
Murray was fascinated by the loneliness of the voyage, a loneliness and
peace which the light whip of the wind, the rush of water down the
gun boat's low-slung sides, and the steady throb of engines seemed to
accentuate. He was a landsman who had been to sea only for the
troopship voyage from New York to Londonderry and on the ferry
boats from Northern Ireland to Scotland. He did not count the training
at Athnacarry where ventures on the nearby lochs had always been
accompanied by the fury of the commandant's so-called practice
firing.

"Never realized before how quiet a combined operation would be,"
he said to no one in particular. As though it were an afterthought and
not something to be concerned about, he added: "What will happen if

we come across the German navy? I hear those E-boats are ferocious goddam beasts."

"We'll just press on regardless," said Wyburd flatly. He had, in fact, decided before sailing that should the enemy be met at sea he would maintain course and speed and try to fight his way through. He had issued orders to all commanding officers in the group to this effect, his motive being, apparently, that any alteration of course or speed would so disorganize the group that it would be impossible to carry out an organized landing. These orders were directly contradictory to those issued for the entire fleet by Hughes-Hallett, who wanted to avoid an encounter at all costs. Surprise at the moment of assault was too vital to be compromised at sea.

Over to the west, the bigger ships of the main assault fleet were nearing the start line where the assault landing-craft would be lowered for the final run into the beaches. They were protected by all the destroyers of which two, *Slazak* and *Brocklesby*, were stationed on the port flank of the fleet in an area just off the port bow of Group 5. No one had seen the two destroyers, of which the Polish commander of *Slazak* was senior officer, since crossing the minefield, something that seemed strange to Wyburd as they were his only protection against German forces.

In fact, *Slazak* and *Brocklesby* were off station about five miles away, and Wyburd would have been even more alarmed had he known that at 1:27 a.m. and at 2:44 a.m. the radar stations at Beachy Head and Newhaven had signalled the warnings of enemy ships moving eastward between Boulogne and Dieppe. Neither of these signals had been received in *Calpe* and, in the absence of orders from Hughes-Hallett, those ships which did receive them, including *Fernie*, took no action.

Instead, Group 5 was allowed to continue on a course leading to a collision with the German convoy which had crossed three miles ahead of the main fleet without either side being aware of the other's presence. It was then about to cross the line Wyburd was following to the Berneval beaches, and the two destroyers intended to cover Group 5 in the event of just this sort of emergency were nowhere in sight.

At precisely 3:47 a.m. the night was brilliantly illuminated by star-shell which exploded high above Group 5. Wyburd gave a single astounded glance upwards before yelling to the military officers: "My God we're in for it. Better get below – quick."

His disbelief that the gamble on an uninterrupted passage had failed was so strong at first that he thought the "lost" destroyers might have somehow reappeared and mistaken the group for an enemy force.

Then every ship in the German convoy opened fire, and he could see that the attack was coming from at least five ships spread in an arc across his bows. The night, so peaceful one minute, had become in the next a brilliantly illuminated inferno of fire. Without *Slazak* and *Brocklesby*, the group were not only outnumbered and outgunned, but they had no means of illuminating the Germans. SGB 5, in particular, was nakedly revealed to an enemy her crew could neither see nor properly engage.

The LCP's broke formation and scattered, mostly unseen by the Germans because of their low silhouettes, while the gun boat, because of Wyburd's orders, steamed directly towards the centre of the enemy arc of fire. The sheer futility of persisting in an attempt to fight a way through became increasingly apparent with each passing minute as heavy shell fire spewed plumes of cordite-filled water over her bridge, and streams of tracer bullets swept the decks.

An armed support landing-craft engaged the nearest German sub-chaser which blew up and retired from the battlefield, but that was also the end of SGB 5's resistance. Enemy fire increased in ferocity, silencing her guns as the crews fell dead or dying around the turrets.

Durnford-Slater, trying to find protection on deck, heard a shout from the bridge and looked up to see an officer beckoning him. He raced up the bridge ladder to be met by Wyburd who said: "Better stay with me. This place is armour-plated." The Commando colonel was not reassured when he looked about to see ten officers and men lying on the deck seriously wounded. One officer, pale and shaken, screamed at him: "This is it. This is the end," and he thought it so likely to be true that he unlaced his army boots and blew up his Mae West.

At 3:57, only ten minutes after the action had begun, SGB 5 received a direct hit in the boiler room and drifted to a stop, helpless and at the mercy of the enemy. Wyburd waited amid the carnage on the wrecked bridge for the German ships to close in for the kill, all the while cursing savagely at the absence of *Slazak and Brocklesby*. To his slowly mounting astonishment the firing diminished and finally ceased, as the enemy ships moved on into the night, evidently having had enough.

The little gun boat was alone in the darkness, but instead of the peace of fifteen minutes before, there was now the loud hissing of escaping steam, the cries of those in pain, and the shouted oaths of men stumbling about in the darkness trying to repair damage and help the wounded.

Scattering had not saved all the LCP's. Four had been so badly damaged they were returning to England, one under the command of a Commando sergeant who had taken over when her entire naval crew were killed. This left fifteen LCP's unaccounted for, and Durnford-Slater concluded that whatever their fate No. 3 Commando could have no further part to play in the raid.

He was wrong. Throughout the action ML 346 had been trying to shepherd the remaining LCP's into some sort of order, eventually managing to round up five which she was now leading at full speed towards Yellow Beach.

A sixth landing-craft, LCP 15, commanded by Lieutenant H. T. Duckee RNVR and carrying three officers and seventeen men of No. 3 Commando's Troop Six, had maintained course and speed in accordance with Wyburd's instructions and had, amazingly, driven undetected through the middle of the enemy convoy. Now she sailed on alone for Yellow Beach, a solitary remnant of a highly trained Commando unit, feeling very naked, impotent, and very forsaken.

Sub-Lieutenant David Lewis RCNVR, of Westmount in the province of Quebec and second in command of the boat, reported: "Our boat was immediately enveloped in the hottest tracer fire I have ever seen. SGB 5's thin armour was riddled, and the shells exploding inside her filled her boiler room with steam. One of the bursts struck LCP 42, killing Sub-Lieutenant Clifford Davidson Wallace of Montreal instantly. In my own boat men threw off the blankets they had used to keep out the night chill and fumbled for their tin hats and weapons. The flak was flying but a few feet ahead and astern of us, some right above us.

"At full speed we tore away from the lashing beams of flak. . . . Astern we could see starshells, flak converging, and a big flash which died down and then blew up and lit the sky. I never found out what this was."

It is often the case in war that a handful of ordinary men are called upon to overcome their private fears and do extraordinary things. The fate of Group 5, by showing how wrong military predictions can be, had precipitated the five sailors under Duckee and the twenty soldiers under Major Peter Young, a veteran Commando raider who had already won the Military Cross, into just this sort of predicament – they could turn back or proceed with an impossible undertaking, one which four hundred and sixty Commandos had considered risky business indeed.

Until the naval encounter, Jubilee had been blessed, from the viewpoint of security, by relatively good fortune. Von Rundstedt's appreciation of the military position prior to 4:00 a.m. on the 19th said:

> Up to the commencement of the battle action . . . enemy air
> operations by day or night did not point in any particular way
> to an impending landing. . . . Interception of operational and
> training wireless traffic in England presented no deviation from
> normal. . . . No identification of enemy forces were reported by
> radar equipment up to receipt of the report of the sea battle off
> Dieppe. . . . Single targets were briefly registered after 0300 hours
> by the equipment at Le Treport as up to 10 miles north of Dieppe
> and taken in connection with engine noises which had been
> earlier reported they were held to be air targets.

But once the Jubilee forces had been irrevocably enmeshed by the
naval encounter, the operation was forsaken by the element of luck
that it needed even before it had properly begun. First there was the
failure of radar to succeed in warning the fleet, then misfortune was
compounded by the absence of *Slazak* and *Brocklesby* from their
proper stations and the Polish commander's subsequent failure to intervene in the battle, because being astern and to port of Group No. 5
he had been under the mistaken impression that the firing was coming
from shore; and finally Wyburd's decision to fight through, instead of
taking avoiding action, achieved what he had hoped to prevent. The
LCP's were scattered, the Berneval landings thoroughly disorganized.

Had *Slazak* and *Brocklesby* been closer in where they were supposed
to be, and had the Polish senior officer at least investigated the flare-up,
the destroyers could have dispersed the enemy force and blasted a way
for Wyburd to follow. While there can be little doubt about Wyburd's
gallantry, when he realized he would get no help from the destroyers, he
would have given his charges better protection had he used his gun boat's
superior speed and smoke-laying capability to hide them from the
enemy while they altered course to avoid contact – which is precisely
what Hughes-Hallett intended they should do. In any event the attack
on Yellow Beach had been weakened even before the action, as four
of the missing LCP's had broken down on passage and had turned back
to England with the majority of the U.S. Rangers carried between them.
Their commanding officer, Captain Murray, never managed to land
either. After leaving SGB 5 in a landing-craft, he was taken on a lengthy
cruise around the fleet and finally back to Newhaven.

Neither Roberts nor Hughes-Hallett were aware of what had happened. They had seen and heard the gun fire to the east of them but
had no idea it involved Group 5 or that it might bear heavily on the
outcome of the operation. Naval Operational Orders stated clearly that

wireless silence could be broken by the senior officer of Group 5 "if by delays or casualties it is the opinion of the senior military officer that the success of the landing at Yellow Beach is seriously jeopardized."

Wyburd, however, never had a chance to use SGB's radio, which was wrecked by the first enemy barrage, and it was not until two hours later, after transferring from one small craft to another, that he and Durnford-Slater reached *Calpe* with a complete report of the incident – too late to influence the raid which was by then moving slowly and inevitably towards its climax.

The effect of the engagement at sea on the Germans ashore, according to von Rundstedt's war diary, was that "the alarm was given in the coastal sector" and the 302nd Division reported troops in the Berneval, Puits, and Dieppe areas "in a higher state of alert." Pourville and Varengeville were too far to the west for defences there to be unduly excited by what appeared to be a minor convoy battle beyond their jurisdiction, and the alert merely served to bring only the coastal batteries in those areas to a state of instant readiness.

The division still refrained from ordering general action stations because, just as Wyburd had no wireless with which to report to *Calpe*, so the German naval forces were unable to report ashore. SGB 5's guns had wrecked their transmitters early in the brief encounter and, lacking any real information, German naval headquarters expressed the opinion that nothing more had happened than "a customary attack on convoy."

The German defences were prepared to resist a raid should it materialize, but they were not expecting it that night in particular, nor did they assume that the flare-up at sea indicated the presence of major assault forces. Surprise was still possible.

However, the initial mistakes were about to multiply.

IV

In far away Canada, where it was either evening or night, thousands of relatives of men about to kill or be killed were washing up supper dishes, putting children to bed, and praying that the lonely days would soon be over. They had become so used to letters from England that it never occurred to most of them that the Army might one day move, might actually fight. After all, apart from training-mishaps or fatal brawls, no Canadian soldier had been killed or wounded in the European war.

They had no way of knowing that the Canadian Army had found its war at last, that it was off the leash and ready to pounce with such ferocity that it would be stunned on impact against a steel-girdled throat. This young, devoted generation of amateur warriors were to discover in nine brutal, bitter hours that war is neither gay nor adventurous, that it consists of only one per cent glory and ninety-nine per cent pure bloody misery. They would be tested in fire, as had other generations before them, as if to prove again that life is a barren existence without the faith and integrity of man to clothe it with dignity. They would learn too that when these qualities are forged in the furnace of human conflict and then cooled to a finely tempered hardness in pools of fear-filled sweat, disaster becomes the birthplace of enduring strength, the fountainhead of a spirit which transcends defeat.

THE

GLORY

At sea, at night, at war. Blacked-out ships, sounds stilled, murmured conversation, and low-pitched orders. Pale moonlight gives visibility up to a mile or so and then accentuates the darkness beyond. More than two hundred ships of all shapes, sizes, and speeds entering hostile waters unseen by even themselves yet conforming to an intangible adhesive called "The Plan."

There is typical Combined Operations thinking about it all: you have a plan, officers and men are told what to do, then communication between units is forbidden and you pray they will somehow be able to do it. These are the principles of small, stealthy raiding parties now being applied to a major military operation, and the dramatic consequences of this most fundamental of all mistakes are about to unfold.

Although the Force Commanders are unaware of it, disintegration of The Plan has already commenced. They can do nothing about it even when they realize it. From this point on, Roberts is a land commander afloat, without a command; Hughes-Hallett is a naval commander who must hide his fleet by using smoke, with the result that the fleet is largely hidden from itself.

To exercise proper command they must have a constant flow of reliable information from the six beaches under assault. The most complicated communications network ever devised for an amphibious operation is designed specifically for this purpose. It is not the equipment that fails. No one had thought the Germans would shoot most of the operators and destroy most of the sets.

The
Commandos
go in

In the pre-dawn darkness, *Calpe* steamed towards Dieppe accompanied by *Fernie*, the bombarding destroyers, and flotillas of landing-craft. The flank attacks fanned out – the Commandos heading left and right to the extremities of the ten-mile front to silence the huge coastal batteries that threatened the fleet; the Royal Regiment of Canada heading for Puits, a beach on the left side of Dieppe Harbour from where they would occupy the East Headland; the South Saskatchewans sailing for Pourville to the right of Dieppe from where they would storm up the right side of the West Headland.

The Force Commanders were together yet curiously apart, each absorbed by his own responsibilities: for Roberts the attack on Dieppe and its flanks; for Hughes-Hallett the business of maintaining and organizing a fleet under the guns of the enemy. He could do it only if the powerful 6-inch batteries at Berneval to the east and Varengeville to the west were destroyed. If the Commando failed, these guns alone could blow destroyers and landing-craft out of the water at the first light of day.

LCP 15 sailed forlornly towards the coast, the men in her silent and strained. Duckee answered a question no one had asked. "My orders," he said, "are quite clear. They are to put you chaps ashore, even if I have to wreck my boat doing it. I intend putting you ashore. O.K.?"

Peter Young, his face blacker than his hair or moustache, replied cheerfully, "Then I think you'd better get us there fast as you can before Jerry wakes up."

Duckee probably had no idea of just how wild this particular three-some of Commando officers really were. Major Young, of medium height, athletic build, and immensely strong, had already earned a reputation for being shrewd, calculating, and inventive, an officer who enjoyed fighting because each action provided him with an oppor-tunity to try out new ideas on how best to refine the art of creating terror along enemy-held coasts. Captain John Selwyn was a veteran raider with a rather awesome contempt for danger, while Lieutenant Buck Ruxton from Northern Ireland had once planned to blow up the German Embassy in Dublin. He had intended visiting the capital of Southern Ireland one weekend in civilian clothes, ostensibly to spend a day at the races, and while there would entice the Irish personnel out of the Embassy with cases of whisky before destroying it with plastic explosives. He had actually received Durnford-Slater's blessing for the project when a raid on Norway came up and his energies were diverted to a more legitimate form of warfare.

Duckee drove the little boat steadily towards a gap in the cliffs which he identified as the western gully leading up to the heights above. As they neared the beach, there was no sign of enemy activity and the troops prepared to land; between them they had one Garand automatic rifle, a present from Roy Murray to Peter Young, a Bren gun which Ruxton nursed lovingly, their tommy guns, and two bandoliers each.

Young whispered to Duckee, "Wait for us if you can. But if Jerry's fire gets too hot clear out. We'll make our way to join the Canadians at Dieppe."

Duckee was too busy navigating to argue, but having come so far he had no intention of abandoning his soldiers ashore if he could help it.

LCP 15 touched down at 4:45 a.m., five minutes before zero, and the twenty Commandos plunged over the bows – a quiet landing, performed neatly as if on exercise, three and a half miles east of Dieppe on a sloping beach 100 yards long and 400 yards wide. Young led the dash across the shale to the rocky ledges at the base of the cliffs and then into the narrow entrance of the gully.

The gully was choked with barbed wire seven feet high behind a wall of thick rabbit-wire lattice work. Young was pretty certain that the footpath leading upwards on the other side so invitingly would be mined and, in any event, his party had neither wire-cutters nor Bangalore torpedoes with which to blow gaps in the fencing. He used sign language to indicate his orders, and the party began climbing up the left-hand side of the gully, using the German wire as rope and the iron stakes securing it as steps. Speed was essential, and the sweating men swore with pain as barbs ripped through gloves and clothing, tearing at their flesh.

Daylight came, exposing them on the cliff face where they clung to ledges of soft, crumbling chalk. They expected to hear the big guns open fire on the main fleet off Dieppe at any moment.

If they were undismayed by their own weakness, they were considerably encouraged at the sight of another small force of landing-craft approaching the eastern beach. These were the five which had been gathered up by ML 346 after the naval action and led towards the coast until they could see the cliffs in silhouette through the early morning haze and half-light of dawn; a high, thin overcast shaded out the waning moon, and the chill of night's end seeped through the battle-dress uniforms of men drenched in spray.

Leading the 96 Commandos and six U.S. Rangers in the five boats was Captain R. L. Wills, now suddenly and unexpectedly responsible for what appeared to be the only major assault likely to take place at Berneval. It worried him not at all, mainly because he was a supremely confident young man who, a year before, during the raid on the Lofoten Islands off Norway, had captured a post office and written out a telegram addressed to Adolf Hitler, Reichschancellery, Berlin. It had said: "You said in your last speech that German troops would meet the English wherever they landed stop I am here stop Where are your troops? . . . Wills, 2nd Lieutenant." He had waited with tommy gun dangling nonchalantly in the crook of his arm while a German army postal clerk had dispatched it "at urgent rates, please."

He had studied photographs of the terrain over which he would have to fight for so long that the details were seared vividly into his mind. The steep 300-foot cliffs were split by the eastern gully that widened into a gorge leading to the high land where open country

surrounded the Goebbels battery. Once reassured that they were heading for the right beach, Wills looked about him at the other boats on
either beam and astern.

Troops were crouched low; only blackened faces showed above the
gunwales. In the leading craft, the flotilla officer, Lieutenant-Commander C. L. Corke, hunched down beside the coxswain giving orders
in a subdued monotone. A specialist navigator, Corke knew that while
he was delivering this remaining section of No. 3 Commando to the
proper beach it was too late – far too late. The Germans at Berneval
were ready, waiting for first light to present them with better targets.

The approach had been reported by a ten-man patrol stationed at a
lookout on the edge of the cliffs, and defences covering the gully had
been manned by 150 men supported by mortars, machine guns, and
anti-tank weapons. Two machine-gun nests were set back on the
beach itself, hard against the foot of the cliff faces. Another 250 men
guarded the Goebbels battery, and three companies of infantry were
held in reserve in a nearby village.

By 5:30 a.m. the glimmer in the east turned into the spreading col-
ours of day, revealing red-tinged clouds, blue sky above green countryside, white chalk cliffs, green-blue water, and grey-painted ships.

The beach was a yellow expanse of shingle sloping for 300 yards
from the entrance to the narrow gully to the water's edge. Nothing on
it or about it moved, and large 25-foot rocks hid the machine-gun
nests from the sight of the approaching raiders. To the right, on the
heights overlooking the beach, were a church and a white-painted
house, a placid scene so deceptively peaceful that the experienced
Commandos tautened instinctively. At 100 yards, they knew their
instincts had served them well. The heights erupted into a fury of
fire, shells cascading down among the landing-craft, machine-gun
bursts whipping the sea between them into spouts of boiling foam.
Men died where they crouched, others screamed as they flopped to
the decks, and the dead were pushed overboard to make more space
for the living.

ML 346 zig-zagged wildly across the line of advance, replying to
unseen targets with her own limited armament until a new danger
crept in from the west – an armed German tanker. The ML raced to
intercept and found herself heavily engaged by both the ship and the
guns ashore.

Lieutenant-Commander Corke collapsed dying beside his coxswain
who, in the next second, was killed outright. A Commando leapt to
the wheel, steadied the boat, and aimed it at the beach. The landing-

craft were hit constantly during those last few yards, some sinking gradually lower in the water but kept afloat by their own momentum and by the will-power of the men they carried.

At 5:35 a.m. and in daylight, all five touched down and the soldiers scrambled ashore, racing headlong into the muzzles of the lower machine-gun nests which now came into the action for the first time. More fire spewed from the white buildings on the cliff, laying down a continuous barrage on the charging Commandos.

Wills covered 150 yards before he died; Edwin Loustalot dashed straight at the right-hand machine gun and died on the run, the first Ranger and U.S. infantry officer to be killed in Europe; Corporal Halls ran blindly at the left-hand machine gun throwing grenades, and when sanity returned he had captured it single-handed without suffering so much as a scratch or a bruise.

ML 346 had seen the fire from the buildings on the cliff and while her small arms engaged the armed tanker, seen to be called *Franz*, she directed her two-pounder at the buildings. When they had been subdued, she turned her attention to *Franz*, closed to within thirty yards, and subjected it to a ferocious hammering until it exploded, caught fire, and drifted ashore. The victorious ML sent a boarding-party across to collect battle trophies – ensign and boat compasses – and then returned to support the troops who were pinned down in the gully. Germans lined the cliff tops lobbing grenades down into the middle of the rocks where they had taken cover.

At 7:00 a.m. an attempt was made to withdraw, the three remaining landing-craft coming in under intense fire only to find that a new hazard had been revealed by the ebbing tide – rows of five-foot iron stakes protruding above the surface in the breaking waves. The naval beach party boarded one of the landing-craft, and about two dozen troops made the dash back across the beach to the other two, both of which were firmly impaled upon rocks and stakes. There could be no further hope of evacuating the eastern Berneval beach; the Commandos trapped in the gully faced annihilation or capture, though they had not reached the stage of admitting to either possibility.

But the inevitable could not be long delayed. Major von Bluecher, commanding three companies of a German mechanized anti-tank regiment, reinforced the defences and led a counter-attack down into the gully. At 10:00 a.m. the Commandos were overwhelmed and eighty-two survivors were marched off into prisoner-of-war camps. One trooper escaped, ran into the surf, and swam three miles before being picked up by the only surviving landing-craft.

II

Peter Young and his small band had seen the landing on the eastern beach, had heard the firing, and had assumed that the bulk of No. 3 Commando were advancing towards Berneval.

They climbed for forty-five minutes, reached the top of the cliff, and gathered in a wood lying at the junction of the gorge and the main Dieppe-Berneval road. Young reconnoitred the road, found it empty, and beckoned the rest to follow him. At the first bend there was a moment of alarm when a 16-year-old French boy appeared on a bicycle and was so startled by the sight of twenty armed, black-faced raiders that he lost control and fell off. Two grinning, French-speaking Commandos lifted him up, dusted him off, and put him back on his saddle. Once reassured, the excited boy offered to guide them to the Battery which, he said, was guarded by at least two hundred Germans. Young declined the offer, deciding that instead of making a lone attack on the Battery he would join up with the force from the eastern beach.

In the southern outskirts of the village the Commandos cut the telephone wires leading to Dieppe and marched towards the main street where they met a crowd of Frenchmen who, according to official records, "showed great friendliness and pointed out the exact location of the Battery."

The Commandos proceeded through Berneval and at the northern end of the village, close to a church, made contact with a machine-gun emplacement on the outer defence perimeter of the Battery. Selwyn and Ruxton counter-attacked, and the whole party were able to escape into the churchyard where the machine gun could no longer see them. Young wanted to get the Bren gun and a pair of snipers up into the belfry of the church from where they could hold the area and snipe down on the Battery itself. But neither stairs nor any other means of getting up could be found.

He led them on a detour through an orchard to a cornfield across which the Battery could be clearly seen two hundred yards away. Although there was precious little cover for the party, Young spread them out into three groups, with orders to keep firing and moving in an attempt to give the impression that the force was much larger than it was. An extraordinary battle ensued.

The Commandos laid down steady harassing fire on the Battery, creating complete confusion among its crews and defenders. The Germans, unable to advance across the open cornfield into their fire, reacted by resorting to the use of their heavy guns which were trained slowly and laboriously around until they faced inland instead of out to sea. Then they opened fire at the Commandos who were so close that the blast and din of each salvo nearly blew them out of their cover.

But the big, powerful guns could not be sufficiently depressed and the shells merely whistled over their heads to land more than a mile away. By way of reply, the Commandos waited for each belching explosion and then poured concentrated fire into the resulting cloud of smoke and cordite fumes. It became a game, a remorseless, deadly game which twenty men armed with tommy guns were winning against two hundred men armed with machine guns, flak guns, and, finally, huge coastal guns. Any attempt to capture the Battery was out of the question, but Young's party was achieving virtually the same result by preventing it being used against the fleet lying off Dieppe.

This incredibly uneven struggle was further aggravated by a danger the Commandos could neither see nor stop. Off the eastern beach ML 346, hearing the sound of the heavy guns and thinking they were being fired at the fleet, hotly engaged the Battery, which it couldn't see, with its two-pounder, and the shells were falling in the cornfield among the Commandos.

The action lasted for an hour and a half, during which the big guns were able to fire only twenty-two rounds at targets they couldn't possibly hit. The Germans never really knew the weakness of the force attacking them and never dared to send a patrol to find out. Finally Young, realizing that ammunition was running short and that the main raid on Dieppe should be nearing its end, decided to withdraw. He sent Selwyn back to the beach with orders to fire three white Verey lights if LCP 15 was still available for evacuation.

Twenty minutes later the signals were seen bursting over the beach, and Young led the retreat at a dignified, unhurried pace. The enemy followed at a respectful distance until they were spotted by the ever-watchful ML 346 which immediately switched targets to cover the withdrawal.

Duckee, in LCP 15, had remained off the beach behind smoke-screens for nearly three hours and now he manœuvred inshore, touching down just as Young's party entered the gully. There was a brief hold-up while the Commandos climbed back over the wire; then they burst out into the beach and dashed for the landing-craft, with Young and Ruxton fighting a two-man rearguard action.

Duckee was already pulling his boat astern when the two officers reached the surf. Heedless of the bullets whipping into the breaking waves around them, they took off their Mae Wests and calmly blew them up. Young placed his Garand automatic rifle on one Mae West while Ruxton laid the Bren gun across the other. Then they pushed their guns ahead of them as they swam out to the landing-craft, in accordance with a Commando rule that weapons must be preserved at all costs.

At 8:20 a.m. LCP 15 vanished behind a self-laid smokescreen and headed back across the Channel to England with twenty happy Commandos on board, some wounded but all alive and proudly conscious that for the two most critical hours of Jubilee they had protected the main fleet from the big guns at Berneval.

Hughes-Hallett was to write in his official report later: "In my judgement this was perhaps the most outstanding incident of the operation."

At the time neither he nor Roberts had the slightest idea of what had happened at Berneval. No beach signals had landed and it was not until Durnford-Slater and Commander Wyburd transferred aboard *Calpe* in the region of 6:00 a.m. to report personally on the naval encounter that the Force Commanders began to cast anxious thoughts towards Berneval. For Hughes-Hallett it was a question of when the big coastal guns would begin to lay their barrage and disperse the fleet; for Roberts, whose forces had by then landed along the entire ten-mile strip of coast, it was a problem of keeping the fleet intact to effect the evacuation. They knew nothing of Young's remarkable exploit until the eventual return to England.

III

Behind and to the south of the village of Varengeville was the formidable Hess Battery which, with the Goebbels Battery at Berneval, constituted the main defences of Dieppe. Each of the six powerful guns, manufactured in 1936 and designed for a maximum range of 24,000 yards, was mounted on a concrete platform revolving on a central pivot. Normal rate of fire was one round per gun per minute, but this could be doubled in emergencies. The special duty of the Battery was to lay a curtain of fire in the sea in front of Dieppe at a fixed range of 8,600 yards. Behind it was a high flak gun and observation tower and on either side were anti-tank and machine-gun emplacements which also covered the sea approaches and beaches. Seven special strongpoints were sited round a barbed-wire perimeter to defend the Battery against infantry attack.

This was the target. Lord Lovat planned to destroy it with 245 Commandos, six U.S. Rangers, and two Free French Commandos as guides.

Even allowing for the relative magnitudes of the tasks and forces involved, the economy of Lovat's military plan, which he code-named "Cauldron," was in startling contrast to the welter of detail in the military plan for Jubilee. In outline it consisted of twelve paragraphs on four pages; in detail it was expanded by only two pages.

Furthermore, it budgeted for such unforeseen eventualities as late landings, wrong landings, lack of surprise, heavier opposition than estimated, and for failure on one of the two beaches to be used. The Jubilee plan provided alternatives only in the event of some infantry landing-ships being sunk on passage. Apart from its brevity, Cauldron was at variance with Jubilee in one important aspect. In Churchill Mann's detailed plan the two brigadiers were allowed to take two copies each ashore, while battalion commanders could carry extracts pertaining to their individual tasks. Lovat's orders were: "No marked maps, operations orders, or any documents whatsoever will be taken ashore."

The Cauldron plan dismissed the possibility of taking prisoners during darkness and continued: "After daybreak . . . as many prisoners as possible will be taken. . . . No prisoner-of-war cage will be established. Prisoners will be securely tied by their thumbs with fish-line in the best Japanese tradition, after which they will be . . . marched down to the beach. Prisoners will always be required to carry Commando wounded."

This particular method of binding prisoners had a definite usefulness to Commandos raiding the enemy coast, but the Canadians were hardly in the same position. It may be that certain officers, Insinger for one and perhaps Churchill Mann for another, preferred to regard as a raid an operation which was really a *bona fide* military amphibious assault.

Zero hour for landing was 4:50 a.m. and re-embarkation was timed for 7:30 – two hours and forty minutes for the operation, for which the Commando was divided into two groups. One group, consisting of seventy men under Major Derek Mills-Roberts, was to land at Orange One Beach near Varengeville and engage the Battery frontally with small-arms fire and mortar bombing. The other group, comprising the main body of the Commando, approximately 180 men under Lord

Lovat himself, would land at Orange Two Beach near Quiberville and approach the Battery from the rear. After a prearranged strike by cannon-firing Hurricanes, this group would then take it by fixed bayonet assault.

Both groups would be in "walkie-talkie" contact with the headquarters ship, and a special intelligence Phantom signals unit would relay information from both beaches direct to the War Office and to Mountbatten at Uxbridge.

The first group would land on a beach that was really just a narrow cove about seventy yards long with the beach sixty yards across. The only exit was a tiny gully, little more than a crack in the cliffs about eight feet wide which led up to the high ground. Lovat's second group would land on a much larger beach some three hundred yards long and four hundred yards deep, one that had several exits, of which the best was an incline to the right leading to the wide valley of the Saane through which the Commandos would pass to reach the Battery.

In charge of navigating these twin forces to their respective beaches was Lieutenant-Commander Hugh Mulleneux, sailing in MGB 312 which would lead in the landing-craft. Acting as close support ship would be SGB 9 commanded by Peter Scott, peacetime painter and naturalist. Between the two beaches was the Pointe d'Ailly Lighthouse, an octagonal tower some eighty feet high and situated on top of the rounded summit of a 250-foot headland. It was camouflaged in green and yellow but its silhouette stood out against the skyline from sea level so starkly that even when not working it could be seen for five miles on a clear night through binoculars.

The troops spent their time in the convoy cleaning weapons, sorting out ammunition, and adjusting woollen caps – this Commando rarely using steel helmets. They painted their faces, some achieving a proper blackness, others emerging with a Red Indian effect, and the snipers using a pale green to merge with the foliage of trees in which they expected to perch.

After the briefing, Lovat spoke quietly with Mills-Roberts. "Do you think you'll find that crack in the cliffs all right, Derek?"

"Yes – no reason why not," replied his second in command who privately felt there were too many reasons why he might not.

The main fleet reached the start point ten miles off Dieppe at precisely 3:00 a.m., and the boatswain's whistle aboard *Prince Albert* summoned the troops to the assault boats, most of which were overloaded with ammunition and equipment. Once lowered, the boats formed up in two columns astern of MGB 312, and because there was still ten miles to go several of the men including Mills-Roberts found convenient corners in which to sleep.

As they headed towards the French coast a light flashed ashore, once . . . twice . . . three times, and Mulleneux chortled with relief. The Pointe d'Ailly Lighthouse was working. For No. 4 Commando, tactical surprise seemed possible, as it was highly improbable that the enemy would be obliging enough to assist an invader he expected, unless he was baiting a trap.

While they watched the lighthouse, starshell burst far away to port, followed by the slow, graceful trajectories of tracer bullets. When the flare-up had died away, they were treated to the spectacle of red and green navigation lights winking steadily on the harbour entrance to Dieppe.

At 4:42 the columns broke up, three landing-craft taking Mills-Roberts and his group straight ahead to their beach and the rest veering off to starboard for the beach near Quiberville where Lovat would land. Two Spitfires of 129 Squadron from Thorney Island roared low overhead and strafed the lighthouse which immediately doused its light. Flak erupted along the coast as more fighters dived down to the Hess Battery, creating a diversion of fire and explosions which covered the approach of the landing-craft.

The first group touched down with immaculate precision – on time, on the proper beach. The soldiers raced ashore and instead of being met by opposing fire there was only the sound of shifting pebbles under their feet. "It was rather like stealing round to the back door of a house where a noisy party is in progress and finding nothing but silence," said Mills-Roberts.

They huddled in the dark shadow of the cliffs to avoid being seen by someone who was clearly visible strolling along the top of a cliff. Their eight-foot wide crack with a pathway leading up to the heights above was crammed with dannert wire through which a gap wide enough to stand the traffic had to be blown by Bangalore torpedoes. They watched the unknown stroller to see how he reacted to the explosions, but he seemed so unconcerned they assumed that he associated the racket with the noise of flak guns farther inland.

Mills-Roberts led the dash through the gap up to the high ground where they found themselves amid a group of white-painted, dirty-looking villas. The sky had lightened, and the local inhabitants were getting up to see how the air raid was progressing. Mills-Roberts placed his defence perimeter, sent another section ahead to conduct a house-to-house search for sleeping German officers, and was then mildly startled by the appearance of two troopers escorting an elderly Frenchman clad in an ankle-length nightgown. He was immediately sorry for the old man who had given up all hope of maintaining even a semblance of dignity and personally led him back to his house where a young girl was waiting on the porch.

"Are you going to shoot Papa?" she asked unemotionally. And Mills-Roberts realized for the first time that to the French people his Commandos must appear to be Germans returning from an exercise. Battle-dress uniforms of any nation are not particularly distinctive, and he hastened to explain that his men were British.

The girl merely shrugged as if soldiers were much the same no matter what they claimed to be and took her father indoors out of sight. Mills-Roberts, not quite certain that he had been as gallant as he might have been, returned to his war and led his men into a wood close to the Battery. They reached it in time to be thoroughly shaken by a series of shattering explosions which hammered on their eardrums. It was the Battery firing its first barrage at the fleet lying off Dieppe.

As there were still fifty minutes to go before Lovat could work round inland to come up from the rear, something had to be done to prevent the Battery firing again. It was no time for stealth, and in their hurry the group crashed through the waist-high undergrowth, making a dreadful din.

All at once they broke out of the wood and had to fall flat on their faces. The Battery perimeter wire was only 100 yards away, and German officers could be heard quite distinctly giving orders to the gunners. Mills-Roberts spotted a two-storey barn to his right. He decided to spread out his men in the scrub facing the Battery while he and a pair of snipers returned to the wood, making their way through it to the barn. On the way they were joined by the house-searchers coming up from the rear and together they broke open the barn door, rushed up some stairs, and charged into a huge room with a window overlooking the Battery, giving an excellent, unobstructed view of the crews of all six guns working in their concrete pits.

One immense German stood in full view issuing a stream of orders – an inviting, irresistible target. At a gesture from Mills-Roberts one of the snipers rested his rifle on a table and took careful aim. Sharpshooters can never be hurried, and the rest of the party fumed silently as he spent an endless time adjusting sights and taking a long look down the barrel. The range was only 170 yards – point blank to a sniper – and having nothing else to think about while he waited,

Mills-Roberts grew acutely aware that once the shot was fired the barn would be an equally easy target for the Germans.

He was looking into the Battery compound through binoculars when the rifle cracked and the victim flopped to the ground. The astonished Germans were even more disconcerted when the men Mills-Roberts had left in the scrub opened fire in unison.

For a minute or so it was a pretty one-sided battle, the Germans preferring to huddle down behind sandbag parapets. Then a heavy machine gun barked angrily from the top of the flak tower behind the Battery, and streams of tracer bullets raked the edge of the wood. Mills-Roberts raced back into it to bring up his own reserves – an anti-tank and mortar detachment.

The anti-tank gun put the flak tower out of commission, and the third mortar bomb landed right in the middle of the cordite charges and shells the Germans had stacked alongside the big guns ready for instant use.

They ignited with a blinding flash followed by a stupendous explosion which silenced the guns for good. It was exactly 6:07 a.m., little more than an hour after touchdown. The Commandos ceased firing temporarily to listen to the cries of the German wounded, to watch survivors rush around the compound carrying fire extinguishers and stretchers.

At this point the Commando attack was being directed from the scrub facing the perimeter defences and from the barn where the snipers upstairs had been reinforced by the anti-tank gunners. Somehow Ranger Corporal Frank Koons had found a slit in the side of the side of the barn on the ground floor and was happily sniping at anything moving within range. "I stayed there until after a mighty goshawful blast and then got out to join Sergeants Stempson and Szima."

The Germans, showing typical resilience to sudden adversity, recovered quickly to lay down an awesome barrage of mortar bombs and machine-gun fire on both the scrub and the barn. There was nothing Mills-Roberts could do but wait until Lovat's main group arrived for the finale.

At 6:25 his mortars lobbed smoke bombs onto the Battery, and one minute later cannon-fighters roared down for a four-minute strike designed to soften up the defences for Lovat's assault – if he reached the rear of the Battery in time.

IV

Lovat's Commandos touched down precisely on time at precisely the right place, and once again tactical surprise was achieved. But as soon as the troops hit the beach a green Verey signal burst overhead, the signal for a pillbox at the eastern end to open fire on the withdrawing landing-craft.

The troops reacted swiftly, like clockwork, one group rushing straight at the pillbox to silence it with hand grenades while another, led by Lieutenant A. S. S. Veasey, ignored the gullies, raced for the cliffs, ran up tubular steel scaling-ladders, climbed to the top and took out two more pillboxes covering the valley leading inland.

Another concealed machine gun pinned them down momentarily until Trooper Bill Finney expressed his contempt for it by climbing a telegraph pole to cut telephone wires while bullets splintered the pole beside him and played a nerve-shattering tune on strands of twanging wire about his head.

Lovat then led his men through the barbed wire barring exit from the beach and avoided a minefield by the simple expedience of obeying signposts which warned civilians in German and French to beware of mines laid in certain directions.

The Commando operated like a thoroughly efficient machine – with one exception. Lieutenant Donald Gilchrist found that while advancing at the head of his section towards the barbed wire his trousers were coming down. He was a very young officer, a newcomer to No. 4 Commando and very conscious of his duty to lead his men into action. The problem was how he could possibly do it with dignity at the risk of being indecently exposed.

He fought his way through the barbed wire entanglements with one hand while holding up his trousers with the other, but more of his metal battle-dress buttons caught in the wire and flew off in all directions.

When he was through at last he gave his temperamental trousers a final angry hitch and lunged forward after his section, who by this time had passed him by. He stumbled, nearly fell, and discovered to his chagrin that his trousers had simply slipped all the way down. After hasty repairs he dashed off in hot and mortified pursuit of the Commando – one hand firmly clutching his tommy gun and the other entwined self-consciously in the folds of his trousers.

"If any one of my Commandos had said one wrong word, I'd probably have shot him dead and then burst into tears," he has since confessed.

The troops ran for half a mile along the banks of the River Saane before turning eastwards to gather in a copse close to the Battery – and be greeted by the shocked faces of thirty-five German assault troops forming up for an attack against the positions held by Mills-Roberts. The Commandos lifted their guns in instinctive, automatic reaction, and before the enemy could recover from their surprise all thirty-five were dead.

Lovat ordered his men to prepare for the charge and a party of Bangalore torpedo carriers crept across the open ground to the Battery perimeter wire where they waited for the confusion which would accompany the air strike to cover their activities when they blew gaps in it.

During a slight lull which followed, a Ranger party consisting of Sergeants Stempson and Szima and Corporals Frank Koons and Haggerty watched idly while a German soldier emerged from a nearby house and began relieving himself in the open. Koons casually lifted his rifle and fired, then all four Rangers rushed over the body into the house, up the stairs and onto the roof where they were presented with a magnificent view of the Battery gun pits. They started sniping and Koons, being the first Ranger to kill a German, if not the first American soldier to do so, was hard put to keep up with his companions who were equally determined to claim their quotas of German dead.

This rather insignificant little cameo suffered an unexpected interlude when the air strike began and a Hurricane's cannon fire overshot the Battery, hit their house, and blasted them off the roof. They fell to the ground in a heap, picked themselves up and, finding no bones broken, dashed back up to their roof to continue the grim business of pouring fire into the Battery. Stempson recalled: "I had nowhere to go anyway. Seven men in my section had been killed outright; only three of us were left."

Donald Gilchrist also remembers a British sniper hitting a German standing on the flak tower at a range of about two hundred yards. While his troop leader watched the victim topple off the tower and fall some eighty feet to the ground, the sniper shouted triumphantly, "Now do I get my bloody proficiency pay, sir?" It had been reduced a week earlier for a bad performance in a practice shoot.

About 6:30 a.m. the Hurricanes finished their strike on the Battery and soared away. Lovat fired three white Verey lights from his copse to warn Mills-Rogers on the other side and then sounded the charge on the hunting-horn always slung over his shoulders. The Commandos, fixed bayonets ready, let out a terrifying battle cry and surged out into the open.

They had 250 yards to cover, each precious yard contested by seven German machine guns firing from behind concrete emplacements. Ugly, black-painted steel took on a dull frightening gleam in the sunlight as the assault line neared the perimeter where a few Commandos fell, the rest plunging on, driven by the appalling fury of the moment. They leapt through gaps in the wire, crossed it on the bodies of their own dead and dying, and when one troop lost its officers, Major Pat Porteous took command by simply crossing on the run to lead them into the first gun pit. Although wounded three times himself he bayoneted the gun's crew virtually single-handed – an exploit for which he would receive the Victoria Cross.

Company Sergeant-Major W. R. Stockdale lost a foot, so he sat down and engaged a machine gun with his rifle. Once through the wire the attackers were almost halted and transfixed by the sight of a German officer using his heavy boots to stomp the life out of a wounded and helpless Commando. The frenzied impetus of the charge slackened, exhilaration evaporated, and it was time for terror. Eyes, set in blackened, sweat-streaked faces, lost all trace of an earlier haunted, hate-filled desperation. They became instead stony and opaque, blank and merciless, reflecting neither triumph, nor pity, nor compassion. Bayonets and knives swept up, down, and across in a rhythmic slashing of bellies, limbs, and throats. Battery Sergeant Holzer and the German sapper rapist who had accused his victim of trying to knife him a few hours before both died by the blade in that attack.

The Battery commandant was the last to die. He was in his office attempting to destroy confidential papers when a Commando trooper burst in and stalked him round a large table. When he was finally cornered, the commandant lost his chance to live as a prisoner by reaching for the pistol in his holster. His hand never completed the movement. Instead, he looked at the Commando in stunned amazement, grasped at the sharp bayonet stuck firmly in his stomach with both hands and tore them to shreds trying to stop the blade twisting and turning inside him.

The shockingly lustful assault was over within ten minutes, and of the 112 Germans in the guns' crews only four were left alive to be taken back to England as prisoners.

Commando casualties totalled forty-five dead and wounded.

Suddenly a squadron of German fighters came in low overhead and, with no time at all in which to take cover, the tensed Commandos contrived to appear relaxed while waving gaily to the pilots. Uniforms look much alike from the air, and the pilots waved amiably in reply, satisfied that all was well below. If the Army looked as if it were taking life easy, why should they be envious? It was, after all, a hot summer's day, a glorious day to be in France by the seaside.

When the aircraft had gone, the big guns were spiked and blown up. Lovat, tall and relaxed in corduroy slacks, grey sweater, and Winchester sporting-rifle tucked carelessly under his arm, looking more like a Highland chieftain out for a day's shooting on the moors than an army officer, gave the surrounding buildings a disapproving glance and ordered: "Burn 'em. Set fire to the lot."

Once he had been given a backdrop of blazing buildings he performed a last ancient ritual reminiscent of the mediæval warrior rites of the Scottish clans. The bodies of the Commando dead were recovered from the places where they had fallen and piled high around the wrecked, smoke-blackened guns. Then, with the fumes of cordite mingling with the smoke of the fires and with the stench of burning flesh in their nostrils, the entire unit stood to attention and saluted while a Union Jack was run up on a makeshift flagstaff.

The enemy made no attempt to counter-attack, confining his interference with the withdrawal to occasional, desultory sniping. The wide, flat beach and rapidly ebbing tide made re-embarkation difficult, and the troops had to wade out up to their necks to reach the landing-craft which had waited unmolested fifty yards off-shore throughout the operation. German prisoners were used to carry the wounded down to the water where they were placed in a collapsible rubber dinghy for the trip out to the boats. The raiders were re-embarked at 7:30 a.m. precisely as laid down in Lovat's timetable.

On the way back to the boat pool around *Calpe* Lovat sent a signal to General Roberts saying formally, "Pigeon destroyed." If this was a junior officer performing his proper duty by reporting to a senior officer he barely knew, his second signal dispatched by the Phantom network directly to Mountbatten was to one hunter from another, the Chief of Clan Fraser. "Every one of gun crews finished with the bayonet. O.K. by you?" it said.

Apparently it was.

A raid, conceived in the classic traditions of the sport and executed brilliantly at the height of the raiding-season, had ended most rewardingly. Another, in and around Dieppe, was finding the hunted too crafty to be brought to bay.

V

The assault on Dieppe began when it was no longer possible to cancel it – at 3:00 a.m., within a few minutes of which the Canadians were delivered to the start point ten miles off the French coast. Once the assault boats had been lowered the force divided, the infantry transports returning by the same route to reach England before daybreak brought the danger of air attack, while *Calpe*, *Fernie*, *Locust*, and *Alresford* led their flocks of landing-craft inshore, protected on the flanks by the remaining destroyers and the assorted coastal support craft.

At Uxbridge, Leigh-Mallory was joined in the control room by Mountbatten and Crerar, neither of whom could do much more than listen to radio-telephone reports and watch the course of the battle being plotted on an immense map. Although it was still early, Leigh-Mallory was already issuing orders for the first intruder attacks, Hurricane bomber raids, and tactical reconnaissance flights. The Kenley and Northolt fighter wings consisting of twelve squadrons were to take off at 4:30 to fly dawn patrol over the Dieppe area and another eight squadrons, including Bobby Oxspring's 222 Squadron at Hornchurch, stood by for take-off fifteen minutes later.

The air plan provided for general fighter cover throughout the daylight hours; close support, bombing, and low-flying attacks on preselected targets; and smoke-laying aircraft to be used to neutralize defences as required by the Army. Tactical reconnaissance would keep Roberts informed on the whereabouts of enemy reinforcements being brought up from the rear and patrol the Channel to warn of any lunge at the fleet by the German navy. The only substantial bomber raid of the day was to be made at 10:00 a.m. on the principal *Luftwaffe* fighter base in the area, the ærodrome at Abbeville-Drucat.

When the three Commanders met in the control room it might have been just another exercise, instead of the early hours of a day destined to influence the tactical concept of war. According to those who were there, Mountbatten was unexpectedly cheerful, almost gay; Crerar, his right to be seated at the summit now recognized, brimmed over with confidence; Leigh-Mallory, with about 800 aircraft to play with, most of them fighters, against an estimated *Luftwaffe* strength of

360 fighters in northern France, had better reason than either of his colleagues to be enthusiastic at the prospects. Yet he was grim, barely speaking and rarely smiling.

The Canadians were then about 120 miles from Uxbridge, only four from Dieppe. The 179 landing-craft of various shapes, sizes, and speeds had manœuvred in the darkness until they were in their proper columns, all pointed at the beaches of Dieppe like the fingers of a hand, the hand Roberts hoped to close into a punishing fist of steel.

They were stretched out with MGB 317 and SGB 6 taking in the South Saskatchewans to Green Beach (Pourville); MGB 326 leading in the RHLI to White Beach (Dieppe right); ML 291 escorting the Essex Scottish to Red Beach (Dieppe left); and MGB 316 leading the Royal Regiment of Canada with its Black Watch attachment to Blue Beach (Puits).

Following close astern of these long, low-hulled columns was the Calgary Regiment in tank landing-craft which also carried the staffs of 4th and 6th Brigades, the beach signals groups, and the engineers. Coming up in the rear were the Camerons, the Fusiliers Mont-Royal, and the Royal Marine Commando.

There was nothing stealthy about the approach, although the calmness and darkness of the night – visibility was two miles through binoculars – made it appear so. Engines vibrated or roared as ships altered speed, but being constant and expected noises they were not alarming. Yet a tin mug dropped on an iron deck or the clash of gun barrels were unexpected enough to startle men whose voices had already dropped to whispers. Suddenly these Canadians realized they were a long way from Sussex, from the fields, the pubs, the girls. Above all they were far from the serenity that comes with the feeling of being safe. Bravado had vanished in the night, to be replaced by fear in some, curiosity in others, and resignation in most.

For Roberts, too, these silent, final minutes of the night had their own unnatural quality, as if they were unreal and unconnected with all that had gone before: the arguments, endless conferences, training, excitement, and everything that had come after those days of voluntary confinement in the Mayfair Hotel. Only yesterday the accumulation of problems had been depressing, but somehow they had dissolved and even the insoluble ones didn't matter anymore.

He was where a practical soldier should be, commanding his troops in battle, where the problems were neither academic nor theoretical, only urgent. He sat in the small cabin under Calpe's bridge, which had become his headquarters, surrounded by officers and yet oddly alone. Even in the midst of constant comings and goings he was alone. Messages would soon arrive asking for help in the many fronts about to be established, and each would require of him an immediate decision. He could seek no advice, nor accept it, yet history would study his actions as a commander and render implacable judgement on the man.

He cared for none of this, enjoying a quiet, private excitement that he had not experienced since the abortive landing in France two years before when he had evacuated all twenty-four of his guns by indulging in justifiable larceny. His mood was marred, however, by an insistent subconscious alarm bell which intruded upon his peace, warning him that all was well but the battlefield.

As a soldier he loved the sea and ships for pleasure, but tanks, artillery, and land for fighting. Now he was fighting from a seaborne headquarters for a precarious foothold on enemy land, something which was singularly unsoldierly and very naval. But this was the new war of streamlined "conjunct expeditions" in which soldiers learned the lore of the sea and sailors were applauded for running aground – a strange war in which only the sound of the guns was familiar.

On a large table before him were charts of the beaches, maps of the towns and of the inland objectives, and a timetable of events in chronological order prepared by Churchill Mann. With him were the special staffs: McBeth, Peter Wright, D. S. F. Bult-Francis, all of 2nd Division, and Captain J. J. Astor, the British War Office representative with direct Phantom radio link to London, to Churchill's war room.

Around the bulkheads were batteries of radio receivers and transmitters which would keep him in touch with Uxbridge and the beaches. There was also space for Hughes-Hallett and his Chief Staff Officer, Commander J. D. Luce, but for most of the day the Naval Force Commander would be on the bridge controlling the movements of the swarms of little boats which would be in constant orbit around Calpe, some always breaking off to proceed on missions while others arrived to take their places in the circle. A mile away was the reserve headquarters ship, Fernie, in which Churchill Mann operated a duplicate headquarters and relay station for urgent signals.

During the night approach the Force Commanders were cut off from their units by the need for wireless silence. They had made their plans, and no new orders would be necessary until the battle began. Until then Roberts and Hughes-Hallett could merely watch the timetable and pray that it was being kept.

They prayed in vain. The landing which Roberts regarded as the hinge of success was already late, and the curtain was rising irrevocably on one of Canada's grandest tragedies. Neither of the Force Commanders knew it – indeed it is doubtful, with the forces already committed, that they could have done anything about it anyway – but at 3:25 a.m. the hinge jammed tight on Jubilee.

The Royal Regiment of Canada, because of a naval error, was then fifteen minutes late in setting off for Blue Beach.

The Abbatoir
at Puits

I

No episode of that day on fire illustrates more tragically the fatuity of military predictions, the disastrous consequences of planning for one set of circumstances to the exclusion of all others, than does the landing of the Royal Regiment of Canada on Blue Beach. Faulty intelligence, human frailty, and a complicated, rigid operational order combined to reduce a trained, eager, disciplined battalion to a scattered litter of men.

Their landing, most vital to the success of Jubilee, was transformed in a few minutes into a sacrificial offering on the altar of war's supreme futility and folly. The records show it; the men who survived know it. Few today will admit it, most of them preferring to wear a mask of pride, and the masquerade is not a pretty one. Tear aside the mask and the haunted face behind it will reveal the truth – that although a not unnatural mistake by an insignificant unit of the Royal

Navy contributed to it, responsibility for permitting this impossible, costly assault rests with the Anglo-Canadian planners.

The gun batteries on the headland overlooking the entrance to Dieppe Harbour bore down on the mile-long beach and esplanade of Dieppe and dominated the sea approaches. Hughes-Hallett wanted the guns silenced so that Ryder's cutting-out force could penetrate into the inner harbour basins and give the assault craft some security in landing and embarking troops. Roberts wanted them destroyed because they might cut to pieces the main assault forces either in the boats or on the beaches.

Given total surprise the Royals might have reached the high ground of the headland without too much opposition. Once there, however, they would have been faced by rings of barbed wire, machine-gun emplacements, anti-tank and flak weapons, and a force of well-trained German marines.

The Royals never achieved surprise, and if the beaches of Dieppe were the schoolrooms where the Allies learned the tactics and techniques of invasion, the one at Puits was the abattoir where the Germans learned how to dismember, dissect, and decimate the anatomy of invasion, how to rip out its heart with clawing fingers of fire.

Of the 554 men from Toronto and surrounding areas who went to Blue Beach, 65 came back, only 32 of them unwounded. In slightly more than three hours of war the Regiment suffered 94.5 per cent casualties.

"The Royal Regiment of Canada," said the Military Plan, *"must secure the East Headland (Bismarck) . . . with the minimum delay."*

Roberts had always believed that if Bismarck were not taken, its guns could lay down so murderous a fire over the main beaches that the battle might be lost. As long lines of assault forces stretched out for Fortress Europe he sat in his operations cabin waiting, hoping, knowing that the report he wanted more than any other must come from the Royals saying they had carried their objectives.

As the seconds flicked by, the minutes dragged into hours, and the sounds of battle reached a fierce crescendo ashore, he still sat – waiting, hoping, yet strangely frightened by a single unexpected development. The Royals were silent. There was no report, none of any kind.

This is why.

II

The regiment would deal with anti-aircraft batteries on the eastern slopes of the valley of Puits, capture the Les Glycines Holiday Camp which the Germans were believed to have turned into a barracks, overrun Bismarck overlooking Dieppe Harbour, and make contact with the Essex Scottish who, after capturing the harbour, would swing eastwards to meet them. Subsequently, the regiment would seize the Dieppe gasworks in the harbour area and protect a part of the Royal Canadian Engineers who would blow it up.

Accompanying the Royals were detachments of the Royal Canadian Artillery who would assist in capturing the guns on Bismarck, man them against the enemy with "prize crews," and dismantle some anti-aircraft guns so that certain parts could be taken back to England. These guns were thought to be fitted with new types of sights which the War Office wanted to know more about. The attached company from the Black Watch of Canada, placed under the temporary command of Captain R. C. Hicks of the Royals, was to land east of Blue Beach to protect the left flank against enemy intrusion. This company and the RCA detachments were grouped into a single component called "Edward Force."

The German defences consisted of few men and many guns. There were two platoons totalling in the region of ninety-four men to defend Puits with machine guns, howitzers, mortars, and anti-tank weapons. In accordance with the "Threatened Danger" state of alert, they had been sleeping in their clothes since August 1 and the guns had been manned that night after the naval engagement had taken place almost opposite their area. This small force capable of powerfully concentrated fire was more than sufficient for the task now at hand.

The Royals were lowered into the water shortly before 3:00 a.m., and the landing-craft flotillas attempted to form up in columns astern of MGB 316, carrying the naval officer responsible for their safe and timely arrival at Blue Beach – Lieutenant-Commander H. W. Goulding, a former merchant marine officer who had already won the Distinguished Service Order. He lay ahead of the infantry landing-ships, *Princess Astrid* and *Queen Emma*, waiting for the assault craft with a shaded blue light burning on his stern to guide them. No other MGB was supposed to be in the immediate vicinity so that there could be no case of mistaken identity. Take-off time for Blue Beach was 3:10 a.m.

There had been no significant mishaps up to this moment, and whereas there would be many serious ones in this quirksome day. none was to have so decisive an effect on the outcome as the appearance that night of MGB 315, groping her way from west to east under the stern of MGB 316 and across the bows of the landing-craft advancing from *Queen Emma*. Cruel, intolerable fate began to envelop the entire operation as five landing-craft, identifying her silhouette as that of an MGB and thinking her to be MGB 316, formed up on her stern and allowed themselves to be led away to the northeast, in the opposite direction to Blue Beach.

Aboard MGB 316 Goulding fumed through his binoculars and shouted angry epithets over his loud-hailer, but his voice was drowned out by the noise of the gun boat's engines. After several minutes, the commander of the errant flotilla, realizing he was being led in the wrong direction and that he must be following the wrong leader, broke away to take his boats back eventually into proper station astern of MGB 316.

The columns then moved out as planned, at 3:25 – too late by fifteen minutes, a delay which could mean touchdown dangerously close to first light. The consequences of allowing this time difference were too obvious for Goulding to miss and he increased speed in an effort to make up for the delay.

The beach at Puits is small and private, running along the base of overhanging cliffs and across the gorge-like valley between them for only two hundred yards. A sea wall built of solid masonry about ten feet high runs for one hundred yards between the cliffs at the bottom of the steep gorge and two flights of steps leading to the top, one about halfway down its length and the other at the southwest end. There are two exits from the beach, a footpath at the northeast end and a country lane winding upwards and inland through the valley to the village of Puits. Villas, mostly painted white, are set back from the lane and the footpath on either side of the gorge so that they can look down upon the sea wall and the beach. Along the top of the wall were thick layers of heavy concertina wire which had not been picked up by air reconnaissance photographs and had not been provided for in the military plan. But Catto had wisely included Bangalore torpedoes in his equipment just in case.

Between the wall and normal high-water mark the beach is usually fifty to seventy-five yards wide and consists mainly of large pebbles up to six inches in diameter. This beach was never over-popular with holiday-makers in peacetime because the pebbles are so big and sharp that walking on them requires the self-control and will-power of an Indian fakir.

At low tide the beach widens to three hundred yards, and the ebbing sea leaves behind a vast expanse of packed sand and huge flat rocks which constitute jutting points flanking the approaches.

Goulding had to deliver his assault craft between these mostly hidden hazards located about two hundred yards apart in darkness, a feat which called for precise navigation. To ensure it, he had deviated from the direct route in from the start point by arranging with the flotilla officers and the captain of MGB 316 that he would proceed directly for Dieppe, fix his position by the harbour moles, and then turn eastwards to make a landfall at Puits.

Although this was the long way round – two sides of a triangle instead of one – it would have the advantage of making accurate navigation possible. If, however, he wanted to recapture lost time he could accept the risk of a miscalculation and cut the corner by sailing down the hypotenuse of the triangle, as Hughes-Hallett had instructed in the naval orders. The confusion at the start point placed him in a box not of his own making. If he took the gamble and hit the wrong beach at the right time, the Royals would be in trouble; if he proceeded as planned and hit the right beach too late the Royals would still be in trouble. Neither Goulding nor anyone else could possibly guess at which course might lead to the least trouble.

In the end, he chose his own plan in the hope that the increase in speed would be enough to cancel out the delay. But two large mechanized landing-craft each carrying a hundred men could not keep up and within half an hour had straggled so far astern that they had lost sight of the main columns chasing MGB 316. Worse, they had four of *Queen Emma*'s assault craft with them. The effect of this was to divide the force into two waves.

MGB 316 steered the faster force straight for the main Dieppe beach as Goulding had intended so that he could recognize the town and get his bearings from buildings on the sea front. The Pointe d'Ailly lighthouse far to the right and the red and green navigation lights at the harbour entrance came on to welcome the expected German convoy and by doing so provided him with unexpected assistance. He fixed his position at 4:20 a.m. as two miles off the harbour, and the columns then altered course eastwards for Puits. As they passed across the front of Dieppe Harbour a port signal station flashed a double A challenge, and in the absence of a reply the Germans reacted by switching off the harbour lights and switching on searchlights, which played their beams across the water in wide, sweeping arcs.

To the men in the boats it seemed that they were bared to the enemy, and faces glowed pallidly in the light reflected from the water, taut-skinned faces of men enduring the strain of some horrible uncertainty. Then the searchlights were extinguished and protective blackness closed down once more upon their passage. German records reveal no indication that the force was actually picked up by searchlights, and it is likely they were far beyond range. But gazing down the beams of these lights can be a disconcerting experience – the hunted feels convinced that the hunters must have seen him when, in fact, they have seen nothing.

At 4:40 a.m., five minutes after zero hour for the touchdown, the first wave was still two miles from Blue Beach and it was time for Goulding to transfer into a landing-craft to direct the final run-in. The Germans, having seen the flare-up at sea and knowing that unidentified ships were in the vicinity, fired flares over the approaches to the harbour, bathing the force in pale, hard light, wrenching aside the cloak of dawn to expose their purpose.

Blue Beach should have been abandoned when the futility of a landing there was apparent. There was, however, no way of doing it. Unlike Lovat's Cauldron plan, which incorporated three alternatives for the Varengeville assault allowing for the use of one of two beaches or both according to conditions such as a late daylight landing heavily opposed, the Canadian military plan demanded that the Royals land on Blue Beach no matter what the circumstances or cost. The Canadian planners had been so confident when drafting operational orders that they had failed to budget for the loss of surprise and had provided no alternatives, thereby denying individual commanders any elasticity in dealing with accidents or minimizing the effect of bad luck. Nor had Catto any means of communicating with Roberts during the run-in were he to wish for a last-time change, which may have been the reason why, when a faint possibility of retrieving an impossible situation still existed, the flotilla officer of the first wave received an urgent message from the second following astern saying that Catto wished to speak with Goulding. It was too late for this too; Goulding was already deploying the boats for the assault.

At 5:00 a.m. it was still dark, and the force had the advantage of approaching from the southwest, the dark side. The general alert had been sounded ashore, yet the force managed to race to within a hundred yards before the first sniping began, desultory at first, but quickening. The noise of the landing-craft engines revving at full speed helped the shore defences pin-point their darkened run-in, and machine-gun fire covered the water's edge, crackled over the heads of the troops, and penetrated through thin hulls to smack frighteningly into soft flesh.

Goulding snapped at the flotilla officer, Lieutenant W. C. Hewitt, RNVR, in the headquarters boat: "For God's sake get the Army to open fire." Hewitt shouted to a Bren-gunner in the bows to cover the approach. The soldier did as he was told, trying to protect himself and fire at the same time, with the result that he fired wildly into the decks. Bullets ricocheted round the inside of the boat, one denting a door runner and jamming the ramp. Major G. P. Scholfield, senior military officer of that first wave, stood next to Goulding one second and was badly wounded the next.

When the craft touched bottom and the ramps came down, the full measure of the enemy's ferocity broke upon the stunned, bewildered soldiers. Guns on the cliffs, in the white-painted villas, and in pillboxes walled in the narrow ramp openings with barriers of fire. There was a brief standstill in time in which nothing moved but the waves. Only the ramp of the senior boat had failed to drop, because of its damaged runner, and the wounded Scholfield climbed painfully to his feet, clutched his Sten gun, cleared the ramp, and stumbled down it into the shallow water. He died there, and the manner of his death was enough to trigger a mad, plunging dash ashore by men bunched in the bows of the seven landing-craft. They shared their gallant major's fate at the water's edge, toppling over in a line a hundred yards long like toy soldiers being knocked down by the impatient hand of a child. According to some reports fewer than twenty reached the treacherous shelter of the sea wall, a man lay dead or dying every three yards along the beach, and those left in the boats were stricken into immobility.

It had been instilled into these men that theirs was the most vital landing of all, that failure would result in untold losses on the main beaches and disaster for the operation. They had been told that everything would be done to help them, that given a proper touchdown they could be over the beach, up through the gorge, and onto the Bismarck headland before the Germans came awake. They would have surprise, smoke-laying aircraft, and the protection of darkness for initial assault.

They had accepted this heavy responsibility on the basis of what all troops require, a fair fighting chance. It is needed during a first encounter with the enemy more than at any other time and, as if in silent testimony to its absence, the dead moved slightly in the gently breaking surf, nudged by the lightly falling waves which came in

white-fringed green and went out streaked wine-red with the blood
of Canada.

To their right was the East Headland from which machine guns spat
viciously without pause; to the left on the sloping side of another cliff
were four concrete pillboxes bearing down on the beach, one of
which was disguised as the summerhouse of a villa – an innocent
camouflage for the core of the inferno from which there could be no
escape.

The ramps were down and empty, the men held back, numbed by the
awful intensity of the enemy's reaction, consumed by quick realization that little of what they had been told to expect had come about.
Huddled in the boats they gazed out at a scene of slaughter compressed into a fragment of earth and time, a narrow strip of shingle on a
strange and foreign shore dominated by towering cliffs sloping inwards
to the green-covered valley of Puits, the natural might of impregnable
cliffs daring man, the pygmy, to advance and die, awe-inspiring head-
stones for a beach that had already become a cemetery.

The appalling price for a combination of errors was being paid.
First light was at 5:15 a.m., which should have given the Royals
twenty-five minutes of darkness in which to land, achieve surprise,
and fight their way from the beach up to the high ground. The boats,
however, had not only failed to make up the lost fifteen minutes but,
in spite of increased speed, the long way round had added two more
precious minutes to the time for the run-in. Touchdown was at 5:07,
clipping seventeen minutes of darkness from the assault and leaving
only eight minutes for the Royals to get off the beach before first
light.

More decisive in terms of life and death for the men from Toronto
was the fact that the enemy, warned by the flare-up at sea and by the
failure of the landing-craft to reply to the challenge from the harbour
pier, had been ordered to the highest state of alert at 5:00 a.m. and
could hear the noise of engines as the assault force approached at full
speed. For at least the final two or three hundred yards of the run-in
the defenders had been at their action stations – ready and waiting.

The grim, sweat-streaked commanders of the landing-craft looked
over the heads of the reluctant Royals at the carnage on the beach,
drew their revolvers, and in sheer, hapless misery delivered their
dreadful ultimatum – land or be shot in the boats.

III

It is August 22, the third day after Dieppe. Britain is proclaiming victory for the Commandos, the United States pays homage to the victorious Rangers, and Canada is wondering why, if the operation was Anglo-American in content, so many Canadians had to die.

An informal inquiry is being held at Portsmouth to find out the truth about the disastrous events at Blue Beach. No attempt is being made to apportion blame or to find a scapegoat; the Navy simply wants to know what went wrong. Giving evidence are twelve naval officers. As it is a naval affair no army officers are present, certainly no Canadians. The witnesses are encouraged to overcome natural reluctance to say anything in such stern official surroundings that might reflect adversely upon members of another service. They have only one obligation: to answer the board's questions as honestly as memory serves them. Their memories are excellent; the events so recent they are etched vividly in their minds.

The first officer is asked to describe the landing of the first flight. He refers to the machine-gun fire which greeted them a hundred yards from touchdown and explains how it proved disconcerting to the troops because the bullets penetrated the hull of his boat, causing casualties. He had shouted to a Bren-gunner in the bows to return the fire but the soldier had fired so wildly that his bullets had hit the inside of the ramp door, jamming its lowering gear.

As the boat beached, he says, Major Scholfield had cleared the door and led the way ashore. The austerity of the ship's wardroom in which the inquiry is being held has much the same barren and controlled atmosphere of a courtroom, and the question about the attitude of the troops after Scholfield had been killed on landing comes so evenly, precisely, and naturally that it has the effect of a whip crack.

The soldiers, says the young witness, appeared to be reluctant to leave the boat. Selecting his words carefully, he adds that they were forced ashore by himself and another naval officer. He saw them run across the beach to the sea wall, leaving behind their scaling-ladders. It seems that this was not significant because once against the wall the troops made no attempt to climb it. He hastens to add that there was heavy firing from pillboxes covering the wall.

In his formal report of proceedings on return from the operation, submitted in the routine manner to the commanding officer of his base, this officer had said: "When the soldiers started to jump onto the beach everything opened up. A number of casualties occurred before the troops reached the shelter of the wall. This discouraged the rest from landing, and only a firm handling of the situation by the naval officers in charge of each landing-craft (there were nine in the first flight) succeeded in compelling the rest to follow their comrades, revolvers having to be used as a threat."

The next officer occupies the witness chair facing the board and describes the approach, the almost certain sighting of the force by the enemy harbour defences, and the fire that broke out when they were about a hundred yards from touchdown. He had also seen Major Scholfield dash ashore followed by several men, but admits that the remainder of the troops had to be urged. He says there was such discouragement among the troops that he had to use force to clear his boat. When it had been cleared, some men were killed while crossing the beach and the rest apparently took shelter against the sea wall.

The others follow in their turn, each giving evidence in the same strain – one saying that his boat was cleared by force, the military officers present joining him in urging the men ashore; another explaining that in his view the reluctance of the men was owing to lack of leadership and lack of experience under fire.

There are four officers with varying evidence to offer. One says his boat was cleared of all but five men immediately on touchdown. These five, he says, were very reluctant. The commanding officer of yet another landing-craft reports that he had no difficulty with the troops, that his boat was cleared quickly at touchdown.

When the questioning is finished the board reaches the conclusion that the landing at Blue Beach was about sixteen minutes late, that the second flight lost touch with the first and consequently beached some twenty minutes later, and that the soldiers had been reluctant to leave some of the boats.

IV

This polite, official verbiage, composed in the aftermath of a torrid, deadly day, hardly reflected the reality of the shambles at Puits. When the first wave of landing-craft were eventually cleared and able to withdraw, they left behind a beach littered with the bodies of men who had died with shocked disbelief frozen into widely staring eyes. The survivors crouched against the sea wall, unable to move or to effectively defend themselves, not even when smoke-laying aircraft came in low from the northeast, dipped below the tops of the cliffs, and swept across the length of the beach laying a billowing curtain of smoke to protect the retreat of the landing-craft.

Among the first to reach the sea wall was Corporal L. G. Ellis, one of the few who, throughout the morning, treated the German fire with calm disdain. He was the first out of his boat, pausing on the way to jump up and down on the ramp which had stuck before touching the beach. When his own weight failed to free it he called out to four other soldiers to come out and jump with him. They held back, and Ellis trailed after a group running for the sea wall, having by this time got his feet wet.

"The wall didn't give us much protection," he said. "It was enfiladed pretty effectively by a machine gun buried into a concrete site in the eastern slope of the gully."

Ellis found the double flight of steps in the western section of the sea wall – a recess in which steps led upwards to the left and right. At the top of the right-hand flight was an oddly silent pillbox. Ellis climbed through a barbed-wire obstacle blocking entry into the recess and went up the right-hand set of steps with his sharpshooter's rifle ready, peered into the pillbox through a gun-slit, and found it empty. He ran back down the steps into the recess and up the left-hand steps to the top of the wall where he found the wire so thick he couldn't see to shoot through it.

He looked down into the recess, saw Captain George Sinclair and a private climbing through the obstacle off the beach as he had done, and shouted down for a Bren gun. Sinclair ordered the men nearest him against the wall to find a Bren, but none would move. Ellis then clambered down into the recess again and suggested quite casually to Sinclair that the only way to silence the guns enfilading the wall would be to "blow the wire and go after them."

The private made his way along the wall, found some Bangalore torpedoes and brought them back. Sinclair set one in the wire at the top of the eastern set of steps and blew a sizable gap. Ellis pushed past him, ran up the steps, and dashed headlong through the gap and into a scrub-filled depression on the western slope where he took cover.

Sinclair, the private, and two other soldiers tried to follow, but the gap had been covered from a large brick house on the left from which fire streamed out of five windows facing the beach. Sinclair and his party were killed or wounded in the gap, leaving Ellis, the first man through the wire, alone in hostile country.

At 5:30, the slower second flight of two mechanized landing-craft and four assault boats ran the gauntlet into touchdown, supported by an armed support landing-craft on each side. Smoke still swirled along the edge of the beach.

"We hit the beach and found the battle really in shape," said Sergeant Legate of Toronto. "When I got off and reached the other side of the smoke, the dead and wounded were lying all over the place. We just had to get to the wall, stay there, and that was that.

"The crossfire coming at us made it impossible to move two feet from the wall else you got it. There was nobody around to look after the wounded, and if there had been it was still impossible to get near them. It turned out to be every man for himself. That's the way I saw it."

Legate also saw Sergeant Preston have his legs shot from under him by a machine-gun burst which continued long enough to chop off his hand at the wrist while he was falling. No one dared to quit the meagre protection of the wall to help, so Preston bled to death. Legate was fascinated by an unnamed soldier who went berserk with a Bren gun, standing in full view and screaming while he fired at the strong-points to the east. Even when there was no more ammunition left he went on screaming – until a stream of bullets lifted him off his feet, spun him around, and ended his magnificent display of madness.

Lieutenant W. G. R. Wedd was followed off his boat by his platoon. When they reached the wall a pillbox built into it which had been silent until now suddenly opened up with devastating effect along the wall, knocking over troops with the precision of an executioner. If total annihilation were to be averted the pillbox had to be taken out. Wedd ran out from the relative shelter of an abutment to the wall, pulled the pin from a hand grenade, and rushed straight into the stream of fire. When he was only feet away he flung the grenade through the gun-slit, killing the crew in the pillbox and destroying it. Inspired by his gallantry, half a dozen soldiers left the sea wall to bring him back to safety.

Sergeant Legate was huddled near the centre of the wall when "Mr Woodhouse, the only officer left where I was," sauntered down the beach, picked up an abandoned Bren gun, and rummaged around among the pebbles while enemy fire splintered them in his face until he found what he wanted, a full magazine. He straightened up, clipped it into the Bren and, still sauntering so slowly that he appeared to the astounded watchers "to be walking in slow motion," he advanced firing from the hip upon a pillbox on the wall above Legate's head. "That Mr Woodhouse took no end of risks," said Legate.

Captain G. A. Browne, an artillery officer accompanying the Royals as a Forward Observation Officer for the bombardment of the Bismarck headland by the destroyer *Garth*, came in with Lieutenant-Colonel Catto in the second flight. They touched down opposite the western extremity of the sea wall, dashed through the smoke, and reached it thinking that the men already there had landed with them. Catto's headquarters' walkie-talkie had been shot into the sea, so Browne immediately ordered his telegraphist to make contact with *Garth* and report via her to *Calpe*: "Doug touched down 0535." This message never reached Roberts who had heard nothing from the Royals since they'd left England. The signal informing him that Doug Catto had landed should have reached *Calpe* shortly after 4:50 a.m. Nearly an hour later the battalion was being slaughtered and he was unaware of it, uncertain of what could have happened, and becoming increasingly alarmed at thoughts of what might happen on the main beaches if the Royals had failed, if the guns on the Bismarck headland were still in action.

It had been impossible for the first wave to report because no beach signals party had landed except two naval signalmen whose set had been knocked out of action within the first few seconds. One of the first killed in the second wave was Catto's battalion signalman. The snipers then destroyed his radio lying in the surf.

Describing the touchdown of the second flight, Browne said later: "In spite of the steady approach to the beach under fire, the Royals in my assault landing-craft appeared cool and steady. It was their first experience under fire, and although I watched them closely, they gave no sign of alarm, and the interior of the boat was illuminated by the enemy flares from the beach and the flash of the Boston bombers. The quiet steady voice of Captain Thompson, seated behind me, held the troops up to a confident and offensive spirit, although shells were whizzing over the craft and you could hear the steady whisper and crackle of small-arms fire over the top of the landing-craft. At the instant of touchdown, small-arms fire was striking the boat, and here there was not unnatural split-second hesitation in the bow in leaping out onto the beach. But only a split second. The troops got onto the beach as fast as in any of the Simmer exercises, and got across the beach to the wall and under the cliff."

The naval officers in the assault boats reported differently. Lieutenant E. C. W. Cook, RNVR, whose mechanized landing-craft carrying one hundred men touched down near the centre of the beach, said: "We took the brunt of the fire, and fifteen casualties were suffered in the boat while the troops were disembarking. The senior army officer was a very early casualty, and this no doubt was the cause of the delay in disembarking owing to lack of leadership. They [the troops] were reluctant to leave the boat and had to be forcibly made to disembark. . . . They left their mortar apparatus behind in the boat but eventually did get it off. . . . There were wounded in the boat and . . . as I pulled off I noticed that the Beachmaster, who was not wounded, and the beach party who had not landed were still in the boat."

Another account of events in this boat says that some fifteen men dashed ashore the moment the ramp went down and reached cover against the face of the cliff – "machine-gun fire holding back the rest."

Captain J. H. C. Anderson of Toronto, who was to be the Military Landing Officer for Blue Beach, was not content to sit helplessly in the boat doing nothing. He grabbed a Bren gun and began returning the fire coming from the summerhouse on the left side of the valley. He was joined by other gunners, including Private J. Murphy and Corporal Ruggles, who had scrambled from the stern of the boat to the bows across the limp bodies of the wounded.

Most of the enemy fire was coming from two houses loftily situated above the beach to the right and to the left, both of which had been clearly revealed in air-reconnaissance photographs prior to the raid but were not shown in the military plan as even likely to be fortified. These two houses, and others to a lesser extent, bristled with automatic weapons of all kinds.

"I first fired into the house on the right," said Private Murphy, "then Corporal Ruggles shouted to look at the house on the left. I saw fire from this one, and fired into each of the windows on the first floor. I think each floor had six windows. By the time I would get to the sixth window the first one would open up again."

Within a very few minutes the Germans were concentrating their fire on the three Bren-gunners in the landing-craft and Anderson was quickly wounded. Murphy and Ruggles, thinking it was time to get ashore, were about to leap across the ramp when the Naval Beachmaster, Lieutenant Warnecke, RNVR, shouted a warning that further attempts to land were impossible, and the boat began withdrawing from the beach.

"As we were backing out," said Ruggles, "I had one brief glimpse of men crouched against the cliff on the western side or against the sea wall and many others lying on the beach, some in the water."

Most of the Royals who returned to England were in this boat.

An ugly scene broke out at the western end of the beach when the assault boats began to withdraw. Private J. E. Creer, who had landed in the first flight and had been hugging the wall ever since, saw a shaking officer suddenly stand up and shout: "It's all hopeless. Get back to the boats."

His action sparked a mad rush down the beach towards the only assault boat still touched down. Sergeant Legate, who had early decided that it was every man for himself, reported afterwards that "fifty of us made the boat, making it too heavy to get off the beach."

The landing-craft was virtually besieged by the men trying to board her. She was overwhelmed to the extent that her small naval crew resorted to repelling boarders with boathooks which were then torn from their hands. The boat, weighed down and overcrowded, stuck in the sand. Ignoring the fire, men jumped back into the water, manhandled it into deeper water, and when it moved astern under its own power they tried to haul themselves back on board over the still lowered ramp. There were so many of them it was impossible to raise the ramp and water poured into the boat.

"The skipper yelled at them to let go or the boat would sink, but they wouldn't listen," said Legate. "He couldn't get the ramp up and she filled full of water. She turned over, and only about ten of us managed to get away and had to swim for it. Myself and another fellow I met out in the water were four and a half hours swimming around before we got picked up. Before then I was ready to give up, there being such a smokescreen around us that the other boats couldn't see us floating about in the water.

"I spotted a rowboat about half a mile from me floating in the water by itself so I swam for it. There were a couple of tommy guns and a Bren gun in it, so I figured somebody else had it and were picked up. There was a canoe paddle in it, so I started rowing out to sea when I saw three heads in the water so I went for them and picked them up. They were Sergeant Thirgood and a corporal from our Intelligence Section and a fellow in the mortars. It was just some minutes after that we got picked up by a flak boat. The MO looked after the wounded I had picked up, and the sailors made me as comfortable as they could. They took all my clothes off me and put me to bed with six blankets, two hot water bottles, and a big shot of rum. It was shortly after that the skipper got his orders to return to England, but before he had those orders he drove his boat to within a hundred yards of the beach and picked up about ten more soldiers from the water."

The corporal Legate saved was, in fact, Corporal Ellis, first of the Royals to cross the sea wall, who had spent an hour roaming about the valley of Puits before deciding to return to the beach and get away. When found by Legate he had been in the water for nearly two hours.

While both these men were experiencing strange adventures, the third flight of landing-craft brought in "Edward Force" consisting of the Black Watch and RCA units, from *Duke of Wellington*. This flotilla of six assault craft had left the mother ship with one boat empty, because the accidental explosion of the hand grenade at Southampton had wounded the troops who were supposed to be carried in it. It was manned by crews of the Royal Canadian Volunteer Reserve whose senior officer was Lieutenant Jack Koyl RCNVR, of Cobourg, Ontario.

According to the plan, this force would only land when requested to do so by Catto ashore. No such signal was received, and when the flotilla was one mile out from Blue Beach, Koyl consulted with Captain Hicks on whether to land even without the expected orders. Hicks replied that he would like to land under the cliffs to the west of the sea wall where it could be seen that the bulk of the surviving Royals were gathered with Bren guns set up in the rocks, concentrating their fire on the top of the eastern cliff and against the houses halfway up its side.

Catto's initiative restored a semblance of order from the chaos on the beach. Once he had reasserted command and imposed discipline on the survivors, the slaughter diminished, and for the first time the bulk of the Royals began fighting back as a cohesive, directed force. They covered the landing of the third flight so effectively that when Koyl's boats touched down at 5:45 a.m. some hundred yards to the west of Catto's defensive positions, only one man was killed, Lieutenant John Coulson of Montreal. His friend in the Black Watch, Lieutenant Murray Mather, said: "I was right beside Jack Coulson when he got his – a burst of machine-gun fire right through the eyes and head. . . . Except for poor Jack, the Black Watch didn't lose a man, but we had a few wounded. . . ."

Private Albert O'Toole ran out of his landing-craft so quickly that he stumbled on the ramp, tripped, and fell with a wrenched ankle. As he could hardly stand, let alone run, he was helped back into the landing-craft by its crew and taken out to sea when it withdrew. He was the only man of those who actually landed to return to England.

V

Above the sea wall, Corporal Ellis, who had watched the second wave
touch down, was crawling through a deep barbed-wire entanglement
which blocked the narrow lane leading up to Puits and shouting warnings to the scattered groups of men still pressed flat against the wall
to "watch out for the house on the right." Only fifty yards away, it
presented two rows of nine windows each to the beach, some being
used for observation and others as gun positions.

Lieutenant W. C. Patterson decided to blow another gap in the wire
through which he could take a party to follow Ellis. He started to join
a pair of Bangalore torpedoes, but pebbles had jammed the locking
device on the coupling. He laid the portion with the fuse on top of
the wall, intending to set it off under the wire; while he was still
holding the length of explosive-filled piping it burst into flames and a
bullet hit him in the shoulder. He fell forward over the piping, his
clothes caught fire and, despite the pain of his wound, he rolled about
on the beach smothering the blazing uniform. He was then seen to
climb to the top of the wall where he died.

Ellis, still the only man over the wall, was finding it slow work
using wire-cutters to make a passage in the wire entanglement when
he noticed that a roll of concertina wire ran through the inside of the
obstacle, providing an easy exit. He managed to crawl into the roll,
using his cutters only where necessary, notably to cut two insulated
signal cables.

The wire ran upwards along a slope to the lip of a hill, and when
he emerged Ellis found himself close to a house near the plateau at
the top of the Bismarck headland. He made his way silently round to
the rear of it, mentally noted the position of a back window in case
of emergencies, returned to the front, and kicked open the door.
Through an open doorway off the entrance hall he could see part of
a room in which smoke swirled in the rays of the sun. He tossed a
grenade into it, and plaster was still falling from the ceiling when he
rushed inside, automatic rifle ready. It was empty, the floor littered
with cartridge cases, still warm and recently ejected. Warily now, he
went back into the hall and started climbing the stairs to the upper
floor, a grenade with the pin already pulled in his hand. He was halfway up when the destroyer *Garth* opened her bombardment of the
headland. With shells exploding in and around the house, Corporal
Ellis threw away his grenade and dived prudently through the back
window. He landed on all fours, ran along a pathway which skirted a

wood behind the house, and to his mild astonishment was suddenly confronted by the Sten-gun-carrying private who had been with Captain Sinclair, and who had somehow passed unscathed through the withering fire at the gap above the sea wall.

They walked together round the wood until they could see that the pathway led towards the sea down the side of the headland in the direction of Blue Beach. They soon reached a fork where a smaller path wound upwards again. Ellis ordered the private to continue down to the beach to bring back a company commander and some troops while he explored the other path.

This trail took him almost to the edge of the dangerous Bismarck headland where he stumbled into a pillbox which, fortunately, also proved to be empty. After that, feeling his luck could hardly hold out much longer, he returned to the intersection of the paths and headed back to the beach.

When he failed to meet the troops he had sent for, he cut off the pathway and entered the woods to the right, found three more empty gun emplacements, eventually emerged close to the house he had left in such unconventional haste, and strolled to the lip of a steep hill where he fell into yet another empty pit. When he recovered, he poked his head cautiously above the parapet and found he could look across the valley. He noticed a concrete pillbox about six hundred yards away on the opposite slope which seemed to be under heavy fire from the Royals; he could also see that the enemy's fire was coming not from the pillbox but from some bushes twenty yards away from it. He thought he could discern the faint white gleam of what could be the German machine-gunner's face through the foliage, an inviting target for a specialist sniper such as Corporal Ellis. He raised his rifle, lined his sights unhurriedly on the patch of white, and fired. The pale white gleam vanished; the stream of tracers from the bushes jerked high into the air as though the gunner had been struck and fallen backwards with his finger still on the trigger. Ellis waited patiently for fire to be resumed. None came.

His next target was the village of Puits itself, which he overlooked from his hill. He could see no signs of movement, so for the sake of something to do he fired several rounds at buildings which looked as if they might harbour snipers. He soon wished he had left the place in peace. A sniper's bullet – he had no idea where it came from – knocked off his helmet. He left the weapon pit in a hurry, crawling back towards the house on his stomach. When he thought it safe to do so, he stood up and was immediately confronted by an officer of the Royals brandishing a Sten gun.

"Anything in this house?" asked the officer.

"No. I've been in and had to get out in a hurry. The Navy's shelling the place," said Ellis.

The officer – Ellis never did find out who he was – either failed to hear the reply or simply chose to ignore it, and plunged through the front door just as a heavy salvo from *Garth* crunched on the ground floor. Ellis dived back into the woods, from where he watched the naval barrage almost demolish the house. It seemed impossible that anyone inside could have survived, so he crawled back to the hill where he had emerged from the roll of concertina wire and looked down on the beach – in time to see a lone assault boat which had come in to take off the wounded being commandeered by the unwounded. It was a chance, too, for him to get off.

He ran down towards the wire obstacle, tripped over a wounded soldier lying paralysed on the side of the hill, dragged him to the wire, and began working him through it. When they were nearly out he came across another signal cable and, believing it to be one of those he had cut previously, he gave it a sharp pull. A violent explosion seared his face, and shrapnel bit sharply into his hands and legs. The wounded soldier he had dragged for some forty feet through wire was killed outright. A German booby trap had done its work.

Ellis continued on by himself and came out of the wire to find the short distance of open country to the gap above the sea wall riddled by enemy fire. He had no choice. Sprinting energetically, he crossed the space, jumped high over the wire barricade, and fell about eighteen feet to the beach.

Unhurt by the fall itself but suffering waves of agony from his wounds and fighting off nausea, he staggered back to his feet and stumbled across the beach to the grounded landing-craft where a mob of soldiers milled about frantically in the water. The young, red-faced naval officer in command was shouting hysterically that the boat was overloaded and that the soldiers in the water would have to let go or push. As Ellis found a place near the ramp, the officer was killed where he stood.

Men were being picked off on all sides, and the water lapping about them was covered in a thin film of sticky, murky-coloured blood. The nauseated Ellis, exhausted through loss of blood, gave up his place and retreated to the water's edge to watch while taking off his boots and uniform. He undressed slowly, ignoring the bullets kicking up pebbles, sand, and water around him and paused only when the landing-craft drew clear of the beach amid a bedlam of screaming from the men struggling to get on board. Heavy artillery shells burst in the water near the boat which quite suddenly swayed lazily, as if in slow motion, and finally capsized.

One of the soldiers inside the boat was Private E. J. Simpson of the Royals who said later: "There was a terrible scramble and nearly everyone still alive on the beach made for the small ramp doors. The slaughter was awful. The boat had to be pushed off the beach. It was so full of holes it began to sink. Bullets were still pouring in, and a bomb landed alongside. Then the boat turned over on its keel and remained afloat upside down. A few men swam away while others and myself clung to the still floating craft. We were only one hundred yards from the ashore and being blasted by enemy fire. From what I could see from there, there was no life on the beach."

Gunner H. J. Rowe, who was among those clinging to the keel of the boat, said: "There weren't more than half a dozen of us, and if anyone moved he was rewarded with a sniper's bullet. That chap hanging on next to me was hit three times immediately after moving because of the pain from earlier wounds."

A naval report of the incident said that the boat was "swamped with soldiers and forced to retire." It was under heavy fire, and most of the soldiers were either killed or wounded once they had climbed aboard. The report continued: "Owing to the jam and excess of personnel in the boat it was impossible for the doors to be housed up and a fair amount of water was shipped. When the craft was about fifty yards out she was hit by fire from heavy guns and capsized. The enemy still continued firing."

This tragic vignette spurred Ellis to get away from the beach. Free of clothing and equipment, he hobbled painfully into the water, pushed aside several bodies which floated coldly, clammily, fattily against him, and began swimming out to sea. Corporal Ellis possessed curiosity and faith to an unusual degree. He had left the beach and gone over the wall because of an instinctive revulsion to dying helplessly. Once in enemy country, he had explored it, examined those defence positions he had found, and had waited for the rest of the battalion to join him. When they had failed to appear he had decided there was little he could do by himself and, therefore, little point in staying. Now he was swimming out to sea, not really having anywhere to go but quite sure that if he didn't want to die he should do something, anything but sit and wait for death.

A powerful swimmer, he began by doing the crawl to get clear of the beach as quickly as possible. This attracted the attention of a sniper, and when bullets came uncomfortably close Ellis flung up his arms and subsided below the surface, pretending he had been hit. When he could no longer hold his breath he surfaced and resumed swimming, confident that the sniper would be concentrating on another target. After all, he was a sniper himself.

He discarded the cumbersome Mae West to quicken his pace and swam until almost exhausted and in desperate need of it. Then he collided with the body of a dead soldier and thankfully stripped a lifebelt from it, as "he couldn't bloody well use it anyway." He floated for another thirty minutes until he drifted into the body of another soldier from which he took another lifebelt, subconsciously noting that both dead men had been killed by shots in the head. Inconsequentially he accorded silent respect to the enemy snipers for being true professionals.

He had been in the water for two and a half hours. His eyes were beginning to close, his mind rambling wildly. Dimly recognizing the symptoms of delirium and approaching unconsciousness he kicked about to keep himself awake, his movements becoming weaker as waves of drowsiness tempted him to succumb and bring an end to pain. Through glazed eyes, he saw a man paddling a dinghy towards him and, summoning his last reserves of will-power and strength, he contorted himself vigorously in the water to attract attention. He thought he heard someone calling faintly and then lapsed into a coma.

Corporal Ellis was the third and last man saved by Sergeant Legate who, after more than four hours in water himself, was nearing the end of his own strength.

Ellis had been on the enemy side of the wire for more than an hour and the only human beings he had seen, apart from the faint gleam of a face in the bushes six hundred yards away, had been the officer who had vanished into the shelled house, the private he had first seen with Captain Sinclair at the gap in the wire, and the wounded soldier who had been finished off by the booby trap. Nowhere had he seen a German, yet on the beach there was no escaping their fire.

VI

After 6:00 a.m. the Germans intensified their fire, quickening the pace of destruction. Mortar bombs and heavy artillery were added to the

machine guns and snipers, making it imperative for the few remaining
Royals to get off the beach, if only to survive. Battalion headquarters,
to which Captain Browne and his telegraphist were attached, had
found a semblance of shelter in a recessed re-entrance at the western
extremity of the sea wall and Catto, realizing that his hastily organized
defensive positions among the rocks at the base of the cliff could afford
only temporary relief, decided to crash out of the trap.

He asked for Bangalore torpedoes. There were none; so, armed with
a pair of wire-cutters each, he and Sergeant Coles climbed to the top
of the wall where they lay flat while clipping steadily at the mass of
tangled barbed wire. They were joined almost immediately by
Lieutenant R. Stewart who opened covering fire with a Bren gun.

The grim, nerve-tautening business of patiently snipping strand after
strand of wire went on for about thirty minutes, each one a lifetime
to the three men who had become the special target of a machine gun
at the opposite end of the wall.

While this display of sustained courage was being enacted above his
head, Browne sent a signal to the destroyer *Garth* for relaying to *Calpe*
saying: "Doug still on beach casualties heavy MG mortars 0610."

There is some evidence to show that this, like the earlier message
reporting the landing, reached *Garth* but not *Calpe*. Roberts, desperately anxious to help the main beaches and alarmed at the havoc being
created by the guns on Bismarck, dared not undertake bombardment
of the headland until he knew where the Royals were. At 6:10 a.m.,
the time of Browne's latest signal, he had no idea.

At approximately 6:30, Coles cut through the last strand, and Catto
crooked a beckoning finger at the soldiers gathered below. They surged
up to follow him through the gap, while Lieutenant Stewart, who had
kept firing his Bren throughout the ordeal at the wire despite being
repeatedly hit, struggled to his feet to cover the break-out. He faced the
machine gun along the wall, firing the Bren from his hip because loss of
blood made him too weak to aim it.

Twenty men went through the gap with Catto: Captain John
Housser, Lieutenant Y. S. Ryerson, Lieutenant T. L. Taylor and Sergeant
Coles with eleven other men of the Royals, Lieutenant J. D. McFetridge
RCA and three of his gunners, and Captain Browne who left his sig-
naller behind with orders to follow with the wireless set after sending
another message.

As the party left the wire on the other side a furious concentration
of fire fell down upon the gap, sealing it behind them. They were now
effectively cut off from the surviving troops on the beach.

At the top of a hill, probably the same one climbed by Corporal Ellis, they entered a small wood which hid them from the view of a German machine-gun crew firing from the lower floor of a fortified house. At a word from Catto, they burst out of the wood and took the house by assault, easily overcoming the half-dozen enemy gunners inside. Two more houses were attacked in similar fashion, but these were both found to be empty.

It was about 7:00 a.m., and the sounds of firing on the left flank of the beach had died away. From the centre and right flank they could hear intermittent bursts of automatic fire and the steady detonations of mortar bombs. In fact, the enemy had sensed that the end was near, that they were the undisputed master butchers at the abattoir of Puits. Casting caution aside, the elated slaughterers refined the art of dissection by gathering at the edge of the cliff immediately above the troops at the western end of the beach and "bombing" them with stick grenades. The more they lobbed their deadly little missiles, the more the troops were forced to dodge among the rocks at the bottom and expose themselves to the machine guns raking the wall of death.

After clearing the last house, Catto's party came under fire from a machine gun on the opposite side of the valley and moved westwards to escape it along the Bismarck heights where they laid up near the six-gun 88-mm battery, one of the regiment's objectives. They watched it open fire on a formation of Hurricane bombers with such proficiency that the impressed Browne rendered professional judgement later by reporting:

> The 88-mm Battery of six guns on the cliff top between Notre Dame de Bon Secours and Puits served its guns magnificently. It was low-level bombed at least four times and machine-gunned oftener by our fighters . . . with us as witnesses, and each time the guns were back in action within a matter of seconds, firing upon departing aircraft. Once, after a low-level attack, only two guns were instantly back in action, the other times always at least four.

The party reconnoitred the road between Puits and Notre Dame de Bon Secours, which overlooked Dieppe Harbour, found it heavily patrolled and covered by machine-gun emplacements, and in consequence entered a small wood near the Battery where they could hide until events elsewhere made their own position less obscure.

VII

After Catto's party left the beach, there was little opportunity left for the Royals to remain a cohesive force. They huddled behind anything that seemed to offer even the slightest protection while the mortar bombs exploded among them, the stick grenades fell down upon them, and the machine guns and snipers picked out exposed parts of their bodies.

One of the battalion's 3-inch mortars had been landed by the second wave and had been left unused at the edge of the water. Sergeant E. Peaks, not a mortar-man himself but weary of being helpless, took advantage of a smokescreen laid by an armed support landing-craft to lead three men out from under the wall and across the beach. Private M. Hamilton, who witnessed the incident, said: "Sergeant Peaks got the mortar set up. I couldn't make out who helped him on account of the smoke but there were three others. They didn't get many more than three bombs away when Heinie found them with his machine guns and they were cut to pieces." Another witness said that this volunteer mortar crew fired fifteen bombs before they were killed.

The Royal Navy had made valiant, vain attempts to relieve the weight of fire on the beach. Two armed support landing-craft had engaged the fortified houses and pillboxes which could be seen for nearly two hours, cruising only one hundred yards off shore to deliver their salvos. By the same token, they had been within easy reach of the heavy coastal artillery batteries and had eventually withdrawn at 7:40 a.m. with guns silenced and most of their crews killed.

Garth, after taking part in the initial bombardment of Dieppe, had switched her fire at 5:35 a.m. to the East Headland and sailed close in under it to fight a three-hour nerve-wracking duel with enemy batteries on the cliff top. In his report of the action, Lieutenant-Commander J. P. Scatchard RN said:

> I found throughout their fire was extremely accurate and it was impossible to go in and carry out a steady bombardment. It was a matter of going in through the smoke till close, squaring off and then retiring, then circling round and repeating the manœuvre. On each occasion we were straddled and it became extraordinary that there were not more of us hit.

Behind this terse commentary lay a dramatic ordeal which began shortly after 6:00 a.m. when the little destroyer, dwarfed by the towering cliffs, tempted a heavy coastal battery into a private battle.

Scatchard sailed *Garth* at full speed parallel with the shore and in the shadow of the East Headland, laying a smokescreen astern and blazing away with his 4-inch guns. When the range opened up, he altered course to port and sailed back in the opposite direction protected by his own smokescreen until it was time to alter course through it and make the mad dash past the battery again, firing broadsides as he passed it.

The German gunners soon recognized the pattern of his manœuvres, and each time the destroyer came out of the smokescreen with all guns blazing, the battery would straddle her with three-gun salvos – one shell going over, one falling short, and the third generally scoring a direct hit.

Goronwy Rees, a spectator aboard *Garth* by courtesy of Montgomery, said: "Calm and unmoved on the bridge, the commander [Scatchard] continued to issue his series of rapid, precise, thin-lipped orders . . . the manœuvre became monotonous and repetitive, and each time harder on the nerves, specially after we had been hit twice, the second time with considerable casualties and damage. Indeed the second time we were hit I thought, and wished, that *Garth* would break off the action. But the commander imperturbably repeated the same orders; once again we emerged from our smokescreen to carry out the same manœuvre. The petty officer on the bridge looked at me, shrugged his shoulders, raised his eyebrows, like a nanny in charge of an obstinate child; under his breath he muttered: 'The old bastard's going in again.' It was spoken in a tone in which wonder, tolerance, and admiration were all equally combined."

At one point during the duel, Scatchard received an urgent message from his Forward Observation Officer, Captain Browne, requesting fire on the white house overlooking Blue Beach. He directed two turrets onto the targets, but the salvos fell short in the cliff face and without Browne, then on the beach with Catto, to spot for him it was impossible to score any hits.

By 8:45 *Garth* was badly damaged and had nearly exhausted her ammunition. As she would no longer maintain her bombardment, she was ordered to take aboard as many survivors as possible from the various beaches and proceed with them back to England.

There is some mystery surrounding the movements of SGB 8 which lay off Blue Beach throughout most of the operation without being able to offer much in the way of effective support to the troops. Shortly after the second wave had landed she had received a message from the beach asking for fire support but had replied that she could not assist as she was to carry out a "warning and cover" patrol against surface attack from the west of Dieppe.

Her commanding officer reported later that he had remained about one thousand yards off Blue Beach to see that the landing-craft were heading in the right direction. Then he added: "Owing to the extremely confused situation on shore I was unable to give fire support without the risk of hitting our own troops. At 0540 I left the vicinity . . . to carry out Task 1, at this time being under fairly heavy fire from small calibre guns."

Some four hours later, however, SGB 8 returned to Blue Beach "and bombarded a field-gun emplacement, RDF [radar], ærials and snipers on cliffs, some hits being scored." This, however, was long after the battle of Puits had ended.

VIII

Aboard Calpe neither Roberts nor Hughes-Hallett were aware of the tragic events taking place on the two eastern flank beaches at Berneval and Puits. So many wireless sets, walkie-talkies, and inter-ship, inter-service, inter-brigade, inter-battalion systems had been superimposed upon the major networks linking Uxbridge, London, Calpe and Fernie that it seemed quite inconceivable that communications should be less than excellent.

The probability of enemy interception of conversation and insinuation of false messages into the various networks had been foreseen, but it does not appear to have occurred to the experts that enemy snipers might give particular attention to wireless operators and their sets.

The silence from Berneval was the result of no beach signals party having landed with the remnants of No. 3 Commando; the silence from Puits was owing in part to Catto's headquarters signalman being killed at touchdown and his set smashed by bullets aimed at it in the water. Furthermore, the Beachmaster, Military Landing Officer, and Beach Signals Group had all failed to land, leaving a communications vacuum between Blue Beach and the vast concourse of shipping lying off Dieppe.

In technical terms the interlocking communications systems were exquisitely designed. All they required in order to function was some means of keeping the operators alive and of preventing ærials being shot away.

The vacuum had been partially filled when Captain Browne landed with his telegraphist and set, both in working condition. For some unexplained reason, however, he reached the bombarding destroyer Garth as planned, but few of his messages were passed on to Roberts — and those that were were so distorted as to be misleading.

Browne's first signal to Garth giving the time of touchdown as 0535 failed to reach Roberts. Had it done so it would have been wrong because the time applied to the second wave, not the first, which had landed twenty-eight minutes earlier. Nevertheless, the enemy was active on the air and at 5:30 a.m. Hughes-Hallett received an R/T message saying, "No landing Puits." Both he and Roberts logged the signal in their situation reports to Uxbridge with qualifying comments that it might be of German origin. None of the battalions ashore were supposed to use place names, only code names.

At 5:54 Hughes-Hallett called MGB 316 with an urgent demand for news from Blue Beach. There was no reply for a long time. Roberts received a signal at 6:10 a.m., without knowing from where or from whom it came, saying: "Royal Regiment of Canada not landed." He suspected it as being of German origin yet felt compelled to report to Uxbridge at 6:20: "All landings made except Blue. Heavy fighting in progress." Simultaneously, he requested that a Hurricane bomber strike be mounted against the East Headland.

By 6:40 a.m. the position ashore was so confused that Roberts could only guess that the Royals might have been repulsed, that if no landing had taken place he had a battalion, or part of one, afloat and able to neutralize the dangerous East Headland if diverted to another landing-place. He checked with Brigadier Lett who had not yet landed from his headquarters in a tank landing-craft.

"Sherwood. No word from Doug. Have you heard?"

"No. Nothing heard Blue Beach."

Coinciding with this exchange was a signal for Hughes-Hallett from the mechanized landing-craft which had touched down in the second wave. It said: "Have only twenty personnel remaining. Can give no report. Have Beachmaster with us. Have about ten soldiers plus beach party and Beachmaster."

Both Force Commanders interpreted this as meaning that no landing had been made, and accordingly Roberts sent signals to Sherwood Lett and to MGB 316 for onward transmission ordering the Royals to reinforce the Essex Scottish on Red Beach, the other side of Dieppe Harbour from Puits.

An entry in the Intelligence log, timed 0640 says: "Blue Beach proceeding to Red Beach." Almost at the same time, Garth contacted Calpe to relay this message from Browne: "Impossible to land any more troops on Blue Beach."

For the first time there was reliable information with an unimpeach-able source providing the Force Commanders with definite indications that the Royals had landed and might be in trouble. Roberts cancelled his orders switching them to Red Beach.

Hughes-Hallett had been impatient all morning at the lack of signals from naval sources close to Blue Beach. He sent a curt message to MGB 316 demanding a full situation report. The reply, at 6:55 a.m., said: "Landing effected with slight casualties and no damage to craft."

It came from Lieutenant-Commander Goulding who had been lying off the beach since touchdown, unable to see what was taking place because of the dense smokescreens laid by the RAF and support landing-craft. It was an optimistic report which, however, reflected what he thought to be the true position. But since it made such little sense when compared with previous information, Hughes-Hallett called an ML and ordered it to "go get Goulding and tell him I want to see him at once."

Goulding reported aboard Calpe at about 7:30 a.m. and gave the Force Commander an encouraging, hopeful, and entirely wrong account based on what he had been unable to see clearly anyway. It was enough, however, for Roberts to cancel his request for bombing on the East Headland as the Royals, so he thought, must be there.

Leigh-Mallory, Mountbatten, and Crerar at Uxbridge received even more confident reports from Churchill Mann on Fernie. Roberts sent a summary of Goulding's report to Fernie which she then duplicated to Uxbridge in a message which became distorted in transmission and compounded the error.

Calpe's signal to Fernie timed 0740 said: "Royal Regiment landed Blue Beach. Doug landed three companies practically intact."

Fernie's message to Uxbridge was: "Doug landed three companies intact Blue Beach 0740 going well." It turned the time of origin from Calpe into the time of the Blue Beach landing – which was also wrong. The entry in Fernie's Intelligence log reveals an even more confident interpretation of Goulding's impressions. Timed at 8:17 a.m. it said: "Calpe reports Doug three companies OK. Heavy fighting for fortified house. Took cover – no further news. No news of 4th company."

While Goulding was still on Calpe, Hughes-Hallett received a call from Garth: "From Blue Beach. Is there any possible chance of getting us off?" This was the signal Browne had ordered his telegraphist to send as he left the sea wall to follow Catto through the wire.

Roberts was jolted into the realization that perhaps the Royals were still on the beach, that they may not have taken the East Headland, and that the main beaches might be in serious danger. The consequences of this unexpected communications muddle between Blue Beach and Calpe were that the Force Commanders were not reliably informed of trouble at Puits until three hours after the first wave had touched down.

Their earlier optimism now thoroughly dispelled, they set in motion strenuous efforts to find out where the Royals really were and, if necessary, to evacuate them. Hughes-Hallett ordered Goulding to take in four landing-craft from the boat pool; Roberts asked Uxbridge to mount an intensive air reconnaissance over Blue Beach and the East Headland. There is no evidence that these special flights were ever undertaken.

IX

Shortly after 8:00 a.m. the Royals made their last offensive bid to reach the top of the East Headland. Two survivors told later of an unknown officer who took five men out into the open to gather up lengths of abandoned rope for an attempt to scale the cliff face. All five soldiers were killed the minute they exposed themselves to enemy fire, but the officer, seemingly a charmed untouchable, clawed his way upwards at a furious pace, pulling out chunks of rock, chalk, and earth yet somehow managing to move up more often than he slipped back.

At first, snipers and machine-gunners chipped at the rock about his body, spraying him with needles of splintering stone. Then the fire gradually eased down, finally stopped, and a simmering quiet settled over the beach as Germans joined Canadians in gazing with fascinated wonderment at this futile bravery. Twenty feet became thirty feet, then forty, and on upwards to seventy-five, perhaps eighty feet. The watchers could see him slowing down, tiring under the strain, the hysterical generator of momentary madness that had driven him to such desperation gradually expiring. He was a speck of weary humanity who would never reach the top and safety, whose precarious holds on the towering cliff were taking longer and longer to find.

A single shot spat flatly across the almost silent beach. The officer convulsed for a brief agonized second, then leaned backwards into space and fell until his body smashed on the rocks below.

Canadians and Germans returned to their war with a sensation of light-headed relief. Movement stopped on the beach. Most of the bodies which carpeted the pebbles were those of the dead; the rest were of the wounded who no longer dared to move. Enemy sharpshooters gloated at the harvest they had reaped and waited cruelly, patiently, for the slightest movement to betray a live body – and a target.

At approximately the same time as the Force Commanders became acutely aware that all was not well on Blue Beach, a dirty white handkerchief tied to a rifle barrel was waved above the western end of the sea wall. Beneath a canopy of drifting smoke, drenched by sweat from the taps of their own fear and warmed by the brilliant morning sun, the Royal Regiment of Canada – or what was left of it – surrendered.

Their colonel was not present. Catto and his party were still hiding out in the wood on the Bismarck plateau where, according to Browne's later report, "shortly aften ten o'clock . . . we heard the survivors of the beach being marched past under guard." It was a humiliating moment for the party lying wretched and hunted in the undergrowth.

The Navy, however, had not yet abandoned hope of evacuating Berneval and Puits. At 9:50 a.m. Commander Wyburd led a group of unarmoured LCP's away from the boat pool for Berneval and twenty minutes later closed what he thought to be Yellow Beach. It was, in fact, Blue Beach. They were greeted by a hurricane of fire from artillery, mortars, and machine guns, sailed into it, and eventually sighted wrecked, capsized landing-craft, one of them with four soldiers still clinging to its upturned keel.

There was no question of stopping to rescue them in so intense a barrage. However, the Canadian commander of one LCP had no intention of leaving his stranded compatriots to be drowned or killed by snipers. Sub-Lieutenant John Boak RCNVR of Vancouver, drove his boat inshore with four heaving lines trailing over the stern. As she passed close alongside the four soldiers, Boak shouted: "Jump for the ropes and hold on."

All four obeyed, caught the lines, and Boak headed back out to sea beyond range of the automatic weapons. When he slowed down only three were brought aboard – the fourth had been too weak to maintain his grip. One of those saved by Boak was Private Simpson who had been in the landing-craft when it had capsized; with him were Privates L. W. Roberts and J. N. Wallace, both of the Royals and Toronto.

The attempt which Hughes-Hallett had ordered Goulding to undertake was not a happy enterprise. Goulding, carried in an armed support craft, led four landing-craft, accompanied by ML 291 to give fire support. As the force approached the smoke-covered beach Lieutenant-

Commander C. W. McMullen, in the ML, beckoned Goulding alongside and suggested he should take in two landing-craft alone to see what conditions were like ashore. Goulding replied that he wanted the ML to go in as well to engage the fortified white house on the eastern slope of the Puits valley. According to Goulding's report, McMullen replied that he would provide what supporting fire was, in his view, necessary.

In any event, this curiously acrimonious exchange ended with Goulding leading a pair of landing-craft towards the beach at about 10:30 a.m., coming up against a wall of enemy fire, and then retiring because, his report said, "it was quite impossible to proceed without fire support. The ML did not exchange the shots."

This implied that ML had given him no support, but McMullen's version is significantly different. He said: "I asked Lieutenant-Commander Goulding to come alongside, suggesting that he go inshore with two boats . . . to see if he could see anything. He replied that he considered it hopeless to approach Blue Beach without the support of a bombarding destroyer. The discussion was terminated by the smoke haze lifting from the cliffs and heavy fire being opened on us . . . and the attempt was abandoned."

More than an hour later, at 11:45 a.m., Hughes-Hallett received a signal from Goulding saying: "Could not see position Blue Beach owing to fog and heavy fire from cliff. . . . Nobody evacuated."

Some Canadian military commentators have chosen to hint strongly that this abortive attempt to evacuate Blue Beach was not a very determined one. Perhaps not – but does it really matter? The Royals had surrendered two hours previously; doubtless by then the abattoir had been cleaned up by enemy scavengers, the pebbles polished, and the beach handed back to those members of the master race whose bathing had been so rudely disturbed.

The tiny German garrison of the 571st Infantry Regiment reported to General Haase at 8:35: "Puits firmly in our hands; enemy has lost about 500 men prisoners and dead."

Above the beach Catto's party lay in hiding for more than six hours, their small wood surrounded by German patrols and gun emplacements. They noticed at 4:00 p.m. that the sound of firing had died away, that there were only occasional faint dull explosions from far out to sea. They knew the surviving Royals had been captured; they knew very little else except that the remainder of the 2nd Division were either returning to England with the fleet or were following the Royals into prison camp. Deciding that it would be merely a matter of time before his party was discovered, Catto advised each man to check his escape kit and run for it if he felt he had a chance.

Half an hour later he led the majority out of the wood to the Puits road where he formally surrendered to a German patrol. The would-be escapers were quickly rounded up, and their capture brought to a dismal end the Royal Regiment's first action against the enemy.

It had been a bloody, brutal affair, one which few can contemplate with equanimity even today. Inquests have brought little in the way of compensation, explanation, or extenuation. The grim truth about the reluctance of some troops to land at the agonizing moment of touchdown has been virtually ignored. Officially it is said to be of comparatively limited importance – and in terms of the operation as a whole this is probably true. The numbers of men involved can be put conservatively at between 150 and 250, representing only 5 per cent of the Canadian force at the most. However, Blue Beach was a self-contained flank assault, the most vital of all, and in this context the attitude of the men is signficant because they numbered at least 20 per cent of the Royal Regiment, perhaps higher than 40 per cent.

This is no way implies that the Toronto regiment had less stomach for fighting than other Canadian units. It means only that a series of unforeseen circumstances had combined to place these unblooded soldiers in the worst possible plight imaginable. It was a crack unit, one of the best in the Canadian Army Overseas, and had been allotted the most difficult landing of all. Pourville, for instance, was a far easier beach to assault. Knowing full well that Puits was but a gully in a long line of cliffs the planners had decided to give it to the regiment most likely to achieve success.

There was no room for error in the timetable of events, and when the naval mistake resulted in a late approach the harm could not be undone. The misdemeanour of a lone gun boat was compounded by subsequent developments into a major felony. Instead of heading direct for Blue Beach the landing-craft were taken across the mouth of Dieppe Harbour where their presence was discovered by an alerted enemy.

When challenged they had been unable to reply, thereby identifying themselves as hostile. Because they were late – although still covered by the last curtain of darkness – the boats had deployed for the final run-in at full speed, engines roaring. Sound carries far in the clear, pre-dawn stillness at sea, and there is no doubt that the enemy gunners followed the growing volume of engine noise until the boats themselves became visible as small dark shapes.

Then came the justification for the fears of some Canadian officers that the enemy would prove to be just as capable of defending his coast as they had been in defence of the Sussex coast. Given a few minutes warning he had welcomed this opportunity to prove his professional ability, and for the Royals the wrong finger was on the trigger.

I have been told that even at this late stage the tragic position might have been saved but for another fateful blow. Catto and his headquarters staff were carried aboard the slower flotilla, and when the first flight beached, the troops were deprived of the leadership of their colonel.

If the events on Blue Beach prove anything in terms of military lessons it is that men naturally hold back when there is no one to show the way, to show them that they have a fair fighting chance. For the Royals there was no fair chance, no fighting chance, no chance of any kind.

General Roberts was to report officially after the operation that the failure of the Royals "considerably affected the success of the landings on the main beaches." Hughes-Hallett was to write to Mountbatten saying of the fruitless landing: "There is little doubt that this was the chief cause of the failure of the Military Plan."

Neither of these Commanders was necessarily right. However, the collapse of the Blue Beach assault had the results both Force Commanders had expected. The guns on the East Headland denied the main beaches to the Essex Scottish and RHLI, prevented Ryder's cutting-out force entering the harbour and ripped the landing-craft flotillas to pieces.

When the sun went down that summer's day the bitter hours were over for the Royals; ahead lay the bitter years of resentment and recrimination which some of their number refuse to decently end.

On another beach at Pourville, west of Dieppe, that same day, the men from the prairies, who had once stood gaping at the impressive figure of Regimental Sergeant-Major Strumm, were about to gape again – this time at their jaunty, helmet-swinging colonel who was about to wrest his country's highest honours from the gold of the morning sun.

Spirit of
the Prairies

I

If Dieppe today is a word with special significance for Canadians, the meaning of it differs vastly from one province to another. Nowhere is this difference more strikingly apparent than in Toronto, where a rekindling of memories is not wholly encouraged, and in the prairie provinces, where men who were there speak of it with quiet, wistful pride. On the one hand, there is likely to be angry dismay, even accusations of betrayal; on the other, perhaps a rueful acknowledgement of youthful inexperience coupled with satisfaction at the lingering sweetness of triumph.

That the failure at Puits was not repeated at Pourville was largely owing to a punctual landing in darkness with a full measure of surprise; the other ingredients of success were the inspired, sustained leadership of Cec Merritt, and the fervent alacrity with which officers and men pressed home every attack. There was another reason, not often heard.

The Germans, knowing that an invader would only land at Pourville to attack Dieppe, had placed their first line of defence on the eastern heights, keeping just a token force in Pourville, one which the South Sasks outnumbered by approximately eight to one – until they moved up to the flanking heights and met the full weight of the enemy's strength. This in no way detracts from the achievements of the regiment, but serves to place them in perspective when related to failures elsewhere. The Germans at Pourville probably regarded these Canadians as the most obstinate of enemies that day; the prairie men, however, discovered within themselves that same indomitable spirit which had enabled earlier generations of sodbusters to wrest uncertain harvests from the dust, drought, snow, and floods. They found too that hands blistered by the plough, calloused by the shovel, could also handle the bayonet with a care and dexterity that the enemy had not the stomach to face. For the South Saskatchewans and the Camerons of Canada at least, the one-day excursion to the "poor man's Monte Carlo" was an exhilarating, if sobering, experience, untarnished by subsequent recrimination.

When the South Saskatchewan Regiment divided itself for the cross-Channel passage in *Princess Beatrix* and *Invicta*, it consisted of 523 officers and men; twenty-four hours later 355 returned to England, more than half of them wounded.

As the Royals were supposed to break westwards out of Puits to occupy the East Headland from the rear and join the Essex Scottish, so the South Sasks were to move eastwards from Pourville to neutralize the West Headland guns and meet the Royal Hamilton Light Infantry. In total, these regiments would form a perimeter round Dieppe through which the Camerons and Calgary Tanks might pass for their assaults on the St Aubin ærodrome and the château at Arques-La-Bataille, suspected of being German divisional headquarters.

The military plan said: "The South Saskatchewan Regiment must secure Green Beach [Pourville] with the minimum delay to enable the Camerons of Canada to pass through without opposition." In the course of doing so, each company in the battalion had specific objectives designed to establish a safe, secure miniature bridgehead.

C Company was to move right to the southwest of the town, destroy a German army motor transport repair shop and several machine-gun positions on the western slopes of the Scie Valley and capture a German officers' mess; B Company would clear the town, deal with a wired compound farther inland and then turn eastwards; A Company would head eastwards to the heights overlooking Dieppe and attack coastal batteries and the radar station; and D Company would also move to the east to capture the Farm of the Four Winds, a strongpoint which dominated the route inland which the Camerons would use to reach St Aubin. There was also a small special force under Lieutenant Leslie England which would assist in the assault on a strongpoint guarding the approach to the radar station and be responsible for evacuating dismantled equipment.

Three extra bodies not listed on the regimental strength were also among them. They wore Canadian uniforms and carried Canadian pay books giving false names and numbers, but in all other aspects they were then, as they remain today, anonymous and faceless – the radar scientist who, if not evacuated would be found by the Germans as just another dead Canadian soldier among hundreds; his official executioner who would never speak to him nor lose sight of him; the soe secret agent who, provided the scientist were evacuated, killed, or executed, would then proceed with his own mysterious activities.

Their presence was disguised by a special order which said: "The R.D.F. [radar] personnel must be given sufficient protection to prevent his falling into enemy hands. F.S. [Field Security] personnel and S.O.E. to assist. . . ."

Boats were lowered at the start point punctually at 3:00 a.m., and the force of ten assault craft and two large mechanized landing-craft sailed for Pourville in two columns under the command of Lieutenant-Commander R. Prior. There was no trouble in finding the beach – nearly half a mile long, seventy-five yards wide, and broken near the middle by the narrow, marshy mouth of the River Scie. Pourville itself lies on what is in effect a dyke between the marshes of the Scie and the Channel and was then separated from the beach by an eight-foot-high sea wall heavily covered by wire.

The Germans had partially dammed the river by installing lock gates so that it had flooded at the eastern end into a sluggish, nearly stagnant lake up to ten feet deep. This had transformed it into a vast anti-tank obstacle, and the only way to cross it was by bridge leading to the main road to Dieppe up the eastern slopes of the Scie Valley. At the narrow exit through the beach, however, the river was comparatively shallow and could be easily waded.

The outer perimeter of the Dieppe defences on the west ran across the eastern high ground overlooking Pourville. The military plan intended that the battalion should touch down in one flight astride the river mouth with the various companies landing on the sides nearest to their objectives – those attacking the eastern heights to be on the east side of the beach, the force assigned to the western slopes to land west of the river mouth.

The approach was eventless, landing-craft deploying about one mile out into line abreast and heading in at full speed for the touchdown. Although the first faint grey of dawn could be perceived in the east it was still dark, and from the boats Pourville was almost indistinguishable from the rearing black ramparts of the cliffs.

Cec Merritt, hunched in the bows of his boat, was quietly encouraged by the lack of movement ashore and the near certainty that the troops would be landed at the right time at the right place. The boats maintained perfect formation as they ran in over the last few hundred yards, each only one hundred feet from the other and their square-cut bows churning the calm sea into swirling waves of fluorescent foam. In every boat the senior officers nodded to NCO's and an order rustled through the men: "Fix Bayonets."

At 4:52 a.m. only two minutes late, the boats grounded, ramps rattled down, and men dashed out across the beach, heavy boots stamping down on the loose pebbles. "We sounded for all the world like a herd of elephants charging across a field of walnuts," said one soldier when he returned to England.

It was not until the landing-craft were pulling astern from the beach that the Germans began firing wildly out to sea, not quite sure what had happened. "We were on the beach before fire opened up," said Major Jim McRae of Weyburn, Merritt's second in command. "We got over it quickly enough and without any opposition." Yet this complete silence from the enemy unnerved some of the men who could hardly credit that they had, in fact, achieved such a full measure of surprise. It seemed just too good to be true – which it was.

A near-perfect touchdown, but too far to the right. Instead of landing astride the river mouth, the force hit the western side of the beach, including those companies whose objectives were on the eastern heights. They had to use scaling-ladders to climb the sea wall, cut gaps in the wire on top of it, scramble through off the beach, turn sharp left, and dash through the town to the bridge over the flooded part of the Scie, on the other side of which lay the road leading up the valley's eastern ridge to Dieppe. Those first few precious moments of surprise in which the defenders were thrown into sleepy-eyed confusion were probably lost, cancelled out by the time wasted in running almost the entire breadth of Pourville from west to east. Long before these companies reached the bridge, the enemy had come awake and manned the machine-gun posts covering it on fixed lines of fire.

Once across the sea wall and through the wire the battalion fanned out in the town – C Company striking westwards, A and D Companies running headlong to the east down the main street, and B Company cleaning the enemy out of Pourville itself.

Aboard Calpe, a signal at 4:50 a.m. from Green Beach saying "Cecil landed" gave Roberts a feeling of elation which would soon dissipate and never return. While he waited for news from Puits where the Royals were being slaughtered, he wondered about Pourville, about the West Headland, about the ability of the South Sasks to create and maintain a bridgehead for the Camerons. Surrounded by all the paraphernalia modern science had devised to assure him the means to control the battles for the beaches he could only sit and wonder, listening intently to the crackling and spluttering of the loudspeakers as if they might hold some clue that might explain the interminable silence.

The silence dragged on. And whereas he would never really know what had happened on Blue Beach at 8:05 a.m. – after a gap of more than three hours – he would receive a report saying "Camerons and South Sasks cleared Beach."

What sort of information was that for an angry impatient commander? Consumed by an agonizing sense of impotence, he burst out to the astonished signals staff: "What the hell is going on anyway? Why won't someone tell me?"

II

Cec Merritt had inherited a tough, resilient fighting unit accustomed to an easy-going version of army life. Merritt, himself accustomed to the self-discipline required in the courtroom and on the playing-field, had applied the principle of instant obedience to his temporary occupation as battalion commander. If the sodbusters had at first protested, they were about to reap the benefits of it.

He was among the first into the town, followed closely by Major McRae, Lieutenant Dickin, in charge of headquarters defences, Sergeant Blackwell, the battalion signals expert, and Corporal Joe Gregory of Calgary, sniper *par excellence*. Battalion headquarters were set up in a deserted garage, and Merritt set about establishing radio contact with his companies.

A and D Companies raced through the town to the bridge where they were met by vicious streams of fire from pillboxes on the hill leading up to the eastern heights on the other side. Men fell in heaps as Murray Osten persisted in leading a charge over the bridge with D Company covering fire, and those in the rear jumped into the river to swim or raft themselves across. While many of A Company never reached the other side, the bulk did, and gathered around Osten in the shelter of a road block.

Sergeant B. H. Smith whose section had been immediately behind Osten on the bridge said, "I went over the bridge followed by my section and came under very heavy machine-gun fire, the remainder of the platoon then crossing the river under the bridge. . . . As we advanced the fire was very heavy from two pillboxes situated one on top of the other on the forward slope of the hill.

"There were snipers and riflemen firing from the slope along the road leading up the hill. The machine-guns appeared to be firing on fixed arcs and were very accurate and all were mutually supporting, covering all dead ground."

While still behind the road block, A Company was joined by Leslie England's special force who had avoided the bridge by running eastwards along the beach for about one hundred yards, wading across the narrow river mouth, and scaling the lower cliffs. As they headed inland England was hit and had to be carried back to the beachhead by Merritt and a Private Williams.

The combined force was held up at the road block for nearly half an hour by the pillbox on the hill before Private Charles Sawden, a lean, tanned, hard-faced farmer from Consul, Saskatchewan, announced: "I'll take out the bastard, if someone brings up my rifle." It seems that it never occurred to him that he might not live to use the rifle again. At Osten's nod, he pulled the pins from two grenades and, with one in each hand, walked uphill into the lacing fire. Private Victor Story, one of those who watched, said later: "Sawden strolled nonchalantly up the hill to the pillbox, lobbed the two grenades through the gun-slits, and wiped it out, killing four Jerries. We were then able to proceed towards our objectives."

Sawden lived then to recover his rifle. An hour later he was wounded in the legs; four hours later he was dead on the beach.

The Company swung inland and then back towards the edge of the cliffs towards the radar station, fighting every yard of the way and hugging the hedgerows. The whole of the eastern heights was defended by hidden pillboxes, gun emplacements, and sniper nests, none of which could be properly located because the enemy used only smokeless ammunition. Snipers moved about constantly, selecting the targets from among officers and NCO's; enemy mortars, accurate and devastating, were moved from one position to another in horse-drawn vehicles.

They reached one of their objectives, a light anti-aircraft battery being used to shell the assault boats of the approaching Camerons of Canada, and stormed it with fixed bayonets. No prisoners were taken.

By then most of D Company – 70 per cent of it – were across the bridge, impatient to get at the Farm of the Four Winds on the high ground, but were held up by A Company whose progress had been slowed down. B Company, which should also have crossed the bridge, was pinned down west of it with the remnant of D Company, some of whom were making desperate efforts to get over it, although only a few reached the other side. One of these was Private J. Krohn, who said later, "Chiltern, Evenden, Pickford, Carswell, and myself were fired upon when we got halfway across. Carswell and Pickford got it and two boys fell beside me. . . . Another fell at my feet and I flattened out, rolling myself over the side of the bridge into the water, dragging one of the boys with me. We started wading and swimming, and when the rest of our platoon saw what we were doing they jumped into the water and followed. But the snipers had been waiting for it . . . and we were picked off, one or two at a time."

A runner returned to battalion headquarters with news of the hold-up, and Merritt, leaving McRae in charge, ran to the bridge, saw the heaped bodies of the men who had been killed trying to cross it, and knew with sudden, stomach-sickening certainty that it was his job, and only his, to persuade the hundred-odd men sheltering on either side of the road to make a concerted advance. The troops already fighting on the other side needed their help urgently.

Facing them was the bridge, a small bridge, only a few feet wide, about a hundred feet long, and lined by low stone walls – an unimpressive bridge such as those that cross rural streams. But once it left the bridge the road continued on, quite straight, and sloping gently until about two hundred yards away it bore right and headed inland. From where the men were sheltering there was no distinguishing bridge from road; ahead lay just one long, narrow ribbon of concrete upon which nothing moved, no one lived. Merritt noticed that a large grey house well past the bridge would provide temporary cover once the troops reached it. It was about a hundred yards away.

Reacting more by instinct than design, he took off his helmet, wiped the sweat from his face and, while it was still swinging from the chin strap wrapped about his wrist, sprinted to the centre of the bridge,

calling out to the astounded men, "Come on over. They can't hit anything. There's nothing to worry about here." He turned his back contemptuously on the enemy guns and walked towards the men, with
bullets kicking up sparks about his feet. "Now let's go get 'em. We'll
get to that house first." Then he turned about and ran across the
bridge to the house. One group hurtled after him and reached the
house at his side. Only four died during that mad race, but the survivors were not enough; there had to be far more over the bridge if
the pillboxes were to be taken and the way opened to reach the Farm of
the Four Winds.

Still clutching his steel helmet in his right hand, Merritt strolled
over to the men sheltering on the Pourville side, and yelled, "See that.
Hardly anyone got hurt. Now let's have all of you over this time.
Keep your heads down and run like hell. Ready.... Go...." He turned
and ran back into the fire again followed by about forty more troops,
mostly of B Company.

One soldier, having crossed the bridge, suddenly froze in the middle
of the road, shocked into immobility by the intensity of fire and the
sight of so many men lying grotesquely in death about his feet. Merritt ran back, spoke to him and then quickly slapped his face from
side to side. The soldier jerked convulsively, relaxed and raced on to
safety.

Captain H. B. Carswell, Royal Canadian Artillery, who had landed
as Forward Observation Officer for the destroyer *Albrighton* which
was bombarding the eastern heights, was one of those held up at the
bridge. He said later: "Lieutenant-Colonel Merritt led several parties
across the bridge which was swept by machine-gun, mortar, and
field-gun fire continually."

Lieutenant J. S. Edmondson, second in command of D Company,
reported: "The Colonel, when he saw we were being held up, crossed
the bridge several times urging the men forward, and the men followed. The dead were piled two deep for about fifty feet along the
bridge."

Before advancing beyond the grey house, the pillbox covering the
road up the hillside had to be silenced – something so obvious that the
men gathered against the wall staring blankly at Merritt as if it were
his business and none of theirs. He looked back at them, bleakly, and
said: "We've got to get the Hun out of there. When I say go, rush 'em,
and don't stop for anything."

The group rustled with movement, loosening grenades and preparing to move out. Merritt raised a hand, and shouted "Now.... Go."

No one moved. He quickly realized that they had expected him to organize some form of support before rushing 150 yards under fire – the "fair, fighting chance" principle at work again. He ordered one man to collect an abandoned mortar lying near the bridge, and when it arrived smoke bombs were fired to cover the dash forwards.

Merritt has since told me: "Once we fired the smoke, they all followed me very willingly, although the smoke was worth little against a machine gun firing on fixed lines down the road at point-blank range." He was not the only amateur officer to learn this day that given the fair, fighting chance the men would take almost any risks.

This is how Private Thrussell saw the end of the incident: "The Colonel stepped out into the road and loped up to the pillbox and blew it up. We were all behind him and took three Jerries prisoner."

When he returned to battalion headquarters, Merritt's boyish grin was so complacent that his adjutant, Captain G. B. Buchanan, asked him what there was to be amused about. Merritt replied: "I've just bombed out a pillbox. Try it sometime before breakfast. I recommend it for the appetite."

In Pourville, the men of B Company cleared houses of machine-gun nests and snipers. Private F. P. Forness disturbed a French couple in bed and bowed gallantly before departing, search abandoned. Back in the street he was fired at from a house decorated with huge red crosses, and angrily retaliated by heaving a grenade inside, blowing out a live German officer grimly clutching a briefcase. Corporal Mercier burst through a front door, Sten gun ready. He emerged with five provocative young ladies and a huge, smug grin splitting his face. Sergeant Coderre, noticing that enemy snipers concentrated on officers and NCO's and always changed position after firing, made snipers his special business and adopted the same tactics: firing, moving; firing, moving. Eventually he backed cautiously round a corner and bumped into somebody backing from the other direction. He swung round to gaze into the horror-filled face of a German and used his bayonet with admirable skill.

Corporal Joe Gregory and Private Stewart both began cleaning out one side of a street, killing two Germans in the first house, capturing a German Gestapo agent and French collaborator in the second, and spending another thirty minutes convincing French families that they were raiders, not invaders. When they returned to battalion headquarters with their prisoners, they found Corporal Coxford in charge of a section guarding some fifty prisoners, so many in fact that the need for a strong guard was draining troops away from the fighting.

They discussed the possibility of shooting the prisoners but quickly dropped it when Major McRae began casting suspicious glances in their direction.

Sergeant Howard Graham, his battle dress draped with incendiary grenades, turned himself into a one-man house-wrecking firm just to smoke out a particularly troublesome sniper. Graham marched down a street, setting fire to one house after another until the sniper finally ran out with his hands in the air and his clothes on fire.

Private Krohn searched the sleeping-quarters of a captured pillbox and found a German hiding under a bunk. He contemplated shooting the captive but resisted the temptation. Then, to his disgust, he was told to take the prisoner back to headquarters. One machine-gun emplacement buried into the side of the cliffs made certain streets in the town highly dangerous to Canadian traffic. Private M. Rogal took an anti-tank rifle to the second floor of a house east of the bridge then occupied by a group under Lieutenant Edmondson, sighted on the enemy emplacement, and fired fifteen rounds at it. "That should have done the trick," he said, inadequately, "but just as I got out of my building, they replied by firing a mortar at me and blowing in the side of the house." Edmondson and his men managed to stay inside the house covering the advance of D Company inland.

Private Sam Block was one of a section that cleaned out the main street, taking prisoners two or three at a time. "On seeing how this situation was depriving us of manpower for fighting, we started to dispose of the prisoners in the usual way," he reported laconically. "A good German is a dead one."

Corporal Rainville agreed. "There were a lot of Germans in civilian clothes who were obviously pointing out our positions to snipers. Whenever we came across them we shot them out of hand. The German tactics seemed to be that they would keep giving themselves up, thus weakening our fighting power. So we killed them on the spot, thus keeping our fighting power."

Private E. H. Shook, made angry in the first few minutes of the street fighting when an impertinent machine gun in a large hotel split his rifle butt, rushed into the hotel, tossed grenades about indiscriminately, and finally wiped out the machine-gun nest, taking four prisoners. "Somehow they got killed accidentally later," he reported briefly.

Private Rodgers escorted some prisoners through the town to battalion headquarters and reported that French women appeared on balconies to wave at him and give the V sign. In one house he came across four young Frenchmen slightly drunk, with empty bottles of wine scattered about the floor. "They gave me and my pals some drinks and offered to help. Last I saw of them they were out in the streets carrying our wounded back to the beach."

One section of twelve men took up positions in a house occupied by three French girls who offered them wine and biscuits. About an hour later they were still in the house and a full-blooded party was taking shape, but an officer ruined it by barging in and ordering them up front on the double. "It sure was a good battle while it lasted – in that house," said one private.

Private E. A. Clarke's section threw about eight grenades into one house and "several Frenchmen came out dressed in blue denim shirts and trousers and carrying lunch bags. They were panicky and ran gibbering about, waving their hands over their heads. Next door a group of women appeared on a balcony. All were crying until they were calmed by a French Canadian." According to Clarke, the prisoners were mostly "snivelling creatures, although several of the large sullen-looking ones still had that arrogant look which made me want to pull the trigger."

While Merritt toured the fighting fronts, McRae was forced to change the position of battalion headquarters several times, keeping communications intact.

He was being constantly harassed by heavy and accurate mortar fire which forced him to keep on the move. Every time he used his radio-telephones to issue orders or answer calls for help, the Germans located him with Radio Direction Finding equipment and subjected him to quick bombardment. The only solution was to move from one site to another before they could do too much damage. According to Captain Buchanan, "McRae was gifted with a sixth sense. Every time we moved, the previous spot was bombed out by mortars. He controlled the battle at headquarters . . . as only an old and skilled soldier can." It was during one of these moves that RSM Strumm of the mighty voice was struck down.

On the right of Pourville, Major Claude Orme, commanding C Company, was handling the assault against the western slopes of the Scie Valley by controlling his platoons and sections in a manner which would have delighted a management efficiency expert. His officers always led, and because there was leadership the men followed. They crashed off the beach, swung right in the town, and headed for the first objective: a large hotel overlooking the right end of the beach that was suspected of being quarters for German officers. Orme carried out the frontal attack with his headquarters platoon while other groups moved around the hotel right and left to deliver an assault from the rear.

Sergeant H. E. Long commanded the platoon which went round the east side with Privates W. A. Haggard of Tisdale, Saskatchewan, and French-speaking G. B. Berthelot of Fife Lake, Saskatchewan, bringing up the rear. By the time this pair reached the back entrance the German sentries had been shot, and all resistance was ended. Orme's men had been equally successful, and there was little else for a third platoon under Lieutenant L. R. McIlveen from Gull Lake, Saskatchewan, to do but go inside to search the place. They found it occupied by nearly a hundred French and Belgian slave labourers brought into Pourville to build the Todt Organization's anti-invasion defences. These very frightened civilians were herded out of the hotel and allowed to disperse.

During this period Lieutenant L. G. Kempton's platoon had occupied the motor transport works farther inland, and the bulk of C Company now converged on La Maison Blanche, high up on a hilltop overlooking the town. Sergeant Long's men left the hotel, paused briefly while a group of French women told Private Berthelot that the Germans were dug in at the top of the slope, and then continued up to the suspected German headquarters in single file. As the column topped the ridge, the enemy opened fire, wounding Long in the head and killing the Bren-gunner next to him.

Berthelot's account, given later, said: "Another sergeant took command but he was uncertain of what to do, and we wasted a few minutes of very precious time. I thought if we do not do something very soon we will soon all be dead. As we were all in a pretty compact bunch we could have been wiped out by a mortar bomb. I called Private Haggard and told him we should advance, one section to the right and two sections to the left."

Haggard agreed and, in the absence of any leadership from the NCO's, took charge of the situation. He reconnoitred ahead of the platoon, finding that the enemy were dispersed along the ridge in front of the headquarters in weapon pits occupied by machine guns and linked by slit trenches. He returned, placed one section under the command of Corporal Scotty Mathieson, from Braddock, Saskatchewan, another under Berthelot, and took a third section himself to attack the Germans from the rear. Both Mathieson and Berthelot were to charge when they heard his section open fire.

It took him fifteen minutes to work round behind the Germans, who could see the encirclement taking place and were prepared to meet it. A stand-off resulted, with futile exchanges of fire merely serving to consume more valuable minutes. Haggard decided suddenly to end the stalemate, and at his signal Berthelot stormed out from cover, rushing at the row of weapons pits and firing a Bren gun from the hip.

He reached the lip of the first and fired straight down into a blur of white faces, then on to the second and the third, repeating the stuttering bursts of execution until he met Mathieson, tommy gun at the hip, coming from the other end of the row and firing into the pits in the same manner. One machine-gun emplacement was set apart from the rest behind a hedge. Private Mattock of Haggard's section could see the gunners but could not shoot without exposing himself. Haggard, however, could not see the gunners but was in a position to shoot at the hedge. With Mattock calling out instructions, Haggard stood up and fired until four of the enemy were killed and the two privates were able to rush the emplacement to destroy it with grenades.

Some twenty Germans were killed in the assault and thirty taken prisoner. Haggard arranged for the platoon to search La Maison Blanche, handed back command to an NCO, and then set off to find the wounded Sergeant Long. The core of resistance on the western hills of the valley had been crushed by an extravagant display of initiative by two privates and a corporal. When Claude Orme came up with the remainder of the company and cleaned out two light coastal batteries, all the objectives to the west of Pourville were achieved.

Although the western approaches to Pourville were now secured and the town itself occupied, the South Sasks were precariously placed on the eastern heights. They had not yet reached the Farm of the Four Winds, and while it remained in enemy hands there was little chance of the Camerons getting past it to St Aubin. Time was becoming the critical factor – for the Camerons were already approaching touchdown.

III

The Camerons were supposed to hit Green Beach at 5:20 a.m., the same time as the assault over the main beaches at Dieppe. The regiment's crossing in the LCP's had been uneventful and there was nothing to prevent their safe arrival. Colonel Alfred Gostling, however, had never been convinced that the South Sasks could properly secure a bridgehead in just thirty minutes and had no intention of making an opposed daylight landing in unarmoured, wooden assault boats which Combined Operations had intended to be used for training purposes only. That they were being used in battle underscored the acute shortage of vessels of all kinds for amphibious operations.

To give Merritt more time in which to open up the bridgehead, Gostling requested the naval officer in charge of the LCP's, Commander H. V. P. McClintock, to land late rather than early. McClintock's later report said:

> Had we trusted to our dead reckoning and continued at a steady course and speed . . . we would have made the correct beach about 10 minutes late, which was the time we were aiming for. Unfortunately, when we sighted the coast we thought we seemed rather close and made a reduction in speed because the O/C Troops preferred to arrive late rather than early. Later, when we could see a bit more, we thought that we were rather too far to the eastward and made an unnecessary alteration of course which we later had to correct. The Camerons of Canada were, however, eventually landed on the right beach about a half-hour late (0550 instead of 0520).

Gostling was in a large LCP commanded by Sub-Lieutenant Johnny O'Rourke RCNVR of Calgary, when the force deployed about two miles off shore for the run in to touchdown. In those final few minutes shells from the eastern heights fell among the boats, and it was clear that the bridgehead was by no means secure.

Gostling calmed the lightly nervous men in O'Rourke's boat by standing exposed on deck and coolly explaining how to recognize the calibre of the guns firing at them. "Listen to that," he said once. "It's mobile artillery. When we get closer they'll use mortars. They'll be a bit noisier than ours."

When only a few hundred yards away, the Camerons' piper stood tall in the bows, braced himself like some Viking figurehead, and began to play, and the wild lilt of Highlands war music was lifted up by the morning breeze and carried ashore where the smiling soldiers of the South Sasks recognized the sound of "The Hundred Pipers."

However, there was only one piper, and at least two men ashore failed to identify the thin, reedy sound. Private Haggard was wheeling the wounded Sergeant Long down the western hillside towards the beach in a wheelbarrow borrowed from an effusive Frenchman. When the faint notes of the pipes reached him he nearly toppled his astonished sergeant into the nearest ditch as he frantically thrust the wheelbarrow behind a hedge.

Long demanded an explanation for such callous indifference to his wounds, and Haggard replied: "Listen. Horsedrawn artillery coming up. Listen hard, you'll hear the squeaking of the wheels."

They huddled silently behind the hedge, hearts thumping, and intent upon the "squeaking" while blessing the German who had forgotten to use axle grease on the gun cart. Then the noise became unmistakably the bleating of bagpipes and the red-faced Haggard resumed his journey to the accompaniment of a verbal tongue-lashing from the pained sergeant.

Although thirty minutes late, partly by request, the assault boats hit Green Beach in perfect formation but wrongly placed. Instead of touching down as a unit on one side of the river mouth, they landed astride it, O'Rourke's boat being at the eastern end of the beach nearly under the eastern heights still held by the enemy. As Gostling led his men in a lunging rush for the sea wall, a pillbox in the face of the cliffs opened fire. Both O'Rourke and Private J. Coll reported that Alfred Gostling was fatally wounded by the first burst, almost as he stepped ashore. Captain John Runcie, a company commander who was close beside his colonel, confirmed that Gostling was the first to be hit and had died instantly.

The manner of their landing presented difficulties for the Camerons who were now divided into two groups: the bulk of the battalion on the western side of the beach where there was almost no opposition at all, owing to Claude Orme's occupation of the western hills, and a miscellaneous group on the eastern side where their passage through the wire was heavily opposed from the flanking heights. The military plan for Green Beach was effectively wrecked at this point and, in the absence of alternatives, future events were decided by junior officers.

Captains Runcie and Campbell led a party of thirty men off the eastern side of the beach into Pourville where they met the indefatigable Merritt who immediately placed them under his own command.

Another group of Camerons commanded by Captain Young had landed so far to the east they were able to scale the extremity of the sea wall and follow the same route inland up to the eastern heights that had been taken earlier by the special force of the South Sasks under Leslie England.

Company Sergeant-Major George Gouk had this to say of the landing and subsequent events:

> As we neared the coast of France we saw the finest fireworks display, coloured lights, bursting shells, tracer bullets – well, all it takes to make what we call a modern war.
>
> About 1000 yards from shore, the Coy Commander gave the order to prepare to land. We scrambled up on deck of the boats after being cramped up in the bottom for over nine hours; gee but it sure felt good to think that we would be able to stretch our legs again on land. Everyone feeling in the best of spirits and to make us feel still better our Coy piper starts playing "The Hundred Pipers." The boat grounds on a gravel beach with shells bursting pretty close. Everyone jumps off at the bow, led by our Coy Commander, rush forward a matter of 50 yards to an eight foot wall. It sure was a disappointment on getting there to find the ugliest looking barbed wire stretching right from the top of the wall a distance of 12 feet. Well the boys didn't hesitate long, as some of us kept firing at the German pillboxes, where snipers and MG's were busy. Those with wire cutters got working and within 10 minutes had two pathways cut through the wire. Now was our chance to get going. Over the wall we went and rushed across the main road and took cover on the river bank. Casualties were small. Up to now a few of the men had slight wounds but that did not keep them back. We worked our way under cover for about 200 yards. Then the Coy Commander thought it was about time we called a halt and got organized before going further. On checking up I found we had only 12 platoon with us and a platoon of "D" Coy. The Coy Commander had no way of communicating with anyone; so decided we would carry on and do as much damage as possible, so we swung left from the river towards a small village where we knew the enemy were. Snipers and MG's seemed to be in every house so we got busy on them and were doing a fairly good job cleaning them out with rifles and grenades when all of a sudden they opened up on us with their mortars. It sure was hell. Our casualties sure started mounting then. Every corner you turned you seemed to run into mortar fire and they sure could place their shots. Well, there was no stopping the boys then. They were seeing their pals for the first time being killed and wounded at their side and the only thought that seemed to be in every-

one's mind was to have revenge. It sure was great to see the boys with blood all over their faces and running from wounds in their arms and legs not worrying about getting first aid but carrying on in a systematic manner, clearing out the "Nazis" from the houses just the same way as they learned to do on the Isle of Wight.

Young's group had, in fact, struck inland along the eastern bank of the river for some five hundred yards and then swung left and uphill to the group of houses Gouk called a village. These were so heavily defended that Private Flemington admitted, "I was kind of worried about all those bullets, but Captain Young told us they weren't very good shots during the last war and that he didn't think they had had much practice since, so I took his word for it and kept going."

Beyond these houses were a series of slit trenches and weapon pits which held up further attempts to reach the heights. Young called for volunteers and led them in a magnificently hopeless fixed bayonets charge across one hundred yards of open country. He died only a few feet from the nearest trench.

By this time the operation on the east side had taken a fluid turn with mixed parties of Camerons and South Sasks acting independently, coalescing or separating as circumstances dictated but always seeking and probing for ways to advance which would enable them to come to grips with an enemy who remained invisible on higher ground, an enemy whose mortar, artillery, and machine-gun fire was constantly inflicting casualties and decimating their numbers. Throughout the morning, Pourville and the surrounding areas were under heavy and accurate mortar fire aimed so effectively that wherever the troops moved it followed them, and whenever a radio-telephone was used mortar bombs would follow.

IV

When news reached Major A. T. Law of Winnipeg, commanding the main body of the Camerons on the west side of the town, that Gostling had been killed, he realized that there was no hope of reaching the rendezvous with the Calgary Tanks, south of the Farm of the Four Winds via the eastern route laid down in the military plan. As an alternative he decided to penetrate southwards along the western banks of the Scie and try to cross it farther inland.

As soon as the advance companies left the town they were forced
to cross open territory under observation from the Farm of the Four
Winds on the other side of the valley. Law ordered the unit to take
cover in the woods, and the troops moved forward keeping the trees
between them and the machine-gun and mortar fire coming from the
farm. Without warning, they stumbled out of the woods into open
fields, covered by a series of enemy machine-gun emplacements. One
of these was cleaned out by assault, and the unit moved left-handed
towards the river and a road leading across a bridge to the village of
Bas de Hautot. In the course of this movement they passed a small
farmhouse from which two half-dressed Germans appeared. An entire
platoon of Camerons opened fire, like a firing squad, and according to
battalion records, "practically every man could claim a hit."

Eventually the Camerons drew up on a ridge overlooking Bas de
Hautot village. They were close enough to the rendezvous to see the
tanks, if they had arrived. Instead of the Calgary Tanks, however,
they saw the village crawling with enemy soldiers and what appeared
to be a cyclist company deploying on the eastern outskirts.

It was nearly 9:00 a.m., and Law, abandoning all hope of attacking
the ærodrome, decided to cross the river, secure the high ground to
the east, and turn northwards to come up on the Farm of the Four
Winds from the rear – a bold plan which would have taken the
Camerons in a vast encircling movement from Pourville down the
western side of the valley, then across to the east to retrace their steps
back to the sea.

However, as the Camerons moved downhill a large German force
was seen heading along the road from Pourville – obviously reinforcements for the garrison at Bas de Hautot. The leading sections of
the Camerons tried to turn back, ran unexpectedly into a German
horse-drawn mortar detachment, wiped it out, and then found themselves engaged by the van of the enemy formation. Private Ted Barnes,
who had wrecked the mortar, killed three Germans in rapid succession, and Law's later report said that two snipers, Privates Alex Huppe
and E. Herbert, "killed fifteen of the enemy between them."

More enemy units moved out of Bas de Hautot to attack the rear of
the Camerons, one group getting above them on higher ground and
firing down with machine guns. Law had to change his plans hurriedly
and issue orders for an immediate withdrawal to the beach. Immediately afterwards his signalman intercepted a message from Sherwood
Lett's 6th Brigade Headquarters to the South Sasks saying: "Vanquish
from Green Beach at 1000 hours. Get in touch with Camerons." Law

managed to raise Jim McRae at Merritt's headquarters in Pourville and inform him that the Camerons were withdrawing back to the beach.

During the retreat, they were harassed by snipers and machine guns firing smokeless ammunition from concealed positions impossible to locate. A party of South Sasks sent out to contact Law with the order to withdraw were met just south of Pourville and joined the Camerons for the last dash back to the sea wall. It was then a few minutes before 10:00 a.m.

While the Camerons were retreating on the west, the South Sasks on the eastern slopes were still struggling to reach the radar station and the Farm of the Four Winds. Osten led a small party of A Company to within yards of the radar station before he was halted by several rows of wire and determined defences. One of this party, Corporal A. F. Sales, said: "We reached the station and found it much too heavily defended. The enemy was far stronger than we had expected, and if we were to take it at all we needed artillery support."

Although D Company never managed to get close to the Farm of the Four Winds, several flanking movements were attempted without success. Private O. O. Fenner crawled through fields up the hill almost to the wire perimeter of the farm, then stood up and walked straight at the enemy positions firing a Bren gun from his hip. Witnesses said he killed about twelve Germans before his legs were shot from under him.

A section led by Sergeant K. Williams tried to take the farm by storming up the hill across open ground, but they were quickly stopped. Williams lived to give a laconic account of the charge. "After we crossed the bridge we turned right, followed road for 500 yards. Consolidated with some Camerons. . . . Made our way over road, up hill, and reached our objective. We killed several Germans and were later forced to withdraw, and fought a rearguard action. . . ."

When it became apparent that D Company would not be able to take the farm, Merritt ordered it to swing left to assist A Company at the radar station. The combined efforts of both companies, however, were still inadequate in the face of the enemy's skilfully placed machine guns and mortars. They had used up their own mortar ammunition and were without naval support fire that might have silenced the enemy.

During the morning, two mechanized landing-craft and MGB 317 had given all the support they could, engaging the batteries in the eastern cliff with their puny fire-power until most of their crews were dead or wounded and their Vickers machine guns so overheated that they jammed.

Requests to Jim McRae at battalion headquarters for fire support from the destroyer *Albrighton* were passed on to Captain Carswell, the Forward Observation Officer, but as he was in no position to observe, the results were not effective. Carswell was hampered by never knowing quite where the South Sasks were and was constantly fearful that his instructions to *Albrighton* would bring down fire upon friends rather than foes.

The captain of *Albrighton* wrote in his official report: "Three indirect shoots were started, but the F.O.O. was unable to spot. He also indicated targets on the cliff between Dieppe and Green Beach for direct bombardment and I think the ship did silence the fire of one light gun position. The ship could not remain stationary for long as enemy fire was always accurate and always close."

The only alternative was effective use of the South Sasks' mortars. Several attempts were made to drop bombs east of the bridge, but most of the targets were out of range and the mortars became quite useless when all the ammunition was expended. This, coupled with the ineffectual and sporadic fire from *Albrighton*, meant that the troops never did have the support of a really worthwhile bombardment throughout the day at Pourville.

At 9:45 a.m. Merritt received a message ordering "Vanquish" for 11:00 a.m. and called off the attacks on the eastern heights, instructing the companies to take up defensive positions east of the bridge. The enemy, however, secure in his strategically sited and well-constructed fire positions dominating the battlefield, had no intention of initiating counter-attacks which would only serve to bring him within reach of Canadian bayonets.

Now it was time for the prairie men to leave Occupied France; unlike their rising from the sea in darkness, departure would take place under a bright, cruel sun, in dreadful circumstances.

V

Roberts and Hughes-Hallett received little more in the way of information from Green Beach than from Blue. After the initial report that the South Sasks had landed, nothing further reached Calpe until an hour later when a false, curiously worded message arrived saying that the radar station had been captured. McRae denied that it was ever sent from battalion headquarters, yet it referred to the word "Study," code name for the radar station and a word unlikely to be known to the Germans. It had the effect of encouraging Roberts to believe that the South Sasks might soon occupy the West Headland overlooking Dieppe proper and be in a position to assist the RHLI on White Beach.

Churchill Mann included the fall of the radar station in a situation report to Uxbridge from where this entirely misleading morsel found its way into the official Combined Operations communiques. Further contact with Green Beach was fragmentary, as snipers were picking off wireless operators and their sets, and the Force Commanders could only assume that limited successes had been achieved. At 8:05 a.m. an entry in Calpe's Intelligence log said: "Camerons and South Sasks cleared beach. No further news."

Waning optimism was given a further rude shock when Calpe intercepted a signal from the South Sasks to Lovat's Commando at Varengeville saying: "We are in serious difficulties on our left flank" (the eastern heights). Roberts was immediately confronted by a contradictory picture of the South Sasks swarming towards Dieppe to capture the radar station, yet in "serious difficulties."

Frantic attempts were made to make contact with Merritt and when these failed, Churchill Mann requested Uxbridge to undertake tactical reconnaissance flights over the West Headland to establish the front positions. These flights produced no useful information, and in the meantime Roberts was forced to accept the likelihood of the Germans having delivered a successful counter-attack with powerful reinforcements.

Yet even this assumption seemed incorrect when, at 8:46, the South Sasks informed Roberts that they had consolidated their objectives and were ready to begin the withdrawal – at least that is how the signal reached Calpe. In fact, however, it was again distorted in transmission because McRae at battalion headquarters in Pourville had only indicated that casualties were ready for evacuation.

The extremely complicated, intricate communications network may have been efficient in design, but it was hardly providing the Force Commanders with the constant stream of accurate information they required for sound decision-making. The military plan was being shattered with every passing minute and the alternatives could be improvized successfully only if Roberts and Hughes-Hallett were provided with reliable information, which was conspicuously absent.

Although he could see little of what was happening ashore, Hughes-Hallett was at least commanding a naval operation from the bridge of

*a ship; it was worse, much worse, for Roberts, removed from the
battlefields where he yearned to be with every tough fibre of his body
and cooped in the headquarters ship where he could only pray that no
news was good – because the little that came was terrible.*

Events elsewhere had already resulted in a Force Commanders' conference in which an overall withdrawal had been discussed and, after
the last distorted message from Green Beach, Merritt was told: "Goose
is to come back to Green Beach – relay by any means possible. Will
give time later." Then Uxbridge was informed that the South Sasks
and Camerons had been "ordered off Green Beach."

Further messages to the South Sasks gave the time for the withdrawal as "Vanquish 1030 hours," which was changed a few minutes
later to "Vanquish 1100 hours." This alteration became confused in
transmission, and led to the Camerons interception and interpretation
of the signals to mean that the withdrawal was to be at 1000 hours,
a mistake that was also made on the western slopes, where Claude
Orme's C Company signallers also heard the amended orders and
informed him that the withdrawal was ordered for 10:00 a.m.

Orme, having achieved his objectives and thinking it much too
early for a withdrawal, suspected that the message might be false and
decided to check personally with Merritt or McRae. However, a runner arrived with news that a battalion of German reinforcements
were deploying along the ridges of the western hills and he was
immediately occupied in organizing a gradual withdrawal.

Lieutenant McIlveen took charge of the rearguard while the rest of
the company retired back to Pourville "as a large force of the enemy
were approaching down the road from the motor transport works."
By 10:00 a.m., therefore, the time which Orme was compelled to accept as "Vanquish" hour in the absence of further information, C
Company had abandoned the gun positions it had captured and had
formed a defensive perimeter in the western outskirts of the town,
where they were joined by groups of the Camerons.

The high ground overlooking the beach was immediately reoccupied by the enemy, with disastrous results when the withdrawal
actually began.

Reporting on the withdrawal from the western slopes, Sergeant
M. Lehman said: "At approximately 0945 hours a lone car was seen
coming down the road into the town which we covered, but Mr
Kempton [the officer in charge of his platoon] was not to be fooled by
it and did not give orders to fire on it. It soon turned around and went

back the way it had come and disappeared into the bush about two thousand yards away. Soon we were able to see the enemy moving out of the trees, and a section started down the road in our direction, followed shortly afterwards by larger bodies of troops. We allowed them to get in range and opened fire with all we had, taking a toll of them before they had a chance to get cover on the sides of the road.

"They moved back to the cover of the trees again and proceeded to pull a pincer on us. Mr Kempton said to me: 'Now we are in a hell of a fix as our flanks are unprotected. I hate to keep the boys but we will have to stick it out until they get in on top of us and then make the best of getting out, as they are relying on us in the town.' Mr Kempton told us to start moving back a few at a time, until all that was left was one Bren gun, which covered him when he came back. One of the boys on this Bren was hit as he crossed the road. Mr Kempton headed out to get him as the other chap on the Bren could not make it. I stopped Mr Kempton and told him he was needed worse than I was, so to give me covering fire and I would get him. He said 'Okay' and that he would tell the mortar to lay some smoke. As I was moving out towards the Bren-gunner they opened fire on me but I was lucky and only got hit in the pack, so carried on to the Bren-gunner. He had only a flesh wound in the leg and was able to make it back under cover of smoke. On the way back I found Mr Kempton lying on the road and found that he had been hit when they opened fire on me. He had died instantly. . . ."

With the exception of Lieutenant Kempton and the wounded Bren-gunner, Sergeant Lehman's platoon reached the town safely. Last of C Company to retire off the slopes was the platoon commanded by Lieutenant McIlveen, which immediately joined with the Camerons to form the centre of the rearguard perimeter.

At 9:30 a lone assault boat attempted to reach the beach, but was driven off by a sudden concentration of mortar and machine-gun fire from the east cliffs. Half an hour later another boat attempted to land, and one soldier dashed from under the sea wall towards it. He was killed only a few feet from the wall, and the boat was then forced to retire seawards.

Merritt hinted strongly to the Force Commanders that they should undertake an early evacuation, when he informed *Calpe* shortly after 10:00 a.m. that both the South Sasks and the Camerons were re-grouped in Pourville ready to withdraw. But so many interdependent factors were involved in rescheduling the withdrawal that forty-five minutes elapsed before Hughes-Hallett could signal the boat pool: "Landing-craft should go to east side of Green Beach."

During this interval, German gunners, now on the edge of the western cliffs from which they could spray the sea wall, harassed the improvized beach organization, which had collected the wounded against it to await arrival of the landing-craft.

The Germans had by then decided to clear up the Pourville situation. General Haase had ordered a regiment stationed in reserve four miles south of the town to move up from the rear and close the jaws of a pincer from the eastern and western heights; furthermore, Von Rundstedt had ordered the 10th Panzer Division out of Amiens, and it was then rumbling towards the battlefield where Haase intended committing it in the Pourville area.

A curious stalemate had developed. The Germans were thoroughly alarmed by the success of the South Sasks and convinced that the invading force was far stronger than it really was. The South Sasks, on the other hand, were only too conscious of their weakness and of the precarious position they were in should a determined counter-attack develop. There was an hour to wait – the longest hour of the day. Officers and men dug in facing left and right, determined to hold on until the arrival of the boats at 11:00 a.m.

For Merritt, the problem had narrowed down to a simple matter of time and attrition. There was no longer room to manœuvre; he could only let his units fall back slowly into the town and gamble on the reluctance of the enemy to engage in hand-to-hand combat.

There were already nearly two hundred wounded huddled against the sea wall under the care of Merritt's medical officer, Captain Frank Hayter, and Lieutenant-Commander Prior, both of whom were performing Herculean feats of organization under constant fire. Stray privates who found their own ways back to the beach were commandeered by Prior to cut gaps in the wire over the sea wall in readiness for the evacuation; others were turned into temporary stretcher-bearers; even the fifty-odd German prisoners were pressed into service to lay out the wounded in priority groups for the withdrawal.

Merritt and Law set up a combined battalion headquarters in the Grand Central Hotel from where they could direct the compression of their defences into a tight, close arc about the town. Their troops ebbed away from the ground they had taken no faster than the ebbing tide widened the gauntlet between the sea wall and the water's edge, now nearly two hundred yards and increasing as the receding sea uncovered slimy, seaweed-covered rocks protruding from a soft bed of sand.

The hunters were themselves at bay, hemmed in by an enemy who, having been cowed earlier, had never been completely subdued and was now closing the ring, scenting victory. As soon as the prairie men abandoned a captured gun position he reoccupied it, and fire intensified into a booming, chattering cacophony, rising to a fearful crescendo as he hurled his hate at the weary raiders.

A lone figure worked heedlessly on the sea wall, widening a gap in the wire above Lieutenant-Commander Prior's head. It was Private Haggard who, after a brief, apprehensive glance at the eastern cliffs, muttered to the equally reckless naval officer: "Don't seem Jerry likes us, do it, sir?"

VI

Shortly before 11:00 a.m. the first wave of boats approached the beach, the tide being so far out that they ran aground 150 yards from the water's edge. This meant that the troops would have to cross 200 yards of pebbles and rocks and then wade out up to their necks or swim to the boats. Merritt sent runners from the Grand Central Hotel carrying the evacuation order to the troops on the east and west flanks, Captains Runcie and Edmondson receiving it in the inn they had turned into a headquarters east of the bridge. They decided to stay where they were with some sixteen men to cover the withdrawal of troops dropping over the lower cliff to the beach.

The whole of the east flank was cleared by a few minutes past "Vanquish" hour, and after waiting a further twenty minutes this spontaneous rearguard party evacuated the inn and became the last of the eastern assault forces to reach the beach.

The arrival of the first four boats was the signal for a furious barrage of crossfire to be laid down on the beach from the heights at both ends – mortars, machine guns, rifles, even heavy artillery. Until then the numbers of killed in both battalions had been comparatively light, and approximately eight hundred men lined the sea wall ready for the dash to the water.

Remembering their Isle of Wight training principle "a body, a boat" – another way of saying that once a raider is ready to leave he simply finds his own way to the boats – the men surged forward into the stream of tracers, into the plumes of sand and splintering pebbles thrown up by bursting bombs in a blind, lunging rush for the water. So many fell in the first fifty yards that the long dark line recoiled and flowed back to the wall, leaving scattered groups to plunge on. The unwounded supported the walking wounded; Lieutenant-Commander Prior literally marched at the head of a column of German prisoners carrying stretcher cases; and when these involuntary helpers were killed by their own bullets, the prairie men raced to take their places at the handles of the stretchers.

Within five minutes one boat was so badly holed it had to be abandoned, and another was so swamped by troops that it rested on the bottom. Men clambered out, shoved it into deeper water, and immediately became a choice target for snipers. They tried to clamber back in over the ramp while those inside tried to keep them out to avoid sinking the boat. Men died with bullets in their backs and hate for their friends in their eyes. Their bodies lay across the open ramp, water poured in, and finally the boat sank two hundred yards from shore. The other two boats, repeatedly hit and taking in water, were filled, and the troops bailed furiously while the crews nursed them out to waiting destroyers where both went down after transferring their men. A fifth boat steered into the crowd of men swimming aimlessly over the boat which had sunk under their weight. So many had been killed in the water that when the survivors were rescued they barely filled the boat.

A British naval officer, Lieutenant David Flory, commanding a sixth boat, wrote in his report:

> I proceeded to the beach which lay under a thick smokescreen; an ML warned me of men in the water and coming through the smoke I found the men swimming out from the beaches to get away from the machine-gunning at the flanks. There were some corpses in the water and those that were alive had little strength left. I picked up about 20 men from the water and proceeded into the beach. . . . By this time one engine was not working and the steering apparatus was defective. I stopped the boat before a group of men who had waded one hundred yards out; four were carrying a severely wounded man on a stretcher. We were now bow on to a machine-gun post and it was impossible to manœuvre the craft owing to the mechanical defect and the weight of men clambering over the bow and stern; many were shot in the back as we pulled them over the bow. When every man in the vicinity was on board we had great difficulty in dragging the

injured men from the lowered door. I gave orders to go astern on one engine which was slow process, but by this time the steering had improved and we were able to put out to sea.

As the toll of death mounted under the warm sun and on the wet sand laid bare by the ebbing tide, fear hovered over the beach, unseen yet as thick as the curtains of smoke and the milling throng of men compressed into a tight motionless mass by the wall east of the river mouth. Claude Orme, who throughout the morning had not once allowed a situation to explode beyond his control, formed a small rearguard perimeter on the town side of the wall.

Merritt and Law, with their combined headquarters at the Grand Central Hotel, were fighting off the enemy's advance patrols into the east and west outskirts when a runner arrived with news that the evacuation was proceeding according to plan. To Merritt this meant his men were getting away in reasonably good order and he led a march down to the lower east cliff from where they could drop down to the beach. It was literally a march. When one platoon seemed inclined to hurry, he ordered the men to "Slope Arms" and proceed as if drilling on a parade ground.

"I was shocked at the sight on the beach," he has since told me. "Instead of finding a few scattered remnants still hanging back, the place was swarming with men, hundreds of them. That was my mistake. I should have gone down to the beach earlier to see for myself that they were re-embarking as fast as they reached the beach."

He shouldered his way through the mass to the wall and was told that two machine guns firing from an emplacement on the western cliff were causing most of the damage. He glanced briefly at the officers and men gathered about him and said: "Right. A lot of us are going to get killed if we don't silence the bloody thing. I need a few men for covering fire. Who's coming?" One soldier was to report in England: "By then he could have got volunteers to clean out hell. He was everywhere and never took cover."

In fact, Orme, McIlveen, and three Bren-gunners answered his call and he led them back through the town, up the hill past the hotel where the foreign slave labourers had been found, and onto the terrace above it, careless of caution, always exposed. The German machine-gunners could see them coming and lobbed down two grenades, one exploding two feet from Orme.

"Hurt?" shouted Merritt.

"No," replied Orme, who now confesses that his left ear has given trouble ever since.

The only way to reach the emplacement was by circling round a ledge on one side of a high wall which separated the terrace garden from the cliff face. Merritt led the party forwards in single file until he reached a series of gaps in the wall. He had crept abreast of the first gap when a German appeared through the second. Canadian and German were equally startled, and both ducked through the gaps to the other side of the wall where they faced each other again. They were at close quarters, only feet apart, the German unable to use his rifle and Merritt unable to pull the pin of the grenade in his right hand. They dropped their weapons and started swinging wildly at each other with their fists – hardly a fair fight because Merritt was big, hard, and heavy and the German was light, slight, and very frightened.

The tussle ended on the ground with Merritt lying on top of his opponent. The rest of the party came up, and Orme pulled Merritt off while McIlveen bent down to help the German. An expression of sheer horror settled on the wretched little man's face and he screamed "*Nein, nein, nein,*" obviously expecting to be beaten to death.

"He was quite wrong," said Orme afterwards. "We didn't have time."

While McIlveen and the Bren-gunners kept the enemy guns occupied, Merritt and Orme came up from behind and blew up the emplacement with grenades.

When they returned to the beach more boats were touching down and the men were leaving the protection of the sea wall to run the bullet-strewn gauntlet before the enemy closed it. They had done the job ashore to the best of their ability; now it was either every man for himself on the body-a-boat principle or certain imprisonment for the rest of the war – and a bid for freedom seemed a chance worth taking.

The wounded Lieutenant England was propped up against the sea wall waving away stretcher-bearers and insisting that other wounded be taken out first. An exasperated doctor cut short his protests by bundling the astonished young officer over his shoulders and galloping across the beach into the water and loading him into a landing-craft. England, now serving with Canada's NATO forces in Europe, was then only midway through his adventures. On the way home his boat was bombed and sunk; he was picked up by a gun boat which transferred him to a destroyer; the destroyer was bombed and so crippled that she had to be sunk by her sister ships; and England was eventually picked up by another landing-craft which deposited him ashore at Newhaven.

Farther off shore Commander Ryder brought *Locust* into range and began bombarding the western slopes while firing smoke bombs to lay a screen across the scene of evacuation. The destroyer *Bleasedale* was also there, engaging the cliffs at both ends while "coming under unpleasantly accurate fire from shore batteries on the cliffs." Her captain reported after the operation: "We did the best we could by firing smoke shell at the cliffs."

The captain of the bombarding destroyer *Albrighton* said, "During the final withdrawal . . . men were lying under the sea wall and dashing down under fire to the sea. Permission to bombard the flanks was obtained from *Calpe*, and positions of some enemy forces in houses to right of beach was established from soldiers brought off. Smoke shell was also fired on high ground to right of beach. After this, ship picked up stragglers and survivors until retirement. During withdrawal communications were difficult due to great quantities of smoke."

Albrighton rescued 190 men, of whom eight died on the passage back to England.

The destroyer *Brocklesby* bombarded the eastern cliffs while picking up more survivors and saw the *Luftwaffe* attack the beach with what appeared to be flame-throwing aircraft. Her captain reported: "At about 1150 an attack by German flame-throwing aircraft was observed on the western side of Green Beach. The attack was delivered by three Junker 88's which flew in low from the west, about half the height of the cliff."

Despite the awful intensity of the enemy's constant fire on the beach, the prairie men declined to stampede. McIlveen organized a mass movement of 120 men down the beach and into the water. Although they had to swim 600 yards, most of them survived.

Captain Campbell of the Camerons helped to carry a stretcher case out to a boat which had stuck on the bottom and was among those pushing it into deeper water when he was hit in both legs. The boat failed to put up its ramp, filled with water and sank. "Another officer blew up my Mae West for me and then helped me swim to another boat," he said. "But there was no room for me there so I swam back to the other one which had by then overturned. Some soldiers pulled me up over its hull and we sat on the keel until another boat came in and took us off. . . ."

Company Sergeant-Major Gouk said he returned to the beach to find those able to walk helping those who couldn't, some crawling across the beach and dragging wounded comrades with them. . . .

Private Haggard had become so attached to Lieutenant-Commander Prior that he was reluctant to leave him behind. He subsequently reported that Prior had risked himself time and time again in persuading men to run for the boats, at one time climbing to the top of a German pillbox and signalling to the boats with flags. Haggard was another who reached a boat and, having survived the whole day without so much as a scratch, was wounded in the arms while swimming.

Corporal Joe Gregory was pushing a boat off the ground when a bullet ricocheted off the steel hull, hit him in the forehead and tore out his left eye. He said later: "I got to a destroyer and then was hit by a bomb splinter. Lost left wrist. Better luck next time."

Sergeant Coderre was in a boat hit by a bomb and was the only survivor. Corporal Ford carried RSM Strumm out to a boat where they were helped aboard by McRae and England. Privates Krohn and Evendon carried their wounded partner, Chilton, out to a boat and laid him on deck where a mortar bomb exploded in his stomach. Murray Osten, fighting on the left flank of the rearguard, ordered his signalman, Private Johnson, to evacuate. Johnson survived to say: "I just went down the beach, called a taxi and told the driver to take me home – which he did."

Shortly after midday the rearguard withdrew behind the sea wall, using it as a fire trench from where they could keep the enemy at bay while the last troops were evacuated. A large group lunged down the beach to the sea and a machine gun erupted from a new position in a house on the eastern cliff, cutting down the van of the group and spreading confusion among the rest.

Merritt, tommy gun under his arm, torn battle dress, blouse unbuttoned, and sweating redly where blood oozed from a flesh wound in his shoulder, called for volunteers to silence it. Lieutenant W. G. Cunningham from Oxbow, although wounded in the head and legs, stumbled forwards and replied: "I'll go, sir. I'd like to."

Then he handed his rifle to a soldier, took a revolver from his holster, and turned on the dirty, fierce-eyed troops nearest to him. "Just one man. Who will it be?" Several feet down the wall, Corporal Coxford, a trouser belt acting as a rough sling for a wounded arm, took out his own revolver and lurched on the pebbles to Cunningham's side. The officer gave the corporal a slight, flickering grin and led the way through the wire back to slopes crawling with Germans.

The watchers at the wall saw Coxford walking close to Cunningham as they vanished out of sight, one hobbling painfully and the other with only one good hand.

Private I. R. Kohaly, who witnessed the incident, said: "It was the most gallant scene I saw. . . . The two quickly and without a word walked round the corner of a house and out of view in the general direction of at least certain capture. . . . They went to do the job as men were moving off, and we were the last boat."

The machine gun was silenced temporarily – long enough to ease the weight of fire on the beach while the last group reached the water – by two cripples who, as Kohaly had foreseen, were both captured.

By then, all except the rearguard were off the beach and in the water. The beach itself was devoid of life, only the bodies of the dead lying in silent testimony to the devastating effect of the enemy fire. Merritt turned from the wall to see if his men had reached the water and noticed instead that a seemingly lifeless body at the edge of the surf was moving. The tide had turned and was now coming in; if left there the wounded man would be drowned.

Without hesitation, Merritt ran across the empty beach, a lone challenge to the German gunners who accepted it by making him the target for machine guns and snipers. As he ran, Merritt called out to the man wading towards the boats but his voice was lost in the noise of battle. He reached the unconscious soldier, an unnamed corporal, just as a bullet hit his shoulder, knocking him flat. Private Renwick of the Camerons, who is now a police officer in Vancouver, raced down the beach, grabbed Merritt by the waist and half dragged, half carried him back to safety. Two more soldiers ran to the water's edge, picked up the unconscious corporal, and carried him out to the boats.

Among the first to be evacuated was the radar scientist, whose strange bodyguard had quickly seen to it that there was a boat for this invaluable body. But a Corporal Stanley Jones would never leave France, and there was no one in Canada to mourn his death. The self-confessed murderer who had killed with the knife was himself killed by bullets.

VII

Around 12:15 Peter Scott in SGB 9 signalled Locust: "Can we help you support Green Beach?" When Ryder replied "Yes – go in," Scott conned his gun boat through the thick, white smokescreens of the destroyers and emerged on the other side in brilliant sunlight about six hundred yards off the beach. While his gunners engaged batteries on the east cliff, he scanned the beach through binoculars searching for signs of movement to indicate the need for further evacuation. There were none, and

Scott remained in the vicinity for another fifteen minutes before quitting the deserted scene to seek excitement elsewhere. From the low vantage point of his bridge he had been unable to see over a ridge of pebbles in the shingle on the east side of the river mouth which hid the wall and the rearguard standing against it.

Sub-Lieutenant Kenneth Tew of assault boat 187 had brought off the last group of forty survivors and transferred them to a destroyer. His report said: "An officer in the destroyer told me it was impracticable to beach again, and this tallied with my own theory, but I took craft beyond smokescreen where I had a good view of the beach. There was no one there . . ."

In spite of these impressions, Merritt had nearly 180 men with him in the rearguard force, including Camerons whose senior officer was Captain John Runcie. His own officers included Claude Orme, Lefty White, MacTavish, Murray Osten, and John Edmondson who had only eight men of his eastern rearguard left when he fell back to the beach.

By 1:00 p.m. Merritt's only hope was to hold on for as long as humanly possible to give the Navy a chance to send in more boats or for some miracle to happen – such as the sight of the RHLI storming towards Pourville from the east. A small party of Germans made tentative attempts to occupy buildings facing the beach, and half a dozen Camerons climbed scaffoldings put up for repairs to the sea wall and drove them off with accurate Bren-gun fire.

One enemy group rushing down from the eastern heights was cut to pieces by Corporal H. L. Keyes who grabbed a Bren gun, ran out to the beach for a better view, and stayed there alone and fully exposed for fifteen minutes until he had been so badly wounded he could no longer fire his gun – but not before he had forced the enemy to withdraw back to the heights.

Their plight was becoming increasingly desperate by the minute, something that was equally apparent to the Germans. At 1:37 p.m. the 571st German Infantry Regiment reported to General Haase at Evenmeu: "Pourville now firmly in our hands." If it was a bit premature then, it was soon to be true enough. Sometime after two o'clock the rearguard, nearly all wounded and being steadily whittled down by the enemy, were further decimated by RAF Spitfires which strafed the beach, apparently under the impression that it was held by the enemy. As ammunition was nearly exhausted, Merritt called a conference of officers at which he gave it as his considered view that as further fighting would soon be futile he proposed to surrender.

It was a bitter disappointment to men who had fought so well and achieved so much to be forced into such a repugnant position. A white bandage was tied to a rifle barrel and waved above the wall, while Merritt pulled a bottle of Sloan's liniment from a pocket and handed it to Osten.

"Here," he said. "Have a drink. It'll make you feel better." The young captain from Oxbow had not earned his reputation by refusing drinks and may have been even a little disappointed to discover that the liniment was really Scotch. Because he was wound up emotionally, still over-tensed by battle, the raw alcohol exploded inside him, and for the first time in his life a drink made Murray Osten sick.

When the grim-faced, still jittery Germans reached the top of the wall to look down nervously at the desolate beach, the dishevelled, wild-looking Canadians were convulsed. Where there had been the violent sounds of guns and shocked, pain-filled screams, there was now only laughter.

A proud, defiant surrender.

When the South Sasks failed to break through over the West Headland the last hope for success vanished. Roberts, suspecting he might have been repulsed on the East Headland – but still never quite sure – had hoped for success at the western end of the beach with the RHLI *being joined by the South Sasks swarming towards Dieppe on the high ground. But the guns of the West Headland remained intact and their fire down onto the main beach deprived the* RHLI *of assault impetus, and the two regiments supposed to storm into the town lay down to die instead.*

Main Assault

I

The test tubes in which the catalysis of future victory was about to take place were the cauterized main beaches of Dieppe. Four of the young colonels were taking approximately two thousand men into the searing holocaust of an infamous frontal assault.

That same morning a group of high-ranking officers were basking with towels wrapped round their waists on the white, sandy, far-away beaches of North Africa, near El Alamein. One of them was Winston Churchill, at whose reputed insistence Jubilee was undertaken without previous air bombardment; another was Montgomery who, having decreed the frontal assault, had then acquiesced to, and presided over, the elimination of the air bombardment.

After an invigorating swim and sunbathe, the former Army Commander of Reigate gave the Prime Minister a summary of his grand design for the defeat of Rommel. Churchill recorded in his memoirs:

"Above all, artillery would be used as had never been possible before. . . . Every crevice in the desert was packed with camouflaged concealed batteries. Three or four hundred guns would fire at the German armour. . . ."

At Dieppe the main assault forces carrying out an earlier Montgomery plan were supported by fewer guns – the eight 4-inch guns of four very small destroyers!

The Germans had not been so considerate as the British in their treatment of the French people of Dieppe. They had razed buildings ruthlessly at either end of the mile-long beach to provide their guns with unobstructed arcs of fire. Hotels had been requisitioned along the sea front and transformed into sandbagged machine-gun nests and snipers' hideouts; even the Casino at the western end of the beach had been half demolished and concrete pillboxes built among the debris. Halfway up the steeply sloping beach were fences of barbed wire six to ten feet thick; more of it was strung along the top of the sea wall, which ranged in height from three to six feet according to how deeply the pebbles were piled against it. More wire criss-crossed the 200-yards-wide promenade, otherwise a barren expanse running the entire length of the sea front from harbour mouth to the old Castle set into the side of the West Headland. Only the Casino, its seaward side on the beach and its inland side only a few yards from the row of sea-front hotels and boarding-houses, gave any protection for troops crossing from beach to town.

Had the Germans really expected an attack on Dieppe that day the remainder of the Casino would have been quickly wrecked; twenty-four hours after the raid it was non-existent.

The harbour entrance at the eastern end of the beach consisted of two large jutting moles three hundred yards long, the gap between them one hundred yards wide. It lay under the shadow of the East Headland which, like the West Headland, was pitted with caves at its base and across its face. Heavy guns, light guns, and long-range machine guns on both these headlands, which the attackers knew about, enfiladed the entire length of the beach; other weapons of the same capability, which the attackers knew nothing about, were concealed in the caves: anti-tank guns, machine guns, and light artillery which could be run out to fire and withdrawn in the face of bombardment.

Particularly dangerous were the big guns on the headlands, the machine-gun emplacements constructed into the Castle battlements on the western end, the old French tank cemented into a harbour mole, and strongpoints built into the tobacco factory on the esplanade facing the east side of the beach.

This was the formidable defensive system that faced the Essex Scots who would land on Red Beach, the eastern one thousand yards, and the RHLI on White Beach, the western one thousand yards. They would, of course, be followed by miscellaneous sapper and demolition groups, the Calgary Tanks, and eventually the Fusiliers Mont-Royal.

There would be neither darkness nor surprise. General Haase had brought his whole sector to maximum alert at 5:00 a.m.; the assault was planned for the grey daylight of 5:20 a.m.

After their cool swim in the Mediterranean, Churchill and Montgomery compared the approaching battle at Alamein with Napoleon's defeat in 1814. It is a pity no army authority had thought about Napoleon in the planning of Jubilee. In days prior to Combined Operations, when Britain knew all there was to know about the art of "conjunct expeditions," Napoleon had said: "All the great captains of antiquity, and those who in modern times have successfully trodden in their steps, performed vast achievements only by conforming to the rules and principles of the art: that is to say, by correct combinations, and by justly comparing the relation between means and consequences, effects and obstacles."

Apparently the force sailing towards Dieppe under Ham Roberts was the means but where was the correct combination of fire-power? It seemed, too, that in this frontal assault not much regard had been given to the consequences of failing to conform with the "rules and principles of the art."

The sun that blazed down upon the sands of El Alamein also glowed warmly on the stones of Dieppe. It was not the only link.

II

The operations orders for the landings said: "It is vital to the success of the operation as a whole that White and Red Beaches be in our hands with the minimum delay." The troops landed in the first flights were to carry the beaches by assault and secure a bridgehead in which engineers and beach assault detachments could off-load the explosives they would use to destroy the road blocks barring the entry of tanks into the town. The Calgary Tanks would land almost simultaneously with the Essex Scots and the RHLI to assist the troops in silencing beach pillboxes before crossing the sea wall.

The Essex Scottish, code-named "Fred," were to move through the eastern half of the town, swing left into the harbour, assist the Royal Marine Commando in cutting out invasion barges from the inner basins, and move up to the East Headland to join the Royal Regiment of Canada breaking west from Puits. The battalion's right flank would be consolidated at a race course behind Dieppe where it would meet the left flank of the RHLI. The race course would be marked out as an emergency landing-strip for RAF fighter pilots in distress.

The RHLI, code-named "Bob," would swing right from the town to the top of the West Headland where it would join the South Saskatchewans in their assault on the Farm of the Four Winds. Other elements of the battalion would penetrate behind the town to join the Essex Scottish at the race course.

The Calgary Tanks, coming astern of the assault battalions with the code name "Johnny," would land in four flights: two consisting of nine tanks each, the third of twelve tanks, and the fourth to comprise "up to sixteen tanks." Each tank landing-craft carried three tanks and assorted scout cars, blitz buggies, and baby-carriage radio sets.

The first tank out of each craft was equipped with chespaling tracks that it could lay ahead of itself as it trundled up the beach and over the sea wall. Second and third tanks would follow their leaders, using the same tracks to reach the esplanade.

Both brigade headquarters would land from tank landing-craft, Bill Southam establishing his shore headquarters at the Church of St Remy from where he would direct the South Saskatchewans, the Fusiliers Mont-Royal, and the Camerons; and Sherwood Lett setting up his headquarters at the Church of St Jacques from where he could control operations of the RHLI, Royal Regiment of Canada, and the Essex Scottish. Johnny Andrews sailed with Lett's brigade headquarters, still openly angry at having to waste his tanks in an operation he had no reason at all to like.

The Fusiliers Mont-Royal were, in effect, the sole strength of the floating reserve, to be committed only when Roberts was assured of a success they might be used to exploit. Yet even this elementary "principle of the art" was to prove a fleeting, elusive, and illusory thing.

Roberts joined Hughes-Hallett on the bridge of Calpe, *neither of them knowing what had taken place at Berneval or at Puits. They did* know, however, that Lovat had landed at Varengeville and the South Sasks at Pourville and, knowing it, there was nothing to do but wait as the last fingers of assault boats reached out for the main beaches to close the mailed fist from the sea.

It was too early yet for danger signs, for evidence that the enemy stood with blade upraised ready to bring it sweeping down to sever the fist from the arm and the arm from the nerve centre which controlled it.

The Force Commanders spoke little because there was nothing to say. The weeks of endless conferences, of endless argument, of seemingly constant friction, of hopes and of fears freely expressed, had drained them of words. Now that the show was on, what could be said that had not been said already? Their thoughts were the same – had the flank attacks succeeded? Because if so the fleet was safe; the troops driving in to the main beaches were safe from the guns of the wing headlands. If not? But it was also too early to doubt.

At Uxbridge fighter control headquarters loudspeakers were alive with static, bursts of excited chatter between pilots. Flags were moved along flight patterns, and for the three supreme commanders there was coffee, tea, or cocoa. They sipped their choice in silence, for what could Mountbatten say to Crerar that had not been said before, and Leigh-Mallory was much too busy anyway. Like the Force Commanders in Calpe they were experiencing the frustration of seeing success on the western flanks while those on the eastern side of Dieppe remained mysteriously, enigmatically silent.

So far, the eager thrusting of the Canadian generals for seats at the summit had merely provided Crerar with an opportunity to drink tea with the Chief of Combined Operations.

The Essex Scottish and RHLI were carried across the Channel in the transports, *Prince Leopold, Prince Charles*, and *Glengyle*. Neither Jasperson nor Labatt were entirely sanguine.

Aboard *Leopold*, a sergeant had reported to Jasperson: "Some damn fool's really done it this time, sir. The Stens are still in their bloody manufacturer's packing. Full of grease."

"Then you'll have to clean 'em," he had replied.

"What about time? Besides there's nowhere near enough ammunition and we're short on Bangalores too."

When we discussed it, Jasperson said: "It was a stupid, blundering ordnance mess. I had to tell the sergeant to get cracking on the guns while I went to the ship's captain and begged everything I could from his stores. We went into battle with about twenty of the *Leopold*'s tommy guns, and just about all our ammunition came from her."

He gave his officers their final briefing an hour before lowering time. They listened in jaded silence to details they knew by heart. Then it was time for the troops to take their places in the boats already swung out on davits and at 3:00 a.m. they were lowered into the water. The vast, looming bulks of *Prince Leopold* and *Prince Charles* vanished in the darkness, leaving the flotillas of the Essex Scottish on their own and on their way.

The voyage had been less eventful for Bob Labatt, whose quarters in *Glengyle* were the "admiral's suite" – fine cabin with comfortable bunk and a tiled bathroom. An hour before lowering time, he was called by the captain's steward who brought tea and biscuits. Then he took a bath before dressing in clean shirt, socks, and underwear – a naval custom to prevent infection caused by dirty clothes next to torn skin.

He joined his adjutant, Captain Herb Poag, for a breakfast of porridge, bacon, eggs, and kidneys followed by hot buttered toast, marmalade, and coffee. This meal had some significance for both. Labatt would not see one like it again for three years; Poag would never eat again.

Both officers were at once excited and repelled by thoughts of what the dawn would bring. Labatt has since told me: "It was fantastic. Units were being launched into an involved operation, the success of which depended upon surprise and each man's thorough knowledge of the several operations to be carried out by his sub-unit and himself. Yet he had been given no time since the cancellation of Rutter to study his tasks."

While they ate, a steward stuffed a packet of sandwiches into Labatt's haversack, saying: "No need to fight on an empty stomach, sir. I've put in something extra to eat on the way home, if the weather keeps fine." Feeling slightly light-headed, Labatt prepared himself for battle – pistol with two magazines, water bottle, field message books, pencils, torch, cigarettes, chocolate, Sten gun magazines, hand grenades, sheath knife, smoke canisters, Mae West, and binoculars. Then he climbed to the bridge to prepare for the lowering of the assault boats. His own account reads:

> Everything was at peace, everything seemed to be going according to plan. Perhaps I had been wrong to confront General Roberts with my objections. Perhaps we would achieve surprise

and this was the proper way to do it. Then came the time to take our positions in the boats. We were lowered on time and for better or for worse were on our way – next stop France.

During the run-in, Labatt suffered a slight attack of conscience about John Foote, the chaplain who had approached him the day before with the same request that Major Savoy had made to Menard. He had said: "I know what's in the wind, Bob. I want to go." Labatt had refused, knowing only too well that when it was over the most popular padre in the regiment's history might be needed more than ever before. Foote had replied: "Well, I'll make my own arrangements, and if you see me on the beach you can order me off." Somewhere in the columns of dark silhouettes, John Foote, stowaway by common consent, was sitting on a hard bench, being carried towards high honours.

Landing-craft of all sorts joined that final approach to the beaches of Dieppe – some in line abreast, some in columns, and others scattered in closely packed groups. In the lead were the coastal support craft, the ML's, MGB's, and SGB's, showing the way to the lines of assault boats following immediately astern with the Essex Scottish and the RHLI; behind them came the columns of tank landing-craft and the destroyers, including *Calpe* and *Fernie*, the only two which would not bombard because of the incredible number of delicate wireless sets they carried. In the rear were *Locust* and her French *chasseurs* (steel-plated motor launches), carrying the Royal Marine cutting-out party, and the Fusiliers Mont-Royal distributed among twenty-six LCP's.

They filled a block of the Channel about two miles wide and five miles deep. When the range had narrowed to three miles and targets could be clearly distinguished, the four bombarding destroyers – *Garth*, *Bleasdale*, *Berkeley*, and *Albrighton* – opened fire with a series of broadsides that whistled over the heads of the assault flights and burst among the buildings lining the promenade.

The men in the boats were quiet, confident, with gas capes draped over their shoulders as protection against the spray. Both Labatt and Jasperson found their misgivings being replaced by that curious immediate pre-battle elation that grips innocent and experienced alike. The only fear in the boats then was that of stage fright, each man nervously rehearsing in his mind his particular assignments, the code words, the times and places affecting his platoon or company.

Radio receivers were switched on to keep communications open in case of last-minute alterations to the plan, and in the various headquarters boats the startling sound of dance music was made even more eerie by an announcement that it came from Radio Berlin.

The first naval salvo was fired at 5:12 a.m., eight minutes before touchdown. Simultaneously, the RAF laid smokescreens over the East Headland to neutralize the defences, attacked gun emplacements with cannon fire, and strafed the sea front. Lieutenant-Commander Mc-Mullen, responsible for seeing that the assault flights touched down on the right beaches at the right time, reported, "The flotillas started deploying for the final run-in just as the RAF dropped smoke bombs on the East Cliff. The bombardment, bombing, and cannoning of the beaches commenced, excellently timed, and although fire appeared to be coming at us from all directions we were on time. . . ."

The East Headland was wreathed in heavy, white billowing smoke, flames flashed from exploding cannon shells as Hurricanes swooped low across the promenade, the naval salvos burst in yellow, fire-filled clouds against the buildings. The blue-grey hem of dawn pushing aside the night was the backdrop for a fury of flak fire, enemy tracers crisscrossing the sky, lurid with the yellows and reds of sudden destruction.

The armada of tiny ships fanned out into lines abreast, the men standing upright to witness what they believed to be the pummelling of the enemy into a state of broken, cowed confusion. Instead, the first defensive barrage exploded in their midst sending great spumes of water filled with cordite fumes high above their heads. Steel hulls were ripped and torn by the impact of artillery; mortar shrapnel cut through the exposed men and, as if controlled by some master puppeteer, they dropped low, crouching behind the bulwarks of the boats while gazing blankly at the necks of the men in front of them.

Three red Verey lights burst overhead and the roar of the Hurricanes diminished, the naval bombardment ceased, and an enemy, rudely awakened and ill-tempered, vented his spite against these unwelcome intruders.

Two hundred yards to go – and was that all? Was that the extent of the heavy air bombardment that had been promised? On every pale, muscle-tightened face there was shock, disbelief, and accusation. For some inexplicable reason, only the senior regimental officers had been informed of the decision to cancel the air bombardment in favour of tactical surprise. The men had not been told; they had been allowed to believe that the conditions of the attack would be the same as those explained to them at the briefings on Rutter. Not even the junior naval officers in charge of the asssault boats knew. One of them reported later: "Aircraft cannon fire seemed to be excellent, but the bombing didn't appear to have had much effect. Did they really bomb the place?"

Realization that they were now riding through a spray of fire towards an opposed landing, fully exposed by the inexorable dawning of another fine, warm summer's day, rippled through the boats. In that instant, with one hundred yards to go, there were some whose eager, nervous excitement gave way to outcries of impotent anger. In fact the synchronization of the Hurricane attack with the landing was almost perfect. Most German gun crews had bolted for cover when the fighter bombers arrived and were still hiding their heads when the assault craft came in. The fire that greeted the troops was bad enough – particularly when any volume of fire can seem heavy to troops who have never seen action before – but it was nothing like as heavy as it might have been.

Mortars placed in the bows of the landing-craft lobbed smoke bombs in a long line down the beach to cover the touchdown. They hit the beach, compressed into a mile of surf, in near-perfect formation within a three-minute bracket – the first at 5:20, the last at 5:23 a.m. Troops debouched from the boats to scramble frenziedly forwards up the steep incline of the broad, sweeping beach, the Essex Scottish scattering across one thousand yards in a thin, sprawling line, guns spitting from hips to keep down the fire from the facing buildings until they could find shelter in which to pause.

Jasperson was first out of his boat, pistol in hand, and urging on those who were beside him one second and dead the next. Men stumbled, pitched forwards on their faces, and lay still on either side of him. He reached the sea wall, four feet high at this end, threw himself behind it, and swore loudly at the large flat expanse of wire-filled space separating the wall from the buildings on the other side of the esplanade.

His battalion headquarters, or what remained of it, had kept up with him, and he ordered a Bangalore under the wire. As it exploded the group swarmed over the wall. But the Bangalore had been too short, and the wire had parted to a depth of only three feet, leaving another three feet of it intact, impassable. Working frantically, they tried to cut through it, while in the buildings they hoped to reach – the hotels and the tobacco factory with its tall chimney opposite them – the snipers and machine-gunners took careful aim.

The converging lines of enemy fire met at the cutting-group, found their flesh, and the men were suddenly stilled, arms outstretched and dangling on the cruel barbs of the wire, their crooked fingers clutching at emptiness.

On the western side of the beach, Labatt came out of his boat, vaguely heard a naval officer at the ramp shout "Drinks – Newhaven – Tonight – Luck," and was then sliding and slithering over a ridge of pebbles twenty-five yards away to the left of the Casino where he fell flat. His signallers were with him, and to each side his companies were spreading out, blasting their way through the first wire.

The right company under Major Bud Bowery, landing west of the Casino almost under the West Headland, was immediately in trouble. Its landing-craft had been hit, their crews killed, and men had come off late. The boats were swung broadside onto the beach, listless and sinking. Captain Tony Hill, second in command of the centre company led a mad dash directly into the face of fire coming from a pillbox against the face of the Casino. Bangalores exploded the wire fences and a group headed by Captain Denny Whitaker, a slight, fast-moving figure in a footballer's rushing crouch, closed in on the pillbox. Private T. E. Greaves reached it first with a length of Bangalore smouldering and ready in his right hand. He thrust it through the loophole and killed the gunners, and the rest of the company moved onto a heavy concrete machine-gun emplacement to their right.

Fire poured out and down from every window in the Casino facing the beach, yet one section calmly began snipping a hole through the rabbit-wire screen of the Casino patio.

The left company under Major Waldron of Hamilton had landed near the centre of the beach alongside the right flank of the Essex Scottish and, like them, had tried to cross the sea wall onto the promenade. It had been stopped cold and the survivors had gone to ground.

Labatt searched the beach anxiously for a suitable battalion headquarters position from where he might watch progress left and right. He rose to his feet, ran in the direction of the Casino, and stuck halfway through the line of wire running along the crest of a roll in the beach. Although trapped and exposed, he commanded an excellent view of proceedings. He could see the entire beach with whatever equanimity he could summon – and that quickly drained away at the scenes of carnage wherever he looked.

One section lay in a hollow ahead of him firing furiously at a pillbox on the left corner of the Casino and at the windows above it. The enemy machine-gun post was protected by a thick jungle of barbed wire, and he was transfixed into quick amazement at the sight of a lone soldier crawling on his belly under the lower strands. As he watched the man's painfully slow progress all sense of personal danger vanished. He ached to shout encouragement.

After a seemingly interminable pause in which nothing seemed to move – actually only a few minutes – the solitary soldier cleared the last strand, squatted on his haunches to pull a grenade from his belt and arm it, stood up, and casually shoved it through the gun slit. Labatt had time to recognize Private Hugh McCourt who then dashed round to the rear of the pillbox which suddenly belched forth smoke and flame. A tin hat on the end of a bayonet bobbed up and down behind the destroyed enemy position, a joyful signal of victory, and the grinning McCourt reappeared to beckon the section in the hollow to join him. They couldn't. In those brief few minutes all had been killed or wounded, a tragic vignette on a beach where already some two hundred soldiers were lying lifeless or in pain as the Calgary Tanks came in.

III

For the Toronto-Scottish machine-gunners giving covering fire from the bows of the approaching tank landing-craft, it was the beginning of a frustrating day. They fired diligently at buildings, pillboxes, and aircraft without ever knowing how accurate or effective they were being. Someone had forgotten to include tracer bullets in their ammunition belts.

Three tank landing-craft (LCT's) touched down on Red Beach fifteen minutes after the Essex Scottish. The first disembarked its tanks safely but was so badly hit while unloading explosives that when it withdrew into deeper water it sank. The tanks – Company, Calgary, and Chief – were seen at this stage to be probing the sea wall for a suitable place to cross it onto the esplanade.

Incredibly, throughout the training for Dieppe, sappers and explosives engineers had worked out complicated plans for blasting down the road blocks, but had not, it seems, pursued the original Combined Operations outline plan for using explosives to blow gaps in the sea wall. Hughes-Hallett has said: "I cannot think why this was not pursued during the detailed planning, but presumably the Canadian Division and Home Forces Staff thought it would be unnecessary."

Sucharov's sappers were supposed to ignore the enemy and erect prefabricated timber ramps. Sucharov's sappers, however, were not ashore.

The tanks had to roam the beach searching for a crossing where the shingle was piled high enough as to be almost level with the top of the wall. The self-laying chespaling device had been received with mixed feelings by the tank commanders, some of whom thought it might work and others who simply refused to use it in case it fouled the tank tracks. Major Alan Glenn, leading the tanks of the first landing-craft, preferred not to use his.

The second landing-craft took so long to unload that it became the prime target for a concentration of heavy artillery fire. According to Sucharov, who was aboard with his assault engineers, the delay was caused by failure to warm up the tank engines prior to touchdown. Each of the three tanks stalled while rumbling down the ramp and it was fifteen minutes before they were clear. Once ashore, however, the leading tank, Cougar, laid its chespaling track and was seen to cross the wall and crank laboriously down the promenade with the other two, Cheeta and Cat, in hot pursuit.

It was already apparent to these first crews that the Churchill tank, experiencing its first major beach battle, was capable of withstanding any shells the Germans at Dieppe could fire. Throughout the day not one tank was penetrated by bullet or shell and none of the crews were hit while inside.

Sergeant J. W. Marsh of the Black Watch, who watched the unloading from the second craft, said: "The first tank was hit three or four times but kept going. It went through the wire, but much to my surprise the wire seemed to spring back into place after the weight of the tank had passed over it. After receiving a couple of hits from the French tank cemented into the mole alongside where we had landed, our tank opened fire and must have scored a direct hit as the French tank seemed to explode into the air. While this was going on, our second tank, Cheeta, was on the way out and headed for an enemy pillbox slightly to our left. The Jerries immediately ran from the pillbox and were promptly mowed down by the Toronto Scottish. Our third tank which was towing the scout car seemed to get stuck half on the beach and half on the ramp. Our captain reversed the boat and so pulled the ramp from under the tank, but at the same moment a shell burst on the ramp and broke the winch cables. The tank, now released, rapidly pulled the scout car through the wire and also tore through the sea wall. The last I saw of the scout car it was tearing like hell up Foch Boulevard."

With the landing-craft beached and empty, it was time for Sucharov's party to land. Their complex responsibilities in assisting the

tanks to enter the town were vital to the operation. They were, however, unable to get ashore.

Sucharov reported later: "I waited for a number of minutes having
previously ordered all ranks . . . to wait on my orders to 'Go.' I was
in the forward part of the LCT and had a fair view of the beach through
a window. The fire did not decrease – but increased. The sapper task
had been accomplished at this part of the beach since all the tanks
were over the esplanade. . . . To land here meant to carry all timber
and materials to right. Under existing fire the loss in men would have
been heavy. I decided to ask the skipper to put us in . . . to the west.
But in that five minutes a direct hit in the vicinity of the door cut the
chains. . . . The craft had already drifted back a few yards and the door
dropped underneath in deep water. It could not be raised; and the
skipper had put the LCT astern. I went back to see him. He said most of
his crew were wiped out and two guns out of action as well as two
engines out of action. . . . The skipper advised that the craft was out
of action and could not put in again."

This particular tank landing-craft drifted out to sea for nearly two
miles before the destroyer *Slazak* drew alongside and rescued the troops
and the survivors of the naval crew.

The third LCT carried three tanks to which the special flame-throwing
equipment had been fitted. The British Ministry of Supply were fortunate to have discovered the loss of the blueprints in time for new
ones to be drawn. By nightfall, the Germans would be making their
own copies. Also aboard were a bulldozer, scout car, five tons of
explosives for breaching road blocks, and sixty sappers and infantry-
men. The LCT touched down east of the Casino, at the junction of
Red and White Beaches, under heavy fire, artillery shells wrecking the
wheelhouse, killing the captain and his officers, setting her ablaze at the
stern, and killing her guns' crews. Mortar bombs dropped into the
hold among the troops. Captain C. R. Eldred, who would act as Major
McCool's liaison with the tank battalion as part of the Military Landing Officers' group, went forward to speak with Captain B. G. Purdy,
commander of the leading tank. When he returned to the stern of the
hold nearly all the soldiers were dead or wounded.

By previous arrangement the LCT doors were opened just before
touchdown to give the tank commander a preview of the beach. Purdy
must have forgotten the arrangement because when the doors swung
wide and the ramp went down he gunned his tank. As the Churchill
rumbled over it a shell burst near the winch, the wire cables snapped,

and the tank "drowned" in ten feet of water. The LCT's bows bounced off the sunken tank and swung into the beach at an angle.

Inside the hold, Lieutenant Jerry Wood and his sappers and Eldred and his beach party could see the rising sun shining low from the east almost into the eyes of the attackers. Machine-gun bullets spattered against the open doors, ricocheted into and around the hold, bouncing from tank turrets to steel sides to a final destination – flesh. For Wood it was more exciting than *The Last Train from Berlin*, now tucked inside his battle dress.

The second flame-throwing Churchill lumbered out, lurched heavily to the beach off the rampless bows, and eventually reached the anti-tank ditch in front of the sea wall, with sparks streaming from the striking of shells against its turrets and the flame-throwing equipment wrecked, including the blazing gasoline containers which supplied it.

Someone forgot to remove the chocks under the tracks of the third Churchill, which started up and slithered backwards, crushing two wounded soldiers lying in its path. It reached the beach, flame-throwing equipment already on fire; after turning westwards a direct hit on a track put it out of action.

Wood lay flat in the bows as the stricken LCT, most of her crew and gunners dead, swung around in the tide and beached broadside on. A naval officer crawled forwards with a Sten gun, and Wood shouted: "Stay down. My orders are to stay inside until it quietens down." The naval officer said: "It's no good here. Let's do something." Wood looked at this eighteen-year-old youngster in amazement and feeling slightly ashamed of himself replied: "You stay. I'll go and make a recce." With that he dropped over the bows into the water and swam ashore.

Once ashore, Wood crawled to the top of a rise in the beach for a view of the promenade. He saw the Essex Scottish huddled behind the wall in the anti-tank ditch and decided there was little for him to do at that moment. As an assault engineer, he could not very well blow up road blocks until the sea front had been secured.

"I saw that my ship was obviously out of action having turned sideways to the shore," he wrote later. "Down by the Casino, LCT 4 was blazing furiously, another on Red Beach had been sunk, and a scout car was on fire nearby. It seemed advisable to get our own explosives ashore in case they were needed so I swam back to the boat and told my men to start ferrying the explosives in on rafts of chespaling."

When he ordered half his men out of the boat to assist in the water, four engineers and three soldiers appeared. Explosives, small-arms ammunition, and spare Sten guns were taken ashore by forming a chain of men in the water, placing the stores on the rolls of chespaling and pushing them from man to man, the shortest in the shallow water and the tallest – Wood himself – by the landing-craft. When there was no more chespaling, Wood ordered the rest of his men from the boat. None came. They were all casualties.

Wood was hit below the left shoulder as he tried to climb back into the LCT to see for himself what conditions were like. A man in the water helped him over the bows and he froze there, horrified at the sight. Men had been parted from their limbs, blood ran thickly down the gutters of the tankhold, and two naval medical orderlies, both wounded themselves, were picking up pieces and trying to bandage mashed bodies into human form.

"What I saw made my head spin," he said afterwards. "What I looked at was quite as fantastic a scene as the Confederate hospital church in the movie 'Gone with the Wind.' The medical orderlies moved unobtrusively about their work in the worst shambles of their experience."

The second wave of tank landing-craft touched down a few minutes after the first, LCT 4 lowering her ramp just east of the tobacco factory. She attracted her quota of artillery fire, received several hits near the stern, and began to blaze. Major C. E. Page, commanding the leading tank, Burns, disembarked successfully, crawled over the first line of wire, topped a rise, and pulled up at the edge of a seven-foot deep, partly completed anti-tank ditch. An excavator was still sitting nearby, indicating that work on the ditch had been recent. Page swung Burns right to avoid it and collided with a heavy artillery shell that might otherwise have missed. It knocked off one of his tracks, wrecked wireless and electrical equipment inside, and the tank, unable to proceed farther, was abandoned, Page and his crew manning the sea wall with their automatic weapons.

The second tank, Backer, which had been following Burns, swivelled past heading westwards but ten yards farther on received a direct hit on one of its tracks and came to a full stop. Bolster, the third, was still climbing up the beach when both of its tracks were broken and, though tilted at a crazy angle, it continued to fire at enemy positions on the West Headland and along the sea front.

B Company of the Essex Scottish commanded by Major David Deziel had crossed the Channel in LCT 4, and once the tanks were clear he led the men in a wild rush through the gaps they had made in the wire and succeeded in reaching the sea wall with only light casualties.

LCT 4 was then ablaze from stem to stern with spare cans of gasoline bursting into flame and stores of explosives blowing up at intervals. An assault boat crept inshore through the haze of smoke, sidled alongside her, and took off the wounded. The stricken LCT drifted away from the beach into deeper water and gradually subsided below the surface.

LCT 5 hit the beach just east of the Casino and was immediately the victim of a mortar and artillery bombardment which killed her crew and set her furiously afire. The first tank cleared the ramp, laid its chespaling, and was gunned up the beach, over the wire and onto the sea wall. The second, commanded by Captain Marcel Lambert, tried to use the same chespaling, swerved off it, threw a track, and came to a halt broadside on across it. The third tank, trying to negotiate around the second, experienced difficulty manœuvring in the loose shingle and finally bellied down among the stones immediately opposite the Casino, unable to move more than a few feet forwards and backwards.

LCT 6 was the only landing-craft of the second wave to survive. Her first three attempts to touch down were frustrated by barrages of shell fire, but she finally hit the beach on her fourth attempt. Her three tanks – Bob, Bert, and Bill – trundled off within three minutes and were seen to head across the sea wall onto the promenade in single file. They turned westwards towards the rear of the Casino where Bert stalled at an anti-tank ditch and had one track blown off while turning away. Bob and Bill drew up on either side of it and covered the evacuation of the crew.

One group of soldiers ran to the beach in the wake of the tanks, seeking their protection. But thirty men remained on board grouped in the empty hold, reluctant to face the awful intensity of fire across the beach. The captain of the landing-craft, his bridge wreathed in smoke and flames licking upwards from stores lashed down on deck, his helmsman wounded and wheelhouse strewn with dead, stood above, looking down and shouting at them to get ashore. They stared ahead into space, not daring to look up at him, yet refusing to move. It required only one to take the plunge into the open and the rest would follow; that man was not among them. Not even the spasmodic shuddering of the boat as shells thumped into and around it could persuade them to leave.

The captain returned to his sand-bagged wheelhouse . . . and waited. For fifteen minutes, an eternity when men were dying by the second and ships sinking by the minute, he waited for the troops to move out, risking the survivors of his crew, himself, and his ship. Then the doors were winched in and LCT 6 pulled astern, away from the beach and headed for open sea where her fires could be fought, her leaks plugged, just so that she could return once more when the time came to withdraw the troops.

Thirty soldiers, most of them probably not more than boys, had recoiled from the sights they had glimpsed in the sunlight beyond the ramp. The captain of the landing-craft expressed neither anger nor blame in his official report, which said briefly: "All the infantry except thirty were landed, and after waiting fifteen minutes for the remainder to go ashore, I withdrew from the beach."

Shortly after 6:00 a.m. the third flight approached, bringing Brigadiers Sherwood Lett and Bill Southam, their staffs, and Lieutenant-Colonel Johnny Andrews with his tank battalion headquarters. Lett's landing-craft came under immediate shell and mortar fire as it touched down, and Captain A. G. Stanton drove off the first tank, only to bog down in the loose shale of the beach. Sappers rushed out to help it without success, seven out of twelve being killed immediately in the process.

Andrews, his beloved tanks in action, his faith in the development of a Canadian armoured force justified, and his career likely now to be meteoric, even if this was not the battleground he would have preferred, leapt from the landing-craft, scrambled to the top of a rise in the beach, and scanned it for signs of the tanks already ashore. Most were immobile, trackless, and helpless, contributing something, however, by firing at unseen targets with their 6-pounders. He returned to the landing-craft just as it began pulling astern, badly hit, and unable to land other tanks while the first blocked exit from the ramp.

Lett, anxious to give Roberts a clear account of the situation on the beach, instructed his staff captain, Paul Garneau, to see what was happening. Garneau cautiously surveyed the beach through binoculars and reported that for the entire mile from West Headland to harbour entrance it was a scene of lifeless desolation in which nothing moved. He could not see the sea wall from the low level of the water line but his information was enough to indicate that despite the astounding profusion of bodies, the lack of movement on the beach might in itself be the result of assaulting troops having crossed the promenade to the buildings on the sea front. The ferocity of fire from the Casino fostered the illusion of success, seeping slowly back from the beach to *Calpe* where the truth was not known then and never would be until the battle was over.

Lett contacted Labatt by R/T to announce his intention to attempt another landing. "For Christ sake, don't," was all he heard before the line went dead.

Another landing-craft in this flight managed to unload its tanks, one of which reached the esplanade mainly through the mad fury of one young officer. His face burned, one eye missing, and his tank badly hit and helpless, he climbed from the turret while machine-gun bullets rattled about it and dropped to the beach, blood streaming down his burned face. He slithered across to an abandoned tank, vanished inside it, traversed the turret, and fought a single-handed duel with the guns on the harbour moles which were concentrating on the landing-craft.

Another craft carried Major Gordon Rolfe, Tank Battalion Signals Officer, whose equipment was in the scout car, Hunter, to be towed off by the last tank. The approach was made through a vicious artillery bombardment, one shell piercing through the side of the craft, ricocheting off a tank turret, and exploding inside the barrage balloon storage space. The flaming nylon balloon wafted momentarily into the air and then settled over one of the tanks, badly burning its commander, Lieutenant Edwin Bennett.

Rolfe organized a party to deal with the fire inside the landing-craft which by the time the balloon had been thrown overboard, had touched down. All three tanks were landed and turned westwards to engage heavy opposition from the Casino. They trundled up the beach towards the esplanade and Rolfe, seeing the sea wall approaching, pulled the lever which released his scout car. As he came free, the tank suddenly stopped at the edge of the anti-tank ditch, reversed, and backed into the car, crushing its front end and burrowing it down into the shale. Signals equipment in the back of the car was undamaged, so it was there, in the middle of the beach, protected only by a rising shingle on three sides, that Rolfe had to establish a communications headquarters.

For the next seven hours the wounded scout car, the calm officer, and his wireless operator, Corporal A. G. Wills, were the only effective link between the beach and Calpe, the beach and Sherwood Lett, the tanks and the infantry.

Brigadier Southam followed the last tank out of the landing-craft, copy 37 of the military plan encased in a waterproofed packet under one arm. His signallers managed to wheel the heavy brigade communications sets ashore in their baby carriage, eventually taking shelter in a hollow about one hundred yards from the Casino. A tank came lumbering up the beach, dipped quickly down into the hollow, smashed the equipment, crushed the signallers, and then rattled off towards the fight raging around the Casino.

Southam, a brigade commander stranded in the centre of the beach without any means of contact with his battalions, unable to take control of events, scrambled over to Rolfe's half-buried scout car. Rolfe was standing outside the car and his operator was inside at the radios when Southam explained that his own sets had been smashed by a tank. Rolfe offered to supply any communications he might require and the Brigadier, having found the means to communicate, decided not to at that stage. Instead, he walked across to a disabled tank and a voice from a half-opened turret top shouted:

"Bloody waterproofing didn't come off properly. We can't see to fire. Get it off for us, will you?"

By the time Southam had cut away the waterproofing from the front of the tank, those inside realized that their good Samaritan on the outside was a brigadier. After the tank commander apologized, Southam ordered him to make his way to the promenade and return with a report on the situation.

Witnesses of the incident have since suggested that the Brigadier might have been able to exercise greater authority by climbing into the tank, turning it into his headquarters, and making the reconnaissance along the promenade himself. Instead, he remained in the vicinity of Rolfe's scout car.

The tank Southam had assisted came from the fourth landing-craft in the flight which managed to disembark its load and withdraw. The other two tanks from this craft gunned their way up the beach, headed straight for the sea wall and fell into the anti-tank ditch.

Twenty-eight tanks were now ashore and one had been drowned; one more was still with Andrews aboard Sherwood Lett's landing-craft, then bitterly engaged by batteries on the West Headland. Their arrival had not improved the temper of the infantry pinned to the beach. Most of the tanks were crippled, scattered about the beach, and had become the primary targets for artillery batteries. Troops, already suffering from machine-gun and mortar fire were forced to move as far away from the tanks as possible to avoid being blown to pieces by shells aimed at the tanks.

At 6:15 a.m. the Essex Scottish were still held to the sea wall; the RHLI were being massacred left and right, but were making headway into the Casino in the centre; approximately twelve tanks had broken through to the esplanade; one brigadier was ashore and another afloat; and the two beachmasters, Major Brian McCool for the Army and Commander Lambert for the Navy, had set up headquarters near the junction of Red and White Beaches without having too much to be

masters of. There was no traffic to control other than the collection
and disposal of the wounded, so McCool became an extra link in the
communications chain, acting as liaison between the various commanders and summoning fire support wherever it was most urgently
needed. It was unlikely indeed that any of the strange characters
armed with special authority from Churchill Mann would return from
their clandestine activities in the town to demand priority evacuation.
None had landed – as far as anyone who really cared could tell. In fact,
even at that early hour it was obvious that none of the special assignments inserted into the military plan could be carried out, that the only
ambition of the men ashore was to hang on where they were until the
withdrawal.

The meagre information reaching *Calpe*, however, was providing
Roberts with an entirely different picture.

From their Commander down, the Canadians were paying shock-
ingly for the failure of Allied leaders in London and Washington to
to recognize and conform to the new "rules and principles" the enemy
had injected into the art of war. Unknowingly, unwittingly, General
Roberts was about to become the instrument for stripping the fat of
obsolescent thinking from all levels of Allied military leadership. The
wasted years of apathy and idleness in which outdated tactics had been
obstinately preserved, in which the lessons of centuries of "conjunct
expeditions" had been forgotten, would not again in this war exact
the appalling toll then being taken on the beaches of Dieppe.

With the assault forces ashore and the little information that filtered
back to Calpe providing a woolly, yet encouraging canvas of tentative
success, the decisions of Ham Roberts from now onwards would be
written into the military textbooks, subjects for endless unresolved
debate.

Calpe, festooned with wireless ærials from equipment set up not
only in the operations cabin but also on her decks, should have been
able to maintain contact with every unit ashore or afloat and even listen
in on conversations between them. Instead, Hughes-Hallett, unsatisfied
at the limited information available to Roberts, remained on the bridge,
constantly probing the thick air and naval smokescreens obscuring
Dieppe; Roberts himself was forced to remain at receivers which
crackled and spluttered but rarely spoke.

No reports came in from Puits or Pourville and only the Essex
Scottish seemed to be poised for a thrust into Dieppe itself.

IV

From the moment he had reached the sea wall after landing, Jasperson had made successive attempts to organize assaults through the wire and across the esplanade. There was no Casino at the eastern end of the beach to facilitate infiltration into the town. The beach and the esplanade were wide, open and flat, covered by guns on the East Headland, by guns firing from the caves in its face and at its base, and by guns firing from the harbour moles to the left of the troops.

At the instant this immense concentration of enemy fire had burst upon his battalion, Jasperson realized he had been landed into a death trap from which few could escape. He was shocked by the sudden fury with which the enemy had cut down the wire-cutting party, yet he persisted in establishing loose control of the companies spread along the wall. Within twenty minutes even this was lost, his sets smashed, and his headquarters signallers killed.

Mortar detachments tried to lob smoke bombs along the harbour side of the esplanade to cover further abortive assaults. Before they could fire more than a handful of bombs they were wrecked and the crews killed. By that time, about 5:45 a.m., one third of the battalion were casualties, officers being picked off with relentless precision by snipers in the buildings opposite them. Only one small walkie-talkie was working.

Then Company Sergeant-Major Cornelius Stapleton exploded a Bangalore under the wire on the wall, let forth a mighty battle cry, and charged through the gap with about fifteen men hard on his heels. They crossed the Boulevard Maréchal Foch immediately beyond the wire, made a mad, crouching, zig-zagging dash for more than a hundred yards across the promenade, and stormed over the Boulevard Verdun, throwing grenades at the windows of buildings facing them, firing guns from their hips and all the while bellowing their hate. At the sea wall a section of men, shouting their encouragement, stood up from their shelter and fired incendiary grenades, attempting to cover the charge by setting fire to the buildings. The tobacco factory exploded into flames just as Stapleton and his men broke into a building east of it, blowing down the doors, blowing out the shuttered windows, and leaping into smoke-filled infernos of their own creation.

For the first time they met the enemy face to face. It was no longer Canadian fear of a fire-swept beach, but German fear of the Canadians at close quarters. Wildness gave way to hard, merciless execution.

Short staccato bursts from room to room, from floor to floor, from house to house, were the sounds of it.

A handful of the group – Corporals Grondin and Stevenson and Privates Fleming and Hood – splintered off to another building, exacting terrible retribution for the slaughter on the beach; and yet a third party reached the eastern end of the Boulevard, and there, as if by divine decree, were enemy troops de-bussing from truck transports. The Canadians were inside, at the windows; the Germans were unsuspecting, on the outside. Combined fire of Sten guns, rifles, and pistols sustained a wicked roar, punctuated by the explosions of grenades and accompanied by the screams of the dying. When the concerto of war ended, trucks were ablaze and the only evidence of life where once there had been a human throng was an unseen cat, hit by a stray bullet and about to die, giving out at first a low, throaty moan of protest which gradually reached a high, shrill, harrowing finale.

Their own voices stilled by the havoc they had wrought, their ammunition all but expended, and their triumphant feelings tempered by the knowledge that since no others had followed them from the beach to which they would have to return, the small, bloodied, dirt-streaked, tattered party rejoined the house-cleaning group and steeled themselves for the race across that fire-filled esplanade.

Almost exactly thirty minutes after their exodus from behind the sea wall, Stapleton was back, reporting to Jasperson that it had been a most rewarding excursion indeed. Neither Colonel nor Warrant Officer could foresee the extent to which this brief foray into enemy territory would influence the operation. Shortly after 6:00 a.m. Jasperson had used the only walkie-talkie still working to inform the RHLI: "Twelve of our men in the buildings. Have not heard from them for some time."

Calpe intercepted this signal which, when placed in the context of reports from elsewhere, pointed to the only success yet achieved: occupation of the buildings facing Red Beach and partial consolidation of the beach itself.

Roberts wanted the East Headland. At 6:10 the intercepted message was reinforced by solid evidence that he might get it via Red Beach. This was a report from Fernie saying: "Essex Scot across beaches and in houses."

It was an inexplicable magnification of Stapleton's skirmish that provided Roberts with news of a success he could reinforce, news so grossly exaggerated that it enticed him toward the quicksand of disaster, toward the fatal assumption that even limited success warranted exploitation.

At 6:15 his hopes were given further encouragement when Labatt reported via brigade headquarters that the RHLI *were at the Casino. When I discussed this with Roberts he told me: "I recall that I queried this and was then satisfied that the* RHLI *were actually in the Casino."*

Five minutes later he received the distorted signal from the naval Beachmaster with the Royals, who had not himself landed, saying: "Impossible land troops." The words "any more" preceding "troops" had been omitted. After a brief conference with Hughes-Hallett, Roberts decided to commit the Royals – whom he now thought to be lying off Puits in assault boats – to Red Beach from where they might still assault the East Headland.

It may well be that Roberts, obsessed as he was by the need to capture the East Headland, was reading too much into the fragmentary information reaching him. He had no way of knowing that he was receiving the blacks and the whites of events but not the greys in between – and the truth was always somewhere in the obscurity of the greys. At this stage, however, he thought he could see a way through the mist of uncertainty; the door, seemingly forced ajar, should require but a single mighty punch to swing it wide open. The Fusiliers Mont-Royal and the two flights of reserve tanks were waiting for just this opportunity.

Lieutenant-Colonel Menard had already transferred to *Calpe* from an ML to receive his orders. While waiting he had joined the 2nd Division staff officers in the wardroom for breakfast – Captain Bult-Francis and Lieutenant W. R. Scott, both of the 8th Recce Regiment, who would go ashore as liaison officers between the brigade headquarters and the Force Commanders, Alex Hayes, staff captain to Roberts, and Dan Doheny, the Montrealer who had been a regular rail commuter between London and the Isle of Wight.

Although Peter Wright, in the operations cabin, had not been able to feed them with too many morsels of information, the general mood was one of optimism, reassuring for Menard. According to Doheny's diary:

> I was glad the steward offered me a cup of tea laced with Scotch. I had that funny feeling in my stomach and a dryness in my throat that made a bully beef sandwich impossible to finish. The

steward fixed me up a couple of ginger-ale bottles filled with Scotch which I put in my haversack. It was now nearly 6:30 and Francis, Scott, and myself would be taken ashore any minute. Joe was waiting on the General.

A beer failed to wash down the sandwich and I began to get nervous for the first time . . . had a distinct feeling for a trip to the "heads" and had been there only two minutes when Alex shouted that the boat had arrived and the beach was secure, so it all looked promising.

The ML had been summoned for Menard. Roberts had by then decided, after consideration of the naval problems outlined by Hughes-Hallett, to commit the Fusiliers Mont-Royal on Red Beach. Conscious, however, of the RHLI success at the Casino, the Fusiliers Mont-Royal would deploy westwards to take advantage of any success on White Beach at Menard's discretion.

Rigid, powerful obligations had swayed Roberts in reaching this decision. The timetable had already gone awry, indeed time had become a predominating factor. If Dieppe were to be taken at all, the floating reserves had to be committed somewhere by 7:00 a.m. – a time limit set not by Roberts but by the anticipated rate of German reinforcement.

If the town did not fall by 9:00 a.m. its defences would be so strengthened that an overwhelming counter-attack could be expected; and to avoid being trapped by the 10th Panzer Division, which might arrive between 12:30 and 1:30, the withdrawal would have to begin by 11:00 a.m. at the latest.

With no news at all from Pourville, having ordered the Royals to Red Beach and knowing the tanks were ashore, Roberts decided to exploit the only success of which he had certain knowledge. The Royals would be followed by the Fusiliers Mont-Royal and then the reserve flights of tanks, delivering in sum a blow which, had it been based upon reliable information, would undoubtedly have forced the door.

The most controversial decision in modern Canadian military history had been made. Critics of it say that Pourville was the only success-warranting exploitation. They forget that Roberts knew nothing of the bridgehead there until ninety minutes later when a scrappy report reached him after 8:00 a.m. saying that the South Sasks and the Camerons "are off the beach." However, even if at 6:30 a.m. he could have foreseen Merritt's success he might still have refrained from landing reinforcements at Pourville – for good reasons.

First, the Fusiliers Mont-Royal were in twenty-six wooden LCP's, designed as reconnaissance boats but used for assault because no others were available. The German coastal batteries would have quickly awakened to the threat presented by the sight of so large an assault convoy heading for Pourville, and the unprotected troops would have been subjected to a continuous, immense barrage of fire throughout the five-mile passage – in terms of time, for forty or fifty minutes. How many of the twenty-six boats would have got through? How many troops would have survived to land? And of those who did, how many would be in a fit state to fight?

It is very probable that a demoralizing massacre at sea would have had far worse repercussions than those that actually occurred – which were bad enough.

Second, Combined Operations, at the urging of the Admiralty, had requested that if a time came when Roberts had to make a choice between the demolitions in the town, the torpedo dump under the East Headland should have priority over all other targets for destruction. Winning the U-boat war was the most supreme strategical objective, and in August 1942 the Allies were still losing it. Roberts intended carrying out this request, if possible, because it fitted neatly into his preoccupation with the East Headland.

Third, and most decisive, a cogent reason for avoiding Pourville had been supplied by Combined Operations Intelligence experts, one that had influenced planning from the outset. They had repeated again and again that to attack Dieppe by means of flank landings would fail for a number of reasons, not least of which that the bridges of the Scie and the Saane would not carry the weight of a Churchill tank. Wherever Roberts landed the Fusiliers Mont-Royal, he also intended following through the exploitation of success by landing his reserve tanks, something the best Intelligence opinion available stated categorically he could not do at Pourville. The tanks, they insisted, could not cross the bridge, nor the flooded areas of the Scie valley.

In fact, this Intelligence opinion was probably inaccurate. Merritt's bridge over the River Scie was said by the troops who returned to be capable of carrying far heavier vehicles than the Churchills.

These reasons narrowed the choice of beaches for reinforcement to Red and White. By selecting Red on the evidence of success in his hands, Roberts was wholly conforming to the accepted rules of war.

Blame for the faults – and dangerous faults there were – lay elsewhere than with Roberts, in the distortion of the Essex-Scottish information and in faulty intelligence about a small and sturdy bridge. This error has been improperly overlooked, for had it not been made, the frontal assault over those murderous main beaches might never have taken place and the story of Dieppe would then read differently today.

V

From *Calpe* to the LCP's of the Fusiliers Mont-Royal, circling three miles off shore under intermittent bombardment from batteries on the West Headland, Menard, standing on the ML's bridge, beckoned the small fleet to close in around him and then shouted in French over the loud-hailer: "The plan is altered. We're going in right now to Red Beach. We'll land opposite the tobacco factory, and our objectives are the buildings along the sea front. If we can't get to them across the promenade we will go through the Casino. Our comrades are there already. This is your chance to show what French Canadians can do. When you land, charge with your bayonets fixed. I will be at your head, leading you to victory."

A chorus of cheers welled up from the boats while Menard grinned hugely down from the bridge to the foredeck where Doheny, Bult-Francis, and Scott were standing in mock salute. Dollard Menard, twenty-nine years old, elder son of a Canadian National Railways engineer from Notre-Dame-du-Lac and named after the French-Canadian hero, Dollard des Ormeaux who had fought the Iroquois in 1660, was enjoying himself. The Khyber Pass had been scorched, dusty exile for a self-assured Latin bred among the snows and pines of Quebec; and, where the British Indian Army might have been faintly amused by his typically French enthusiasm for life, his fellow countrymen openly loved him for it.

On the bridge of the streamlined, powerful motor launch, with steel helmet tilted over his right eye and tommy gun held carelessly under an arm, he was a darkly rakish figure – recruiting poster model of a soldier braced for battle. At this melodramatic moment he was in his element, displaying such outward trappings of leadership that his men happily fixed their bayonets, joked with their officers and with Father Sabourin, the smiling padre whose grin then was wider than ever. The honour of Quebec would be in safe hands for the next few precious hours. They had Menard's word for it.

At least one officer who witnessed this seeming braggadocio knew it to be superficial, knew that behind the swaggering façade Joe Menard felt deeply that his Fusiliers Mont-Royal were about to fight for the first time in this war as part of the Canadian Armed Forces. Politics and separatist ideology apart, Menard was a Canadian, proud of his heritage from France and tolerant of its Anglo-Saxon bed-fellow. At the moment when he appeared in his most fearsome light, the big Quebec commander prayed within the sound of the guns for fusion by fire.

During the approach from under the West Headland there was no way of seeing through the thick haze of low-lying smoke; only the tops of the cliff were visible in the sunlight. Aircraft were everywhere, fighters racing across the dawning blue of the sky, jigging about in innumerable dog fights and swooping down on Dieppe; formations of enemy bombers dropped their loads and then hurried home to bomb up for a return trip. Tracers streamed upwards from the German flak defences and streamed down again from the strafing close-support fighters, while tiny black clouds of smoke burst overhead from the guns of the fleet. The constant chatter and boom of guns was above, on either side and ahead – at Dieppe.

As the LCP's formed into long columns astern of the ML, shells burst among them, and Dan Doheny, feeling slightly exposed, quit the foredeck for what appeared to be a safer position behind the bridge where he could quietly contemplate that if things ashore were as encouraging as they had appeared to be aboard *Calpe*, how strange it was that the enemy should be able to devote so much time and energy to the destruction of his particular ML.

Then it was time to transfer to an LCP for the final run-in, for the boats to deploy into line abreast – a long, thin assault line which vanished into the smoke. When Menard had announced the switch in beaches from the ML he had used French, which is not the official language of the Royal Navy. The young officers commanding the boats remained ignorant of the change. However, the set of the tide and the ferocity of fire from the East Headland were decisive, keeping most of the boats down towards the western end of the beach.

The approach had been made under artillery bombardment; when they emerged from the smoke only one hundred yards from the beach, the immense fury of the water-line barrage fell upon them. They were strung out along the entire length of the beach, but most of them so far to the west that even White Beach was to their left.

A wall of bullets greeted them, ripping through the thin wooden hulls to spread bewilderment and terror. In Menard's boat, coming in west of the Casino, Doheny shouted above the din: "Let's load our Stens. Looks like we'll need 'em." The soldiers snapped in their ammunition clips, someone fumbled, and a short burst came from the stern of the boat. Lieutenant Scott, standing between Bult-Francis and Doheny pitched forward, a bullet in his back.

At touchdown, whether in answer to Menard's call to uphold the traditions of French Canada or simply because nowhere could be as unprotected as the boats, the Fusiliers Mont-Royal charged onto the beach in a scattered line, their eyes screwed into thin slits against the searing blaze of the rising sun. They raced to wherever there was shelter and there they stopped, benumbed by the reception. One small group joined the Essex Scottish at the sea wall, another found the anti-tank ditch opposite the burning tobacco factory, a considerable number made it to the wall slightly west of the Casino, but the bulk of the battalion, nearly two hundred of them, reached the base of the West Headland and huddled under the overhang against the face of the cliffs. They were so far west they had found a beach of their own, a new one bared by the ebbing tide and on the right fringe of the battle. Bewilderment replaced fear. Was this the success they had been sent to exploit?

One of the LCP's which touched down under the cliff was commanded by Lieutenant McRae, senior Canadian naval officer at Dieppe. The boat, riddled by machine-gun fire and with huge holes in its sides gulping in the sea, was a wreck at the instant of landing. Major Sarto Marchand led a handful of the troops to the protection of the cliff face, the rest remaining aboard either dead or dying. Major Painchaud, in peace a Montreal lawyer, in war Menard's second in command, was wounded in thighs and legs as he landed; but Lieutenant Erskine Eaton was cut down before he left his boat, and his body was taken back to England for burial.

McRae and his small naval crew worked among the wounded, giving morphine, bandaging, and whispering words of hope. The Germans came to the edge of the cliff above them, looked down, and saw that the stricken boat was little more than a stranded first-aid post. It was not fired on again.

Menard followed Doheny up towards the Casino and was wounded in his right arm before reaching the wall. In that first wild rush a kaleidoscope of tragedy flickered before them. The beach was littered with dead and wounded, small parties of men hugging the hollows for protection, a Bren gun carrier burning fiercely, its crew dead and transfixed in weird, petrified positions. One man with head and body mutilated had one leg over the side of the carrier as if he had been about to step out. In front of the Casino, bare-headed young Marcel Lambert was sitting on the turret of his immobilized tank directing the crew's machine-gun fire.

Doheny joined a group of twenty men gathered behind another helpless tank and found Lieutenant John Counsell of the RHLI flat on the beach with arms outstretched to make himself as small a target as possible.

"What the hell is happening?" he asked.

"It's a proper bloody foul-up," replied Counsell. "They were waiting for us, must have been. We've not been able to do anything. The whole bloody place is under fire. Anyway what do you know? What have you come here for?"

"It must be a local hold-up," said Doheny, quite sincerely. "When I left *Calpe* things seemed to be going well. We thought you chaps had captured part of the town, especially on the left flank of the beach."

"That's a break," said Counsell. "Maybe they'll get round behind these bloody sea-front houses and cut some of the fire out. We sure as hell need some help here."

They were lying face down, ten feet behind the tank with shoulders touching. A burst of machine-gun fire flashed like summer lightning across the beach kicking up a tiny trail of dust and pebbles. Counsell moaned, and Doheny looked round to see blood oozing from a wound in the young lieutenant's back.

Standing beside Rolfe at his scout-car signals station in the centre of the beach, Brigadier Southam watched the touchdown and said: "I wonder what the Fusiliers Mont-Royal are doing here?" Rolfe suggested that as the Force Commanders might be unaware of the true situation, he could contact *Calpe* for the Brigadier.

"No point," replied Southam. "I'll wait until things sort themselves out a bit." In retrospect it is painfully obvious that a report from Southam then would have done much to dispel the uncertainty plaguing both Roberts and Hughes-Hallett.

VI

The assault troops were ashore, the tanks were ashore, the assault engineers were ashore, and the Fusiliers Mont-Royal were ashore. Wireless sets, stores of explosives, mortars, and special equipment had been lost overboard in landings, wrecked on the beaches by enemy fire or destroyed while still in the boats. The assault sappers had died in droves at touchdown – one group so massacred that only nine out of seventy survived unhurt within a few minutes of landing. It was a battle of independent groups, of platoons intermingling, companies breaking up and coalescing, of men fighting alongside strangers and dying in their arms. Because wireless and radio-telephone sets were smashed, commanders used runners who were almost always killed; Sten guns jammed, were thrown away; and pebble splinters caused as much havoc as bullets.

Neither Labatt, Jasperson, nor Menard could exercise direct control of their battalions until the battle stabilized – which it never did. Throughout the morning no organized assault could be made, no special task undertaken. In the far-off days of the Isle of Wight training, General Roberts had insisted that the tanks should be landed with the assault battalions to give them armoured fire support. Now the troops were reluctant to leave shelter and go forwards without the tanks; the tanks could not go forwards until the engineers had blown the road blocks; the engineers, loaded down with their prepared 60-pound charges, could not go forwards until the troops had secured the immediate vicinities of the road blocks.

Checkmate.

Battle for
the Beaches

At 7:00 a.m. Georges Guibon, formerly director of the Dieppe Tourist Bureau and a fluent speaker of German, sits in the living-room of his house on Jean Ribault Street, watching the frenzied antics of a panic-stricken bat. They are old acquaintances, this tall, emaciated, middle-aged Frenchman and the repulsive mammal, because the bat has so far eluded all Guibon's efforts to catch and kill it. Now it is behaving imbecilically, hurling itself from wall to wall, from ceiling to floor, and Guibon is hoping it will refrain from doing something foolish, such as killing itself. At the dawn of an ugly day, the bat is a companionable link with more normal times, a symbol of permanency.

Outside, the constant roar of aircraft, the crump of bombs and the spine-chilling drumbeat of fighter cannons make him anxious and he occasionally winces. The house shakes alarmingly, doors rattle, and a shell explodes on the roof of the German Field Security headquarters next door, pieces of slate crashing into his garden. Smoke filters into the room, flames reflect in the windows, and to the deep throb of engines overhead is now added the loud hissing of steam escaping from locomotives wrecked in the nearby railway yards.

The bat traps itself behind a cabinet, but Guibon no longer wishes to seize it, certainly not under such unfair circumstances. Neither can he bear to listen while it beats its wings stupidly and emits pitiful squeaks. He goes to his kitchen, controlling the surge of hope that perhaps all this is the prelude to invasion, and switches on his gas stove. It works – and hope fades. If an invasion were imminent, surely they would not leave the main gas supply uninterrupted?

His thoughts are dangerous, but he does not mind. For two years now he has been working as an interpreter at German headquarters and has stored information for the day when it will be useful to the Allies. He is very good at storing information, so good in fact that the Germans have not the faintest idea that their obliging interpreter is a link in the local underground. Because of his secret work, Guibon is slightly concerned that the Allies may have launched an invasion without informing the Resistance. Then he shrugs. Perhaps they have, but there are so many organizations, so much internal conflict between them.

The Todt Organization engineer billeted in his house comes downstairs. "*Haben Sie ein Keller?*" he asks. Guibon murmurs "*Nein.*" No cellar, so his lodger joins the dust pan and brooms in the closet under the stairs.

After breakfast, Guibon goes into the street and shuffles against the house fronts to where a group of neighbours are standing in a doorway. They greet him with an excited chatter – "The Allies are landing in the West." Two elderly German soldiers motion to the group to stay inside. One says, "*Der Tommy ist da, am Hafen! Zu Fuss!*" (The Tommies are here, at the harbour, on foot.)

Inside the house the mother of a family of six occupies herself by making jam which she knows will be confiscated when it is finished, but it keeps her busy. Therapy for overwrought nerves. The first civilian casualties are being rushed up the street to the hospital, an open car goes by with a German soldier sitting in the back holding a wounded little girl in his arms. A horse-drawn ammunition wagon goes galloping past in the other direction towards the beach, and there are now groups in doorways and at windows all along Jean Ribault Street shouting questions at each other.

Ambling slowly along the street in its customary fashion is the aging horse that pulls the once-weekly milk wagon. It belongs to a farmer who is permitted to deliver a small amount of milk to cripples and the bedridden. He makes three stops in the street, fills the dirty pots held out to him, and continues on with the bulk of his load for the hospital. A piece of shrapnel falls near Guibon and he picks it up, intending to give it to a neighbour as a souvenir. It is hot; he is burned and drops it. It will be lunchtime soon and the neighbour invites him to share thin vegetable soup with her family.

Georges Guibon and the residents of Rue Jean Ribault are not yet aware that on a beach where English honeymoon couples once frolicked by day, in a Casino where they once sipped blood-red wine by romantic candlelight at night, a Canadian generation is gambling for its life.

II

Advance sections of the RHLI crashed through the sun verandah of the Casino, blew down doors, and rushed inside, some singly, some in pairs, others in groups. In that first desperate dash off the beach it was obvious that the capture of the Casino would provide the only protection from the relentless fury of enemy fire sweeping the vast expanse of the beach. They left a desolate trail of assault behind them – soft, lifeless bodies moving jerkily in the rippling surf, broken bodies scattered on the slopes of the beach, fences of rolled barbed wire blown apart, the bits strewn about like bundles of tumbleweed.

On the northeast corner of the Casino a huge, two-storey concrete emplacement armed with a powerful artillery gun laid down a non-stop barrage along the water line; machine-gun pillboxes flanked it protectively. Farther to the left Labatt and his headquarters staff were two hundred yards from the Casino, in a hollow near the wall from where they could see the progress of individual units.

Denny Whitaker led one group from the beach over the verandah, grenades blowing a pathway ahead of them into the Casino – from sunlight to sudden shade. They stopped, hugging the walls of the entrance, blinking to adjust their eyes; a rifle fired from the depths of the gloom, and Private Henderson collapsed, fatally wounded. Private T. W. Graham, knowing he would be clearly silhouetted against the light outside, moved quickly away from the wall to throw grenades in rapid succession. When the swirling smoke from the explosions receded, five Germans were standing with hands in the air, fear in their eyes. Rifle fire from an upstairs landing chipped the panelling near Whitaker's head, and the nervous, light-footed stalking began, down long narrow corridors, across balconies, and from room to room.

Corporal C. A. McDermott, with a miscellaneous party of sappers and infantry, caught a brief glimpse of three Germans near a raised stage at the far end of an auditorium. To his astonishment one of them held a rifle pointed straight at him. At once indignant, he crept down one side of the auditorium behind a long bar until he was close enough to throw a grenade. The Germans threw one back and then leapt for cover. When the grenade landed on his right foot, McDermott leapt also. He was forty feet away and still sprinting when it went off, the blast knocking the rifle from his grasp. He squatted on the floor behind the bar, nursing his sore foot and pondering the situation, and after due deliberation returned to his party for another grenade. Armed with this, he returned to the stage, approached the wreckage cautiously, and found that the enemy had vanished, leaving behind a rifle, three stick grenades, two bayonets, and a trail of blood. He was joined by Captain John Currie, and they followed the trail through a maze of backstage dressing-rooms. When they could waste no more time, McDermott took up a defensive firing position at a window overlooking a half-demolished wall to the right of the Casino and saw the heads of a line of German soldiers behind it. He fired, knocking the helmet off one head whose owner dropped his own weapon and clapped his hands about his ears, obviously hurt by the concussion.

Private A. W. Oldfield joined three stray soldiers from the Fusiliers Mont-Royal. They started to run lightly up a wide, circling staircase and at the first bend met four Germans running lightly down. The enemy turned about in sudden flight, with the Canadians in close pursuit. The chase ended when the Germans went to ground in a cubbyhole where grenades blew them to pieces.

Oldfield found a sniper hiding nearby and went after him with his bayonet. For the first time in his life, this young soldier killed a man while looking into his face, watching him die, while trying to free the bayonet before he vomited over his victim's head.

Private F. E. A. Jenner reached the third floor all on his own. "The only two Germans I ran into I shot because they wouldn't come out of their hiding-place when I wanted them to," he reported later. Private R. W. Wilkinson found himself at one end of a corridor with a German at the other, both with tommy guns at the ready. They faced each other with the hard, tensed expectancy of gunfighters. The idea that neither could win occurred to both at the same time and they dodged back to shelter simultaneously.

Corporals Bowles, Lissen, and Billings, accompanied by Private Johnson, roamed the building as a team. They crept stealthily to one closed door after another, one of them always throwing it quickly open while the other three poured fire into whatever room or cupboard happened to be revealed. Their score mounted steadily.

Whitaker led his group to the rear of the Casino where they found that a covered arcade, lined with shops on one side and spaced with columns on the other, led out across the promenade to the Boulevard Verdun which separated it from the sea-front buildings. It was covered by converging fire from four machine guns in the Royal Hotel opposite the Casino.

The quiet, nerveless Private Graham, armed with a heavy anti-tank gun this time, placed the weapon casually across a window ledge, aimed it carefully and let go three shots at each enemy gun. In the pause that followed, a German sergeant-major came up behind the group, all intent upon watching the results of Graham's shooting, and startled them by announcing in a loud voice that he wished to surrender. Ignored, he went away in a huff to find more obliging troops. Whitaker pointed to a slit trench about three feet deep, ten yards away to the left, so without further hesitation Graham jumped into the open, threw his anti-tank gun into the ditch, and dived in after it. Whitaker followed with the rest of the group and they crawled to the right where the trench curved towards the town. Graham reached the bend first, peered round it, saw two Germans gazing at the Casino. One shot from his anti-tank gun killed one, wounded the other. Only then did the group realize the trench they were in was a latrine drain.

Whitaker, anxious to be rid of such unpleasant surroundings, led a rush to a shack on the fringe of the demolished half of the Casino. Machine-gun bursts kicked up tiny spurts of dust about their feet as they crashed through the flimsy door to slither about on a wet surface, finally tumbling down in a confused flurry of legs and arms. This time they had found the latrine itself.

The certainty of nausea inside outweighed the certainty of death outside and they quit the shack along another ditch to take shelter across the Boulevard Verdun beside an ordinary rabbit-wire fence covered by a hedge, from where they were able to maintain intense fire at point-blank range into the nearest sea-front buildings. Sergeant H. Lowe tensed as he caught the blur of movement behind the hedge, his eyes gleaming in anticipation, while the muzzle of his Sten gun followed the progress of two German soldiers creeping stealthily along the other side to the rear of the group. The pair leapt suddenly through a gate onto the Boulevard, potato-masher grenades held above their shoulders ready for throwing. Before either could properly register his horror, both were cut down by Lowe's prolonged burst of fire, already dead when the grenades exploded, dismembering their bodies.

Mortar bombs began falling uncomfortably close, and the nauseous trenches were all of a sudden more inviting than the Boulevard Verdun. The group ran back across the road, fell into the first ditch — more carefully than before — and were still there when joined by Dan Doheny, who has reported his experiences after leaving the wounded Lieutenant Counsell on the beach:

"Taking advantage of a quiet spell — in other words no direct machine-gun fire aimed at me — I set out for the Casino one hundred yards away. While scrambling and stumbling as fast as I could, I noticed a big sergeant of the RHLI standing with his back to where enemy fire had come from a few seconds before and calmly waving and calling up his men sheltering in hollows along the beach. The men, seeing him standing alone and apparently unharmed, rushed for the Casino and seemed to make it without too many casualties.

"When I got there, the Casino was bare except for our troops and Germans — dead, wounded, and prisoners. The Germans still alive were cowering in a corner with all the fight knocked out of them. Every time one of our chaps came near them they would holler 'Kamerad.' I met Denny Whitaker and having nothing else to do joined him. The narrow trench running inland from the Casino to the promenade was filled with dead or dying Germans. Denny, with about twenty men, had already been across the promenade once. Now we tried it again.

"We made our way along the trench to a hedge adjoining a concrete abri. We crossed a gap in the hedge and ran over the road and flung ourselves in grass — about forty yards of grass. Then the road [Boulevard Verdun] lay between us and the houses which were set back from the road. In front of them was a small yard with a grilled fence stretching along the sidewalk.

"After a few exhortations from Denny, about eight of us ran across in the hope of getting into the houses. It was a mad skelter to a concrete wall only about two feet high. A machine gun opened fire from behind us, the bullets chipping cement from the wall into our faces. I tried to climb over the wall to the protection of the other side, but couldn't squeeze between the grill-work of the fence above it. It was most uncomfortable. Denny yelled: 'Let's get out of here.' We turned back across the road and flung ourselves into the grass again. . . . I rather think now that it might have been one of our own troops seeing us running and pressing his trigger instinctively."

On the beach itself, Sergeant George Hickson, the dark-haired sapper from Kitchener, Ontario, was scrambling towards the wire guarding the left side of the Casino. With him were the six sappers of his party loaded down with the plastic explosives with which they hoped to blow up the Dieppe telephone exchange, the post office, and eventually assist with the destruction of the torpedo dump under the East Headland. One of the men, a slender, blond, tow-headed youngster, insisted upon wearing his helmet tilted back on his head. Hickson had told him repeatedly: "That tin hat's got a purpose. Wear it right and it might save your lousy life." The sapper's customary reply had been to push it back on his head even farther.

The small party were scrambling after an RHLI platoon commanded by Lieutenant Webster, already at the wire of the sea wall and preparing to blow it up with Bangalores. Unexpectedly another sapper stopped, frozen rigid with fear, by the awesome intensity of the fire covering that body-strewn beach. Hickson ran back, shouted at him, shook him hard. The sapper's unblinking eyes gazed blankly ahead until suddenly he gave a slight high-pitched cry and dived behind a trackless tank, his body quivering, his face burrowed painfully into the pebbles, his fingers clawing frantically, convulsively.

Hickson followed in the wake of his party to the wall where Lieutenant Webster's men had already laid the first Bangalore under the wire. While waiting for it to explode, he noticed that only a few yards away another sapper was hung up on the wire, lying half across it with arms windmilling sluggishly and legs digging spasmodically at the pebbles. The Germans had stopped firing at the stricken, helpless man. They had already hit his pack of explosives and it was burning on his back, the flames licking around him. He was burning to death and there was nothing anyone could do.

The Bangalore under the wire failed to go off and a soldier laid another alongside it. This too smouldered for an interminable number of seconds until the soldier, thinking it a dud, stood up to investigate. Then it exploded – and his head rolled down the slope of the beach towards the sea.

Corporal Weaver was first of this section of RHLI through the gap, followed by Webster who collapsed on the other side, hit by four bullets. Hickson was about to dash through when a pillbox to the right opened fire and closed the gap. Accompanied by two infantry-men, he crawled towards the pillbox, reached a blind side of it, and at his signal all three lobbed grenades through the loophole. When they returned to the gap in the wire. Hickson saw with a sense of quick shock a familiar sapper lying face down. The helmet was pushed far back on the head. Dropping to one knee, he turned the body over and looked down into a life-like expression of wide-eyed astonish-ment. A huge black hole gaped high up on the forehead, the blood from it staining the blond hair a dirty, dark red.

Wiping sweat from his own face, now suffused by savage rage, Hickson loosened the bag of plastic charges from his back, stalked through the gap and on into the Casino, oblivious of danger until a soldier shouted, "Take cover, you bloody fool! They're rolling gre-nades down the corridors. There's snipers up there too."

Beckoning to this soldier and about half a dozen others to follow him, Hickson led the way into a room already cleared and announced, "If we can't get down the corridors, we'll blast a way through the walls." Then he began to march through the Casino, using his charges to blow down the walls between the rooms. By the time he ran out of walls and rooms there was little left on one side of the ground floor except wreckage, falling masonry and dead Germans.

By 8:00 a.m. some twenty-odd prisoners were hunched along a wall, their thumbs tied behind their backs with fishline and passed round their necks in the manner the stout Captain Insinger had re-commended on the Isle of Wight and in accordance with the opera-tional orders.

Hickson was now joined by Private Johnson, separated from his winkling-out team of corporals, who showed him an immense steel door that led to the two-storey concrete gun emplacement built into the Casino wall. They could hear the dull detonations inside as the heavy gun fired at landing-craft off the beach. Hickson placed a 3-pound limpet charge against the door, detonated it, and the door blew outwards, the concussion of the explosion in so confined a space kill-ing some of the German crew inside and stunning others. Hickson, Johnson, and Corporal Vermette of the Fusiliers Mont-Royal who had joined them, rushed into the smoke-filled emplacement and, while the live Germans were pulled out, Hickson placed a 1-pound clam charge in the breach of the gun and wrecked it. The German crew were wearing gas masks because, according to one of the prisoners who recovered, they had been told that the Allies might invade under cover of poison gas.

Private Johnson's later report said: "We rushed in and under a corporal's orders tied the thumbs of our prisoners behind their backs and sent them down to the beach to join the collection point for the wounded where they might be of use." Two of these prisoners were Poles, one of whom could speak English. He said the gun's crew had been locked in the emplacement for four days on meagre rations. Private J. A. Taylor, who was listening, threw a bar of chocolate at the prisoners, and the Canadian watched grimly as they fought and clawed each other for possession of it.

Hickson returned to the south side of the Casino where he saw a German running across the end of a corridor. He followed, trapped him under some stairs from where the enemy soldier fought back ferociously. There were some eighteen men with Hickson then and, undaunted by their combined fire, the German rolled a saucer-shaped grenade at them. Hickson was to say of this incident: "The grenade shook us up somewhat, but Corporal Vermette, the French Canadian who had been with me when I blew down the steel door, charged with his bayonet and the enemy came out with his hands up."

Sergeant-Major Lucien Dumais of the Fusiliers Mont-Royal also had a busy day. He had landed with five others on the centre of the beach between two wrecked tank landing-craft, one of which was burning furiously. They came under heavy fire from the flanking headlands, three men being killed in as many seconds, and Dumais led a dash for the Casino. On the ground floor he searched a room used by the Germans as living-quarters, "to see if there was anything worth taking," then received a message from Corporal Vermette that some Germans had taken refuge in a strongroom or vault. He found the corporal, tried to open the door, found it locked, and beckoned to a nearby sapper. The sapper not only blew down the door, but most of the ceiling as well. Dumais was to say later:

"We couldn't see anything for dust. We could not go into the strongroom as I had no torch at hand. We let things go for the moment as the explosion had been strong enough to kill anyone inside."

On the second floor, Dumais went to a window on the west side that overlooked a house 150 yards away in which he saw movement. He opened fire with his Sten gun, which jammed after three bursts. He changed clips and tried again. It jammed once more, so he threw the gun away, picked up some German grenades left lying on the

floor, and returned to the strongroom to toss them inside. "I did this
to make sure that there were no live Germans left," he said.

At the rear of the Casino he was told to watch out for a sniper in
the steeple of the St Remy Church and decided he should do something about it. He found an abandoned Bren gun, worked himself into
a comfortable, protected position, and let loose experimental bursts
at the steeple to entice the sniper to reveal his whereabouts. His
scheme worked, the sniper replying from between two grey columns
under the coping. This lone duel continued for about thirty minutes
before Dumais gave up, the Bren-gun fire having little effect. For the
rest of the morning he rounded up fifteen Fusiliers Mont-Royal, stationed them at windows on the second floor, and became *de facto*
commander of the Casino's upper defences against counter-attack.

The Casino was never quite cleared of the enemy. More than one
hundred assorted RHLI, Fusiliers Mont-Royal, sappers, and signallers
occupied the ground and first floors, but enemy snipers continued to
fire from the third floor and the roof. However, it was enough that
the ground floor was available for those sections intent upon entering
the town to pass through to the Boulevard Verdun. Labatt, receiving
news of Whitaker's attempts, reported to *Calpe* at 7:12 a.m. "Casino
taken," thereby confirming what Roberts already thought to be the
case.

III

Throughout the day sporadic attempts were made to use the Casino
as the wide end of a funnel through which troops could be poured
across the promenade into the town. First of these was made by four-
teen men under Captain Tony Hill of Hamilton who had no intention
of leaving Dieppe without seeing the town, and being a determined
young man he used the sustained fire of Whitaker's party at the rear
of the Casino to cover a wild run across the open esplanade to the
buildings at the western end of the sea front. No one was hit while
they were fast-moving exposed targets, but once they reached the
buildings and paused, a machine-gun burst drew a line of holes across
Private Clausen's chest.

They tried to negotiate through a barbed-wire entanglement at the
entrance to the Rue de Sygogne and climb over the anti-tank road
block. Without Bangalores or cutters, however, the heavy wire proved
impassable, so they broke into a large building on the east side of the

street by smashing a window and found themselves in what Company Sergeant-Major J. Stewart subsequently described as "the storeroom of a cinema theatre."

They passed into the main amphitheatre, crossed it by the front row of seats, and plummeted through an exit into the Rue Couronne – a narrow, dark little street less than one hundred yards long and lined by tall buildings that closed out the sky. They spread out on either side against the buildings and edged slowly southwards in the stop-start-stop movement taught so well on the Isle of Wight, expectant and waiting for the enemy to open fire. Nothing happened until they turned westwards along the Rue St Remy and reached the Rue de Sygogne, main north-south artery on the west side of Dieppe, which they had already tried to enter over the road block.

A patrol of Germans ran, but only hesitantly, towards them, and Hill shouted: "Let's get 'em." A Sten-gunner threw his jammed weapon away in disgust and loped at Hill's heels bowling grenades at the enemy while shouting encouragement to Stewart, who was firing the Bren gun from his hip. The Germans took one look at the fixed bayonets, turned about and fled, leaving four bodies lying still on the roadway. Stewart stopped to recover his breath and saw a Frenchwoman, shawl over her head and basket over her arm, come out of a house and walk calmly along the road, ignoring the sound and signs of battle. While he gaped, she vanished into a shop, emerged a few moments later, and walked back to her house. Stewart couldn't take his eyes from her basket. Protruding from it was the tapering end of a lengthy loaf of bread. It was her family's weekly ration, and such was their need that the war could wait while she collected it.

The party now back-tracked along the Rue St Remy, crossed the square dominated by the Church of St Remy and turned southwards along the Rue de la Barre. Stewart killed a sniper, and a group of Frenchmen on the corner of the Rue des Baines shouted warnings of approaching Germans. They tried to withdraw but were not quick enough. The enemy patrol caught them in mid street, fired a volley which brought down Private Harris, and forced them to fight a slow, vicious rearguard action back to the cinema.

They reached it safely and, finding Major Harold Lazier there with four sappers, Hill sent Private Liss outside to keep watch while the two officers worked out a plan to blow down the Rue de Sygogne road block. While they were talking an elderly French floorsweeper came in and went to work, sweeping up debris, cleaning out ashtrays, and dusting the seats. He gave no attention to the Canadians, nor did he attempt to speak or interfere. Lazier and Hill had agreed on a plan, when it was discovered that although the sappers carried 60-pound packs of explosives they had forgotten to bring the detonating charges. Private Liss ended the frustrated cursing with a shout: "Jerries – more than I can count."

The combined force prepared for the return dash across the promenade to the Casino. At Lazier's signal they ran, Stewart bringing up the rear and stopping every few yards to turn, fire a burst from his Bren gun, and then chase after the rest. When they landed in the ditch once occupied by Whitaker's group only one man was wounded – and the total cost of a stubbornly persistent 300-yard penetration into Dieppe had cost only one life.

While Hill's party were sight-seeing for more than an hour in the town, Sergeant Hickson, with his eighteen men, attempted to carry out his primary mission, destruction of the telephone exchange. A tank lumbered off the beach over the sea wall and blew a track on the esplanade near the Casino. The tank commander, new to the scene and not daring to lift the lid of his turret for a look, had no way of knowing where enemy fire was coming from – until Whitaker, with his party at a hedge on the Casino side of the promenade, found a solution. Seeing the tank firing wildly, he signalled Private Graham to fire bursts of tracer at the most dangerous enemy gun positions. The tank commander, quick to notice the pattern of tracer bullets moving from one place to another, and to guess the purpose, traversed his 6-pounder at the points indicated by Graham's shooting.

A perceptible lessening in the weight of enemy fire followed, enabling Hickson's group to reach the cinema without loss. They passed through it and penetrated as far as the Church of St Remy, making their way cautiously down the Rue Couronne, then being used by French civilians who made no attempt to take cover.

In the Rue de la Martinière sniper fire became less erratic, more accurate, pinning them against buildings. Machine guns added to their discomfort and it seemed likely they would soon be trapped, unable to move forwards or backwards. They noticed that most of the French civilians in the vicinity wore arms bands with an insignia looking suspiciously like a swastika. Hickson's subsequent report said: "We watched the situation carefully for some time before deciding that these 'civilians' were really collaborators giving away our individual positions to the Germans."

The group wasted no time in clearing the streets. A Bren-gunner aimed low across the St Remy square, sweeping it with a long, sustained burst. The "civilians" scattered, running for cover, the slower ones being bowled over by bullets chopping into legs and feet.

After that the sniper fire grew erratic again and they were able to retreat towards the cinema – but not far. Fifty yards away a German patrol had occupied a house they would have to pass, and the only way to do so safely would be to storm the place.

They rushed the house in a tight bunch, broke down the door, sprayed the hall with tommy guns, threw grenades into rooms, and plunged into the clouds of smoke and dust with bayonets ready. On the second floor, a dozen Germans attacked with their own bayonets as the Canadians came up the stairs.

Blades clashed and when the fight ended every German was dead, every Canadian wounded. Only then could they reach the cinema, cross the esplanade, and stumble through the friendly portals of the Casino. Eighteen men under a sapper sergeant had also penetrated substantially into the town; but there were some two thousand troops clinging to dubious protection on the beaches and being decimated every minute. They stayed in their hollows, behind the walls, in the shelter of derelict tanks and landing-craft, waiting for orders from junior officers who were waiting for orders from senior officers who were waiting for orders by even more senior commanders who were in no position to give orders at all.

Sergeant Pierre Dubuc, of medium height, slimly built with dark, curly hair and slight moustache, landed west of the Casino, ran one hundred yards up the beach to a depression where he took cover, staying there for "a long hour." Enemy fire had quite convinced him that movement in any direction would bring a quick end to his young life. Facing him were two pillboxes set into the sea wall which fired continuously over his hollow into its pebbled rim; moreover, fire which fell, as he was to say later, "like a never-ending hail storm" from the West Headland and the Castle made his decision simple to reach. This son of a Montreal doctor and one of a family of seven children had a powerful, abiding respect for the joys of life. He stayed in his hollow, pressed flat on the stones.

Private N. Daudelin, also of the Fusiliers Mont-Royal and also from Montreal, crawled into the hollow, dragging behind him a self-generating smoke-making machine. The sergeant and the private discussed the immediate danger from the pillboxes, Dubuc insisting that if Daudelin would put up a smokescreen they could use it as cover. Naturally, the private argued that if the sergeant wanted smoke he should damn well make it himself – as whoever made it would have to expose himself. Equally naturally, the sergeant ordered the private to make smoke and Daudelin, bitterly resenting a system which gives sergeants authority over privates, raised himself to his knees and, while contorting his body into a tight ball, cranked the handle of the machine furiously. The astonished Germans in the pillboxes fired, also furiously, splintering the stones about him until a fog bank of smoke hid him from sight.

Daudelin, trembling under the strain and in no mood to take Dubuc's kindly pat of encouragement in the same spirit in which it was made, nevertheless nodded agreement when the sergeant said: "Follow me. We'll crawl up and grenade 'em." Which was precisely what they did – wriggling on their stomachs to the sides of the pillboxes, standing up quickly, and virtually putting their hands through the gun-slits to let the grenades fall inside.

Then it dawned on Dubuc that as a derelict tank some 150 yards away to the right of the Casino had been silent for most of his sojourn in the hollow it must have been abandoned. Beckoning Daudelin to follow, he crossed the intervening expanse of beach, alternately running and crawling, reached the tank, and both men vanished inside. For the next twenty minutes they fired the tank's 6-pounder at enemy guns on the West Headland, stopping only when there was no more ammunition.

At this stage, the private wanted no further part of the sergeant and the pair split up, Dubuc deciding to join a group of Fusiliers Mont-Royal against the western cliff face. But on the way he veered to the sea wall, waved to the group, and they followed him across the Rue Alexandre Dumas, the western extension of the Boulevard Marechal Foch running along the sea front. Dubuc, now accompanied by eleven men, passed between houses on the inland side of the road, turned eastwards through the back gardens towards the Casino, and emerged at the esplanade corner of the Rue de Sygogne.

The Germans had in the meantime opened a gap in the road block to pass through reinforcements for gun positions in the sea-front buildings. For some odd reason it was still open, unguarded. Dubuc's party dashed through and ran southwards down the street until they were brought to a sudden, scattering halt by machine-gun fire from a small municipal garden in the centre of a road junction. Six grenades thrown hastily and wide of the machine gun so disconcerted its three-man crew that when the Canadians charged, the Germans were alive, uninjured, and very frightened.

As Dubuc intended penetrating through to the harbour, where he believed the Royal Marines would be cutting out invasion barges, his small force would be slowed down if prisoners were taken. Sten guns roared, the Germans died, and the twelve Canadians headed at a steady trot to the southeast along Rue Claude Groulard, a long street leading past the main public park to the inner harbour docks: Bassin Duquesne and Bassin du Canada, so named because the harbour had been for centuries the loading port for ships taking freight and French settlers to the New World.

A sniper fired from a schoolhouse window as they passed by the park, hitting one man in his right heel. Dubuc ordered him back to the beach, and for the second time that morning he was sworn at by a private, one who had no intention of being left on his own, a stranger in a hostile town. At the Bassin Duquesne they turned inland to skirt the edge of the docks until reaching the Bassin du Canada where they found two large barges tied up alongside a quay on which a group of gesticulating dockers were gathered. To their amazement, the civilians were arguing with two men, both wearing Canadian army uniform with Fusiliers Mont-Royal badges, lying on the ground, battledress blouses open, sunbathing. Dubuc approached them; the pair smiled while claiming to be members of B Company. None of his party recognized the men; their French had not been taught in Canada but, there being no time for discussion, the matter was tactfully dropped. It seems likely, however, that the two sun worshippers were members of a mysterious attachment to Jubilee who had elected to facilitate their landing by wearing Canadian uniform.

Four of Dubuc's men boarded the two barges while the rest stood guard on the quay, fought a spirited duel with sailors firing from below decks and, when ammunition was all but expended, the party withdrew to look for cover until the Marines appeared. Dubuc has since said: "Just then fifteen Germans rushed at us from three sides. As we had no ammunition left for the automatic weapons and little enough for the rifles, we surrendered, throwing down the weapons and raising our hands. We were taken into a courtyard behind a house where the Germans shouted orders we couldn't understand."

Dubuc smiled apologetically, and an obviously exasperated German burst out in English: "Undress or we shoot." The captives needed time in which to search feverishly for a way to escape. The well-known political conflict between Quebec and the rest of Canada came to their rescue. Dubuc, speaking French, explained that as French Canadians they could never accept an order given offensively in English. Why, to do so would be an unforgivable sin against their national pride. The Germans, thoroughly confused, shouted among themselves until one eventually confronted Dubuc to say curtly, in French: "Undress."

The party stripped down to their underwear and were told to stand with faces to a wall, their hands raised and placed against it. All but one of the Germans then departed taking the clothes and equipment with them. Dubuc turned his head until he could see which of their captors had been left in charge and quick hope welled up inside him. The guard was a boy, probably no more than seventeen years old. Using limited German, Dubuc asked politely:

"Do you speak English or French?"

"English a bit, I speak."

"It's a rotten war. I suppose you're just as hot and thirsty as we are. How about a drink of water?"

The German swung round automatically to see if there was an outside garden tap, and the Canadians sprang upon him. He was young but he could kill, probably had done so already that morning. Someone lifted a short length of iron piping, and the boy died, his head cleaved neatly in half.

The group started running, each man for himself, back to the beach more than half a mile away. Dubuc lost contact with the others almost immediately as he scampered down one street after another, heedless of astonished stares from Frenchmen, of squeals from French girls, and of the trail of merriment he left in his wake. Turning one corner he sped into a German patrol, swerved round them, his heart pounding with anticipation of the blow of bullets whipping into his back. However, the sight of an unarmed man galloping through the town in his underwear convulsed the Germans no less than the French. He may have been a lodger surprised by a jealous husband, and their catcalls followed him as he vanished into another street, legs churning mightily, hurtling him across the cobblestones.

Guided now by flames from the burning tobacco factory, he headed for the promenade, changed course quickly to avoid a heavily guarded road block, entered a house through a side window, emerged from the front door onto the esplanade, and swung westwards towards the Casino.

There was a slight pause in the gun duel between Canadians in the Casino and Germans in the sea-front buildings, as the sweating, light-skinned figure in white shorts and vest sprinted across their lines of fire. Once he was clear and over the sea wall to the beach, the opposing forces shook off an eerie, light-headed feeling of having witnessed something inexplicably peculiar, and resumed firing at each other.

Dubuc lay panting on the stones of the beach, nursing the ache in his side and dripping wet from the exertion of his run. A voice said: "Who are you?" He looked up into the grim, smoke-blackened face of an RHLI sergeant and weakly replied: "Sergeant Dubuc, Fusiliers Mont-Royal."

"Then where the hell have you been out of uniform."

IV

Roberts and Hughes-Hallett were frustrated in their control of the battle by two elements: disrupted and suspect communications, and smoke – the endless smoke obscuring the beach from the view of all aboard Calpe. *While there was no beach to see, Roberts dared not leave his operations cabin; Hughes-Hallett preferred to be on the bridge anyway.* Calpe *was being navigated so close inshore that, had it not been for the smoke, control would have been comparatively simple. As it was, troops fired smoke bombs from mortars, generated smoke from machines, threw smoke grenades and canisters; ships laid smoke-screens to protect themselves from enemy batteries, laid down more screens to protect the landing-craft, fired smoke shells to neutralize the guns on the headlands; aircraft laid smoke along the edge of the sea, over the sea-front buildings and also on the headlands. To all this was added smoke from burning houses, the tobacco factory, and the blazing tank landing-craft stranded on the beach.*

The battlefield was a cauldron, the beaches sealed off by the tall flanking cliffs, the sea, and the mile-long line of buildings comprising an impregnable rampart guarding the town. Inside the narrow stretch of beach and promenade confined by these barriers the cauldron seethed, simmering with the fire, smoke, and white heat of death, destruction, and pain.

At 6:30 a.m. Commander Ryder had transferred from *Locust* to *Calpe* to inform the Force Commanders that attempts to lead the *chasseurs* carrying the Royal Marine cutting-out force into the harbour had been frustrated by heavy barrages from the East Headland. *Locust* had been severely damaged, and it was his considered opinion that neither *Locust* nor the *chasseurs* would survive another attempt.

Hughes-Hallett knew that if the man who had achieved so much at

St Nazaire said entry into the harbour was impossible, then there was little to be gained by persisting with the mission. Accordingly, he had offered the Royal Marine Commando to Roberts as an additional reserve unit. Roberts had accepted, and at his request the Marines had been transferred to landing-craft and were now awaiting orders to plunge into the battle. Their commander, Lieutenant-Colonel J. P. Phillips, being unaware of the slaughter inside the cauldron, shared the optimism with which Menard had vanished behind the smoke to reinforce Red Beach.

Despite the lack of hard news, and with what there was of it likely to have originated with the enemy – the picture as seen from *Calpe* was encouraging. A series of reports between 7:00 and 8:30 a.m. gave Roberts the impression that the Essex Scottish were across the esplanade into the sea-front buildings; that the RHLI had secured White Beach and taken the Casino; and that the tanks were off the beach, operating along the promenade.

During this period, Lieutenant-Commander Goulding reported aboard *Calpe* to paint a bright picture of events at Puits, on the strength of which Roberts cancelled his earlier orders, thereby switching the Royals to Red Beach, and told Uxbridge there was no further need for a planned air strike against the East Headland. It seemed possible that the Royals were already there in contact with the enemy.

These factors constituted an added reason for not exploiting the success at Pourville – which Roberts still knew nothing about – as it was unlikely that reinforcing the South Sasks could have much effect on the battle at Dieppe. There was insufficient time remaining for a reserve force to leave the boat pool, reach Pourville, land, and then fight back into Dieppe. Such a course might have been valid were it a two-tide operation and had the Force Commanders known what was happening ashore.

The Fusiliers Mont-Royal had given additional weight to the push off Red Beach, and it seemed logical to Roberts that the assault should then develop into a two-pronged thrust by giving the RHLI extra help on White Beach. At 7:35 a.m. a report from Major Rolfe's radio station in his derelict scout car said a hole had been punched across the esplanade into the town near the Casino, through which Brigadier Southam had ordered the tanks.

In fact, Southam had been informed by a runner from Labatt's headquarters that troops were entering the town via a cinema on the sea front. He had interpreted this message as meaning that a way into town had been opened and had instructed Rolfe to order all tanks through the gap. Southam made no effort to reach the Casino to find out for himself how wide the gap really was, nor did he keep Roberts informed about the progress of the tanks thereafter. He paced the beach, indifferent to danger, encouraging the wounded and, according to Rolfe, this unwittingly exaggerated report was one of the only two occasions that morning on which Southam spoke personally to *Calpe*.

It was the first report Roberts had received from so reliable a source as one of his two brigadiers. Hope for success bounded when the other, Sherwood Lett, reported at 8:00 a.m.: "We are going in with Johnny to land on White Beach." To the Force Commanders this implied that the tanks must have made sufficient progress – probably through Southam's alleged gap – to warrant Andrews assuming personal command of their operations ashore. There was no reason, therefore, to doubt the credibility of a further message which reached *Calpe* at 8:17: "White Beach under firm control."

Roberts decided to commit the Royal Marines on White Beach. Once again, it was a textbook decision based upon the most reliable intelligence available and therefore conforming to all the "rules and principles of the art." To the best of his knowledge and ability he was reinforcing penetrations, not hold-ups.

Enemy wireless activity on the air was so effective that *Calpe* had considerable difficulty in detecting genuine messages from false. For instance, *Calpe*'s signal log for this period shows that the only four reports purporting to come from the Fusiliers Mont-Royal were suspected of being bogus, and all attempts to challenge the senders resulted in lines going dead.

Communications were failing miserably. Information from battalions was never more than fragmentary and too often non-existent. Junior officers ashore were reluctant to give Roberts too pessimistic an assessment, either because they were unsure themselves or because the position might change radically leaving them forever on record as having admitted defeat too early.

The extent to which the Force Commanders had been misled into believing that success existed where there was only a desperate bid for survival was later revealed by Captain P. W. C. Hellings of the Royal Marine Commando who said: ". . . Commander Ryder reported that Red and White beaches were clear of opposition, and the General wished the Marines to go in . . ."

Ryder, too, had been infected by the confidence pervading *Calpe*.

The assault boats carrying the Marines formed up some five miles off the West Headland and headed in towards the main beach, with Free French *chasseurs* on either beam to give fire support at touchdown. The sun glowed into their eyes, smoke drifted about them, shells threw up columns of water between them – yet there was no hesitant swerving nor break in formation. Two gun boats altered course to intercept the starboard column, one of them signalling: "May we join your shoot? Game is scarce on our beat." Of the ten assault boats which began the run-in nine were left at two miles to go, eight at one mile, and seven at three hundred yards. Lieutenant M. Buist, commander of the *chasseurs*, was to say:

"I realized that this landing was to be a sea parallel to the Charge of the Light Brigade. There was a barrage coming from the East Cliff, another from the West Cliff, and a wall of machine-gun fire from houses along the promenade, which showed only too well that White Beach was under very heavy attack indeed. Added to which there was a blazing LCT on the beach, another abandoned alongside it, and shells were bursting ahead of us. . . . I shouted to Colonel Phillips to ask what he thought about going on; but I doubt that he heard me. Anyway he merely waved his arms and grinned to show that he meant to land at all costs."

This incredibly obstinate little force, manned by sailors who had already made more than one trip into the beaches, one crew after another being shot to pieces, swept through the bank of smoke and rode into the sunlight again to touch down at the edge of the inferno. Phillips, shaken and aghast at what lay starkly bared before them, climbed to the bows of his landing-craft, casually pulling on a pair of immaculate white gloves so that his hands could be all the more clearly seen. Then he turned his back to the enemy fire, raised his hands, and waved the boats back into the smoke. He was shouting: "For God's sake go back . . . ," and those who were beyond range of his voice could hardly fail to understand the motions of his white-gloved hands. His intention was as clear to the men in the boats following astern – as it was to the enemy.

Streams of tracers concentrated on the surf to cut down the assault, lifted to converge upon that tall figure, the lazily floating tracers clawing the life from a man who in that single brief moment died to save the majority of his Commando. Five boats, torn and mangled by the relentless enemy fire, turned away from the beach to re-enter the smoke; for the remaining two it was too late. They touched down, but of the few Marines who charged up the beach with the image of their commander's last gesture seared vividly into their minds, only a handful reached the shelter of a helpless tank. Others died on the ramps, the scene of it so brutal that Lieutenant Buist continued: "When last seen, Colonel Phillips was standing up in his landing-craft . . . with the rest of his headquarters platoon dead in the boat . . . a few men had managed to get ashore and were seen sheltering under the lees of a burnt-out tank."

As Buist turned his own *chasseur* away, a lone tank landing-craft sailed in through the smoke to compound the tragedy, to bring the saga of LCT 8 to a dreadful climax.

V

When Major Rolfe discovered that despite his scout car's nose dive into the pebbles he could still use his wireless equipment, his first action had been to contact LCT 8 carrying Andrews, Sherwood Lett, his staff, and Lieutenant-Colonel J. P. Parks-Smith, a Royal Marine observer from Combined Operations. Extracts from Rolfe's signals diary trace the implacable advance of the events which followed:

TIME	TO	FROM	MESSAGE
0610	JOHNNY (Lt-Col Andrews)	HUNTER (Maj Rolfe)	Have landed on WHITE [Beach] with 10 [Tp 10 Lieut Bennett]. Craft hit badly on way in. Troop 10 manœuvring to right and whole beach under heavy fire from WEST cliffs and promenade. My vehicle bogged in shale. Situation generally confused, over.
	HUNTER	JOHNNY	OK. Keep me informed of progress. Let me know when you think I should land, over.
	JOHNNY	HUNTER	HUNTER OK, off.
0630	JOHNNY	CHARLIE (Maj Page)	My tank track knocked off through gap in sea wall. Tank Tps continue manœuvre on

TIME	TO	FROM	MESSAGE
			main beach. Very heavy opposition, over.
			[No answer heard from JOHNNY]
0635	CHARLIE (Maj Page)	HUNTER	Your troops using main frequency for internal tank communications. Keep main frequency clear as possible. Keep calm, out.
	HUNTER	Various tps	OK out, OK out etc.
0643	JOHNNY	HUNTER	Have made contact with BILL [Brig SOUTHAM] on WHITE [Beach]. His communications destroyed by tank running over baby carriage [a cart on which wireless sets were mounted]. Have agreed cover his frequencies and will come back to this net from time to time, over.
	HUNTER	JOHNNY	OK. Our craft hit several times and we have lost some steerage. Is it worthwhile me coming ashore, over.
	JOHNNY	HUNTER	Will give you reply in about 15 minutes. Now switching to BILL frequency to get situation reports, out.
0812	JOHNNY	HUNTER	Situation here very confused as are reports from BILL outstations [battalions]. Very heavy opposition from all directions particularly from WEST cliffs and damage high. Tank actions appear uncoordinated. Suggest you come in, over.

TIME	TO	FROM	MESSAGE
	HUNTER	JOHNNY	OK, on our way, out.
0835	HUNTER	JOHNNY	About to beach. Be seeing you, cheerio.
0838	All Stations JOHNNY	HUNTER	JOHNNY off in deep water. Crew out on turret and appear OK, out.

Rolfe, reporting from a distance, had seen only the middle of the drama. Sherwood Lett, not much better informed of events on the beaches than Roberts, decided to go ashore with Andrews. As LCT 8 approached the beach, the first hit killed two of his staff, one being Captain Insinger whose refinements in the art of making prisoners talk had made the infantry wince. The second killed Colonel Parks-Smith of Combined Operations, and the toll of life thereafter mounted with dreadful persistence as shells and mortar bombs exploded in the landing-craft at the rate of one a minute.

At touchdown Andrews was in his tank, revved up and ready to move out, when a shell hit the ten-foot-high ramp, breaking the chains. It crashed down through the water, the top of it ramming into the sand beneath the boat which came to a shuddering stop in deep water twenty yards from the beach. Andrews, thinking the fall of the ramp meant that the boat was beached, drove off, and drowned the tank. The crew, including Corporal T. L. Carnie, baled out through the turret lid, as Rolfe had seen, and swam for shore. Carnie last saw his colonel wading waist-deep towards the surf; another member of the crew saw his body floating where the waves roll up and unfurl. Snipers had laid their fire upon Johnny Andrews with such terrible accuracy that the narrow, shifting seas of the English Channel are now his tomb.

The captain, officers, and all but one of the crew of LCT 8 were killed, while the boat rode as if at anchor with the upper rim of the ramp stuck in the sand ten feet beneath it. An explosion in the engine room blew the engineer, sole survivor of the crew, out through a gaping hole in the ship's side. Garneau, not knowing anything about marine engines, rushed below and pulled any lever he could find until finally the engines started up. He pulled more levers and was rewarded by a shout from the wheelhouse: "Your doin' fine, sir. We're movin' astern." It was Sergeant T. J. Badlan of the Marines, now an impromptu helmsman.

When Garneau returned to the main deck, Sherwood Lett was lying on a stretcher, severely wounded, but still trying to reach Roberts by radio-telephone to give him a further situation report. An assault boat pulled alongside at speed, brushed against the helpless LCT, and a dripping wet figure leapt aboard. It was the engineer who, having been knocked senseless by the blast of the explosion, had been quickly revived by his involuntary ducking and had attracted the attention of the boat.

LCT 8 now had a man at the wheel and a man in the engine room. Otherwise she was littered with more than forty soldiers and sailors dead or wounded. As they crept back into the protection of the smoke, Garneau manned an anti-aircraft pom-pom, depressed it, and fired a last angry burst at the West Headland. Sherwood Lett has since told me: "We were eventually taken in tow for the return trip to England. I contacted Bob Labatt's headquarters ashore and instructed him to take command of the brigade. There was, after all, little more that I could do. We were sitting ducks in the LCT for thirty-two direct hits. All naval personnel were hit. A number of the brigade personnel were killed; others, including myself, were wounded."

The landing of the last reserves had failed. Aboard Calpe, *Roberts listened to the terse account of a Royal Marine officer and could scarcely believe the situation ashore could be so bad. Throughout all ranks in* Calpe *there was bewilderment at the sudden turn of events, shock at the enormity of the mistakes and the misjudgements now so starkly apparent. Roberts cancelled the landing of the last wave of tanks and decided to go ashore himself.*

Alongside and about to cast off was a boat carrying Lieutenant-Commander Earl Beatty, commanding the tank landing-craft squadron.

Roberts shouted: "Wait. I want you to take me ashore."

"Sorry, sir," replied Beatty. "Can't do it without orders from the Naval Commander. And I wouldn't advise that you go anyway."

Roberts recognized the truth in the naval officer's advice. Nothing could be gained at this stage by his presence on the beaches and there was still the difficult withdrawal to be undertaken. In addition, like it or not, he was by then the only military officer in the Allied forces who had commanded a major assault against Fortress Europe. The knowledge and experience gained would be invaluable to the invasion planners. He returned to his control cabin.

Lessons had been learned, were still being learned, and more would

unfold during the withdrawal. But as far as Hughes-Hallett was con-
cerned the naval objectives had been already achieved. The Navy had
brought the Army across the Channel, landed the assault troops at the
right places at approximately the right times, and had maintained a
huge fleet off the enemy coast for five hours. In the air, Leigh-Mallory
had the satisfaction of knowing the great battle for the skies in which
he hoped to crush the power of the Luftwaffe in the West was taking
shape. The Army could console itself that if the various assaults had
succeeded with the smoothness of a knife passing through butter,
nothing would have been learned about the problems of invasion.

So pale a truth to emerge from such a livid ordeal!

The three infantry battalions and the Calgary Tanks were now
besieged upon the beaches, struggling to maintain their precarious
foothold in France until the boats came in to take them off. Labatt had
inherited a non-existent command from Sherwood Lett: no contact
with the Royal Regiment at Puits, the Essex Scottish firmly impaled
upon the raking fire from the East Cliff, and his own RHLI steadily
disintegrating between the Casino and the West Headland. Few of his
headquarters company were left.

There was a momentarily satisfying diversion when Sergeant-Major
Harris focused binoculars on the West Headland and shouted in surprise: "By God, sir. Take a look at that." Labatt looked through his own
glasses to see a group of high-ranking German officers, some in white
summer uniforms, standing and drinking; he could see glasses in their
hands. When telling me of the incident, he said: "From the glitter I
judged it included pretty high-priced help. They were standing right
out in the open, obviously enjoying the fun. Some were smoking cigars.
I switched two Brens onto them. Both guns opened fire at the same
time and the group scattered in split seconds. We must have hit some of
them. Anyway they never came back. Their carefree, holiday attitude,
however, confirmed my fears that the South Sasks had not been able
to approach the West Cliff from the west."

These German officers were, in fact, the Commander of the 10th
Panzer Division and his staff, who had arrived in advance of the
armoured column to watch the progress of the battle and decide, in
co-operation with General Haase, where the heavy tanks could be most
usefully employed. According to Haase's war diary, it had already
been decided – around 9:00 a.m. – that the situation in Dieppe was
under control and that the 10th Panzers would be committed only in
the event of a breakthrough from Pourville. This reveals in retrospect

that an even worse massacre might have resulted had Roberts sent the Fusiliers Mont-Royal through Pourville.

Accompanying the German officers were the news correspondents summoned from the all-night dance at the *Luftwaffe*'s women's auxiliary base. They had not had time to change, and the white uniforms Labatt had seen were their formal white evening-dress tunics.

If the correspondents enjoyed watching the battle from their privileged vantage point, the *Luftwaffe* pilots also at the dance were not so pleased at their abrupt recall from leave. One bailed out of his burning fighter, landed in the sea near *Calpe*, and was picked up. He arrived on the bridge bristling with righteous indignation. "Look at the time, sir," he complained reproachfully to Hughes-Hallett. "It is not quite nine o'clock and my leave was not supposed to be over until noon today."

If the remnants of the forces ashore were not to be annihilated it was time to order Vanquish, code name for the withdrawal. Most suitable time for the landing-craft would be half-tide which, as the tide had now turned and would come into the halfway level at 10:30, would also give time for the troops to prepare for embarkation and the RAF time to organize overwhelming air cover.

Hughes-Hallett advised Roberts to issue the order for the withdrawal to begin at 10:30 a.m. – in fact, the sooner the better. The Force Commanders, at this decisive moment, were strikingly dissimilar: Roberts, hunched jacketless in his chair, smoking incessantly and a light sweat dampening his khaki shirt; Hughes-Hallett, somehow contriving to appear coolly immaculate despite the heat of the day and the exertions of command.

Roberts agreed with his naval colleague, reluctantly because he still knew little of the situation ashore, but readily because he knew that any delay could result only in further loss of life. He wished, however, that more information were available concerning the whereabouts of the Fusiliers Mont-Royal. Just then a loudspeaker crackled alive and a voice was faintly heard to say: "Joe in severe difficulties." There was no authentic signature, and even while efforts were being made to trace the source another report came in on a different wave length saying: "Joe is surrendered." As before, there was no indication of the sender and both messages were entered into the Intelligence log as being possibly bogus.

Roberts waited no longer; the order "Vanquish at 1030" was issued shortly after 9 o'clock.

By this time *Calpe* was in touch with only two shore signals stations, both of them wrecked scout cars. One was being used by Major Rolfe, the other by the Principal Military Landing Officer, Brian McCool, but only sporadically as he had to run a gauntlet of fire to reach it each time he reported to *Calpe*. He was to say of his difficulty: "We had most of our party blown up within three minutes of landing, and whenever we collected another half-dozen or so the same thing happened. Finally we established contact from a derelict scout car but had to face intensive fire to reach it. They drew claret out of me five times but nothing more than skin deep. . . . By the way I was grateful to the Navy for a fast reply to one of my urgent appeals. . . . They undoubtedly saved our lives. . . . A sniper had been picking us off each in turn. . . ."

The sniper, firing from the end of a harbour mole, had so exasperated McCool that he had dashed to the scout car on Red Beach with bullets kicking up the pebbles at his heels, grabbed the radio-telephone, and shouted: "Blow hell out of pillboxes at end of pier east of Red Beach." The message had been received by Churchill Mann, aboard *Fernie*, who passed on the request to *Locust*, and Ryder had sailed in to effectively oblige.

Confusion followed the order to withdraw when Air Commodore Cole, the Air Force Commander's representative on the raid, was informed of the decision to Vanquish at 10:30 a.m. and promptly informed Roberts that the timetable would not permit the RAF to provide an adequate air umbrella until 11 o'clock. He pointed out that this was the earliest time contemplated in the military plan and the air arrangements had been made accordingly. There was, in his view, insufficient time remaining to make drastic alterations in these arrangements and he advised that Roberts should adhere to the original schedule. The Dunkirk evacuation two years before loomed frighteningly into sharp focus. Then, as now, troops were gathered on beaches waiting for boats and at the mercy of the Luftwaffe. Roberts wanted no repetition of this predicament at Dieppe. Nor was he certain that the Vanquish order would reach all units ashore by 10:30, so Cole's advice merely contributed to his decision to issue a second order changing the evacuation time to 11:00 a.m. Although the correction reached most units, there were some that did not get it – with the result that at Pourville the western slopes of the Scie valley were relinquished by the South Saskatchewans long before it was necessary.

While Vanquish filtered from Calpe and Fernie to the beaches, to the few remaining radio-telephone sets and from these to the independent companies, platoons, and sections, General Haase reinforced his positions on the headlands with mobile gun batteries. The volume

*of that incredibly concentrated crossfire on the wide mile of beach
and esplanade intensified unbearably, forcing those already lying flat
to wriggle even deeper into the shale, reducing the life span of any
who moved perceptibly to mere seconds.*

Dan Doheny and Whitaker, still firing from behind the hedge at the
rear of the Casino, were immensely impressed when three tanks
waddled towards them along the esplanade. They pointed frantically
at the buildings opposite them and, ignoring the tattoo of bullets
striking the turret, Lieutenant Edwin Bennett lifted the lid of the leading tank, Bellicose, to wave cheerful understanding. With Beefy and
Bloody in company he wheeled towards the enemy positions in the
front gardens of the buildings and had the satisfaction of seeing Germans "pour out from everywhere running like hell for the buildings."
The tank gunners opened fire, dropping enemy soldiers in droves. One
German dodged round the tanks and ran hard down the promenade
with Bellicose giving chase. There was little chance of the soldier,
weighed down by heavy uniform and equipment, outrunning the
cumbersome tank, which Bennett manœuvred after him with the skill
and glee of a racing driver. The fleeing German stumbled and fell,
looked up in helpless horror at his clanking pursuer and died under the
tracks – not flattened, just mangled.

Inside Bellicose, Bennett acknowledged a signal from Rolfe on the
beach – "Vanquish 1100."

Doheny and Whitaker, although fascinated by the spectacle, were
also relieved when the tanks withdrew to the beach to cover the
evacuation. Their presence had brought down heavy artillery fire
behind the Casino, and life had became distinctly uncomfortable by
the time a runner arrived from Labatt's beach headquarters with the
order – "Vanquish 1100."

At 11.00 a.m. Doheny, Whitaker, Lazier, Currie, Hill, Hickson,
Dumais, and 150 others were bunched inside the Casino ready for
the last crossing of the beach. With them were twenty-three German
prisoners, unbound and acting as stretcher-bearers.

On the western fringe of White Beach, hard against the face of the
West Headland, nearly two hundred Fusiliers Mont-Royal were unable
to move, pinned there under bombardment from Germans who were
standing on the cliff edge above, holding grenades in their outstretched
hands and letting them fall. The senior officer, Sarto Marchand, was
searching for a way to reach the end of the sea wall and utterly unaware that farther west of his strip of tidal beach a narrow track led

down from the top of the headland. A German patrol climbed undetected down the track, and the Fusiliers Mont-Royal were startled by
a series of barked commands behind them. They swung about, stared
disbelievingly into the muzzles of a dozen automatic weapons, and
Marchand slowly lifted his hands. One small party under Lieutenant
A. A. Masson had actually reached the wall nearby and were cutting
through the wire above it when, hearing a commotion behind them,
they looked back to see the cause. A long column of their comrades
was shuffling towards them, hands raised, and in reply to Masson's
unspoken question, Marchand called out: "Further resistance is impossible, André. Better surrender now."

Masson obeyed, and the Germans escorted this surviving remnant of
the Fusiliers Mont-Royal back along the beach to the track leading
up the cliffs. The first of the Canadians had surrendered, at 10:30 a.m.,
without ever receiving the order to "Vanquish." Masson, among those
bringing up the rear of the column, glanced over his shoulder for a last
lingering look at the beach; he saw only the bodies of the dead, the
bodies of the living, and there was no distinguishing between them.
Nothing and no one moved along the broad yellow blade of hateful
shale.

The French Canadians left their dead crumpled sadly on and amid
the slippery, slime-covered rocks, bodies of men who so shortly before
had pulsated with eager, finely tempered young life. They, who hoped
for honour and glory, were spared in death the sullen, craven image
of surrender. The merciful sea came in to lap curiously about them,
to cover the forlorn scene with its sparkling blueness, to embrace the
dead, and disperse them along its flowing currents. Among the bodies
were those of Captain Roy Dillon who, fatally wounded and blinded
in both eyes, encouraged the wounded around him until the time came
for him to die; and of the stowaway, Major Savoy, who had been
considered too old to fight, yet had died fighting.

On Red Beach, the Essex Scottish, cut down and sliced apart with
nearly four hundred casualties, kept watch across the wall in five-
minute shifts to forestall an enemy assault across the promenade.
During one five-minute tour, Private J. Maier glimpsed a sniper firing
with devastating accuracy from the tower on the roof of the Casino,
some five hundred yards to his right. All morning this particular sniper
had been singling out officers, NCO's and signalmen for special attention, defying detection himself by using smokeless, flashless ammunition. Maier caught the flash of sun on metal as a bullet threw pebbles
into his face. Regardless of personal danger he stood upright, took

careful aim with a heavy anti-tank rifle, and fired two rounds – sufficient to demolish both tower and sniper.

Jasperson, having organized the wall defences, moved along it giving morphine to the wounded, encouragement to the crying and the praying. Men lay on the beach, white-faced and damp with tears or sweat or both, gazing blankly upwards at the fighters twisting and turning in battle, the formations of bombers, some trailing smoke, falling and shedding wings, as parachutes opened and crews bailed out. One German pilot landing on the beach quickly crawled to the shelter of the wall and stared at the dirty, grim-faced Jasperson with the expectancy of death.

Anger and hate drained from the big Windsor lawyer as he gazed into his enemy's eyes, seeing only a very young, very frightened boy, barely twenty-one, for whom he could feel only compassion. A sergeant tied the pilot's hands behind his back – not in the Insinger fashion – lit a cigarette and placed it in his mouth. The German's shadowy smile of gratitude was a flickering of the lips, the fear remaining in his eyes.

Jasperson's diary records: "We were all afraid. We had been made afraid by the sight of the Fusiliers Mont-Royal coming in to land. They came through the haze like some proud regatta, the boats in line abreast. The firing seemed to stop, and a sergeant said to me: 'My God, they're pretty.' It was as though the Germans felt the same way and had paused to enjoy a moment of sanity in insane, inhuman surroundings. Then the roll of corrugated thunder crashed out again. Launches were demolished into flying wreckage; screams and shouts pierced our ears. Bullets whipped up as many tiny spurts of water as a hail storm, black dots bobbed where the boats had been and then they too were gone. . . ."

At another section of the wall, Lieutenant Jack Prince of Windsor, heard an anguished cry and a moaned "For God's sake, someone surrender." Prince whirled around, his face livid. "No one surrenders, you hear me," he shouted.

Jasperson was to describe those hours on Red Beach in a letter from prison camp to his London banker which said:

> Mortar and shell splinters were whistling all around me . . . but none got me. The most I suffered was periodic showers of stone on my tin hat and body which did me no harm. The experience was quite harrowing and how I was missed God only knows. The scene of it all will be imprinted on my mind for ever . . . personal

acts of bravery in this show are beyond words. I saw no one jittery and all fought splendidly. . . . Major Willis was undoubtedly outstanding. Badly wounded in chest, arms and head he kept on directing his company's fire. . . . Lieutenant Green, with a foot shot off, had it bound up and continued to hobble on leading his platoon when a second mortar bomb finished him. . . ."

Jasperson was attempting to reach *Fernie* with a request that boats be sent to evacuate the wounded when a runner arrived from Labatt's headquarters, a remarkable achievement considering it was nearly half a mile away, to report – "Vanquish 1100."

Throughout the morning Acting Brigadier Labatt's plan had been to send men through the Casino into the town. Major Waldron led one group towards it, reached a wire barricade, cut through it, and found himself alone. His entire party were dead. He ran on alone, crouched with pistol drawn, hurling shrill wild curses at the enemy. Labatt saw him vanish into the smoke lying over the beach and recorded in his diary: "He was a happy warrior."

Labatt was the only unwounded officer at his headquarters, apart from three German pilots who, having been shot down, had paddled ashore in their inflatable rubber dinghies. They cowered near him, gripping the pebbles and miserably awaiting the shot in the back of the head they had been told to expect.

Wounded men, driven by surging instincts of self-preservation, had spent hours inching their way across the beach to the seaward side of a large tank landing-craft left stranded by the ebb of the tide. Hundreds were gathered there, protected by the towering steel hull and tended by doctors, medical orderlies, and Padre John Foote, raider by choice, who was giving more than spiritual help to his flock that day. Heedless of the enemy, careless of his own safety, he walked among them, easing the final moments of dying, giving hope to those pushed to the brink of insanity by sheer pain and despair.

At sea, anti-aircraft gunners were firing at any aircraft flying within their range. Captains of landing-craft, destroyers, and gun boats were roaring hoarse warnings to cease firing on friendly planes, always in vain. Aboard *Fernie*, General Truscott watched a fighter fly in low, at eye level, and was startled when the destroyer's pom-poms barked into wicked action, forcing the aircraft to turn laboriously away, and in doing so reveal itself to be a wounded Spitfire limping home. Before the day was over, six British aircraft would be shot down by a British fleet, in which some of the anti-aircraft gunners were members of the Toronto Scottish. They manned the Vickers guns on the tank landing-craft, and such was their eagerness to fire that their commander, Lieutenant-Colonel Guy Gostling, said later:

"I was standing beneath the bridge in LCT 16 when two Bostons escorted by Spitfires flew very low over us. The naval gunner on deck opened up followed by several of our own machine guns. I dashed up the bridge and asked the first officer why the goddam gunner was firing upon our aircraft. His answer was non-committal, so I then dashed over to the gunner and asked him what he was firing at, and he replied: 'At a Focke Wulf torpedo bomber.' The planes were then out of range and the firing stopped. We were recompensed for our mistakes by having the escort of Spitfires spray us liberally with machine-gun fire."

Truscott witnessed this exasperating cameo from the deck of the nearby *Fernie*, and as he started for the operations cabin a sudden crash threw him off balance. When a nut torn from the superstructure by a heavy artillery shell hit his boot he picked it up as a souvenir. Farther aft where the shell had burst, sixteen men were dead or wounded.

He reached the operations cabin just as the order to "Vanquish 1100" was followed by requests relayed to Uxbridge for extra smoke and fighter cover during the critical evacuation period. Churchill Mann turned to his American guest and said, "General, I'm afraid this operation will go down as one of the great failures of history."

At 10:22 a.m., Hughes-Hallett ordered in the fleet; the withdrawal, most difficult operation of the day, one that is now described as seldom equalled in the history of war, began.

The assault landing-craft were divided into two groups: a western force under Lieutenant-Commander Dathan for White Beach, an eastern force under Commander McClintock for Red Beach. Once filled, each craft would return to a destroyer or LCT, transfer troops, and then return for another load. Smoke again hid the beaches but covered the approach, to the extent that the troops ashore could not see the fleet coming in. Rolfe, convinced by all that he had seen and heard by signal that the enemy knew withdrawal was imminent, suggested to Southam that the full strength of fire-power from the headlands might be unleashed against the boats to prevent evacuation. Throughout the morning he had been scrupulously careful to sign all his reports to *Calpe* or *Fernie* with the Brigadier's code name, Bill. When Southam appeared unconcerned by his warning, he called up *Fernie* at 10:44 a.m. to report: "Enemy along headlands waiting for Vanquish." Twenty minutes later, at Southam's request, he asked

Fernie: "When will boats arrive?" In reply he was told that "all available boats are on way and smoke is being laid."

At 11:10 a.m. a formation of Bostons laid dense smokescreens on the headlands and along the waterfront, which also served to warn the Germans that the boats were approaching. The weight of heavy artillery and mortar bombardment shifted from the beaches to the edge of the sea, the guns firing along pre-fixed lines into the smoke, laying a barrage through which the boats would have to pass to reach touchdown.

It was 11:20 when Rolfe sighted the first assault boats racing in out of the smoke and he immediately reported to *Fernie*: "Boats coming in under intense fire. Want lots of support. They cannot get in. Much smoke and air support wanted." Aboard *Calpe*, a signals breakdown left Ham Roberts with no direct contact with Rolfe, but he could listen in on the conversations between the beach and *Fernie*. At 11:35 he heard Rolfe say without a trace of anxiety evident in his voice: "You'd better rush things. It's getting a bit hot hereabouts. Boats are being hit and sinking. Bill doesn't think it possible to evacuate unless you get everything available in here."

He sounded a little more concerned three minutes later when he came back on the air to say: "Boats are being hit because there's no support. High ground to east and west *must* be bombed or shelled."

Roberts was sending one appeal after another to Uxbridge for immediate air bombardment of the headlands; Hughes-Hallett had taken in five destroyers as close to the smokescreens as possible. Hurricane bombers were on their way but would not be able to reach their targets before noon; and the destroyers, blinded by smoke, were unable to approach closer without running aground.

Another report from Rolfe, also signed "Bill," hinted strongly at the depth of the tragedy taking place on the beaches. Distinctly angry, he told *Fernie*: "Request lots of support. Enemy engaging craft. Need smoke and all support possible for assault craft." Then in a noticeably happier tone, he added: "We're dropping quite a few Boche planes ourselves."

Brian McCool reached the scout car he had been using to make contact with force headquarters during the morning and reported: "Situation here no damn good. Need LCA's, LCS's, LCT's. Lots of smoke and Leigh-Mallory [meaning air bombardment]."

The Hurricanes arrived over the headlands at midday, and a momentary easing of enemy fire allowed several landing-craft to with-

draw. Eleven minutes later, McCool reported: "Very few personnel
have been evacuated. 1000 is maximum."

The final tense moments of a drama the Force Commanders could not
see reached *Calpe* via *Fernie* in a series of brief, highly charged messages
from Rolfe, all couched in the matter-of-fact voice which for so long
had been the only continuous and reliable link between ships and
shore. . . .

1243   White Beach not good, Red not so bad because of fewer
       people there. . . .

1301   Bombard buildings and pillboxes along promenade. Enemy
       closing in.

1305   Give us quick support. Enemy closing in on beach. Hurry
       it up please.

1307   We are evacuating. [Rolfe had by then decided to blow up
       his equipment.]

1308   There seems to be a mass surrender of our troops to the
       Germans on the beach. Our people here have surrendered.

*Rolfe's casual tones, however, could not hide from Roberts and
Hughes-Hallett the desperate plight of the troops, the suffering of the
landing-craft crews, and the implacable advance of disaster under the
sun of high noon. These could be visualized against the vicious, crackling roar of continuous gunfire. What could not be imagined was the
immense confusion in which some boats which should have been at
Red Beach were actually bringing off South Sasks on Green Beach,
others were mistakenly heading back to England, and those that
reached the beaches were being swamped and capsized by a wild,
uncontrollable rush of soldiers. The prime cause of this extraordinary
muddle was a word which is often more filled with meaning than any
other in the English language – the little word "if."*

VI

When the assault boats were organized for their respective beaches,
Commander McClintock was still under the impression that withdrawal would begin at 10:30 a.m. as originally decided by the Force

Commanders. Then a gun boat closed his ML to inform him that the
time had been changed to 11 o'clock. He proceeded to Dathan's craft
and ordered him to pass on the amended time to the western force
while he went off to tell the eastern groups. His official report said:

> I had got about as far as the Dieppe breakwater [harbour en-
> trance] when a bombing and cannon attack developed and I
> rather think we were under fire from ashore. . . . At any rate
> I retired very hurriedly to seaward followed by quite a few
> landing-craft. The end of the attack found us rather disorganized
> as we had three or four rather serious casualties among the craft
> and I decided I must dispose of them as soon as possible. This I
> eventually did to HMS *Alresford*.
>
> I was told by landing-craft that had tried to approach Blue
> Beach that it was held by the enemy, and as I had come to the
> conclusion that it was not possible to evacuate Blue, White, or
> Red Beaches, I told such landing-craft as had followed me to
> form up on a course for home. I then went in search of *Calpe* to
> report what I knew to the Force Commanders and to exchange
> information, but could not find her so made a signal in plain
> language [to the Naval Commander's staff]. The reply apparently
> said: "If no further evacuation possible, withdraw four miles
> from shore." This signal as received by me said: "No further
> evacuation possible, withdraw." Foolishly I made no reply to
> this signal so left the Force Commander in the dark as to what
> I was doing.

There is no question of someone being blameworthy for this mistake.
The battle was fierce; the Germans had launched a heavy air attack
against all elements of the fleet; mistakes in signalling were to be
expected. It was unfortunate, however, that so much depended upon
so small a word as "if." Had McClintock received it correctly it is likely
he would have turned about at once to take his tiny force into Red
Beach. As it was, these few but invaluable landing-craft were lost to
the Essex Scottish. McClintock's report continued:

> I was then joined by an LCP who told me that White Beach was
> held by the enemy. I must admit that I had some difficulty in
> making up my mind at this time as to the exact action to take.
> The difficulty was caused by the fact that I could see nothing to
> shoreward owing to the smoke and did not really know where all

the landing-craft were. I knew . . . Lieutenant-Commander Dathan had a certain number with him and I knew a certain number had already started from home by my orders. There was also a Group consisting largely of LCP's in company with me. These I had difficulty in communicating with because my loud-hailer was out of action, but had no difficulty in keeping together because wherever I went they followed. After a certain amount of hesitation I decided the best thing to do was to withdraw with this group, which I did at about 1230.

Off White Beach, Dathan was cruising about through the smoke and enemy barrages, collecting landing-craft and moving them through to the beach. The first four to touch down were, according to their captains, "literally swamped by the sheer weight of numbers of troops trying to embark." One of these was overturned, blown up by artillery fire, and its occupants either killed, drowned, or wounded. The other three managed to withdraw into the smoke, each carrying seventy soldiers.

Another eight landing-craft, aiming for White beach actually hit Red and came under heavy air attack as well as fire from the East Headland. Within a few minutes, six were total wrecks. The senior officer brought off by the surviving two said afterwards: "My craft was among the six destroyed. I advised my crew to swim away from the beach, and the four of us were eventually picked up a mile and a half from the beach by one of the two which managed to get away. This craft carried more than eighty troops and was so badly damaged that when she had transferred them to a destroyer she had to be sunk by gunfire."

No more boats reached the Essex Scottish. Another flight intended for Red Beach somehow touched down three miles away at Pourville where they rendered excellent service to the South Saskatchewans – something that was of dubious consolation to those Essex Scottish who survived to hear about it. On returning from Green Beach, however, some of these boats ran into Red to see if troops remained ashore. One of these was commanded by Lieutenant Mackenzie Kerr RNVR who reported: "I paused at White Beach but there was no sign of activity. It looked to me as if the Essex Scottish had never moved from where they had got on first landing – but they were dead now. Two men waved at me from behind a derelict tank, but the opposition was too strong for me to touch down without cover of smoke and I had exhausted my supply of smoke."

As Commander McClintock had thought, the Force Commanders were very much in the dark about events ashore. Smoke obscured the fleet from Hughes-Hallett who said later: "It soon became virtually impossible to know how the withdrawal was proceeding but, at about 1130, *Calpe* embarked two landing-craft loads of troops, mostly wounded, from whom it was learned that there were still men waiting to come off at Green Beach. At about the same time the General asked for the ship to proceed to the main beaches and ascertain the position there.

"Accordingly, instructions were issued to round up more landing-craft in the area and send them in again.... *Calpe* then closed the main beaches ... took aboard more troops from a tank landing-craft and, slightly later, I closed two assault boats that had just come off the main beach. Both gave it as their opinion that the conditions ashore precluded further evacuation.

"At about 1220 a signal was received from Commander McClintock indicating that no further evacuation was feasible. However, the military commander asked that a further effort should be made, and although I felt that this might well result in greater losses to troops already embarked than in the embarkation of additional troops, I decided to give Commander McClintock discretion whether to make a further effort. Accordingly, the following signal was made: 'If no further evacuation possible, withdraw.' Actually the signal as reported to Commander McClintock omitted the word 'if,' and from that time onward *Calpe* was unable to get into touch with him. I supposed at the time, his ML must have been sunk, but actually he was able to order the withdrawal of landing-craft to ... four miles off Dieppe. Consequently the two assault boats and *Calpe* were soon the only craft left close inshore, but owing to the low visibility I was not aware of this at the time."

Neither Roberts nor Hughes-Hallett had the slightest intention of leaving the scene while any hope remained of bringing off additional troops. At 12:50 p.m., *Calpe* closed the main beach to give the Force Commanders their first and only personal view of the main beaches. The two assault boats remained in company as she headed for the eastern end of Red Beach and, the need for wireless communications now secondary, opened fire with her main armament on the enemy guns at the end of the harbour moles. When only a few hundred yards off shore, in the murky fringe of smoke, Red Beach came into sight and *Calpe* herself came under concentrated fire from the East Headland. No movement was seen on the beach, and they turned back into the smoke, running out on the seaward side in the alarmingly close vicinity of *Locust*. While Hughes-Hallett discussed with Ryder the possibility of *Locust*, with her shallow draught, making a closer inspection of the beaches, Roberts received the last signal from Rolfe – "Our people here have surrendered."

The Navy had done everything humanly possible in such murderous conditions to effect total withdrawal. The landing-craft, driven by the resolution of Hughes-Hallett, went in time and again; Hughes-Hallett was himself driven by the agony of the Military Commander who passionately urged that the utmost effort was still not enough. But after the final run-in through the smoke, Roberts recorded in his war diary:

> In spite of heavy casualties to both personnel and craft, the Navy went in again and again to every beach until it was heard that our men on White and Red Beaches were either killed or overwhelmed, when any further attempts would have been of no avail. . . . Every possible effort was made to get craft into the beaches, including the Naval Force Commander's destroyer which closed the beach until it almost grounded. In fact, *Calpe* did touch bottom momentarily.

Brocklesby also went aground. Shortly before noon, she approached within five hundred yards of the West Headland to bombard from point-blank range, and was hit so often herself that she had to turn back into the smoke. During the turn her stern swept around and touched bottom. Engine telegraphs rang full speed and her momentum pulled her off.

Final reports from pilots of reconnaissance aircraft confirmed those of the ships – no movement was to be seen on the beaches after 1:00 p.m. By then only the dead and the wounded remained.

VII

At 11:00 a.m. the troops prepared for evacuation. Anxious eyes scanned the haze at sea for a glimpse of the incoming boats and, seeing nothing, turned skywards where German bombers now flew in strength, the air battle rapidly reaching a new crescendo. At sea, water was being lashed into boiling foam by shellfire, mortar bombs, and machine-gun fire, and more than one soldier inwardly recoiled at the prospect of having to pass through that bullet-swept surf to reach the boats. Others, determined to be among the first evacuated, tensed for the final dash, while still more managed to race down the beach to the shelter of the two stranded LCT's from where they would have only a short distance to cover when the boats appeared. They had suffered on the beaches for more than seven hours; now it was time to go and each had but a single thought – to find a boat which could take him home.

Lieutenant Jerry Wood, who had been tending the wounded in the protection of LCT 1, recorded later that the seaward side of it was thronged by a mass of men. "We ran out of stretchers, bodies had to be piled high to make room for the living. . . . A large party of infantry-men, all hale and hearty, blew in with a leather-lunged lieutenant. They all seemed very, very nervous and bewildered. I told him I needed some able-bodied men to load the wounded when the boats came in. It didn't occur to me that this party had been ordered to withdraw for the evacuation. They should not have been at the water's edge until the boats had arrived when they would have been sent for."

Then the first four assault boats sailed out of the smoke and headed in towards the beaches. Before they touched down the great wild rush gathered momentum and hundreds of men came out from cover. Essex Scottish, RHLI, Fusiliers Mont-Royal, sappers, and beach parties rose from the hollows, from behind ridges, from behind derelict tanks and scout cars, from the sea wall, and from the anti-tank ditch to surge in one great dark flowing mass for the sea. The Germans made little attempt to stop them, preferring to wait until they reached the water before cutting down their ranks with relentless precision.

Wood's account continued: "The men were literally running *en masse* for the boats, worse than any moving pictures of a mob flight. In my rage I yelled and yelled. I should have saved my breath. No one was going to help me move my wounded. Machine guns on the cliffs wrought fearful execution. Some of the boats pushed off, all hopelessly overloaded. . . . It was frightful murder. . . . The sea was full of men and bodies."

Some 150 yards away from Wood a soldier was crawling on hands and knees in the surf, so badly wounded that the gentle waves kept knocking him over. The tide was coming in faster than he could crawl, and every few minutes found him struggling painfully through deeper water. Wood and his wounded at the LCT watched fascinated at this one man's race to survive against the tide. Time passed; he moved less often, his body even more submerged. Wood could stand it no longer. Accompanied by two medical helpers he rushed across the beach, pulled the wounded soldier from the water, rescued a second who happened to be floating nearby, and returned to the LCT.

When the dash began Southam left Rolfe's scout car to make his way over to Wood's LCT. His later report said: "The approach of the assault landing-craft was the signal for a headlong rush of several hundred men who waded into the water, shoulder deep, in an attempt to board them. Some boats were hit, some were swamped. It was my thought that certainly none would get away. I walked to that area. A beached LCT was shielding many wounded and unwounded men, both on the seaward side and on board. I ordered them all to be prepared for the arrival of more assault landing-craft – and made it clear (I thought) that priority must go to the wounded. I added that any disobedience would be settled if necessary by pistols in the hands of officers. . . . About this time I met Lieutenant-Colonel Labatt who had just swum ashore after being on the way out to a small boat. He was wearing only a naval duffle coat and was obviously, in his own words – pooped."

In contrast to the "every man for himself" instinct which had triggered off the violent mobbing of the boats, the RHLI retreat from the Casino had been more or less disciplined, controlled. Labatt had moved his headquarters to the beach in front of it for the withdrawal, and under his supervision small groups began running down from the sun verandah, through the wire to the water's edge. The German prisoners carried wounded on stretchers and on doors torn from the Casino, which by then was occupied by an all-officer rearguard – Lazier, Hill, Currie, Whitaker, and Doheny. As the Germans left the buildings on the sea front to cross the esplanade into the rear of the Casino, the small rearguard withdrew to the verandah and manned the windows, keeping the Germans at bay. When the troops had begun to embark, Labatt signalled to the rearguard to follow, and with Herb Poag beside him walked calmly down to the water.

"There was no beach control," he has since told me. "All the boats we could see were overloaded and starting to pull back. We moved to the east to see how things were going there, and were joined by the rearguard from the Casino who waded with us out to some boats trying to manoeuvre off the beach. We got into the last of these boats. It was frightfully crowded. But we were no sooner aboard than the smokescreen lifted and we were fully exposed right under the German guns.

"Every German weapon turned on us, and all hell broke loose. What we had experienced before was nothing to this furious hurricane of fire. In no time the sea was littered with the wreckage of assault boats and dotted with bobbing heads and waving arms. A shell burst inside the boat next to us with ghastly results."

Labatt's boat was hit and he decided to swim for a large tank landing-craft about half a mile away. Poag declined to accompany him, saying, "No thank you, sir. I still don't like water and I'm going ashore if that's okay by you." By then Labatt had stripped off his uniform, and while Poag returned to the beach, he commenced swimming powerfully out to sea, carefully avoiding large groups of swimmers who were providing tempting targets for enemy machine guns. As he neared the LCT, he realized with a sense of sudden anger that it was being shelled. When he was only two hundred yards away, it received two direct hits, sank, and after staring at the sea where it had been, he said aloud: "How bloody silly." Reaction set in and, feeling very tired, very cold, he reluctantly headed back to the beach, emerging from the water close to the LCT where Southam and Wood were trying to organize a defensive position. While he dressed in a dead man's socks, shoes, and duffle coat he saw the futility of their efforts. Most of the men were wounded and incapable of firing guns; the others were unwounded men from the wrecked boats whose weapons had been thrown away when they had left the beach.

Southam's attention was diverted elsewhere and Labatt, with the incoming tide threatening to submerge the wounded, ordered all able-bodied officers and men to lift them into the LCT. Among the wounded was his adjutant, and while he was helping to lift Poag to safety an officer ran out from behind the LCT to stand in the open waving a white cloth. He died instantly, his body riddled by fire from the enemy in front, by fire from his own men behind.

"He had no orders to surrender and it was made all the worse because a trackless tank was still firing and protecting the LCT only twenty yards away," said Labatt.

Farther east behind LCT 3, Padre Foote was saving the lives of at least thirty men. When the boats came in, he lifted the first on his back, walked down the beach into the water, waded out to the nearest one, and despite the jam around it persuaded men to help him transfer the wounded man on board. He waded back to shore, walked up the beach to the LCT, lifted another wounded man to his back and repeated the previous exploit. So it went on for more than an hour, the incredible padre seeking out boats and calling to all who could hear: "Every man carry a man." When only one boat remained, two men grabbed his arms and pulled him into it. The boat had moved astern when suddenly he leapt into the water and returned to the beach because, he said, "It seemed to me the men ashore would in all likelihood need me far more in the months of captivity ahead than any of those going home." The approved stowaway had made his choice, one for which hundreds of soldiers would be grateful and one which made him the most unforgettable Canadian at Dieppe.

Sergeant Hickson had made his own way down the beach from the Casino, wanting no part of the mass rush which had attracted the worst of the enemy's fire. He reached one of the first boats to touch down, but so many men followed him that the ramp jammed under their weight. The crew pulled the boat astern while Hickson shouted to the men to bale out water with their tin hats. He tried to persuade them to sing so that they could work in unison and rhythm, but in the end felt a bit foolish when he realized he was the only one singing The boat stayed afloat long enough to transfer the men to a destroyer; then it sank.

Sergeant-Major Dumais of the Fusiliers Mont-Royal was on his way down to the water when he stumbled over a wounded corporal, a large, heavy man impossible to lift. He returned to the Casino, found two German prisoners who had been left behind with the rearguard, and employed them to take the corporal out to an assault boat. He tried to clamber aboard by pulling himself up by a rope hanging over the boat's stern. He was halfway up when she began to move, forcing him to let go. His waterlogged pack and his sodden uniform dragged him down to the bottom. He struggled to the surface twice and then found he had been carried into shallower water by the backwash from the propellers of the landing-craft.

He waded ashore, collapsed wearily on the beach, and when a machine gun opened fire on him he was too weak to care. Eventually he made his way to the stranded LCT where Padre Foote was still making one mercy trip after another out to the boats.

Sergeant-Major Stewart boarded an assault boat which was so over-loaded it sank minutes later. He swam out to sea for two and a half hours before another boat cruising in search of survivors picked him up. Major MacRae, with the Essex Scottish, loaded wounded into a small, abandoned lifeboat that had washed up on the beach, heaved it into the water with the help of walking wounded, and then swam behind pushing it for two miles. The party was rescued by a gun boat just as he lapsed into unconsciousness through exhaustion.

Sergeant Dubuc, still wearing only his underwear, found his commander, Colonel Menard, lying near the sea wall west of the Casino, badly wounded. He had been hit five times in the arms and head, had persevered in trying to cut through the wire on top of the wall, and had finally collapsed through loss of blood. Four RHLI soldiers had carried him along the wall to the shelter of a stranded tank where, by then almost delirious with pain, he waved off Dubuc's attempts to help him to his feet, shouting angrily that he would not leave the beach until the last of his men had been evacuated. Corporal Berube joined Dubuc and between them they carried Menard to the water, ignoring his threats of dire consequences, and placed him aboard an assault boat. Only later did Menard learn that he had been stretched out on crates of high explosives – for which he was to curse his saviours roundly.

Dubuc then returned to the beach, made his way to a wounded corporal named Cloutier, picked him up, and carried him to another boat which he also boarded himself.

Dan Doheny left the Casino on the run and headed for the protection of the LCT stranded on Red Beach. Pity welled up in him as he witnessed the hundreds of men swamping the first boats in, saw shells and mortar bombs explode in the middle of densely packed groups, throwing arms, legs, and bodies high in the air.

Of the "at least twelve tanks" which reached the esplanade, most found their way back to the beach in those final minutes of evacuation. But by noon all tanks were immobilized by enemy fire, although the crews remained inside and in action, attempting to give fire support to the withdrawal. Throughout, the conversation between them was casual, reflecting none of the strain that must have been generated by the massacre on the beaches. Alan Glenn saw the rush of troops to the first flight of boats, called up Rolfe, and asked "What's happening? Have the boys gone nuts?" Rolfe warned all tank crews to prepare for evacuation and not to forget to blow up their tanks.

At 1:05 p.m. Glenn issued a general order to all tanks: "Unload crews. Get to beach." Most of them reached one or other of the two beached LCT's, both of which were crowded with wounded and men who had been rescued from the sea. Only one member of all the crews who landed swam away from the beach and survived to be picked up and taken back to England, a hull gunner named Trooper G. Volk.

Two miles off shore an LCT took aboard eighty men from a sinking assault boat, among them Menard and Private Leo Belair, who was looking after his colonel. The LCT, already full, was now overloaded. Everything movable was thrown over the side, but she continued to settle lower in the water. Someone shouted: "What about the Jerries?"

Huddled in the hold, half submerged by incoming water, were a group of German prisoners. A strange silence fell momentarily over the boat, and a wall of soldiers automatically formed to block the view from the bridge, where the LCT's commanding officer was intent upon navigation. Neither he nor Menard were aware that in a few brief moments every German aboard was thrown over the side. Nor did they attribute any significance to the burst of Sten gun fire which broke the silence. Of all the prisoners taken on the main beaches, only three arrived in England. Private Belair confirmed the incident in a later statement in which he said with understandable brevity: "We threw several Germans overboard when we found them half submerged."

By 1:00 p.m., when *Calpe* sailed in through the smoke for a final look at the beaches and saw no movement anywhere, there were still more than seven hundred men on the main beaches, most of them wounded and all unable to show themselves. To do so invited death. Five minutes later the beach had quietened, no ships could be seen, and the air battle was drifting farther out over the sea. Tense expectancy settled over the tragic scene as men fixed their eyes on the sea wall over which the Germans could be expected to appear. Enemy fire slackened, becoming almost negligible, and the quiet grated on the edges of jagged, taut nerves.

In the Castle on the West Headland a German officer picked up a telephone, called General Haase at Envermeu, and said: "The British Navy has gone. Remnants of the landing force are still holding out. Request permission to clear up the battlefield." When he put down the telephone, a message was sent to all units of the 571st Infantry Regiment ordering the advance to the main beaches.

A small piece of white fluttered from behind a tank west of the Casino; another flew over LCT 1. Without guidance or direction, the surrender had begun. Rolfe's last signal from the beach told the beginning of the end. He stacked his signals books and codes in a neat pile on the beach, set them on fire and blew up his scout car with a grenade. A few seconds later, while the first Germans, faces grim under bucket helmets, came into view over the sea wall, the bonfire was burning fiercely – just as Rolfe noticed the waterproofed package Southam still carried under one arm. The military plan! The one document that should never fall into enemy hands. Rolfe said: "I raced to the Brigadier, pointed to the bonfire on the beach, and urged that the package be burned immediately. Southam hesitated, saying he might still have further use for it. He refused to part with the package, and instead ordered me to organize a defence of the beach. I asked again to be given the package. Southam suddenly shouted: 'We must not surrender. There's the enemy. Why doesn't someone shoot?' The outburst died as quickly as it had arisen. After a swift glance at the enemy on the sea wall, Southam bent down quickly in an attempt to bury his precious package under the pebbles." His action had not escaped a German officer scanning the beach. In copy 37 of the military plan was the fateful clause: "Wherever possible, prisoners' hands are to be tied. . . ."

Behind Southam and Rolfe a doctor appeared atop the LCT waving a white handkerchief. Labatt as senior officer at the other LCT watched the waving of white cloth spread along the beach and wondered how to accustom himself to the idea of imprisonment. He tied a dirty white handkerchief to a rifle barrel, handed it to a German prisoner, and shoved him out into the open. It was as good a way as any to find out if Germans honoured white flags.

Even though there was now only peace and quietness, the sound and fury of battle was too recent and too terrible to be forgotten. The smoke drifted out to sea, dispersed, and the blue water glistened under the sun. Jubilee was over for the soldiers of both sides; only the dead were there as evidence of the folly of the living. It had taken only nine hours to tear out the heart from a Canadian force which had striven for three years to reach peak battle efficiency. It was for this that Labatt had left his investment brokerage in Hamilton; for this that Whitaker had exchanged the uniform of the Tigers for one of khaki; for this that Jasperson had given up a legal practice "for the duration."

A German interrogator thumbed through Wood's copy of *The Last Train from Berlin*, took it with him to interview the captured colonels and, in answer to a questioning glance from Labatt, explained that he had brought it from Paris to read during the several days of waiting for the Canadians to arrive. The seeds of suspicion and betrayal were casually and easily sown.

Among the last to surrender was Dan Doheny. He sat behind the LCT in shallow water smoking a cigarette and gazing out across the Channel, clinging with lingering deliberation to the last few seconds of freedom. When the cigarette burned his fingers he tossed it away, gripped his Sten gun savagely, and threw it far out beyond the surf, and then walked up the beach with hands high above his head to join the groups already being searched.

Resignation, hate, and the bitter conviction that the enemy had been somehow warned of their coming were the only emotions among the Canadians as they entered captivity, emotions the enemy cunningly fostered in the years ahead. The roll call was fertile soil by itself: the RHLI, 365 dead, wounded, and captured; the Essex Scottish, 500; the Fusiliers Mont-Royal, 513, to which all the auxiliary units contributed another 400 casualties of all kinds.

By 2:00 p.m. the beaches of Dieppe were cleared of the living, the dead being left to be picked up by the tide and deposited farther up the beach. According to a German officer it was a quite rational thing to do because then the bodies would not have to be carried so far by the burial details.

Twenty minutes later a bird flew across the Channel towards England, a lonely bird with a destination and a purpose. It was a carrier pigeon released from *Fernie* with a hand-written message from Churchill Mann to General Crerar attached to one leg. It said:

TO 1st CANADIAN CORPS
FROM HMS *FERNIE*   Date 19 August

Recording opinion now in case of trouble later. Surprise probably lost when naval encounter occurred in early a.m. – if landing-craft spotted.

Strength of enemy: Seems to have been increased. Basic view of all officers on *Fernie* that Bomber Command MUST provide really heavy support in future combined operations. Troops seem to have behaved magnificently – never a trace of panic on R/T.

Failure to succeed in forcing Red and White due to very heavy fire on promenade. Gun fire also on beaches. No news of Yellow and Blue parties since early a.m. Communications worked well throughout.

Are getting reports re casualties by lamp.

Sorry we failed to achieve our hopes.

Navy did grand job.

We want to go again some time too!

C. C. Mann

While the pigeon flew direct for its Combined Operations loft, the fleet straggled across the Channel, subjected to a ferocious bombardment from the air. Group Captain Oxspring flew a close support mission in the afternoon and watched a Spitfire pilot parachute down to the sea. When he hit the water his rubber dinghy inflated and he climbed into it to start paddling furiously after the ships – the last in the long line of what had once been a proud and hopeful fleet.

The last casualty of the day was an American. Colonel Hillsinger, United States Army Air Force observer aboard the destroyer *Berkeley*, was standing on deck when a bomb, jettisoned by a Dornier under attack, exploded within yards of him, blowing off a foot. He had been wearing for the first time a pair of boots hand-made for him in London. While using his tie as a tourniquet he recognized his foot floating away from the ship encased in brand new leather. With an expressive gesture of disgust he took off his other boot and threw it too into the sea. The destroyer was so badly damaged she had to be torpedoed and sunk by *Albrighton*.

VIII

Georges Guibon returns to his home on Rue Jean Ribault. The soup at lunch has been tasteless, and he savours the thought of an iced Cinzano at the bistro on the corner of his street. The bat is still trapped but it makes no noise and he wonders if it has flapped itself into insensibility. On the dining-room table is a letter he has forgotten to post. He picks it up, thinking that he might as well mail it even if the postal services are disrupted and it never reaches Bourgogne.

Outside, the sounds of battle seem to be diminishing and he walks towards the sea front hoping to pick up news on the way. He is told that the tobacco factory is burning, that the Hôtel Regina is wrecked, that M. Verel, owner of the Hôtel des Arcades, has been killed behind the reception desk by a stray shell, that a woman he knows has been half scalped by a piece of shrapnel and is at that moment giving birth to a baby while on a stretcher.

He sees a long column of Canadian prisoners being marched through the streets. They are in a ghastly state, one with an abdominal wound so big that he has to hold in his intestines with his hands. Some raise their arms over their heads while a German cameraman takes pictures, then lower them again. At the railway station there are some Canadian wounded and he leans over one saying: "Bless you and thank you for what you have done."

He makes his way to a mail box and, noticing that the next collection is due in ten minutes, deposits his letter while waiting to see if the postal services are still operating. Thirty minutes pass, and he is about to leave when the postman arrives by bicycle and tells him:

"The Germans have ordered all civil servants to carry on with their duties. I have to collect and deliver your letters."

Guibon returns to his house where he discovers that the Todt engineer has left the broom closet under the stairs, that the bat has freed itself and is now hiding somewhere else, that a neighbour is waiting to join him for a drink at the bistro. Only German aircraft can be seen in the summer sky and the air is filled with the acrid fumes of burning. Guibon sips his iced Cinzano deliberately, then gestures towards the pall of smoke and flame over the sea front and says: "Dieppe will never forget this day."

His letter, mailed amid the dying embers of battle, is delivered the next day without appreciable delay. Like the gas supply, the mails are not interrupted.

Guibon's letter reached its destination before Corporal J. R. Gilchrist of the Essex Scottish was found. He had been wounded by a bullet which ricocheted off a tank crossing the sea wall. He lay as if dead throughout the operation, losing consciousness, regaining it momentarily, and then relapsing into oblivion again. It took the Germans more than twenty-four hours to clear the beaches of bodies and the last Canadian to be found alive was Corporal Gilchrist – at dusk on August 20.

Then the fusion by fire of English-speaking and French-speaking Canadians took place. At a prisoner-of-war assembly point behind Dieppe the Fusiliers Mont-Royal were separated from the rest of their comrades and given an emergency issue of Red Cross parcels, a patent attempt by the Germans to encourage a division between the Canadian races. Sarto Marchand, on behalf of the battalion, gravely thanked the Germans, and then officers and men carried the boxes to the general compound where their contents were shared equally among French and English. It was a gesture of supreme contempt for an enemy who had supposed that at moments of common crisis there could be anything but unity among Canadians.

When the sun had set and the curtain of dusk had blessedly softened the harsh glare of an angry day, the peoples of the Allied Nations were talking, as was their custom then, of war and of the men who were fighting it: the stubborn British, the gallant Americans, the brave Russians, and even with reluctant respect for the coldly efficient Germans. The next morning they received the news of Dieppe with wonderment, mingled with joy and grief. For a few days the truth was obscured by sensational headlines in Britain and the United States, but when the muddle was unravelled it emerged with stark shining brilliance, and the democracies turned to Canada in admiration.

Quite suddenly it seemed that the "Unknown Soldier" of man's most violent conflict had become a Canadian – not for what he had won or lost, but for what he had endured.

Return to
the Muddles

I

They returned to England at dusk: nearly 1,000 Canadians who had never landed, another 600 wounded, and a handful who had come off the beaches unhurt. Military men are prone to predict, and once the frontal assault had been decreed by the Army Commander in Reigate the zealous planners had immediately predicted that losses would be 10 per cent of the forces engaged; 10 to 20 per cent of tanks and armoured vehicles. Actual casualty figures for the whole force reached 60 per cent in men and 100 per cent in tanks. Obviously the predicted casualty estimates were the outcome of pretty over-optimistic, un-educated guesses.

The proportion of casualties to troops engaged among the 2nd Division, the Commandos, the Royal Marine Commando, and United States Rangers was as follows:

| Engaged | | 6,086 | } 59.5 per cent |
| Casualties | | 3,623 | |

The proportion of casualties by Services was as follows:

Naval (excluding minesweeper and troop
transport crews)

| Engaged | | 3,875 | } 14.5 per cent |
| Casualties | | 550 | |

Military
  Canadian Forces

| Engaged | | 4,963 | } 68 per cent |
| Casualties | | 3,367 | |

  Commandos

| Engaged | | 1,075 | } 22.9 per cent |
| Casualties | | 247 | |

  U.S. Rangers

| Engaged | | 50 | } 26 per cent |
| Casualties | | 13 | |

  Royal Air Force

| Engaged | | 1,179 | } 13 per cent |
| Casualties | | 153 | |

These losses so decimated the 2nd Division that it now barely existed
as an organized unit. Two months later, after the injection of raw recruits from Canada, the Royal Regiment was still 6 officers and 218
men below strength; the RHLI needed another 4 officers and 193 men;
the Essex Scottish was short 12 officers and 212 other ranks. The entire
division reverted to a basis of elementary training to the extent that
after a further six months it still held the lowest priority in the
Canadian Army for employment.

It had been intended originally that all casualties should be landed
at Newhaven, the nearest disembarkation port. Ships' doctors, however, advised Hughes-Hallett that many of the wounded carried in the
destroyers would not survive the delay and discomfort of being transferred back into landing-craft and being slowly ferried ashore. He
immediately signalled the Admiralty for another flotilla of destroyers
to take over as escorts for the landing-craft when the force was still
twenty-five miles from Newhaven while *Calpe* led the way direct to
Portsmouth.

A second signal to the Commander-in-Chief, Portsmouth, requested
that arrangements be made to receive "600 to 700" wounded, and by
the time they arrived every available civil and military ambulance

was waiting in the dockyard. It was a remarkable feat of improvization which saved the lives of those Canadians who would not otherwise have withstood the journey from the destroyers into Newhaven.

Five hospitals worked ceaselessly for two days and nights, the nurses
in six-hour shifts, the doctors almost non-stop. In the operating theatre
of one hospital four tables and eight doctors were ceaselessly occupied
with surgery for forty hours. Another hospital admitted 401 patients
in twelve hours, among them 82 urgent surgical cases, and kept its
operating theatre functioning without pause for 36 hours. A soldier
wrote home to Canada: "I broke a bone in my shoulder and the worst
part was waiting for the Doc . . . he had done 167 operations that first
night so I guess I don't complain. Fine now."

Other letters, and in that first week in England more than eight
thousand of them were examined by Canadian censors, told of Dieppe
in terms of sober judgement or in wild condemnation. The censors
reported that those who felt they had been in some way betrayed
were outnumbered in the ratio of 20 to 1 by those who wanted to
"have another crack at Jerry because we know we can lick him next
time."

Encouraging as this may seem, a small nation cannot afford to over-
look the lasting damage caused by the thoughtless words of a minority. Many Canadian families cling to their bitterness and hand it down
to younger generations wherein it reproduces itself. The children left
fatherless by this incident of war have never had the opportunity to
judge for themselves the reasons why their fathers died. Instead they
have become, in some cases at least, the sour soil in which the seeds of
a cruel nationalism have been sown – cruel because the soil is too
bitter to nourish patriotism, which requires the sweeter juices of
dedication to justice and devotion to country.

The sense of betrayal shared by this minority had nothing to
support it. The South Sasks achieved surprise; Lovat's Commando
achieved surprise; Major Young's remnant at Berneval achieved surprise. Documents captured at Varengeville included the German Guard
Book which showed the existence of normal routine up to the last
entry made only an hour before the Commandos landed. In fact, the
off-duty crews of the coastal battery were asleep *undressed* despite
the alert that had been in force since August 1. General Haase issued
the general alarm only at 5:00 a.m. when the flank landings indicated
a major operation developing.

His division had received no reinforcements, indeed it had been
brought up to strength by two batches of low-quality recruits, mostly

Poles, some of whom were medically unfit for strenuous duty. The strengthening of Dieppe's defences had been started as far back as April as part of a general reorganization of the entire West Wall. Most convincing evidence, however, was the fact that the *Luftwaffe* had granted leave to some fighter pilots and that it was unable to launch a major bomber effort against the fleet until 10:00 a.m. – five hours after the first assault.

Moreover, German Military Intelligence had planted agents inside the largest Allied espionage rings in Paris, known respectively as "Alexandria" and "Fromenteaux." These agents reported: "The two principals of these rings are disgruntled because, after all, they had been under orders from the British to make preparations for forthcoming attacks. . . . This proves that enemy agents were neither aware of the Dieppe undertaking, nor were they employed in its execution."

Colonel Rudolph, chief of German Intelligence in Paris, commented later: "We have always been of the opinion that NO agent on the Continent would be informed of any forthcoming operation before it started. Our agencies in France had no reports that the opponent was planning the attack on Dieppe."

More likely culprits were the Allied political warfare experts and propaganda specialists – among whom there were Canadian and American as well as British – who spent several weeks creating a second-front atmosphere by diligently encouraging German fear of attack. They were so successful that at periods when lunar and tidal conditions were right, such as between August 1 and 20, the enemy was alert for it.

Being professional in the art of war, the Germans went about the business of preparing the defences at Dieppe efficiently by giving a few men the proper weapons. The Canadian amateurs failed to grasp that the enemy had done unto them what they had hoped to do unto him had he dared to attempt a landing on the Sussex coast of England.

Fortunately for the Canadian Army, and for the nation itself, for every bitter survivor there were twenty more who acquired a healthy respect for the enemy, a new appreciaton of the value of training and the *élan* of the blooded.

German losses, never fully detailed, were in the region of only 600 dead and wounded. This is a believable figure because the sea front of Dieppe, for instance, was defended by only one company of infantry – one company against three Canadian battalions supported by tanks! As Roberts had always feared, the damage had been done by the guns on the wing headlands supported by those in the caves, which he had known nothing about. He had said that the headlands were the hinges of success, and having been proven right has since received precious little credit for it.

II

Commenting on the raid in the British House of Commons, Churchill said: "The raid, apart from information and reconnaissance value, brought about an extremely satisfactory air battle in the west which Fighter Command wish they could repeat every week." The basis for this statement was a summary of Leigh-Mallory's report which said:

> Throughout the landing, extensive air cover for both ships and landing forces was provided from all Operational Commands of the Royal Air Force, from the U.S. Army Air Force, the Royal Canadian Air Force, the Royal New Zealand Air Force. . . . While the principal objective was to give support to the landings . . . there, in fact, developed one of the greatest air battles of the war. . . . The Germans were forced to call up aircraft reinforcements from all parts of Occupied France, Holland and Belgium. Many of these enemy aircraft were engaged long before they ever reached the area of the operation. During the engagement 91 German aircraft are officially known to have been destroyed and about twice that number have probably been destroyed or damaged. In all these operations 98 of our aircraft were lost and the pilots of 30 of these were saved.

After the war, captured German records gave the *Luftwaffe*'s actual losses that day as only 48 aircraft. Leigh-Mallory, who has since died, never believed this figure. He was convinced to the end that the enemy had deliberately falsified the extent of the losses.

The RCAF contribution consisted of six Fighter Squadrons – Nos 401, 402, 403, 411, 412, and 416 – and two Army Co-operation Squadrons – Nos 400 and 414. The latter, commanded respectively by Wing Commanders R. C. A. Waddell and R. F. Begg, flew forty-two reconnaissance sorties over France to warn of German reinforcements coming up from the rear. They lost only two aircraft. This participation by the RCAF is little known in Canada today mainly because it was submerged by the flood of grief which spread across the country, as news of the enormity of the Canadian sacrifice filtered round the world – most of it inaccurate, distorted, and vague. The public relations plan was quickly shattered into as many fragments as the military plan.

III

If the Western allies and neutral nations were to receive comprehensive and accurate information about the operation, it was essential for the British government to maintain the propaganda initiative. On the eve of the departure of the troops, Combined Operations submitted two draft communiques to McNaughton and Eisenhower. They were approved – although Eisenhower insisted that all releases concerning the role of the U.S Rangers should be made by his headquarters.

The first communique, released at 6:00 a.m. on the 19th, said:

> A raid was launched in the early hours of today on the Dieppe area of enemy-occupied France.
>
> The Operation is still in progress and a further communique will be issued when fuller reports are available.
>
> Meanwhile, the French people are being advised by wireless broadcasts that this raid is not an invasion.

The second, issued at about 1:00 p.m., said:

> The troops taking part in the raid on the Dieppe area have landed at all points selected. Heavy opposition was encountered in some places; and on the left flank one landing party was initially repulsed but reformed later and carried the beach by assault.
>
> The troops on the right flank, having achieved their objective, which included the complete destruction of a six-gun battery and ammunition dump, have now been re-embarked. In the centre, tanks were landed and heavy fighting is proceeding. The military force consists mainly of Canadian troops. Also taking part are British Special Service troops, a detachment from a United States Ranger Battalion and a small contingent of Fighting French.
>
> The force was carried and escorted by units of the Royal Navy. Air support and protection on a large scale is being pro-

vided by bomber and fighter aircraft of the Royal Air Force, in the face of considerable enemy opposition.

A further communique will be issued later.

More than seven hours elapsed before the third communique, a delay caused by political alarm at what seemed to be a major military disaster. Anthony Eden, British Foreign Secretary, intervened with a telephone call to Mountbatten at Uxbridge in which he urged that the role of the American troops "should not be over-stressed . . . since it might harm Anglo-American relations." Eden had no illusions concerning the extent of American reaction to a high percentage loss of the small contingent taking part.

It was too late. Once Eisenhower had insisted that his own headquarters should make all releases about the Rangers, his public relations staff had launched a propaganda field day. Their carefully worded releases were calculated to give the impression that the Rangers had led the way back to the Continent, and United States newspapers were not slow to stress it. Combined Operations admitted later: "We should have suggested the issue of Press Guidance Memoranda by U.S. Army headquarters making clear that only a small number of American troops were participating. Failure to do so caused a temporary over-emphasis in American newspaper headlines. . . ."

Churchill, fearing a disaster of Tobruk magnitude, and angered by German radio broadcasts claiming that an invasion had been repulsed, also telephoned from Downing Street to instruct that further communiques should refer to the operation as a "reconnaissance in force." His motive was to bridge the gap between the Combined Operations description of the operation as "a raid," when it was obviously something bigger, and the enemy claims that an invasion attempt had been made, when obviously the operation was something smaller.

In an effort to correct the false impressions of the communiques that the operation had been primarily a Commando and Ranger affair, the British Ministry of Information issued a series of press guidance memoranda for the "private and confidential" information of editors in Britain and Canada.

The first of these, issued at 1:30 p.m. over the signature of Francis Williams, Controller of Press and Censorship, said:

> Following the news of the Combined Operations raid on Dieppe, certain factors which for obvious reasons could not be previously disclosed, are given for your guidance. They must not be quoted as coming from official sources.

The present raid, in which a more numerous personnel is taking part than on previous raids and in which tanks are being used for the first time marks an important step forward in the planned program of our agreed offensive policy. It is important in commenting on the raid to bear this fact in mind.

In view of the possibility of increased defensive preparations by the enemy, it is difficult to estimate the probable losses we shall incur, but in any case our losses must be seen not only in their relation to German losses in men, material and aircraft, but also in the light of the invaluable experience gained in the employment of substantial forces and in the transport and use of heavy equipment.

For your own information, I may say that while Canadian troops comprise the main body of the landing force, they constitute approximately one-third of the total personnel of all Services participating in the raid.

This example of misguided guidance merely served to compound the public relations muddle. The Canadians comprised not a third of the landing force, but five-sixths of it, although if naval, marine, and air force units were included the Canadian content of the overall force would be about 50 per cent. One can but assume that Mr Williams was shockingly misinformed by Combined Operations about the units actually taking part. The effect of it was to reinforce the belief of Allied newspaper editors that British and American troops had been merely supported by a few Canadians.

The third communique, eventually issued at 8:10 p.m., said:

Despite the clear statement issued in our first communique this morning . . . German propaganda, unable to make other capital out of the turn the operation has taken, is claiming that the raid was an invasion attempt which they have frustrated.

In point of fact the re-embarkation of the main forces engaged was begun six minutes after the time scheduled, and it has been completed nine hours after the initial landing, as planned.

Some tanks have been lost . . . and reports show that the fighting has been very fierce and that casualties are likely to have been heavy on both sides. . . .

In addition to the destruction of the six-gun battery and ammunition dump reported in our earlier communique, a radio-location station and flak battery were destroyed.

Apart from the losses inflicted on the enemy, vital experience has been gained in the employment of a substantial number of troops in an assault and on the transport and use of heavy equipment. . . . Our new tank landing-craft were in use for the first time. From reports so far received 72 enemy aircraft are known to have been destroyed in addition to a number shot down by naval vessels. More than 100 enemy aircraft were also probably destroyed or damaged.

Ninety-five of our aircraft of all Commands are missing, but 21 pilots are known to be safe. . . .

By this time the propaganda specialists were in serious trouble. The news from Dieppe was not good, the Germans were screaming that an invasion had been defeated, and Allied prestige was being seriously undermined. The third communique reflected their concern by revealing a definite political tinge and by including the fallacious, rather stupid remark that the withdrawal had started "six minutes late." Few operations run to that sort of timetable.

The official report of the British Political Warfare Executive said:

The plan for political warfare collapsed with the issue of the third communique. In the ensuing twenty-seven hours we lost the initiative . . . and owing to lack of further material with which to cover angles from which we are being attacked, German propaganda built up a strong position, not dissimilar to their position in the field.

The enemy's political counter-attack was reinforced by the addition of much detail, military and political. . . . When one considers that the raid on Dieppe . . . was undertaken at an unpropitious moment, one cannot help feeling that if there had not been very careful preliminary planning in the initial stages . . . the political effects to ourselves might have been far worse.

Between the third communique and the fourth, which was also the last, nearly three hours were wasted trying to sort out the proper role of the Canadians. Mr Williams obligingly made some effort to counteract the unfortunate effect of his earlier guidance memoranda by issuing another at 9:10 p.m. which said:

It will be very much appreciated if in their stories of the Combined Operations raid on Dieppe, the newspapers will bear in

mind that by far the largest proportion of the troops engaged
were Canadian forces. . . . To emphasize Commandos in headlines and stories would be to give an unfair perspective to the
operations.

Even this was not a clear-cut statement, and the fourth official
communique did little to help the situation. It said in part:

Reports now received from the Force Commanders make it possible to give a full co-ordinated story of the Combined Operations
raid in the Dieppe area.

These reports show that as a Combined Operations the raid
was a successful demonstration of co-ordination of all three
services. . . . The raid was a reconnaissance in force, having a
vital part in our agreed offensive policy.

It was known that as a consequence of our avowed aggressive
policy the Germans had recently been heavily reinforcing the
coastal defences of the whole of the occupied territory.

Heavy opposition was therefore anticipated. . . . The tanks
which had been landed and some of which succeeded in breaking
into the town, were ordered to be blown up and destroyed. . . .

While the principal objectives of the air operations was to
give support to the landing and cover the forces . . . there in fact
developed one of the greatest air battles of the war . . . this
battle had not been planned as one of the objectives.

The propaganda flap had by this time become quite ridiculous.
Combined Operations knew perfectly well that the operation had
been based on Intelligence opinion that Dieppe was *weakly defended*.
It was also known by then that probably no tanks had reached the
town; indeed Roberts was not sure if they had even left the beach.

The Political Warfare Executive used three major excuses for losing
the propaganda battle – in the first place, the raid took place when for
political reasons it would have been better had it not taken place,
which forced them into an explanatory or justification state of mind;
second, the action itself proved anything but a clear victory, and there
was a dearth of success stories to exploit; third, the objectives of the
operation were not of such a nature as to capture public imagination.

It may have been better if these specialists had used a little imagination of their own. For two years the English Channel had been denied

to the English. It was so dominated by the *Luftwaffe* that a German battle fleet had been able to sail through it in February 1942, with something that approached impunity. For three years of war the Allies had been on the defensive, preparing to meet an invasion of England. Dieppe changed this dismal picture of war entirely. Where there had been desperation without hope there was now determination with hope and confidence. For the first time since the outbreak of war we had taken the offensive against the German occupier of Europe. We had driven the *Luftwaffe* from the air above the Channel and had maintained a fleet of more than two hundred ships hard against the much-vaunted West Wall.

Surely, if the ingredients for a magnificent appeal to public imagination were needed, they were here. We could proclaim our contempt for the legend of the enemy's invincibility; we could proudly proclaim that the English Channel had returned to England; we could crow about our victory in the air, point out that we had won a Battle of Britain in reverse; we could exude confidence in our ability to land anywhere we liked along enemy-held coastlines; and above all, we could issue dire warnings of what was in store for the enemy when we decided to cross the Channel to stay in Europe.

This is the very substance of morale-boosting, of prestige-making. Yet none of it was said.

The Canadian role remained misunderstood. One London magazine ran an eleven-page article on September 5 entitled: "Dieppe: The Full Story." It was devoted to the RAF role, the Commando role, and the Ranger role. Two obscure sentences on the tenth page referred to the Canadians. It was this article which inspired Churchill to address Parliament three days later, saying:

"It is a mistake to speak or write of this as a Commando raid, although some Commando troops distinguished themselves remarkably in it. The military credit for this most gallant affair goes to the Canadian troops who formed five-sixths of the assaulting forces, and to the Royal Navy, which carried them all there and which carried most of them back."

Something positive at last!

What of the press party that had accompanied the raid? Were they not encouraged to file stories, to tell a tragic but rewarding tale? Three Canadians were included in this group — Fred Griffin of the *Toronto Star*, Ross Munro of *Canadian Press*, and Wallace Reyburn of the *Montreal Star*. Munro had been in a landing-craft off Blue Beach for a while and had then landed for a few moments on the main beaches. Reyburn had followed the South Sasks ashore at Pourville and had stayed until he was slightly wounded and evacuated.

On return to England they were instructed to report to Combined Operations Headquarters where they arrived at intervals between midnight and 2:00 a.m. on the 20th. Munro was particularly anxious to write for immediate release and made it clear to Major Cliff Wallace, public relations officer for McNaughton's Army headquarters, that he deplored any delay which might give the enemy time to create a false impression of the operation.

Combined Operations intervened with an instruction that no stories could be filed until correspondents had been given a thorough briefing – and the delay Munro had warned against occurred anyway. The first conference was timed for 10:45 a.m. on the 20th, and when the correspondents appeared for it the Combined Operations representatives said that, as it was felt insufficient information was available, the briefing would have to be postponed. Munro and Griffin – Reyburn was not present because of his wounds – were joined by other correspondents in demanding that they be allowed to file their stories at noon.

Combined Operations, however, insisted that the stories be submitted for their approval first. Usually such stories were censored by the Ministry of Information, but Mountbatten employed his own public relations experts. This meant that Dieppe copy had to be cleared, according to official records, "for policy censoring by Combined Ops Public Relations before being submitted to the normal censors."

As a result, the first eye-witness stories by the Canadian correspondents were not filed until 6:05 p.m. that night – twenty-nine hours after the operation had ended, sixteen hours after the correspondents had returned to London. It should have been obvious at the outset that such lengthy delays would lead to an information vacuum which would be filled by the distortions of the enemy.

Combined Operations admitted somewhat ruefully later: "The period of silence . . . enabled the enemy to seize the initiative from us."

The Germans had plenty to support their contention that the operation had been an attempted invasion. They were the first to mention that tanks had been employed, and they used this fact to indicate that the Allies would not risk such valuable armament on anything but a major operation, certainly not on a raid.

While we were still worrying about the contents of our last communique Radio Berlin announced: "Orders found on captured officers contained maps and sketches not only of the area around Dieppe, but also of the entire coastal areas of Northern France, including Paris. . . . Members of the German High Command have shrugged their shoulders at the dilettantism evident in the planning and execution of this action. It is considered that the failure of the enemy Intelligence is well-nigh incomprehensible." They also claimed that Canadian officers carried with them the names of Paris nightclubs.

As usual, Winston Churchill was singled out for spiteful attack, being called the "prisoner of the Kremlin who has placed political motives so far above military considerations that he has muzzled the counsel of his generals."

The Prime Minister, although accustomed to this sort of abuse, was nevertheless a displeased war leader and a worried politician. Because the operation resulted in heavy political attacks upon him, he felt obliged, on November 11, to make a speech in the House of Commons outlining his reasons, within security limits, for approving the Jubilee plan. He said:

> The attack which will be made in due course across the Channel or the North Sea requires an immense degree of preparation, vast numbers of special landing-craft, and a great army trained, division by division, in amphibious warfare. . . . It would have been most improvident for us to attempt such an enterprise before all our preparations were ready. . . . However . . . a joint communique was issued by the United Kingdom with the United States and Russia which spoke of a second front in Europe in 1942. One object of this was to deceive the enemy. . . . Meanwhile, whether or not we were going to attack the Continent in August, September, or October, it was of the utmost consequence to Russia that the enemy should believe that we were so prepared and so resolved. Only in this way have we been able to keep at least 33 German divisions in the West.

The Dieppe operation, he said in another speech, was an indispensable preliminary to such full-scale operations. It had the secondary function of holding the enemy on the French shore.

Not even this could fully counter the adverse effects of allowing the enemy to snatch away the propaganda initiative. Even today Lord Haw-Haw's neat summation persists – "too large to be a symbol, too small to be a success."

IV

By and large the Dieppois remained passive during the raid, as they had been instructed in leaflets handed out by the troops and in messages broadcast by the BBC. In some cases, however, they answered questions, gave information concerning the whereabouts of enemy strongpoints, and provided refreshments in the form of wine and biscuits. On the day after the raid they were uniquely rewarded by receiving first the congratulations of Field Marshal Pétain, then two hours later by congratulations from Hitler, and in the evening by the thanks of the British via the BBC.

The official report to Berlin from Field Marshal von Rundstedt said:

> The bearing of the civilian population during and following the English attack was not only unobjectionable, but was absolutely loyal. Throughout the whole day of battle no sabotage whatever was committed in the battle area. German wounded were cared for and the troops handed refreshments. In addition the population participated in putting out fires and clearing up debris. The French authorities immediately placed themselves at the disposal of the German Military Command. At about 4:00 p.m. normal life returned to the streets of Dieppe. All shops were open.

On the evening of the raid German Military Intelligence in Paris sent special agents to Dieppe who proved more cautious in their estimate of what had motivated the Dieppois.

Their report to *Abwehr* headquarters in Berlin said:

> The French civil population of Dieppe has shown . . . a calm and correct attitude. According to reports so far received civilian casualties amount to approximately 40 dead and 40 seriously wounded. During the fighting the population of Dieppe provided German troops with coffee and food . . . and there were no acts of sabotage. . . . To this it must be added that by means of wireless signals and leaflets the British Intelligence Service had unequivocally requested the French civil population not to participate in any way in the fighting. It cannot be told whether the attitude of the population would have been substantially different had they been asked by the British to participate and commit acts of sabotage.

It must be mentioned that it was established in Rouen, Nantes, Angers and other cities that the population was listening avidly to the BBC and that wide circles were inclined to believe it exclusively. In Rouen, gatherings of French people were seen in the streets during the operation. People were saying with very great enthusiasm that now at long last the hour of liberation from the Boche had struck.

German agents, playing the GV Radio Game Porto 11 in Paris, on August 22 intercepted a message from London saying: "What are the reactions of the French and the Boches to the raid on Dieppe? Urgent."

The following bogus reply was made:

It is most embarrassing for us to report truthfully on the attitude of the population of Dieppe. On the 19th and 20th most of the French listened to London Radio with enthusiasm. After the defeat came the reaction. In general, one hears that the operation has misfired and the prestige of the Allies has suffered. Severe criticism is being expressed, particularly in higher circles, on account of inadequate preparation. Great disappointment. The civil population behaved in a distressing manner, in many instances making common cause witih the enemy by delivering up Allied soldiers to the Boches.

The Boches are laughing – but he who laughs last laughs best.

There must have been considerable chuckling at Von Rundstedt's headquarters when this message was dispatched, because it contained enough truth to be credible.

The assault had an unexpectedly happy ending for the Dieppois. As a token of his appreciation for their behaviour, Hitler ordered the release of seventeen hundred French prisoners of war who came from the Dieppe area and sent them home with immunity from conscription into slave labour forces, regardless of their ages. Then Radio Berlin announced that the German government would give Dieppe ten million marks to pay for damage caused by the Allies.

V

Enemy analysts were not very kind in their criticisms of the Jubilee plan. Copy 37, taken almost literally from the hands of Brigadier

Southam by a German naval intelligence officer, Lieutenant Schuch-
mann, was studied first by Military Intelligence, then by General
Haase, and finally by Von Rundstedt. Their subsequent comments
were anything but flattering to the Anglo-Canadian military planners.

Major Kretschmann of Military Intelligence examined the maps of
Dieppe's defences and reported:

> The items drawn in were on the whole fairly correct, but very
> incomplete and faulty in interpretation. Reconnaissance had
> been made primarily by means of aircraft, but it was comple-
> mented by information from agents. This information would
> hardly be likely to come from an organized, smoothly working
> espionage network on the coast itself. The purveyors might
> rather be sought amongst the civil population and foreign work-
> ers on the construction projects who are not trained to deliver
> exact and reliable material. . . . There has not been in the recent
> past and is not now any smoothly working espionage net in this
> area.

Nor was German Intelligence impressed by the military plan. The
report said it was too detailed and therefore "difficult to visualize as
a whole," and continued: "The planning down to the last detail limits
the independence of action of the subordinate officers and leaves them
no opportunity to make independent decisions in an altered situation."

The report then went on to say that "the enemy's knowledge of the
troop dispositions in the coastal zone was extraordinarily inexact"
and that the "mistaken belief of the British Intelligence Service that
110 Infantry Division had been brought to the Dieppe area is apparently the result of German deceptive measures."

General Haase ended his personal report to Von Rundstedt with an
appreciation of the assault as seen through the eyes of the commander
whose job it was to repulse it:

> The British completely miscalculated the strength of the Ger-
> man defences and tried to grab the bull by the horns by landing
> the main body of their invasion forces, particularly the tanks,
> right in front of Dieppe. They persisted with this plan although
> they were aware of the strength of the Dieppe street defences,
> concrete constructions, anti-tank walls, machine-gun positions
> and coastal guns.
>
> This we know from their maps. It is also inconceivable why

they did not support the battalions which landed near Pourville with tanks. An attack with tanks from Pourville against the hill west of Dieppe and against the *Ferme des Quatre Vents* might have been successful. . . .

The Combined Operations planning disagreement which had begun with the birth of Rutter was brought into sharp focus by this pithy comment. The Navy, led by Hughes-Hallett, had striven to persuade the Army to avoid a frontal encounter, to go in with tanks on the flanks. Indeed they had compiled a plan for it.

The Army, however, had insisted upon the frontal assault, and had used faulty intelligence that there were too many hazards between Dieppe and Quiberville or Pourville for the tanks to overcome. Roberts had been told that the bridges would not carry the weight of a tank. If Haase were right – and it is likely that he was – the Navy plan was better suited for a military operation than the Army's.

Contrary to all expectation [Haase continued], the British did not employ parachutists. . . . If they had attacked Puits simultaneously with airborne troops and from the sea, the initial position of the defenders would probably have been critical. . . . Since fire control observation on the big ships was poor because of the smokescreens, the landing force had no artillery support whatsoever.

The British Operational Order [121 pages] fixed every detail of action for each unit. This method of planning made the failure of the whole raid inevitable in the event of unexpected difficulties.

When these reports and others from specialist analysts had been further studied at his headquarters, Von Rundstedt issued his own appreciation entitled "Basic Observations of the Commander-in-Chief, West." It said:

I have had the captured English Operation Order for Dieppe translated and mimeographed.

According to German ideas this order is not an order, but an *aide-mémoire* or a scheme worked out for a map exercise. Nevertheless it does contain many points of value to us.

First, how much the enemy knows about us.

Second, the peculiarities in his method of landing and fighting.

For that reason this order is to be studied thoroughly by all staffs. . . .

But it would be an error to believe that the enemy will mount his next operation in the same manner. He will draw his lessons from his mistakes in planning and from his failure and next time he will do things differently.

The Field Marshal's prediction, unlike so many associated with Jubilee, was to be proved correct. One of the most important lessons of the war had been learned at Dieppe – how not to go about an invasion. There had to be a different way, and in London the experiences of the Force Commanders were being subjected to a scrutiny that was no less exhaustive than the enemy's.

VI

The process of reaching the right conclusions from the experiences of the men who returned began on August 20, when staff officers began taking statements from all ranks, officers being also assembled at a conference hall near the War Office where Mountbatten listened to their personal accounts.

The Force Commanders were not pleased with Mountbatten for insisting upon the conference so soon after the operation, when feelings were inflammatory and judgements likely to be highly coloured. Leigh-Mallory objected to it on the grounds that surviving officers should make their first reports to the Force Commanders, not to a higher authority. He addressed the RAF officers present, forbidding them to take any further part in the proceedings. Hughes-Hallett was also unhappy but as Mountbatten was his immediate superior he was in a difficult position. Moreover, both he and Roberts were so mystified by the total failure of the Blue Beach landings that they welcomed the opportunity to learn the reason why. He compromised by allowing the naval officers under his command to report what they had actually seen but forbade them to repeat hearsay or to express personal opinions.

It was an oddly tense, electric gathering which could be quickly set alight by thoughtless comment. The Force Commanders sat ready to quench threatened conflagrations before they could properly begin. The first spark flashed when Denny Whitaker rose to state bluntly that in his opinion the enemy had possessed foreknowledge of the operation. Mountbatten cut him off with a curt warning that as he was satisfied no breach of security had occurred he would hear no further comments of this nature. He was interested, he said, in constructive criticism, not excuses. There is little doubt that Mountbatten was right, but the Canadian officers so recently returned were not wholly convinced then – nor are they now.

Lieutenant-Commander Goulding, the naval officer in charge of the Puits landing, provided the second spark. He told the conference that the trouble at Blue Beach had been caused by the troops being afraid to land. He was at once silenced – but not before he had said enough to convince Hughes-Hallett that an informal inquiry should be held at Portsmouth to bring out the truth.

It was at the subsequent investigation that the naval officers in charge of the landing-craft told stories of troops having to be forced ashore at the point of revolvers. Because most of the men concerned were by then either dead or in captivity the report of the inquiry remained private.

In any event, the inquiry in no way diminishes the gallantry of the Royal Regiment and should not be allowed to give a distorted view to those unacquainted with the reactions of young men, such as the landing-craft officers, who had just come through a great ordeal. Once the troops recovered from initial shock, they fought on the beaches with matchless courage.

Yet the inquiry did provide a valuable lesson to the invasion planners – that the employment of troops with no previous battle experience in an exceptionally hazardous assault operation was ill-advised to say the least. This type of battle calls for skill, dash, and professional knowledge, qualities seldom found in any but the most highly seasoned units.

On a higher level it was agreed that the air side had performed faultlessly, that Leigh-Mallory had won a victory reminiscent of the decisive days of the Battle of Britain. Hughes-Hallett and Roberts, however, answered written questionnaires, submitted to cross-examinations, and made recommendations to such authorities as the War Office, the Council of Combined Operations, the Combined Commanders, McNaughton, and Crerar. Only one statement in the formal report made by Roberts was challenged.

The employment of tanks in a raid of short duration is not recommended [the report had said], and it is considered that a bridgehead must be established prior to the disembarkation of tanks.

All landing-craft should have heavier armament, which should be shielded and so positioned that it can support the assaulting troops.

The effect on the population of coastal towns of heavy bombing as a preliminary to landing must be accepted. . . .

It is considered that in all operations of this nature the initial assault should be made by light forces to feel out the soft spots with strong and flexible reserves quickly available.

The very opposite had happened at Dieppe where the inflexible military plan had demanded that the bulk of the assaulting forces be committed in the initial stages, leaving only a weak reserve to exploit success. However, the general who had been at Uxbridge took issue with the general who had been at Dieppe. Crerar wrote to Roberts:

I am not convinced that the tactics you . . . indicate are suitable for "all operations of this nature." There are practical limitations in the way of technical inter-Service difficulties which are bound to impose a certain degree of rigidity in the plan of Combined Operations. It must also be accepted that if our intelligence concerning the enemy is complete, we shall be able to frame an effective plan in advance of the operation. This situation is unlikely but not impossible.

The weakness in the argument put forward by Roberts was that large reserves in amphibious assaults could be usefully employed only if the commander was armed with full, detailed information of events as they developed. Roberts had not been informed of developments ashore at Dieppe, and had he possessed larger reserves their committal would probably have resulted in even greater losses.

The Dieppe planners, however, had nowhere near the sort of complete and reliable intelligence required for the sort of detailed planning in advance which actually took place. Photographic interpretation had produced phenomenal results, but information from espionage sources had been so out-of-date that it was largely worthless.

In any event, the official lesson learned in this respect, as finally produced by Combined Operations, tended to support Roberts by saying: "The chances and opportunities of an assault landing are extremely difficult to gauge in advance. The military plan must, therefore, be flexible in order to enable the Commander to apply force where force has already succeeded."

When asked whether the frontal attack was justified "in view of the fact that we were not taking any steps to pulverize the defences. . . ," Roberts replied: "Very questionable if a frontal attack is justified. Defences were stronger than anticipated and failure at Blue Beach [Royal Regiment] altered the whole situation."

Roberts's answer to a question from the United States staff of the Combined Commanders supplied a direct link to the eventual D-Day invasion. The question was in two parts, the first asking whether the plans had been sufficiently flexible to permit the Commander to exploit soft spots in the defences.

"The plans were not flexible," replied Roberts. "All but one battalion were to be in the initial assault. Only weak forces were left in reserve."

The second part asked: "Is a forced landing practicable on defended beaches without the advantage of surprise or great superiority in fire support?"

"No," said Roberts. "You must have surprise or great superiority in fire-power, preferably surprise with fire support available as required."

On D-Day, the forces that landed in Normandy achieved a measure of surprise with the most overwhelming fire-power in the history of amphibious warfare. This was partly a result of the patient application of lessons learned at Dieppe in planning for the future by Mountbatten, Hughes-Hallett, and the technical staffs of Combined Operations. Hughes-Hallett's conclusions matched those of the Military Commander in these respects:

> Although from a purely military point of view the results achieved were disappointing, and the heavy casualties sustained regrettable, it is considered that the operation was worthwhile provided its lessons are carefully applied when the time comes to re-enter France on a larger scale.
>
> The principal lessons appear to be firstly, that much stronger military forces are required to break through the German coastal defences in any important area; secondly, that a much higher proportion of the military force should be held in reserve until the progress made in the initial assault is known. . . . Unless this is done there is no guarantee that any of the beaches will be secured. . . . Arising out of this is the need for far more effective methods of supporting the troops. . . .

Curiously, the most significant contributions to the success of D-Day were not in Hughes-Hallett's official report. He was by then convinced of two major requirements: the need for a permanent, highly trained fleet of assault boats, including vessels of all kinds necessary to support the initial landing; and the need to avoid further frontal assaults against heavily defended enemy ports.

He reported to Combined Operations that theoretically a successful invasion was now possible, that most of the opinions and beliefs which no one would fully accept until they had been put to a practical test were now proven valid. The main point, however, was that it should be aimed not at a port, but across open beaches. From this concept, War Office engineers designed a long beach pier with a large "speed" pontoon. It received Mountbatten's enthusiastic support, and at his urging a prototype was built in the Solway Firth, being completed by the end of 1942.

In 1943 the Cossack planning organization for D-Day was set up and among the key planners was Hughes-Hallett who, in June of that year, proposed that the invasion force should take with it an impro- vised harbour. He visualized breakwater ships which could be sunk off a stretch of beach to provide sheltered water for the landing of troops and supplies. When this proposal reached Winston Churchill, it was immediately expanded into what is now known as the Mulberry Harbour.

Hughes-Hallett felt so strongly about the creation of a permanent naval assault force that Mountbatten appointed him the creator of it. Using most of the crews who had been to Dieppe as a nucleus and preserving the code name "Force J" (for Jubilee), he spent the two years to D-Day devising the famous standardized assault orders known as "JNO's" which were adopted by the Royal Navy, the United States Navy, and the Royal Canadian Navy. They became not only the stand- ing orders for assault craft operations in the European and Mediter- ranean theatres, but also in the Pacific where they were employed effectively in the United States island-hopping campaign.

The development of Force J into the skilled organization it became under Hughes-Hallett's direction, and of the Mulberry from his original conception, made it possible to plan D-Day as a major assault across open beaches, which in turn gave the Allies a measure of tactical surprise. This was because the Germans had reached different con- clusions from their experiences at Dieppe. They assumed that whereas the Allies would not be so foolish as to attempt another frontal assault, they would land on either flank of a port and then encircle it. From

Dieppe onwards their defences were reorganized and concentrated to cover likely invasion ports, thus weakening the defences along open beaches where the landings actually took place. They also concluded that an assault could be destroyed at the moment of landing and therefore sacrificed defence in depth in order to reinforce the West Wall.

Additionally, many enemy divisions were tied down after Dieppe on coastal defences as a precaution against further Allied incursions, divisions which otherwise might well have been sent to Russia.

The technical staffs of Combined Operations devised a wide variety of landing-craft for D-Day – mechanized landing-craft to land armoured support swiftly; engineer craft designed to take sappers ashore and give them protection while they were demolishing obstructions on the beaches; flail tanks to lead troops through minefields. These were but a few of the machines which grew from the experiences of Dieppe, not least of which were the craft designed to provide pulverizing fire-power.

Inspiration for some of these weird-looking vessels was a medical analysis of the wounds sustained by the Canadians who returned from Dieppe. It showed that in this kind of operation the chances of a soldier being hit by a flying missile of some sort were one in four – a rate which also indicated that frontal assaults were not the most economical in terms of loss of life.

The analysis showed that most casualties at Dieppe had occurred during the landing and re-embarkation, and that troops were most likely to be wounded in lower limbs, upper limbs, thorax, head and neck, and abdomen, in that order of frequency. Combined Operations, therefore, set about designing landing-craft with sufficient protection to cut down casualties.

Most of the lessons learned at Dieppe have been quoted many times and need only brief mention here – although we may occasionally pray that they be indelibly scarred into the military conscience. There is no doubt at all that they were applied well to the business of winning the war. Had there been no Dieppe, those who died in August 1942 might have lived for two more years simply to be killed in June 1944. There would have been no legacy of life-saving information to inherit.

Mountbatten has said that for every soldier who died at Dieppe, ten were saved on D-Day. This may be one of those vague scraps of statistical information impossible to prove or disprove, but in the absence of something more concrete the ratio can be accepted as reasonable. There is every reason to believe today that without Dieppe, and without such men as Mountbatten and Hughes-Hallett to see that the lessons were put to practical use, ultimate victory might have been long delayed.

Lord Lovat, commander of the successful assault against the Varengeville guns, has certain reservations about the operation in its purely military sense. "Looking back," he says, "one thing is certain – never postpone an operation and then remount it after an appreciable delay. I also consider it was a mistake to concentrate shipping in Newhaven, immediately opposite the target. It was quite certain that reconnaissance aircraft never lost sight of this fact, although the German High Command were maybe unaware of the exact target, and it stands to reason that precautions were redoubled on the opposite side.

"With respect to the Canadian Forces, I do not think they were sufficiently aware of the magnitude of their task. High courage and ordinary infantry training are no answer to machine-gun fire and impregnable fortifications, set in cliffs. By the same token I do not think either the planners at Combined Operations, or the tie-up between Army, Navy, and Air Force had at that time reached the high standard that was subsequently achieved.

"It taught many invaluable lessons, the main one being (and this stood us in good stead on D-Day) that it was quite impossible to capture an occupied harbour or railhead which at that time the High Command thought necessary in order to supply expeditionary forces re-entering Europe."

On June 10, 1944 – D-Day plus four – six men crossed the English Channel to spend a day watching the Allied armada feeding the invasion armies ashore. While travelling back to London by train in the evening the group composed a letter to Mountbatten, then Supreme Allied Commander, South-East Asia. It said:

> Today we visited the British and American armies on the soil of France. We sailed through vast fleets of ships with landing-craft of many types pouring men, vehicles, and stores ashore. We saw clearly the manœuvre in progress and in process of rapid development.
>
> We have shared our secrets in common and helped each other all we could. We wish to tell you at this moment that we realize that much of this remarkable technique, and therefore the success of the venture, has its origins in developments effected by you and your staff of Combined Operations.

Each of the six men signed the letter in the following order – Winston Churchill, Field Marshal Lord Alanbrooke, Field Marshal Smuts, General George Marshall, Admiral Ernest King, and General Hap Arnold.

None of the techniques, equipment, or assault tactics which contributed so vastly to the "success of the venture" on D-Day could have been developed had the need for them failed to have emerged from Dieppe. To denigrate the Canadian sacrifice at Dieppe is to label the signatories of the letter as fools and by doing so proclaim oneself the biggest fool of all.

The young hunters of Rutter, of Jubilee, of Dieppe, are no longer young. Mountbatten still wears his uniform with formidable presence and serves England in the capacity of a supreme commander. Hughes-Hallett also serves, but in the decorous manner of a Tory Member of Parliament. McNaughton has retired as soldier, as statesman, and as scientist yet remains frisky in public life; Crerar, having gathered up the rewards of a distinguished career, has also laid aside his uniform; so has Baillie-Grohman, now an addition to the country gentlemen of Sussex, the English county his fellow Canadians defended and delighted.

What of General Ham Roberts – the only Allied military commander until 1943 to have led a major offensive against enemy-occupied Europe, the only Allied military commander then with the practical know-how of assault? After Dieppe Roberts was relegated to command of a training camp in England for Canadian recruits and reinforcements – still a major-general in 1945 when he retired to Jersey in the Channel Islands.

Ottawa is not likely to confess that Roberts was in any way sacrificed to quieten public tumult; nor is Roberts likely to admit that there is any need for it. Yet to many, including survivors of Dieppe, the quiet Canadian gentleman now living in the Channel Islands symbolizes the shame of man's folly, the glory of his conduct.

Epilogue

The Canadians left nearly a thousand dead on the pebbles of France. There were, as well, more than two thousand living, men who entered Dieppe in strength for the first time that day as prisoners of war. Southam, Merritt, Labatt, Jasperson, and Catto were there; Menard was the only battalion commander to get away. Also among the rows upon rows of prisoners were Brian McCool, Marcel Lambert, Dan Doheny, Gordon Rolfe, Jerry Wood, Tony Hill, Harold Lazier, Padre Foote, Sarto Marchand, André Masson, Lucien Dumais, and Corporal Vermette. Mention a name from the 2nd Division, and the likelihood was that the owner of it would be either dead or amid these bruised, bewildered ranks.

Some had stripped to their underclothes when trying to swim to safety and had nothing else to wear. Lengths of rubber torn from useless Mae Wests were bound about their feet as shoes. Others had stripped to the waist while sweating out the battle in the heat of the sun and now marched erect, lean, and hard, their bronzed young bodies gleaming with health under thin damp coats of dirt.

The prisoners were taken first to a hospital behind Dieppe, where the wounded were treated by German and captured Canadian doctors. Then they were assembled farther inland at a bricks factory to be searched and documented, before moving on to Verneuil where they spent a week in a disused French barracks while the interrogations continued.

German counter-intelligence officers, their attempts to divide French-speaking and English-speaking Canadians having failed, devoted much of their time to Canadians with German names, with no success whatsoever. It transpired after the war that the only three Canadians to be seduced into collaboration bore thoroughly commonplace Anglo-Saxon names.

One interrogator, Major Koestner, reported that a Canadian officer had stated he was passionately anti-Bolshevik, that he had been forced to emigrate from Scotland to Canada because of his political persuasions. According to Koestner, the officer said his fiancée in Canada was of German blood and the couple had made a pact to do anything in their power to help Germany's fight against the Russians. The officer had suggested that he could be usefully employed as an agent in England.

The Germans took this nonsense seriously, but there is no evidence that the officer achieved his purpose: to have his return ticket to England paid for by the enemy.

The prisoners were separated for the journey to Germany, officers being sent to Oflag VII B at Eichstatt in Bavaria, while NCO's and other ranks were sent to Stalag Landsdorf in eastern Germany. But not all the Canadians were present when the trains pulled into their destinations.

Captain Browne, who had been Forward Observation Officer with the Royal Regiment, escaped before the train filled with officers crossed the border into Germany, and made his way into Unoccupied France. He found Vichy agents to be as enthusiastic manhunters as the *Gestapo*. A few weeks earlier, the Vichy government had announced that persons caught assisting escaped Allied prisoners would be sentenced to death by beheading. This was a return to the days when Madame Guillotine reigned with dreadful power, and in these circumstances it was hardly surprising that Browne should be quickly captured and interned. He escaped a second time, but was recaptured shortly before the remainder of France was occupied by the enemy in November 1942 and handed over with other prisoners into the hands of the Italians. While being moved to Grenoble by bus on December 7, Browne escaped yet again and made his way via Toulouse to the Pyrenees where he joined two Spanish smugglers who guided him across the snow-covered mountains into the tiny independent republic of Andorra, which lies between Spain and France. He was subsequently repatriated via Gibraltar, and arrived in England on January 26, 1943.

Captain John Runcie of the Camerons also escaped while the Canadians were still in France. Feigning illness, he managed to have himself transferred to a hospital in Paris where he was given a private room adjoining a ward filled with German wounded from the Russian front. The doctors could find nothing wrong with him and instructed that he should be returned to Verneuil within forty-eight hours. By then Runcie had persuaded a hospital orderly to have a friend bring civilian clothes and wait one night in the shadow of a nearby church.

The evening of September 5 was dark and rainy, but at 10:00 p.m. Runcie, dressed only in pyjamas, escaped through a French window at the end of a corridor, climbed over a low garden wall, and met the orderly's friend. This Frenchman led the way to an apartment in Montmartre, occupied by a family who cared for him for the next ten days. Then came the long, lonely flight across France to the Spanish border – Paris, Fontainebleau, Orléans, Blois, Tours, Poitiers, Bordeaux, Biarritz, and so on. At first he slept in woods by day and travelled only at night. He reversed the procedure when he found that bridges and road blocks were guarded at night, unguarded by day. He received lifts from French truck-drivers to whom he always confessed his real identity, yet he was never betrayed. Towards the end of November he crossed the frontier by moonlight into Spain and eventually reported to the British Consul at San Sebastian. He was taken from there to the British Embassy in Madrid and subsequently repatriated back to England via Gibraltar.

Several French Canadians, having a natural language advantage, attempted to escape from the train heading for Germany and four were successful. Lieutenant Masson, Sergeant-Major Dumais, and Privates C. Joly, C. Lafleur, and R. Vanier, all of the Fusiliers Mont-Royal, evaded the Germans and made contact with the French Resistance through whom they were returned to England. For some of them the secret war of intelligence beckoned. Although carrying the scars of Dieppe and imprisonment, they volunteered for Special Operations

Executive and were parachuted back into France to help organize the escape routes out of Occupied Europe.

Oflag VII B was probably not much different from many other prison camps in Germany except that it was situated in lovely Bavarian countryside rather than in bleaker areas of Germany. Southam, because of his rank, was given a room to himself, and the Colonels – Merritt, Labatt, Jasperson, and Catto – shared another room above him. For some reason, still unexplained, Southam did not insist upon recognition as senior British officer of the camp, although the English officer in charge was a major. By agreement with the Brigadier, the Major continued to command, and naturally he knew nothing about Copy 37 of the operational orders for Dieppe.

After the raid the German Intelligence examined several of their own soldiers and members of the Todt Organization who had been captured temporarily by the Canadians and left behind during the evacuation. The report said:

> O.T. men [Todt] wore Swastika armbands in the battle zone. This brought about the result that the Canadian soldiers who had landed at Pourville made an immediate dash of particular ferocity on these men. One O.T. man (Schneider) was thereby wounded by a dagger stab in the chin and then killed by a shot in the stomach. Some other O.T. men were fettered in the following manner: a cord was laid twice round the neck, then across the shoulders and carried back to the thumbs, which were bound at the height of the hips in such a manner that strangulation must result from the slightest downward motion. An order of this tenor had been given to the soldiers of 2nd Canadian Division in copy of captured British Operations Order for operation "Jubilee". . . . It seems therefore that the enemy attached great importance to taking prisoners as quickly as possible in order to lead them away to a certain spot for interrogation. . . .

The Germans were pretty angry about this, and on September 2, Radio Berlin broadcast a communique which said:

> In the British order captured at Dieppe, Appendix L, paragraph 4, reads: "Wherever possible, prisoners' hands are to be tied so that they cannot destroy their papers."
> In the official exposition by the High Command of 30th

August, 1942, this paragraph in the British order of operations was published.

The British government have not stated their attitude on this question. The High Command has therefore ordered that all British officers and men captured at Dieppe shall be put in chains from 3rd September, at 2 o'clock.

The reason for this treatment will be told to the prisoners. This measure will be revoked as soon as the British government officially withdraws the above-mentioned order on the binding of German prisoners.

The High Command further reports that all future wild-west measures of this kind, which represent a disgrace and lack of respect for gallant soldiers, will be immediately answered with sharp reprisals.

The German troops have so far, as has been proved by a number of photographs of Dieppe, always treated their British prisoners as opponents to be respected.

It rests with the British leaders to decide whether this change in the treatment of prisoners evoked by them will, in the light of the experience of Dieppe, hit the British or the German prisoners more.

The appalled, confused British War Office issued a reply the same evening saying: "Investigations are being made as to whether in fact any such order was issued. It is categorically denied that any German prisoner had his hands tied. Any such order, if it was issued, will be cancelled."

The War Office clearly knew very well that prisoners hands had been tied but were using permissible subterfuge to play for time. The ruse partially succeeded because next day the Germans announced they had cancelled their proposed reprisals. But on October 7, the German government announced that in view of further investigation into events at Dieppe and because Commandos had bound prisoners taken during the raid on Sark in the Channel Islands three days earlier, officers captured at Dieppe would be placed in shackles. The text of this statement follows:

After the abortive landing attempts at Dieppe, a captured British order demanding that German prisoners be fettered, forced the High Command of the Armed Forces to announce suitable counter measures for the protection of German soldiers' honour. Thereupon the British War Office declared on the 2nd

September: "It is emphatically denied that any German prisoner has had his hands fettered. Any such order, if it should have been issued, will be revoked."

In the meantime, both declarations of the British War Office have proved to be either frivolous, unverified assertions or conscious lies.

For the examination in court of a German lance sergeant, a corporal and five privates as well as five men of the organization Todt, who temporarily fell into British captivity at Dieppe, and who were later freed, makes it clear that they had all been fettered from ten minutes up to one hour and a half. Either their hands had been tied on their backs, or their wrists, in some instances even their individual fingers had been tied together over their chests.

This was not all; a similar dastardly incident took place on the Channel Island of Sark on the 4th October. In the early hours of the morning, 16 British raided a German Labour Squad of one NCO and four men. These, dressed only in their shorts, were tied up with a thin but very strong plaited rope, prevented from putting on any further clothes and marched to the beach. When the German soldiers resisted this unheard-of treatment, the NCO and one man were killed by shots and by thrusts with the bayonet, and another soldier was wounded. These facts are confirmed by the evidence of a sapper, who managed to escape in the affray. The investigation has evinced that the fetterings had been prepared systematically.

The German High Command of the Armed Forces had thus in its hands irrefutable proof of the two British War Office statements of 2nd September having been made untruthfully.

The High Command of the Armed Forces therefore finds itself compelled as follows:—

As from 12 o'clock noon of the 8th October, all British officers and soldiers captured at Dieppe will be fettered. This measure shall remain in force until such time as the British War Office will give evidence that in future it will make truthful statements on the fettering of German prisoners of war or that it has assumed authority to make sure its orders are enforced with the troops.

In future, all terror and sabotage units of the British and their henchmen, who behave not like soldiers but like bandits, will be treated as such by the German troops and, wherever they appear, they will be ruthlessly finished off.

The same day that the British government decided to undertake reprisals against an equivalent number of enemy prisoners then in Canadian prison camps, Ottawa was asked to agree and co-operate, although the Canadian government had not been consulted during the preliminary sparring. Ottawa doubted the wisdom of the British decision, but nevertheless acquiesced and, on Otober 10, German prisoners in both the United Kingdom and Canada were shackled, in spite of resistance by prisoners in such camps as Bowmanville, Ontario. A further British statement said:

> In order that the true facts of the controversy about tying the hands of prisoners of war may be clearly before the public, the following statement is issued by His Majesty's Goverment:
>
> In the Dieppe raid, an order was issued, without authority, to the effect that "Wherever possible the hands of prisoners of war will be bound, so that they cannot destroy their papers." On the complaint of the German government the War Office at once, before there had been time to make enquiry, issued a statement that, if any such order had been issued, it would be countermanded, because they considered that such an order might be held to imply that, irrespective of the circumstances, the hands of prisoners of war should be bound.
>
> On enquiries being made, no evidence was found that any of the prisoners brought back from Dieppe had had their hands tied. But the existence of the order came to light, and it was countermanded.
>
> The raid on Sark was carried out by a party of ten officers and men. Seven of the party captured five Germans. The hands of the Germans were tied in order that arms might be linked with the captors. No orders, written or otherwise, had been issued. But the prisoners had to be taken past a German-occupied barracks on the way to the boats, and precautions were therefore necessary. In spite of the precautions, four of the five German prisoners of war broke away, shouting, and had to be shot to prevent them raising the alarm.
>
> The Geneva Convention contains no statement about tying the hands of prisoners, but prescribes humane treatment. The question at issue is, therefore, what constitutes humane treatment.
>
> Clearly this differs according to circumstances. There is a wide difference between what is appropriate to a prisoner in safe

custody and to prisoners in the course of battle. It will be observed that the actions complained of by the German government
relate to action in the course of battle.

The German government have, however, themselves taken
action to tie the hands of prisoners of war in their custody and
far removed from the battlefield as an act of reprisal. Acts of
reprisal against prisoners of war are specifically forbidden by the
Geneva Convention.

A series of conferences was held at the War Office in London,
attended by McNaughton, to decide whether the tying of prisoners'
hands in certain types of operations did, in fact, contravene the
Geneva Convention. In January 1943 McNaughton advised the Canadian government that Canada should not agree to an undertaking not
to shackle in the field. A month later the British Army Council issued
a secret letter to Commonwealth army commanders setting out the
types of operations in which prisoners could be legitimately bound.
The Dieppe operation was not one of them, and the letter described
the clause in the Jubilee plan as "objectionable." The letter also provided that troops destined to make contact with the enemy would not
in future carry written orders dealing with the treatment of prisoners.

Negotiations with the Germans through Switzerland were mostly
fruitless because the Germans insisted upon an unconditional Allied
order against shackling, something the Allies were not prepared to do.
While the diplomatic stalemate persisted, the plight of three hundred
Canadian and British officers at Oflag VII B was a sorry one.

They were separated from the rest of the camp, confined in the
storeroom of a nearby castle, and bound with rope. After a while they
graduated from rope to handcuffs, which kept their wrists tight together. Then the handcuffs were replaced by chains with padlocks at
each end, and finally the proper shackles arrived – two steel bands for
each wrist connected by eighteen inches of chain.

Shackling time was from 8:00 a.m. to 9:00 p.m. each day, but despite
the special guards, homemade keys were smuggled from the camp to
the castle. As the days dragged on, even the guards became fed up with
the prisoners' ability to unshackle themselves whenever the opportunity arose.

Labatt had since told me: "The effect of shackling on health, both
physical and mental, was extremely bad, particularly during the winter
months. However, things got much better in June 1943, when the
Allies won their great victory in Tunisia, taking hundreds of thousands

of prisoners. For the first time, the British had more German prisoners than the Germans had Allied. The effect was instantaneous. Wire barriers separating us from the rest of the camp were taken down and the special guards disappeared.

"True, the shackles arrived each morning, so many to a room. But they were just dumped on a table for each prisoner to select a chain and hang it on a nail. Every evening he would solemnly take the chain down from the nail and place it back on the table for the guards to collect at 9:00 p.m."

On November 22, 1943, more than a year after the shackling incident had flared up, 8:00 a.m. came and passed with no signs of shackles being brought to the rooms. They were never seen again — and no one missed them at Oflag VII B.

In 1945 the men who had fought for nine hours in a war that had lasted six years were released by the Allied armies to join the hundreds of thousands of ex-prisoners streaming across Europe. Kindly Americans flew them to England where they submitted to interrogation and then embarked in troopships for the voyage home to Canada.

One ordeal had ended; ahead lay another — that of peace, of adjusting the Oflag mind to environments which should have been familiar but which were suddenly strange, even hostile; of adjustment to people who had to share with them the nervous days of getting to know each other all over again.

Bill Southam came home and died, as did many others. The rest dispersed to their homes across Canada: Labatt to Hamilton, Jasperson to Windsor, Merritt to Vancouver with a Victoria Cross, Catto and McCool to Toronto. The integration of the amateur warriors into professional civilian life took weeks, months, years to accomplish. In some cases it has not yet been completed and may never be.

If you should ever visit Dieppe, you may ask yourself what made this place worth so many Canadians lives. The rich pass through it by rail and car or over it by air, heading for more luxurious playgrounds. The not-so-rich might stay simply because Dieppe, being a comparatively insignificant resort on the wrong side of France, offers a cheap holiday. In fact, the place would probably be regarded as a pretty poor real-estate investment by North American standards.

Yet once it held the "priceless secret of victory." And if you really want to know why so many Canadians died to unlock that secret, then ask any American, Englishman, or Canadian who landed over the open beaches of Normandy on D-Day.

That he lives will be reason enough.

Bibliography

Much of the literature on so controversial an episode of war as this is curiously sterile, which may explain why the image of the event has remained distorted for so long. This bibliography includes the best books referring to the subject, and I have raided most of them quite ruthlessly, taking full advantage of authors and publishers generous enough to tolerate my predatory instincts.

Bryant, Arthur. *The Turn of the Tide*. New York: Doubleday & Co. Inc., 1957.

Buchanan, Lieutenant-Colonel G. B., MBE. *March of the Prairie Men. The Official History of the South Saskatchewan Regiment*. Privately printed, 1957.

Canada, The Department of National Defence. *The Canadians in Britain*. Ottawa: The King's Printer, by authority of the Minister of National Defence, 1945.

Churchill, Winston S. *Memoirs of the Second World War*. London: Cassell & Co. Ltd., 1959; Boston: Houghton Mifflin Company, 1959.

Combined Operations. *The Official History of Combined Operations*. London: H.M. Stationery Office, 1943.

Durnford-Slater, Brigadier John. *Commando*. London: William Kimber & Co. Ltd., 1953.

Gilchrist, Donald. *Castle Commando*. Edinburgh: Oliver & Boyd Limited, 1960.

Goodspeed, Major D. J. *Battle Royal*, Official History of the Royal Regiment of Canada. Privately printed, 1962.

Mills-Roberts, Derek. *Clash By Night: A Commando Chronicle*. London: William Kimber, 1957.

Montgomery, Field Marshal the Viscount of Alamein, K. G. *Memoirs*. London: William Collins Sons & Co. Ltd., 1958.

Munro, Ross. *Gauntlett to Overlord*. Toronto: Macmillan Company of Canada Ltd., 1946.

Pickersgill, J. W. *The Mackenzie King Record, Vol. I. 1939-1944*. Chicago: University of Chicago Press, 1960.

Rees, Goronwy. *A Bundle of Sensations*. Toronto: Clarke Irwin & Company, Ltd., 1960.

Reyburn, Wallace. *Glorious Chapter*. London: George G. Harrap & Co. Ltd., 1943.

Reynolds, Quentin. *Dress Rehearsal*. Toronto: Random House of Canada, Ltd., 1944.

Ryder, Commander R. E. D., VC, RN. *The Attack on St Nazaire*. London: John Murray Ltd., 1947.

Scott, Peter. *Eye of the Wind*. New York: Houghton-Mifflin Co., 1961.

Stacey, Colonel C. P. *Official History of the Canadian Army at War*. Ottawa: The Queen's Printer, 1948.

Thompson, R. W. *Dieppe at Dawn*. London: Hutchinson & Co. Ltd., 1957.

Truscott, Lieutenant-Colonel L. K. Jr. *Command Missions*. New York: E. P. Dutton & Co., 1954.

Wilmott, Chester. *The Struggle For Europe*. London: Collins & Co. Ltd., 1952.

Acknowledgements

More than sixty people in Canada, Britain, the United States, France, and West Germany have helped me, giving generously of their time. Private papers, correspondence, documents, and diaries have been made readily available. I feel it necessary, therefore, to state clearly that all comments and opinions in this book are my own. They do not reflect the views of any government department, of any organization, or of any individual other than myself. They have been made in accordance with a writer's privilege to comment fairly upon matters of public interest. I have considered them essential here because in official histories the truth sometimes becomes veiled by documents and statistics, whereas it may emerge more vividly if personalities are permitted to dominate the event.

I do not propose to name everyone who co-operated with me because many of them would prefer anonymity and are already aware that my gratitude is poor recompense for their unselfish assistance and unfailing courtesy. It would be churlish, however, not to express particular thanks to the Right Honourable Douglas S. Harkness, ED, MP, Canadian Minister of National Defence, who permitted me access to the official records in Ottawa and to those officers and men of his Department who proved so helpful at all times.

I am grateful too for the patience of the following who undertook to read my draft manuscript to ensure accuracy of mood as well as of fact:

Lt-Col C. C. I. Merritt, vc
Maj-Gen J. H. Roberts, cb, dso, mc
Vice-Adm John Hughes-Hallett, cb, dso, mp
Vice-Adm H. T. Baillie-Grohman, cb, dso, obe
Brig Dollard Menard, dso
Brig D. Whitaker, dso, ed
Lt-Col J. S. Edmondson, cd
Lt-Col F. K. Jasperson, dso
Lt-Col R. R. Labatt, dso
Maj Claude Orme, dso, ed
Capt Murray Osten, mc

I am indebted to the following for their invaluable advice, constant assistance, and guidance:

Maj John Foote, vc
Gen H. D. G. Crerar, ch, cb, dso
Brig Sherwood Lett, cbe, dso, mc, ed, cd
Brig S. C. J. F. The Lord Lovat
Gp Capt R. Oxspring
Cmdr R. Hayden, rcn, cd
Lt-Col Gordon Rolfe, dso, mbe, cd
Lt-Col F. Reesor, mbe, ed, cd
Lt-Col H. F. Wood, cd
Lt-Cmdr R. F. MacRae, rcnvr
Maj Brian McCool, mbe, ed
Maj J. Robinson
Capt Lucien Dumais, mc, mm
Capt George Hickson, dcm, mm
Mr Ronald M. Bell, mp
Mr David Deziel
Mr Dan Doheny
Mr Jim Green
Mr Douglas Kendall
Mr Sarto Marchand
Mr Goronwy Rees
Mr Peter Scott
Mr Peter Wright
M. Georges Guibon of Dieppe

For permission to quote from *The History of the Second World War* by Sir Winston Churchill, I wish to thank Cassell & Co., Ltd., of London, England, and Houghton Mifflin Company of Boston, U.S.A.

Index